Little Michigan

100 Towns POPULATION **BELOW 600**

A NOSTALGIC LOOK AT MICHIGAN'S SMALLEST TOWNS

by Kathryn Houghton

Adventure Publications
Cambridge, MN

Dedication

For my family, who believe in me even when I doubt.

Acknowledgments

This book could not have happened without the help of many people. The following people were instrumental in writing this book: Virginia Burleson, Kari DeVerney, Cathryn Fitz-Jung, Linda Gutzki, Mike Hosey, Robert Houseman, Judy Jones, Lynn Jordan, Shaun Lausby, Jerry McDiarmid, Don Moore, Dick Morgan, Julie Morgan, Jane Mueller, Janette Weimer, JoAnn Zerilli. In addition, I'd like to thank all of the local historical societies from these one hundred towns for giving me information I could not have found anywhere else, and for the residents that stopped on the street to answer quick questions and point me toward interesting places. There truly are too many of you to name.

I'd also like to thank Brett Ortler and the entire team at Adventure Publications, without whom this book would not be nearly as much as it is. Finally, I'd like to thank Steve Houghton for accompanying me on many of the long hours of driving I put into researching this book, and Melissa Houghton for keeping me company while I did much of the writing and editing.

Photo Credits

All photos by Kathryn Houghton

Cover and book design by Jonathan Norberg

Edited by Brett Ortler

10 9 8 7 6 5 4 3 2 1

Little Michigan: A Nostalgic Look At Michigan's Smallest Towns
Copyright © 2018 by Kathryn Houghton
Published by Adventure Publications
An imprint of AdventureKEEN
(800) 678-7006
www.adventurepublications.net
Printed in the China
ISBN 978-1-59193-768-5 (pbk.); ISBN 978-1-59193-769-2 (ebook)

Table of Contents

Introduction

When I travel outside of Michigan, people generally think they know two sure things about my state. First, they know about the perceived tragedy of Detroit and, second, that it's cold and we get a lot of snow. My first winter as a graduate student in Spokane, Washington, saw more than 90 inches of snow fall, and people would tell me how lucky I was that I was used to getting so much snow. When I told them that no, we didn't often get winters like that—at least not in the Lansing area, where I grew up—they never quite believed me. I would get defensive for my state. Michigan was nothing like what they thought; Detroit isn't a stain upon our identity, and we aren't these mythical winter beings that are used to driving in a few feet of snow. I chose to go to Washington for graduate school so that I could get away from Michigan, but the more I found myself defending and describing my home state, the more I missed it. I realized that Michigan hadn't just been my home—it would always be my home. The day after I graduated, I moved back.

I take great pride in my state, but for a long time I barely knew more than my out-of-state friends. To me, Michigan was Lansing and its suburbs, it was Michigan State's campus and the interstate rivalry with the University of Michigan, it was lakes and vacationing "up north." It was, in a sense, the same thing outsiders saw.

Then I started researching this book. The first town I visited was Pewamo, a town I'd never before visited or even driven through, though it was only forty minutes away from where I'd grown up. It was a sunny September day, and I decided to walk around, taking notes on what I saw and photographing some of the buildings. Within five minutes, the first person approached me. He was taking a break from a bike ride and he'd noticed me walking around. I thought at first that he was going to challenge me on my right to be there, an outsider in this small and close-knit community.

Instead, he wanted to know if he could help in any way.

It was like that everywhere I went. People smiled and said hello. They pointed me toward their towns' hidden gems and told me stories about people and events from the past, some of which are now told here in this book.

What I found most remarkable, however, was the enthusiasm of the residents of these small towns. When I told them I was from the Lansing area, and that I worked at Michigan State, their enthusiasm became shaded with something almost akin to disbelief. I didn't understand at first, and then it hit me that, to them, I was the same as the out-of-staters I met in graduate school. Sure, I was from Michigan, but the town where I'd grown up, the town I'd called a "small town" until I started working on this book, had 11,000 people. Small town indeed.

As I continued my work on this book, a second pattern began to emerge. Usually the people I spoke with were in their 60s or 70s. They'd lived a lot of the town's history, seen so many changes. Theirs were the hands that had shaped their communities, both during the good days and the challenging ones, and they weren't sure who would be left to do so once they were gone. The younger generations, they told me, were moving away, and most of those who stayed were much more interested in the community's present and future than in its past.

I never found the courage to admit it to the people I spoke with, but before I started working on this book, I was much the same way. But I've learned that it matters immensely where we've been and where we come from. I've learned that to truly understand and appreciate my state, I need to hear so many more of its stories than simply those told in the Lansing suburbs. I need to hear the stories that often go overlooked by any but those who lived them. It is stories that tell us who we are.

Today, I see Michigan in a different light. I see it as a vibrant and tenacious state with so many different people and communities. I see it as a place with a humble past and a dignified future. It's still my home, but it's now a bigger and more varied home than it was before. As you read this book, I hope you discover some of the same things that I did and, in doing so, that Michigan feels a bit more like home, whether you've lived here all your life or only visited for a day. Welcome to Michigan. We have so much to tell you.

Locator Map

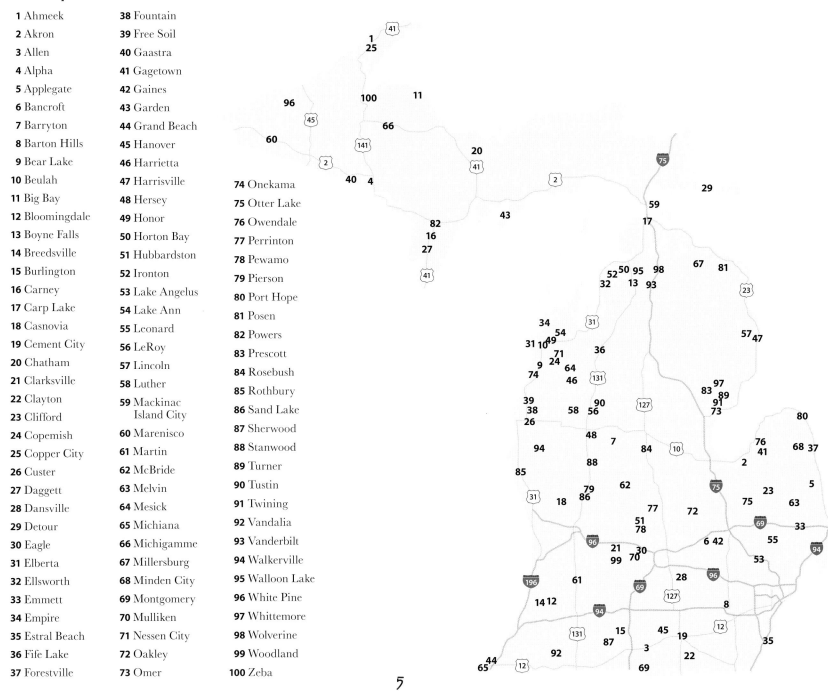

TOP: A row of company houses built by the Ahmeek Mining Company in the early 1900s

Population: 146[1]   Incorporated: 1909[2]

INSETS L to R: The old streetcar station now houses a vacation rental, an ice cream store, and a nature center • A plaque commemorating Gabriel J. Chopp, a late Ahmeek resident after whom the local park is named • Some of the playground equipment at Gabriel Chopp Park • The Ahmeek Village Hall

The name Ahmeek comes from the Ojibwe word for beaver, though a closer spelling of the word might be Ahmuk. At its founding, there was an abundance of beavers in the area.

Ahmeek

The Last Manned Lighthouse

ADVANCES IN TECHNOLOGY can come with the benefits of added convenience and decreased cost, but they can also cause once-common ways of life to all but disappear. For the Great Lakes, lighthouse keeping is one occupation that has disappeared. Ahmeek is home to the last manned lighthouse that was built on the lakes. Built in 1917, the Sand Hills Lighthouse, like lighthouses almost everywhere, fell victim to electrification and automation.[3] The Coast Guard bought and automated the lighthouse in 1939, but after World War II, the lighthouse was abandoned —until Bill Frabotta bought it.[4] He and his wife, Mary, restored and renovated the property and opened a bed and breakfast at the lighthouse, which is now listed on the National Register of Historic Places.

History of Ahmeek

Like many towns in Michigan's western Upper Peninsula, Ahmeek, part of Copper Country, was first settled due to the mineral deposits in the area. The first mine opened in 1902, and the Ahmeek Mining Company began building five-room homes for miners in 1904.[5] The cost of building one of these early homes was $95.[6] In 1907, the village hall, containing a jail, a courtroom, and offices, was built, and the village began to take shape [7]. The village was incorporated two years later in 1909 and held its first elections in March of that year.[8] Maurice Kenel was elected the first village president.[9] With the success of the nearby mine, the village grew quickly. By 1910, the census recorded 760 people living in Ahmeek.[10]

The Copper Miners' Strike of 1913–1914

As Ahmeek grew through the success of the mines in the early 1900s, area miners began to push for unionization. Like many mining towns in the Upper Peninsula, Ahmeek was home to people from a variety of European countries, including Ireland, Finland, Poland, Sweden, Russia, and Hungary,[11] and the cultural and linguistic differences inherent in the international communities made unionization more difficult, particularly when faced with the opposition from the mine bosses.[12] Growing tensions throughout Copper Country, particularly in nearby Calumet, boiled over into the Copper Miner's Strike of 1913 and 1914. Thousands of miners throughout the region, including many in Ahmeek, went on strike to protest wages and working conditions, and many women in the area protested alongside the men.[13]

The strike, however, was accompanied by multiple acts of violence, including the Italian Hall disaster in nearby Calumet when someone shouted "fire" at a Christmas event.[14] There had not, in fact, been a fire, but the panic that ensued led to a stampede that caused the deaths of 73 people, most of them children.[15] In Ahmeek, strikers fired on a train of detectives hired by the mining companies and set off an explosion at a smokestack at the Ahmeek mine.[16] Numerous officials bemoaned the lack of law and order, but Judge Patrick O'Brien, who presided over cases related to the violence, noted that while the strikers were violating the law, the mining companies had done little to calm the situation and had instead acted in ways that had increased the "bitterness and hostility."[17]

The strike continued until early spring of 1914, and one factor in its end was the lack of funds for strike relief—money that was provided to strikers to support them while they were not collecting wages.[18] A vote to end the strike was held on April 12, and in Ahmeek, 600 of the 617 votes cast were to end the strike. The official end of the strike did not end tensions, however, though community members in Ahmeek worked to put the strike behind them.[19]

Decline and Persistence

Ahmeek's boom years faded with the decline of the copper industry, which suffered in the 1920s, and the Great Depression shook the industry still further.[20] The Ahmeek mine closed in 1966.[21]

The decline in mining coincided with a decrease in population in Ahmeek, but the village was determined to hold on. Entrepreneurs attempted a variety of business ventures in the town, including an ice cream factory, an ice company, a meat market, multiple grocery stores, a restaurant, and even a shop that sold agates.[22] Some of these businesses, such as the meat market and the agate shop, were successful, while others were not.

Ahmeek Today

Though the Ahmeek Mine has been closed for decades, the village of Ahmeek still holds reminders of its days as a mining town. Many of the houses are those first built by the Ahmeek Mining Company, and the older roads even have a copper color to them.

Village events are held at the village hall or at Gabriel Chopp Park. Local businesses include the Dairy Bar (an ice cream shop) and two antique shops. Visitors can stay at the old streetcar station, which now is a vacation rental that also houses a visitor center for the North Woods Conservancy Center and an ice cream shop.[23] The village also has a Catholic church, a post office, a fire station, and, of course, the lighthouse, which is now a popular bed and breakfast.

A mineral compound called mohawkite has been mined in the Mohawk-Ahmeek area. This is the only known place in the world where the specific compound of silver, arsenic, cobalt, iron, nickel, and, of course, copper can be found.[24]

Population: 402[1]   **Incorporated:** 1910[2]

INSETS L to R: As part of the veterans' memorial, American flags decorate the plaques recognizing local soldiers who fought in America's wars • This building was completed over one hundred years ago in 1905 • A park and playground area along Beach Street • The Pariahs Motorcycle Club has a meeting place in Akron

The main road running through Akron is known as Beach Street, no doubt in reference to Charles Beach, one of the first settlers in town.

TOP: The grain elevator near the downtown area of Akron

Akron

History of Akron

AKRON WAS FIRST SETTLED BY A EUROPEAN IN 1854, when Charles Beach came to the area and named the settlement there Beach's Corners.[3] Three years later, when the town received its first post office, the name was changed to Akron after Akron Township, where it was located.[4] The township in turn was named after Akron, Ohio.[5] Akron's first postmaster was Samuel B. Covey, though not long after he took the role, the post office was moved from Akron.[6] It did not return to the village until 1882, and at that time George Simmons became postmaster.[7]

Samuel Lynn first platted the village in 1882, and that was also the year the Saginaw, Tuscola & Huron Railroad came to Akron.[8] 1882 was also the year Akron gained its first true business enterprise, a store built by G. W. Crane.[9] The next year saw the start of a second store, a lumber company, a stave bolt mill, a sawmill, and a cheese box factory.[10] Another year saw the addition of a blacksmith shop and a wagon shop.[11]

By the early part of the twentieth century, the town also had a flour mill, a cider mill, a hay and grain company, a furniture store, two drugstores, a barber, a hotel, a boarding stable, a jeweler, a photographer, a bank, two physicians, and a milliner.[12] Within another fifteen years, the village had added a confectioner, a cooperative cheese factory, a grain elevator, a pool hall, and a restaurant.[13] There was also a coal mining operation.[14]

Akron Today

The land around Akron today is primarily used for agriculture. There is a large grain elevator, and the local farmland grows a variety of crops, including sugar beets, corn, wheat, and dry beans. Some of the farmland also has wind turbines to generate wind energy. In the summer, there is a farmers market in the village itself.

The community in Akron is close knit, and there are a variety of community-wide events that take place. They hold a softball tournament over Labor Day weekend, and each December there is a Christmas parade and bake sale.

On the west side of the village, there is a community park with playground equipment and plenty of shade trees. Businesses in the town include a post office, a hair salon, a gas station, a restaurant, a car wash, a motorcycle club, and a bank. There is also a county road commission, a police department, and a fire department. Churches in the town include the Akron Community Church of God, the Wisner United Methodist Church, and the Great Lakes Baptist Church. The Akron-Fairgrove Elementary School, which serves students from kindergarten through fifth grade, also makes its home in Akron.

Many of the businesses in Akron help sponsor the annual Michigan Bean Festival in nearby Fairgrove.

Population: 191[1]   **Incorporated:** 1950[2]

INSETS L to R: A mural remembering Captain Moses Allen, who founded the village • A shop at the site of the old Allen Township Hall • The Allen Antique Mall Plus along US 12 • A brick-faced shop front in the downtown area

TOP: One of the many popular antique shops along US-12

Allen built its first high school in 1869.[15] Though the building burned down in 1913, the community came together to approve the building of a new school within a few weeks of the fire.[16]

First built in 1879, the Robert and Barbara Watkins Home still stands in Allen.[17] The house has recently undergone extensive restoration to ensure it continues to stand in Allen.[18]

Allen

An Important Crossroads

TODAY ALLEN IS A SMALL COMMUNITY OF UNDER 200 PEOPLE, but it is located at a historically important location. Before European settlers came to the area, the town's present location was the intersection of two main trails, the Great Trail and the Sauk Trail.[3] The American Indians called the area where Allen now sits *Mascootah-siac*, roughly translated as Sand Prairie Creek.[4]

The area was first surveyed by a team that included Captain Moses Allen, a veteran of the War of 1812.[5] When he came to the area where Allen now sits, he found it to be a prime place to bring his family.[6] He settled there in 1827 and called the place Allen's Prairie, though today the village is simply known as Allen.[7]

Allen was the first full settlement in Hillsdale County, and the first school in Hillsdale County was also in Allen, opening in 1831.[8] A hotel opened in the village in 1837, and after it was painted pink, locals called it the Old Pink Tavern.[9] Another famous early dwelling was the Allen House, first built in the late 1830s and which held a tavern in the mid-1840s.[10] By the 1860s, the town had grown to include a blacksmith, a carriage shop, a few smaller stores, a mercantile, a drugstore, and two churches.[11]

The first post office at Allen was opened when the settlement was still called Allen's Prairie, but the post office itself was called Sylvanus.[12] It did not change to the name Allen until 1849, and the village was not officially platted until 1868.[13] Two additions to the plat followed, first in 1869 and then in 1871.[14]

Antique Capital of the World

Allen may be a small town, but in one area, it's the biggest. Known as the Antique Capital of the World, Allen has dozens of historic buildings and antique shops. There is the Hog Creek Antique Mall, the Allen Antique Barn, Capital Antiques, Preston's Antique Gaslight Village, and the Allen Antique Mall, among others.

Allen Today

Today, Allen is located on U.S. Highway 12, with Railroad Street being the main north-south road, leaving the village looking a bit like a cross. The antique stores are on US-12, but Allen is not only a town for antiques. Madigan's Sports Pub is located on the western side of town, and closer to downtown there is also an oil and gas company, a fire department, a post office, and a historical museum. A building in the downtown area is for the Knights of Pythias and Pythias Sisters. There is a park in the middle of town that has a gazebo and a playground. The park also includes a memorial to Assistant Chief Wilson of the Allen Police Department who was killed in the line of duty in 1954.

Allen is also served by two churches. There is a Baptist church and a United Methodist church.

Allen is located along the US 12 Heritage Trail, which bills itself as the road "meant for Michigan memories."[19]

TOP: The Porter School, built in 1914, now houses small businesses and community events

Population: 145[1] **Incorporated:** 1914[2]

INSETS L to R: The Mastodon Township Veteran's Memorial • The First National Bank building now houses the Alpha Museum • Between 1932 and 1954, Alpha's high school basketball team won three state championships • The Village Hall building

Alpha is known for its Fourth of July activities, which include a flag-raising ceremony, a parade, children's activities, and speeches.[16] The day ends with a community-purchased fireworks display.

In 2005, Alpha sold the Porter School to Charles Hoogland for $1.[17] Hoogland restored the old school and moved his woodshop business into the building. Today, other small businesses have joined Hoogland in the old school.

Alpha

History of Alpha

IN 1884, OVERLY OPTIMISTIC EXPLORERS indicated that the area near Alpha contained ample amounts of iron.[3] The Alpha mine was started to mine the iron, but only a tenth of the explorers' expected ore was ever discovered there, making the mining expedition there a failure.[4] Still, Alpha was a mining town. Around 1910, the Pickands & Mather Company began construction on a large mine, and people came from all over, hoping to find work.[5] The area where they settled was the newly platted village of Alpha, about a half mile north of the development. Three years later, the village received a post office, then in 1914 it officially became incorporated and held its first elections.[6] E. J. Pearce was elected the first village president.[7]

With an official village government, the town quickly saw improvements. A school had already been opened, but within the first year of being an incorporated village, Alpha had two new hand pumps for water, funding for street improvements, and plans to bring power to Alpha by the formation of the Alpha Light and Power Company.[8] The traffic circle in the middle of town was also established that year.[9] In the fall of 1915, the village also got its first concrete sidewalks, and in 1917 they set their first regulations for cars in the village.[10] The last mine in the Alpha area closed in 1958,[11] and today Alpha is primarily a bedroom community served by Crystal Falls and Iron Mountain.

The Mastodon Mine

One of the first mines opened in the Alpha area was known as the Mastodon mine, named for the mastodon bones that were found during the sinking of a mine shaft. That find later gave its name to nearby Mastodon, just a few miles down the road from Alpha.[12]

The Balkan Mine

Disaster struck at another area mine in 1914. While drilling to drain a water from the mine, miners accidentally released quicksand instead, which poured into the mine, creating an avalanche. Twelve men were trapped, and seven of those, aged 22 to 45, died in the cave-in.[13]

Alpha Today

Alpha is built around a large traffic circle, called the Alpha Circle, and the Porter School, first built in 1914, still stands proudly, just back from the road. It no longer houses school children but instead has been remodeled to allow small businesses to use the old classrooms.[14] In addition, the space is sometimes used for community events or gatherings.

The village also has a community and senior center, a water tower, a township hall, a veterans memorial, an inn, and a shooting range. A newer business is the Alpha Michigan Brewing Company, which is in the old Alpha General Store building.[15] Also of note in the town is the historic First National Bank building, which currently houses the village museum.

Alpha is not the only village in Michigan named after a Greek letter. There have also been communities named Epsilon, Delta, and Sigma.

TOP: An old brick building on the corner of Main and Sherman Streets in downtown Applegate

Population: 248[1]   Incorporated: 1903[2]

INSETS L to R: A humorous sign outside the Applegate Market •
Apples decorate the address sign outside of one of Applegate's
buildings • Looking south down Sherman Street • A veterans'
memorial near the train tracks

A local institution for more than a century,
the Applegate Inn's basement still partially has
a dirt floor.

Applegate

History of Applegate

APPLEGATE CAN TRACE ITS BEGINNINGS BACK TO 1856,
when George Pack built a sawmill in the area that would later become
the village.[3] In 1858, the first church in the area near Applegate opened,
a United Brethren church.[4] The post office opened in 1880, and the
village was named at that time for Jesse Applegate, a pioneer who had
helped establish part of a settlement trail into Oregon.[5] As some residents say that Applegate was once known as Andersonville, it seems
likely that the area known as Anderson Station was near the current site
of Applegate.

The Applegate Inn is over one hundred years old, and it's seen
much of Applegate's history discussed at the bar in the evenings, and in
1974 it became a part of that history when a man was shot in the bar.[6]

In its heyday, Applegate was a thriving town, with a big railroad
station on the Pere Marquette Railway and a grain elevator.[7, 8] The
foundations from the station are still visible by the railroad tracks that
cut through town. In the 1940s, a man named Sam Elliott—no not
that Sam Elliott—owned a gas station, and by the 1980s, there were
two gas stations.[9]

A Mob in Applegate

John J. Cornish was an early Mormon Missionary who traveled
widely throughout Canada and Michigan. Relations between Mormons
and non-Mormons were tense during much of the 1800s, and attacks
and assaults weren't uncommon. In fact, when Cornish and a colleague

were in Applegate, they were confronted by a mob that pelted them with rotten eggs.[10]

Applegate Today

Applegate, like many small towns, has encountered some obstacles lately. The funding simply isn't there, and that causes businesses to often choose elsewhere to operate.[11] However, the long-term residents, often from legacy families in the village, feel a strong connection to Applegate. "It's not about how much money you have but what you mean to people," says JoAnn Zerilli, owner of the Applegate Inn.[12] "People are quick to help each other."[13]

Applegate has a post office, a general store, a bank, a hair salon, a thrift store, an inn, a veterans memorial, and a fire department. The old fire station, from 1914, is now a museum that contains information about Applegate's past. The village is served by two churches, the Applegate Wesleyan Church and a United Methodist church.

The village has recently begun holding an annual Summer Festival in August that brings together residents of Applegate and nearby communities. The festival includes tractor and wagon rides, a car and tractor show, a variety of children's activities, a selection of vendors, and, of course, food.

TOP: The baseball field in Bancroft

Population: 545[1]   **Incorporated:** 1883[2]

INSETS L to R: The residential streets in Bancroft are shaded by many mature trees • The railroad tracks run diagonally through the town • The United Methodist church • Many of the buildings in the town date back to its earlier days

Bancroft is home to the Van Agen Sod & Tree Farm, a sixth-generation family-owned farm. The Van Agen family, originally from Belgium, first started their farm in Roseville, Michigan, but when the construction of I-94 broke the farmland into three sections, they moved to Bancroft, where they have been selling sod ever since.[22]

Bancroft

Mat Wixom's Great Show

AS A CHILD, MAT WIXOM DREW A PICTURE OF A HORSE painted with stripes and, calling it a zebra, charged people an admission to see it.[3] Though as an adult he was a lawyer in Bancroft, he still held a fascination with things related to the circus, and, in 1874, while Mat was in his early thirties, he organized a circus.[4] The first season was a financial failure, but Mat, undeterred, tried again, and this time he found success.[5] His circus, which he ran with various family members for over twenty years, showed under a variety of names, including Wixom Bros. Palace Show and Congress of Stars, and Wixom Brothers Great Shows.[6] He eventually passed management of the show on to his sons, who continued the circus through 1907.[7]

History of Bancroft

In 1877, the Chicago and Lake Huron Railroad extended to the place where Bancroft now stands.[8] N. S. VanTuyl selected the site to begin a lumbering business, and he built the first frame structure in the area.[9] The village was officially platted in that year,[10] after a previous platting had gone unrecorded,[11] and its post office, which is still in operation today, opened.[12] John L. Simonson was named the first postmaster,[13] and the first village elections were held in the spring of 1877.[14] L. C. Shelley was elected the first president.[15]

Within the first few years of its founding, the village had a hotel, a school, two planing mills, a sawmill, and a flouring mill.[16] A series of fires impeded Bancroft's growth[17] but were not enough to stop the success of the town. Bancroft was in a desirable location, and the Ann Arbor Railroad was considering the village for the site of a junction.[18] Indeed, the village leaders had so much confidence that Bancroft would be selected for the site of the junction that they refused to give in to the railroad's requests and, in the end, lost the junction.[19] It was a setback, but not one that would cripple the town. The village was still a stop on the Chicago and Lake Huron Railroad, and, by the early 1900s, Bancroft had gained a second hotel, a furniture factory, a screen factory, a foundry, a grist mill, and an elevator, and had also signed a contract with an electricity company to bring public and private electricity services to the town.[20] Still, in the early part of the twentieth century, the population of the town began to decline slightly and the lumbering business began to taper off.[21]

Bancroft Today

Though the village is no longer the thriving lumber town it once was, the community has not given up. The village council is working with residents to enact a plan of revitalization for the town.

In the meantime, Bancroft has a fire station, a village hall, a post office, a gas station, a party store, a library, and a funeral home. There are three churches in the community, the First Congregational Church, the First Baptist Church, and Bancroft United Methodist Church. Village residents and visitors alike can enjoy a cup of coffee at the Village Coffee Cup or relax with an adult beverage at Woody's Bancroft Tavern. The community hall is available for rent for community events, and there are two parks as well.

A recent survey sent to residents and posted at a town notice board identified proposed future improvements to town, including updating the sidewalks, parks, flower beds, and the town veterans' memorial.

Population: 355[1]   **Incorporated:** 1908[2]

INSETS L to R: Fall colors along the Chippewa River • The Barryton Elementary school, built in 1935 • Looking west down Northern Avenue • The Barryton Public Library

Barryton held a celebration on its fourth birthday, and a notice in the *Alma Record* promised "balloon ascensions, bicycle races and parade, bandmusic, bowery dances, baseball games, and . . . 'bumptious orators.'"[19]

TOP: This gazebo, which overlooks the Chippewa River, is located near the village offices

Barryton

A Famous Market That Has Survived

BARRYTON'S MACKERSIE BROTHERS' MARKET first opened in 1920.[3] Six years after it opened, disaster struck. Within a six-week timeframe, the store burned down and both brothers passed away.[4] Even that was not enough for the family to give up, and the market, now run by the fifth generation of the family, is a fixture of current-day Barryton. The year 2020 will mark the store's centennial.

History of Barryton

Barryton was founded in 1894 when Frank Barry and his wife Marion first came to the area.[5] He registered the plat that year, an area of approximately twelve blocks, though he originally wanted the town to be called simply Barry.[6] A post office opened in Barryton the same year

it was platted, and within two more years, the town had grown to include a livery stable, a sawmill, a planing mill, a pharmacy, a hardware store, two hotels, and two general stores.[7] By the turn of the century, the village had approximately 500 residents, and transportation options to and from the village had expanded to include a stagecoach trail and service on the Pere Marquette Railroad.[8]

Barry was a businessman involved in the grocery and pharmacy industries, and in real estate as well.[9] He had no training in medicine but still offered to treat local residents, earning him the nickname Doc.[10] He also was occasionally involved in the lumber business.[11]

Three early school buildings still stand in the village today. The first is the Titus School, a one-room building built in 1882 that is now part of the Barryton Area Museum. The Covert School, built two years later, in 1884, is also attached to the museum. The Barryton Elementary School, which still stands today, was built in 1935 and is still in use.[12]

Annual Barryton Lilac Festival

Barryton has numerous community gatherings each year, including Barryton Homecoming Days, Taste of Barryton, and the Barryton Lilac Festival. Perhaps the largest of these events is the Lilac Festival, held in late spring of each year. It includes a parade, a petting zoo, a talent show, a car show, shopping opportunities with a selection of craft vendors, and a variety of other family-friendly activities.[13] There is live music, and other Mecosta County–area organizations get involved, too, such as the Mt. Pleasant Discovery Museum.[14]

Barryton Today

Two branches of the Chippewa River meet in Barryton, and the sign welcoming you to the village proclaims, "Life is good where the rivers meet."

In addition to fishing opportunities, Barryton also has a gas station, a grocery store, a dentist, a car wash, a pizza shop, an auto sales and service store, a bank, a hardware store, and two dollar stores, among other businesses. The village has a library, a township hall, a township community center, and a senior center. The Barryton Elementary School is part of the Chippewa Hill School District, and the Chippewa Hills Board of Education has plans to build a new elementary school in Barryton.[15] The school serves children from kindergarten through fourth grade.[16]

Across from the school there is a park with a playground, a pavilion, and tennis courts. The Barryton Area Museum, right next to the park, is open to visitors on weekends from May through the end of September.[17] The museum is attached to a one-room schoolhouse.[18] The village is also served by a few churches, including a United Methodist church, a Free Methodist church, and the Barryton Church of God.

In 2011, a woman named Heather Holland helped solve the case of Kristin Spires, a 20-year-old from Barryton who had gone missing the year previous.[20] Holland worked with Spires' stepmother, Carolyn.[21]

TOP: This one-lane bridge was built by the Wrought Iron Bridge Company in 1876

Population: 294[1] **Incorporated:** 1973[2]

INSETS L to R: The Barton Hills Country Club • A look toward Barton Pond from Barton Shore Drive • One of the buildings at the Barton Hills Country Club • Flowers growing along the Huron River

Unlike many affluent communities of the early 1900s, Barton Hills never enacted any race-based restrictions on residents, and today it has residents from a variety of racial and ethnic backgrounds.[23]

Barton Hills

History of Barton Hills

BARTON HILLS LIES ON THE HURON RIVER, and it is because of the Huron River that the village exists. The first land sold in the area was in the late 1820s, and the Towar's Wayne County Creamery bought a farm there in 1896.[3] With its steep hills, the area was not well suited to farming, but it was fine for cows, and the farm maintained operations until 1912, when it was sold to Huron Farms, a subsidiary of the Detroit Edison Company.[4] Some of the buildings from the creamery still stand today.[5]

The real start of the community, however, came with the construction of the Barton Dam. The Detroit Edison Company, an offshoot of the original Edison Illuminating Company started by Thomas Edison, soon began building a series of hydroelectric dams and generating stations across Michigan, including one in Barton. The original plan was to sell off any land not needed for the operation and maintenance of the dams, but the president of Detroit Edison instead chose to use the property for several different purposes, including as a retreat for female employees of the company.[6] After the construction of the dam, the company retained the services of the Olmsted Brothers to design a residential community on the land.[7]

The First Landscape Architects

The Olmsted Brothers are one of the most illustrious landscape architecture companies in the history of the United States. The Olmsted brothers were the son and stepson of famous landscape architect Frederick Law Olmsted, who designed Central Park in New York and the expansion to the U.S. Capitol Grounds. They followed in his revolutionary footsteps, designing parks, college campuses, and facilities around the country, and even portions of some of the national park system. They often also provided their services to smaller communities that were influenced by the "City Beautiful" movement.[8] Proponents of the movement argue that beautiful, well-ordered cities and parks can produce well-ordered civic societies.

Transforming "Barren Hills"

The Olmsted Brothers had ambitious plans, and, at first, some people thought the job a hopeless one and joked about the proposed community being called "Barren Hills."[9] The plan called for large lots that were laid out with the view and geography in mind, the construction of a pond, and a country club on one of the higher points, looking down over the community.[10] After a few years of planning, work began on the community in 1919.[11]

The village grew, and eventually families not tied to Detroit Edison came to the village. The oversight of the Detroit Edison Company was to be short lived, however. During the Depression and into the beginning of World War II, the dam and utility service had become a liability for the company, and with materials needed for the war, construction on new houses nearly halted. Finally, in 1944, the company made the village residents an offer: Detroit Edison would give the village $10,000 in exchange for their taking over the costs related to community maintenance.[12] In a sense, the company had given the village to its residents. In 1973, the village decided to seek status as a home rule village (a village with a large amount of control over its own charter, laws, and ordinances), and became the first such municipality in the county.[13]

The Olmsted Brothers' Impact on Barton Hills

The Olmsted Brothers did a lot more than simply designing lots and adding a pond. They designed the layout of roads by balancing artistic concerns with the more mundane matters of drainage and grading,[14] and they made all design decisions with the goal of making the manmade and natural elements work in harmony.[15] Some residents even consulted them for decisions related to the landscape design of their own lots.[16]

In the years that followed the completion of the Olmsted Brothers' work on the community, residents slowly began to forget about the work they'd done.[17] In recent years, however, they have tried to return to the roots first laid down in the early 1900s, though their problems now stem mostly from maintenance, such as how to handle plant overgrowth in Barton Pond and what to do about the size of the area's deer herd.[18]

Barton Hills Today

True to its roots as a community built around nature and with an artistic eye, all homes in Barton Hills must be individually designed by a registered architect and all plans must be approved by an architectural review community.[19] The community is quiet, set in among the trees, and is almost entirely residential.

The Barton Hills Country Club, which celebrated its one-hundred-year anniversary in 2017, provides social and athletic services to residents of Barton Hills and the surrounding Ann Arbor area.[20] It occupies land first donated to the village by the president of the Detroit Edison Company and still strives to meet its mission of serving families.[21] The community also has the Barton Boat Club, first established in 1937, which offers opportunities to sail on Barton Pond.[22]

In 1998, building excavations in Barton Hills revealed the grave of an American Indian woman who lived over one thousand years ago.[24]

Population: 286[1]   Incorporated: 1893[2]

INSETS L to R: This bear holds the sign for a local store • Niizh Makwa Traders sells "unique cultural treasures" • This sign welcomes visitors to both the village and the lake • Hopkins Park

Despite its many changes over the years, several Bear Lake families have seen it all. Bear Lake is home to more than half a dozen Centennial Farms—farms that have been in the same family for at least one hundred years.[24] As of 2014, the Centennial Farms in the area were owned by Mabel Schimke, Hazel Briske, Winston S. Churchill EST, Donovan and Bernice Anderson, Harold and Joyce Johnson, Earl and Dorothy Osborn, and Douglas and Linda Alkire.[25]

TOP: The veterans' memorial, located on Lake Street, overlooks the lake

Bear Lake

History of Bear Lake

PEOPLE HAVE LIVED ALONGSIDE MICHIGAN'S BEAR LAKE for thousands of years. This long history is attested to by a number of burial mounds discovered on the west shore of the lake, including one that had a diameter of approximately twenty feet and a height of around seven feet.[3]

The first European settler in the area where Bear Lake village now sits was Russell F. Smith.[4] He first came to the Grand Traverse area of Michigan in 1863 but then followed an American Indian trail to Bear Lake.[5] He was so taken with the area that he bought land and moved his family there.[6] Their early years homesteading in the area proved to be difficult, though the difficulties lessened as more settlers came to the area.[7] Smith was essential in this effort, providing encouragement and assistance to new settlers.[8]

The true start of the village, however, came when Smith sold part of his farm to the Hopkins Brothers in 1873.[9] The Hopkins brothers brought businesses to the town. They provided the money to build a sawmill and a grist mill and also oversaw construction of a large store.[10] By the end of the 1870s, they had also been instrumental in building the horse-powered Bear Lake Tram Railway, which featured maple rails and transported cargo to and from the nearby town of Pierport on Lake Michigan.[11] They also built a livery stable, a manufacturing company, and, eventually, the Bear Lake and Eastern Railroad.[12]

As technology and building methods changed, they kept Bear Lake on the forefront of change by rebuilding or improving businesses as necessary. Their rebuilt grist mill in 1881 became the first roller-style mill in all of northern Michigan.[13]

Theirs were not the only business enterprises in Bear Lake. The Hopkins brothers were supportive of others in the town, sometimes even loaning money to help with the start of a new business.[14] By the late 1870s, the village had over 70 buildings.[15] The growth could not last forever, though, and once all the trees in the area had been cleared, the village had to find a new purpose, as the mills closed and the railroad ceased to operate.[16] By the 1920s, the population had begun to drop drastically.[17]

The Lake that Gave the Town Its Name

The village of Bear Lake sits on the southern side of its namesake lake. Like many Michigan lakes, Bear Lake was formed by glaciers, though it is a small lake of approximately 1800 acres.[18] Reports from the late 1800s list the water to be "clear as crystal,"[19] and while the lake isn't as clear as it once was, it is still a beautiful blue, and a recent planning document for Bear Lake Township identified steps that could further improve water quality.

At its maximum, Bear Lake is 24 feet deep, and while not particularly deep, it's enough for the use of watercraft on the lake, both for leisure and fishing.[20] The lake has walleye, bass, perch, bluegill, and a variety of other fish and is considered one of the better fishing lakes in its part of the state.[21]

Bear Lake Today

Today, Bear Lake focuses on agriculture and tourism rather than logging, and the population fluctuates between the winter and the summer months. The village and its surrounding area have a golf course, a campground, a bed and breakfast, and lake access, and the food options in the area include a café, a restaurant, and an ice cream shop. There is also a bank, a hardware store, a design center, a gas station, a dollar store, an insurance agency, a health center, a car wash, a hair salon, and a barber. Services in the area include a post office, a library, a school, and a township hall. The Bear Lake area is served by a United Methodist church.

The oldest business in Bear Lake is the local drugstore, Richmond Drug, which first opened in 1877.[22] At one point in the store's history it suffered damage from a fire and had to use the back door as the customers' main entrance for a time.[23]

Population: 349[1]   **Incorporated:** 1932[2]

INSETS L to R: The former Benzie County Courthouse • Looking northeast down South Benzie Road • A row of brightly colored birdhouses decorate a fence in Beulah • Myers Granary Antique Market

TOP: The Beulah Public Beach is located on the southeast shore of Crystal Lake

In 1873, an attempt to connect Crystal Lake to the Betsie River went awry. The "Tragedy of Crystal Lake" led to a massive flood, and one not without casualties; an out-of-towner known as "Peacock" drowned while trying to cross the still-raging stream.[22]

Beulah

Changing Crystal Lake

THE AREA WHERE BEULAH NOW STANDS, on the shores of Crystal Lake, was not always habitable. Prior to 1873, the water level of Crystal Lake was much higher—about 20 feet higher—and there was almost no shoreline to speak of.[3] The forest ran right up to the shore, and even slight winds caused whitecaps on the lake—giving the lake the nickname "Cap Lake."[4]

The town fathers soon hatched something of a wild plan. They wanted to connect Crystal Lake to the Betsie River; if they did so, they'd have access to the nearby port of Frankfort on Lake Michigan.[5] To this end, the Betsie River Improvement Company was founded,[6] but things didn't exactly go as planned. The company successfully cleared a chan-

nel below the lake's outlet to the Betsie River, and they then widened the connection between the outlet and the waiting canal.[7] They even commissioned the construction of a steamboat that was intended to carry cargo down the river and back.[8] At first, just a trickle of water passed through, but that stream quickly widened, and soon it was a deluge.[9] The *Onward*, a steamboat in port at Frankfort at the time, made the trip up the raging river and into Crystal Lake.[10] The return trip, with the full current, was more perilous, but the vessel survived.[11]

Once the stream quieted, the proponents of the new canal were disappointed. The water level in the lake had dropped by 20 feet, and the steamboat was barely able to make one voyage downstream.[12] The lake, it seemed, had lost some of its appeal, but in retrospect, the change

24

has helped Beulah survive. It expanded the beach, opening up new area for settlement.[13] The change in geography also brought the Ann Arbor Railroad to the area.[14] Even today, the town's relationship with the lake is what allows it to succeed.

History of Beulah

Reverend Charles E. Bailey founded the town around 1880. He named the town after the Bible verse Isaiah 62:4.[15] Beulah used to be attached to Benzonia, another village in Benzie county. Benzonia's railroad station was named Beulah, but they officially became two separate communities in 1892.[16] As a village in its own right, Beulah received its first post office at the time of the split;[17] Charles S. Merritt was the first postmaster.[18] The Benzie County Courthouse in Beulah, now listed on the National Register of Historic Places, was also built early in Beulah's history, and while it was in use, it was variously used as a courthouse, a hotel, and a restaurant.[19]

Celebrating Crystal Lake

The seminal event in Beulah's history—the lowering of the lake —is still celebrated in the town today. Each year, the village celebrates Archibald Jones Day, named for the man supposedly responsible for the lowering of the lake.[20] On that day, the village gets together for a sort of reenactment of the event. In addition, there is a bridge walk, a selection of food and entertainment, and games from the 1870s.[21]

Beulah Today

Today, Beulah is the county seat of Benzie County, giving it an important significance in the county. However, it is more well known for its proximity to the Sleeping Bear Dunes and the nearby Interlochen Center for the Arts, and both bring visitors to the town. There are a variety of thriving businesses in Beulah, and many have names that recall the Bible verse for which the town was named. These include Eden Brook Place Apartments and Eden Bible Church.

There is a real sense of community in Beulah, which holds a wide variety of community events each year. They hold a fall festival, a Fourth of July celebration, a juried art fair, a team marathon, and two winter festivals.

The Darcy Library of Beulah is named in honor of the founder's dog. Though Darcy is no longer alive, the library still has a therapy dog come in for children to practice reading to.

TOP: The Powell Township School building was built in 1938

Population: 319[1]   **Unincorporated**

INSETS L to R: The Big Bay boat launch • The Big Bay Lighthouse • Big Bay Outfitters is located in the building that once housed Big Bay's jail • This marker is part of the Kcymaerxthaere parallel universe art project, one of nearly 100 installed worldwide

The Big Bay Lighthouse was converted into a bed and breakfast in 1986, though three lighthouse keepers still reside there.[22]

Big Bay

Anatomy of a Murder

BIG BAY MAY BE A SMALL TOWN in Michigan's Upper Peninsula, but it has had big publicity over the years—most particularly in the 1950s. In July of 1952, Korean War veteran 1st Lieutenant Coleman Peterson walked into the Lumberjack Tavern in Big Bay, pointed a gun at the bartender, a man named Mike Chenoweth, and shot six times.[2] Peterson's wife had come home bruised and told her husband that Chenoweth had raped her.[3] Peterson was found not guilty of the murder by reason of temporary insanity.[4] After the trial, however, doctors determined that Peterson's actions had been a one-time event, and after a one-month stay at an asylum, Peterson was free to go his own way.[5]

That alone might not have been enough for Big Bay to be remembered in infamy, but Peterson's defense attorney, John Voelker, writing under a pen name, published the book *Anatomy of a Murder* in 1956, drawing inspiration from the events of Peterson's crime and trial.[6] The book topped the bestseller lists for weeks on end, prompting director Otto Preminger to turn the book into a movie.[7] And the movie? Parts of it were filmed right in Big Bay. The Lumberjack Tavern didn't quite work for Preminger's vision, so many of the events were filmed in the Thunder Bay Inn down the block instead.[8]

History of Big Bay

Before Big Bay was known for its Hollywood ties, the area in and around where the village now sits was first known as a site where French traders and American Indians would exchange goods.[9] In the mid-1870s, a group of lumber workers came to the area and started the town, naming it after Big Bay on Lake Superior.[10] At the beginning of the twentieth century, the Big Bay post office opened, and Andrew McAfee was the first postmaster.

The Big Bay Lighthouse

Big Bay's lighthouse is another town fixture. The Big Bay Light was completed in 1897 and was in active service until 1956.[11] In 1986 it opened as a bed and breakfast and its light now serves as a private aid to navigation. When first built, it was an incredibly isolated spot, and it saw its share of tragedy. Its first lighthouse keeper ended up taking his own life after the assistant keeper, his son, died due to injuries from a fall.[12] The keeper's ghost is reputed to haunt the site today.[13]

The Henry Ford Connection

Big Bay was a lumber town, and the first industry in town was a mill for Brunswick Bowling Pins.[14] In the early 1940s, the lumber focus in the area changed to car manufacturing when Henry Ford came to town and built a sawmill for the creation of boards for the panels of Ford's station wagons.[15] He did not stop at just the sawmill, however, and also purchased the nearby power plant and a number of buildings in Big Bay.[16] Ford also purchased what is now the Thunder Bay Inn. Built in 1911, the building originally housed a lumber warehouse and store, but when Henry Ford bought it in 1940, it became a vacation home.[17] He was so determined to have his vacation home be an ideal place for him that he went so far as to have several local houses and buildings—including the railroad depot—moved, so as to not interfere with his view.[18] His family sold the building in 1947 after Ford passed away.[19]

By the 1960s, the building's use had changed again, this time to become a hotel called the Big Bay Hotel.[20] Unfortunately, Big Bay had begun to go into decline. When the inn's present owner purchased the property in 1986, only two businesses were open in the whole town.[21] Another town might have given up, but Big Bay held on, and in recent years, it has been making a true comeback.

Big Bay Today

In addition to the Thunder Bay Inn and the Lumberjack Tavern, Big Bay contains a number of businesses. There is a bed and breakfast in the old lighthouse, a campground, and motels. There is a gas station, a general store, the Hungry Hollow Café, a laundromat, Big Bay Outfitters, and a few art and gift shops. There is public beach access for visitors to the town, and Burns Landing Historical Park is nearby. In the winter months, snowmobiling and other winter sports are popular. The Powell Township Hall is in Big Bay, and there is also a volunteer fire department and a road commission building. There is a Catholic church and a Presbyterian church in Big Bay, and the Bay Cliff Health Camp is nearby.

The film version of *Anatomy of a Murder* was filmed just a block away from the original crime scene. Today, the Lumberjack Tavern boasts movie memorabilia on its walls and three bullet holes still visible in the wall.[23]

INSETS L to R: Augustus Haven Park is named after Augustus Haven, one of the earlier settlers of Bloomingdale • The local grocery store • A mural adorns the side of one of the buildings near the downtown area of Bloomingdale • The Depot Museum

Bloomingdale has had a telephone company for over 100 years.[23] It began in 1908 when the Bloomingdale Telephone Company was organized to oversee the telephone and switchboard communications in the area. Today the company, under a new name, provides telephone and high-speed internet services.

TOP: This caboose is part of the Bloomingdale Depot Museum

Bloomingdale

The Oil Boom in Michigan

THE POPULATION PEAK IN BLOOMINGDALE'S HISTORY was not due to a flourishing lumber industry or copious mineral resources like in other Michigan towns.[3] It was the discovery of oil in 1938 that led to Bloomingdale's population boom.[4] Everyone in Bloomingdale wanted their own oil well, and most people eventually came to have one.[5] A total of 437 wells were drilled, with a few dozen right inside the village itself, and the Bloomingdale Field, as the oil discovery was called, ended up producing more than ten million barrels of oil.[6] There were few regulations at the time, however, and development was aggressive—eventually leading to new regulations for oil drilling for the entirety of the state.[7] The Oil and Gas Act, Michigan Act 61 of 1939, is still used to guide oil and gas drilling today.[8]

History of Bloomingdale

Bloomingdale's history goes back long before the oil boom. The first European settler in the area was Henry Kilhefer. He moved after another man in the area gave him an acre of land in 1855.[9] Two other early settlers were Samuel and Orrit Lane.[10] Orrit, after seeing the beautiful scenery, especially the multitude of wildflowers, declared the place should be called Bloomingdale.[11]

In the early years of the village, the only way to get to and from Bloomingdale was on American Indian trails, as there were no roads, and the railroad had not yet come to town.[12] The first business enterprise in the town was a store opened by Kilhefer in the late 1850s.[13] Within a few years, a drugstore, a mercantile, a dressmaking shop, and two hotels had also opened in the town.[14] The Michigan Central Railroad placed a depot in Bloomingdale in 1870.[15]

A Pair of Professional Baseball Players

Bill and Wade Killefer, brothers born in the late 1800s, were two professional baseball players from Bloomingdale and direct descendents of town father Henry Kilhefer. (The surname changed spellings several times over the years.) They played baseball at nearby Paw Paw High School, winning state championships, before moving on to the pros.[16] Bill "Reindeer" Killefer, the younger of the brothers, is best known for being a talented catcher who played for a time with the Chicago Cubs alongside Grover Cleveland Alexander, a Hall of Fame pitcher.[17] Bill often led the National League in throwing out base runners.[18] After his playing career was over, he served as a manager and as a coach for major league teams, winning a World Series as a pitching coach with the 1926 St. Louis Cardinals.

Older brother Wade "Red" Killefer was a versatile player, and during his career he played all nine positions.[19] He is best known for his time playing with the Detroit Tigers in 1908 when they won the American League pennant.[20] After he left professional baseball, he went on to become a manager in the minor leagues.[21] Over time the brothers became overlooked in baseball lore, but in 2009 the Society for American Baseball Research dedicated a pair of monuments to the brothers in Paw Paw.[22]

Bloomingdale Today

The oil reserves are now exhausted, but the town still remembers its past. There is an old oil derrick (not one from Bloomingdale) behind the old train depot on Kalamazoo Street. The depot itself is now a historical museum with a wide variety of historical items from the village's past. The railroad has become a trail, as part of the Rails to Trails program in Michigan, and the Kal-Haven Trail now runs through the village, right beside the derrick and museum.

The town also has two schools, a municipal center with offices for both the village and the township, a library, and a post office. Local businesses include Goldie Ray's Café, Classy Creations, a grocery store, a telephone company, a technology store, a real estate office, a gas station, a funeral home, and several churches.

Film and television actress Betsy Palmer, perhaps best known for her role as Mrs. Voorhees in *Friday the 13th*, used to spend summers in Bloomingdale.[24]

TOP: The town veterans' memorial

Population: 294[1]   Incorporated: 1893[2]

INSETS L to R: These ski runs at Boyne Mountain overlook the town • A local hotel • The Boyne Falls United Methodist Church, built in 1892 • Some older structures line one of the roads out of town

The main tourist draw in Boyne Falls may be Boyne Mountain, but the area is also a prime location for fishing and hunting, and people come from all over the country to enjoy these sports.[26]

Boyne Falls

History of Boyne Falls

SOME OF THE FIRST EUROPEANS in the area where Boyne Falls village now stands were followers of Jacob Strang, who came to Michigan from Wisconsin in the 1840s, though most stayed on and near Beaver Island.[3] The first settler who played a role in the history of the Boyne Falls settlement was John Miller, who came to the area in 1857.[4] The river and surrounding forests made the area good for logging, and within a short time, a dam, a mill, and a millpond had all been built.[5] However, the village of Boyne Falls did not begin in earnest until 1874 when the Grand Rapids & Indiana Railroad came to the area.[6] That same year saw the establishment of a post office and the first store in the village.[7] The village was incorporated in 1893,[8] and within a few years it had five general stores, three hotels, a hardware store, a pharmacy, a barber, a livery stable, a bank, and a number of saloons.[9]

In its early days, Boyne Falls was a logging town, but the village supported more than just loggers and their families. In 1902, Guy C. Conkle, a doctor, came to Boyne Falls and opened a practice that served people in Boyne Falls as well as in several surrounding communities, including nearby Boyne City.[10] During the early part of the twentieth century the village also supported farming, brickmaking, and milling industries.[11] The village also had a telephone office, though before the arrival of the railroad, it was run out of a boxcar.[12]

The Boyne Mountain Ski Resort

The Boyne Mountain resort can trace its roots back to 1947 when Everett Kircher built a small lodge on 40 acres of land he purchased for $1.[13] Kircher called the place the Boyne Ski Club and set out to make his ski resort one of the best in the Midwest.[14] At first, the resort only had one lift and one run,[15] though it began to grow almost at once, helped by an increase in skiers to the area in the 1950s, including then-Congressman Gerald Ford.[16] Over the years the resort has earned many honors and achieved many firsts. The resort saw the world's first installation of both a triple and a four-person chair in 1964.[17] Kircher died in 2002, but his sons now manage the company, making it a true family endeavor.[18]

Where are the Falls in Boyne Falls?

Boyne Falls is named for the falls on the Boyne River that runs on the west side of town.[19] However, the falls are so small that even many residents aren't sure where they are—though no doubt this confusion is also caused by the falls' location: where the river flows underneath M-75.

The Boyne Falls Annual Polish Festival

Every summer, Boyne Falls holds a Polish Festival in the downtown area of the village. Begun in 1975, the festival spans four days and has a variety of activities for everyone in the family.[20] In addition to the Polish food, Polish music, and plenty of opportunities to polka, there is also bingo, a carnival, a car show, a bike parade, live music, a four-wheel-drive mud run, and a parade.[21] On Sunday, the last day of the festival, they also hold a mass in one of the tents.[22] The festival also offers the community a chance to honor some of its residents, and each year they select "Polish Royalty," including honored citizens, a grand marshal, a Little Miss, and a Little Mister.[23]

Boyne Falls Today

Today Boyne Falls is best known for being the site of Boyne Mountain, one of Michigan's top skiing destinations. The resort is not only for skiing, however, and summer activities, including scenic chairlift rides and golfing, bring tourists to the Boyne Falls area year-round.[24] In addition, families can visit Avalanche Bay, the largest indoor waterpark in Michigan.[25]

Still, Boyne Falls is not all about the local resort. It's a community in its own right, located right on US-131. It has its own K-12 school district. There is a market, a repair shop, a gas station and E-Z Mart, a custom builder, a self-storage facility, a post office, a fire department, a village hall, a library, and a food pantry. Just outside of the village limits there is a greenhouse. In addition, there are various food and lodging options throughout the village.

Though the now-defunct Grand Rapids & Indiana Railroad no longer travels to Boyne Falls, the Great Lakes Central Railroad runs through the village.

Boyne Falls is also home to Avalanche Bay, the largest waterpark in Michigan.

TOP: The Pine Street Bridge

Population: 199[1] **Incorporated:** 1883[2]

INSETS L to R: The Breedsville Community Park • Some older
buildings near the main intersection in Breedsville • Playground
equipment in town • An area fruit farm

Early in Breedsville's history, the Agricultural
Department gave away maple trees, and many
were planted all over Breedsville. Unfortunately,
this meant that over a hundred years later,
many of the trees in the village all began to
die around the same time.[27]

Breedsville

History of Breedsville

BARNARD M. HOWARD AND REVEREND JONATHAN N.
HINCKLEY were the first people to purchase land in the area that is
now Breedsville.[3] They built a log cabin on the land and then returned
to their native New York, but they did not intend the land to sit idle.[4]
That same year, 1835, around 25 people from New York came to the
land to form a settlement there, including Hinckley.[5] This was the beginning of Breedsville, and at the time the settlement was the first "of any
importance" in northern Van Buren County.[6]

One settler in the group was Silas Breed, who had come with his
wife and children.[7] He and the other settlers quickly built two more
houses, but that was all they had done when winter came, and they spent
their first winter with only those three houses.[8] Sarah Taylor, Breed's
adopted daughter, did not survive the winter.[9]

The following year, Breed built the first sawmill, and soon the
settlement received a post office.[10] By the early 1840s, there were a number of houses in the village that would welcome travelers, and in 1848,
Thomas P. Page opened a hostelry (an inn) to service the increased travelers through the town, with the advent of a stagecoach line that passed
through the village.[11]

By the early 1900s, Breedsville had a blacksmith, a Methodist
church, a few mills, four doctors, and a variety of other businesses.[12]
There was a two-story school. In 1913, the first telephone office opened

in the town.[13] Electricity came to Breedsville a little over a decade later, in 1925.[14]

An Unsolved Mystery

In 1916, a 12-year-old boy was sent to the attic by his mother to bring down an ironing board.[15] While looking for the ironing board, he found a collection of human bones wrapped up in a newspaper from 1893.[16] Local investigators located some of the previous residents of the house, which had been used as a rental for many years, but they were unable to solve the mystery of the bones.[17]

Surviving the Depression

The Depression hit Breedsville in the 1930s, but the townfolk were determined not to let it destroy their community. They organized a large farmers market and drew up plans for a canning factory, but the government refused to fund the project.[18] When oil was discovered in nearby Bloomingdale in 1938, some Breedsville residents tried for themselves to find oil, but there wasn't much, if any, to find.[19]

The village underwent many changes over the next few decades as the lumber industry declined. The dam on the nearby Black River was torn down when the need for it—and the local sawmill—disappeared. In addition, many of the older buildings were replaced during this time, including the Breedsville School, which was replaced in 1960.[20]

The Importance of a Bridge

Breedsville has one main intersection, with Main Street running east and west through the town and Pine Street running north and south. Pine Street also features a bridge just south of town, where the roadway crosses over the south branch of Black River. In December of 2015, the bridge on Pine Street was shut down for repairs after metal footings on the bridge failed. The cause of the failing was not known, but some in Breedsville suspected an overweight truck had driven over the bridge.[21, 22] Repairs took 18 months, and according to the village clerk, Linda Norton, the closure of the bridge caused a hardship for those in the village and the surrounding area, particularly the blueberry farmers who often had to go well out of their way to get to town.[23]

Breedsville Today

Today Breedsville is largely an agricultural community, and the land surrounding the village is made up largely of farms, particularly farms that grow fruit, such as blueberries and apples. The downtown area is small in Breedsville, but there is a general store, an automotive store, a motorcycle club, village offices, a post office, a Methodist church, and a park. At the park, which is on the south bank of the Black River, it's not uncommon to see people fishing. Michigan's famous Kal-Haven Trail also runs north of town.

The village holds a number of events each year, with those at Halloween and Memorial Day being the biggest.[24] In 2017, Breedsville also hosted its first ever Easter Egg hunt.[25]

The first Methodist church in Breedsville was built in 1877 and burned down in 1953.[26] A new Methodist church was built on the site of the original church and still stands today.

TOP: Barnes' General Store is located on Main Street

Burlington Village was home to the first bridge built in all of Burlington Township. It was the bridge that passed over the St. Joseph River, and it was built in 1838.[23]

In 1896, the village of Burlington experienced a religious revival after more than fifty people converted in the early part of the year.[24]

Burlington

History of Burlington

THE AREA THAT WOULD BECOME THE VILLAGE OF BURLINGTON was first settled by Europeans in 1833, though it was not platted for another nine years.[3] The village was formed on land originally purchased by William and Ansel Adams (not the artist), and it was their frame house that was the first house in the village in 1838.[4] The same year saw the opening of the Burlington post office, and Levi Houghtaling was selected as the first postmaster.[5] Many of the early male residents in the town had come to Michigan after the War of 1812, and some say the town is named after a gunboat many of the men served on together.[6]

The first schoolhouse in the village was built in 1837, and Mary Buckingham was the first teacher.[7] By 1842 the village also had a church and a blacksmith.[8] The first true store in the village was built in 1843; before that time there had only been a man who traded goods with both settlers and American Indians in the area.[9]

The village was incorporated in 1869, and J. D. Spoor was elected as Burlington's first president.[10] By the late 1870s, the village had grown to also include four general stores, a shoe store, a drugstore, a hardware store, a sawmill, a grist mill, three blacksmiths, two physicians, a carriage and wagon shop, two factories, and a school, among other facilities.[11] Rather than the railroad bringing growth to Burlington, it was Burlington's growth that brought the railroad, and eventually the Mansfield, Coldwater, and Lake Michigan Railroad built a depot in Burlington.[12]

A Rough and Tumble Town at Times

In 1904, two men from the Burlington area who had been feuding for a few years were in the village drinking.[13] One man followed the other back to his farm where the two began to argue, and the owner of the farm, a man named Engle, returned to his house for a gun and killed the other man, who was named Barrington. Engle claimed he shot in self-defense, but as there were no witnesses, he was not tried, as guilt would have been difficult to prove.[14]

Burlington Farm Leading the Organic Push in Calhoun County

The Hiday Family Farm, located just outside of Burlington, has been a leading player in the push for organic farming in Calhoun County. In 1987, Dan Hiday began raising beef cattle on his farm, but in the early 1990s, he found himself uneasy with some of the farming practices he followed, such as extensive chemical use and feeding cows grain rather than grass.[15] He switched his farm to an organic operation.[16] As one of the early farms to switch to organic, Hiday at first struggled with the new business operation.[17] But when the culture began to shift to embrace organic methods, his struggle began to pay off.[18]

In 2014, Hiday decided to change his business model again, this time adding dairy cows to his farm.[19] Rather than milk, however, his new product of choice is yogurt.[20] But what truly guides the farm's products, though, is the desires of its customers.[21] This means that they raise animals to meet the needs of customers rather than trying to find enough customers for all the animals they want to raise. In addition to beef and dairy cows, the farm also raises chickens, turkeys, and pigs, and they sometimes sell other products, such as jam and salsa.[22]

Burlington Today

Today, Burlington is located on M-60 in Calhoun County, right on the St. Joseph River. The downtown area comprises a few blocks and has a variety of businesses, including a gas station, a tavern, a library, a body shop, and a post office. Also in and around the area you can find a florist, a general store, a hair salon, an auto sales business, and a place giving archery lessons. The Burlington area is served by a Church of God and a Seventh Day Adventist church.

Some sources claim that the village got its name after a group of men who had served on the gunboat *Burlington* during the War of 1812 came to the area.[25]

Population: 192[1]   **Incorporated:** Unknown

INSETS L to R: Carney is still an active logging town • The Carney Village Hall building • This railroad building is no longer in use • A mural painted on the side of one of the village's buildings

Carney no longer has its own school system, but the combined Carney-Nadeau Public School, founded in 2012, is still located in Carney.[25]

TOP: One of the village's older structures

Carney

History of Carney

CARNEY'S HISTORY CAN BE TRACED BACK to the arrival of the Chicago & North Western Railway to the area in 1879.[2] The village was named after Fred Carney, who owned a great deal of land and business interests in the areas near the eventual site of the village.[3] As with many towns in the Upper Peninsula, the early industry of the village was logging.[4] Three years after the railroad came to town, Carney received a post office, and Charles A. Brown served as postmaster.

Not much has been recorded about its first years, but by the early 1920s, Carney had grown to hold over 300 people.[5] There were no judicial or banking services in Carney at the time, but the residents of Carney had other perks. They had a public school, two churches, and both phone and telegraph services.[6] In addition, the town had a hardware store, two general stores, two well drillers, a hotel, a blacksmith, a stationery store, a potato warehouse, and a cheese manufactory.[7] The town also had at least one sawmill, but it seems to have shifted its industry to be primarily agricultural in nature some years before.[8]

Like many towns in the Upper Peninsula, Carney had a sizeable population of families from Scandinavia.[9] These immigrants and their descendants formed strong communities, and one of the aspects shared by the people in those communities was religion. In 1885, Suzanna Moseson wrote to a pastor in Norway, Michigan, and he agreed to come to Carney and help found a Methodist church.[10] The church was finished a year later.[11] Due to poor road conditions near the church for much of the year, a second church was constructed in 1892.[12] The church reorganized in March of that year as a nondenominational group and called itself the Carney Bible Church.[13] In 1959 they reorganized again, this time voting to become associated with the Evangelical Free Church of America.[14] The church celebrated its 125th anniversary in 2010.[15]

A U.S. Scandal

In 1912, William Lorimer, a congressman from Illinois, was unseated following two investigations into how he had earned his seat in the Senate.[16] Fred Carney was called as one of the witnesses in the 1911 congressional investigation and testified.

Farming in and around Carney

Much of the area in and around Carney today is used for farming. One local farm is the Miller Family Farm, which was established in 2012.[17] The farm grows lettuce, kale, and tomatoes, raises tilapia, and incorporates both hydroponics and aquaponics as farming techniques.[18] Another local farming operation is the Castle Cattle Company, which raises Hereford cattle for breeding.[19]

Carney farms have also been the sites of agricultural research performed by Michigan State University. In 2017, Carney was selected as one of the sites for a research trial on forage oats and forage peas.[20] Unfortunately, however, the Carney growing site suffered from excessive deer feeding and had to be excluded from the research trial.[21]

Carney Today

Today, Carney has returned somewhat to its lumber roots. Performance, an area lumber corporation, has a sawmill operation near town, and the wood from that location gets turned into a wide variety of products, including pallets, firewood, animal bedding, and wood pellets for grills.[22] The company's location in Carney produces "over 12 million board feet of natural hardwood materials annually."[23]

Lumber is not the only business in town, however. There is also a village hall, a township hall, a market, a bank, a gas company, a general store, a scrapbooking center, a self-storage unit, a Legion hall, a collision center, a telephone and broadband company, and a post office. The Carney Round-Up Rodeo is located in the village. There is also an outreach center for Tri-County Safe Harbor, Inc., a program that supports victims of sexual assault and domestic violence.[24]

An old postcard from Carney, from about the 1920s, declares Carney to be "Lovers' Lane."[26]

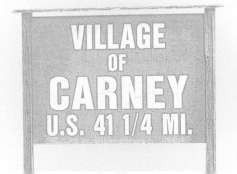

Population: 357[1]   Unincorporated

INSETS L to R: One of the fishing piers on Paradise Lake • A sign welcomes visitors to Bear Lake • The Carp Lake General Store • This wooden model of a lighthouse is taller than a person

There is a saying in Carp Lake and the surrounding area that "you will find paradise in Carp Lake, but you won't find any carp in Paradise Lake."[13]

TOP: This sculpture was created by artist Virginia Stevens and is called "a day in bear-adise"

Carp Lake

A Misnamed Lake

THOUGH THIS TOWN IS CALLED CARP LAKE, it's actually located on Paradise Lake, which also goes by Lake Paradise, depending on the map you're looking at. (To add to the confusion, the lake was historically known as Carp Lake, too.)

History of Carp Lake

Carp Lake Village was founded around 1880 by Octave Terrian from Quebec.[2] He originally came to Mackinaw City from Quebec and then later moved to Carp Lake Township, where he homesteaded the farm on which he lived until his death.[3]

Around the same time that he founded the village, the Grand Rapids & Indiana Railroad opened a depot in Carp Lake and the village also received its first post office.[4] Alpheus B. Hendricks was appointed the first postmaster.

Even from its beginnings, Carp Lake was a tourist and resort town, with Paradise Lake (then Carp Lake) only a few miles south of the Lake Michigan shoreline.[5] By the early 1900s, the village had a population of approximately 150 and supported a lake house and a hotel.[6] It also had other businesses, including a sawmill, a lath mill, a grocer, and a saloon.[7] By 1922, Carp Lake also had a potato company, a well driller, and a moving picture theater.[8]

Carp Lake is still a resort community today, and it has also become a community focused on nature. Three different nature preserves can be found within the village limits, and in addition to the Carp Lake Township Park on the southeast side of the village, there are a variety of other parks within only a few minutes' drive.

Preserving Nature in Carp Lake

The residents in Carp Lake know that the surrounding scenery is what makes the village and local area so enjoyable—for both them and visitors to the town. One of the preserves, the William and Stephanie Veling Nature Preserve, was sold by the Velings to the Little Traverse Conservancy in 2011 because the couple had always wanted their land to remain as natural as possible.[9] The Stony Point Nature Preserve has been home to a pair of bald eagles.[10]

But nature doesn't always make things easy and peaceful. Invasive species can come to an area and cause problems for native plants, animals, and ecosystems, and Carp Lake has been dealing with the invasive plant Eurasian water milfoil. In 2012, however, the community became the first in the state to introduce the milfoil weevil to the lake in an effort to combat the spread of the invasive plant.[11] The work done on Paradise Lake, all with an eye toward preserving the natural state of the lake and the land, has resulted in the Paradise Lake Improvement Board being recognized for its eco-friendly approach to lake management.[12]

Carp Lake Today

Because of the way the village is laid out, much of the community wraps around the lake's shoreline. There are residents who live near the water, but there are also a number of hotels and cabins either right on the lake or across the street from it. With the area's own beauty and Mackinaw City and the stunning Mackinac Bridge only around a ten-minute drive away, it is a prime place for visitors to stay. There is also a marina where you can purchase fishing or hunting licenses or also rent a boat. There is public beach access, too.

In addition to the more than ten options for lodging in Carp Lake, the village also has a restaurant and bar, a real estate office, a plumbing and heating business, a construction company, a general store, a post office, a taxidermist, a quilt shop, a self-storage company, and a township hall. The Petoskey to Mackinaw Trail, running right along US-31, passes right through Carp Lake, on the west side of the lake.

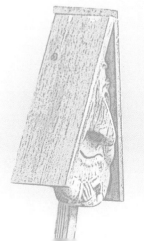

In Carp Lake you can find a statue of a bear. This piece of art, created by Virginia Stevens, is titled "a day in bear-adise" and was sponsored by the Paradise Lake Association.

TOP: Daniel H. Schroeder Memorial Park was dedicated in honor of local veterans

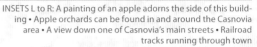

Population: 319[1]   **Incorporated:** 1875[2]

INSETS L to R: A painting of an apple adorns the side of this building • Apple orchards can be found in and around the Casnovia area • A view down one of Casnovia's main streets • Railroad tracks running through town

The name Casnovia comes from the Latin words for *casa* (home) and *nova* (new) and roughly translates to *new home*. Other early spellings of the village name included *Casinova* and *Cazenovia*.[24]

The first village election in Casnovia was contested, after surprising results and several voting tickets that had been left blank.[25] The issue went all the way to the Michigan State Attorney General, who agreed with how the elections officials in town had counted the votes.[26]

Casnovia

History of Casnovia

THE VILLAGE OF CASNOVIA was founded in 1850 by Lot Fulkerson, the first European settler in the area. He welcomed travelers into his log cabin and also operated a tavern out of his home.[3] In the early 1850s, the village, then called Casnovia Corners, received a post office, and Daniel Bennett was appointed as its first postmaster.[4]

The town grew quickly. The tavern moved from Fulkerson's home to a building of its own, and a hall was later constructed alongside.[5] By 1870, Casnovia had a blacksmith, a handful of stores, and three mills either in or nearby the village.[6] Within another five years, there was also a pump factory and a cider mill.[7]

The village was officially platted in 1862,[8] and the Pere Marquette Railroad brought its line to Casnovia in 1872, giving residents a railway connection to Grand Rapids.[9] The town was also on a carriage road.[10] Three years later, with a population of approximately 300 people,[11] Casnovia incorporated as a village,[12] with part of the village in Kent County and the rest of the village in Muskegon County. The village elected A. C. Ayer as the first village president.[13] By that time it had grown to contain a brick schoolhouse, a grain elevator, a livery stable, a hotel, and a variety of stores, including hardware, general goods, drug, and military stores.[14]

Saving the Old School

Casnovia's original elementary school burned down in the early 1930s, and in 1934 the village constructed and opened a new elementary school.[15] That elementary school served the community until Casnovia Schools merged with another local school district.[16] Now called the Old School, the old school continues to serve the village as a reminder of both what has been and what can still be. In 1986, the Casnovia Old School Foundation formed,[17] and since then it has worked to raise money to maintain the old building.

So far, their work has been successful. The school now hosts a variety of activities, such as arts and crafts classes and meetings for community groups, including the Masonic Lodge, Red Hat Society, and Lions Club.[18] The school is available to rent for parties and gatherings, and it also hosts fundraising events for the Old School Foundation, such as a Santa Day and a My School Color Run.

Bion J. Arnold

Born in Casnovia in 1861, Bion J. Arnold is remembered as one of the premier electrical engineers of the early years of the twentieth century.[19] He primarily worked with electrical transit systems in cities, serving as a consultant in Chicago and other cities.[20] In addition, he developed easier and more pragmatic methods for railroads to make the shift from steam power to electrical power.[21]

Casnovia Today

Since its early days as a railroad town, Casnovia has rebilded itself as the "Gateway to Michigan's Apple Country." The village is surrounded by apple orchards that grow more than a dozen varieties of apples, and images of apples decorate the village. In addition, many people in the village are tied to the apple business in one way or another.

Casnovia has a post office, a village hall, and a public works building. There is also an attorney, an insurance agency, a graphic design company, Kazz Bar & Grill, and two hair salons. There is a memorial to honor community veterans. The village is served by two Baptist churches and a Reformed Church.

The heart of the town, though, is the local apple country. Caveman Sawmill & Pallets makes apple crates and boxes used by many nearby orchards,[22] and Precise Manufacturing engineers and produces a variety of machinery used for growing and harvesting the fruit from orchards, including oranges, cherries, peaches, and, of course, apples.[23]

In 1891, a man from Casnovia by the name of Dr. Bosanko was arrested.[27] He was drunk, had a pocketful of false teeth, and claimed that the people of Casnovia would "turn out en masse" to avenge his arrest.[28] Unmoved by his protests, Bosanko was taken to jail and had to present himself at a hearing the following morning. From the historical record it's not clear what happened next.[29]

TOP: The Depot in Cement City

Population: 438[1]   **Incorporated:** 1953[2]

INSETS L to R: The village fire department • Cement City still has its own post office • A view down one of the residential streets in the village • The Cement City Baptist Church

Before it was razed, exploring the abandoned factory was a favorite pastime of teenagers in the area.[18] No doubt safety concerns were one reason the factory was torn down.

Cement City

History of Cement City

THE AREA WHERE CEMENT CITY is now located received its first post office in 1838, but it bore the name of Woodstock, as the post office was located in what was then Woodstock Township.[3] That post office opened and closed with some degree of regularity through the 1880s, and the town changed names several times. The present village seems to have first formed as the town of Woodstock sometime around 1868.[4]

The Railroad and the Cement Industry Come to Town

The Lake Shore and Michigan Southern Railway came to the village in the mid- to late-1800s, and the Cincinnati Northern Railroad arrived in 1896.[5] In 1901, the town officially changed its name to Cement City, in honor of the arrival of William Cowham's cement company, the Peninsular Portland Cement Company.[6] Cowham picked the location near Cement City for his cement company plant because there were numerous sources of marl, a material needed to make cement, in the surrounding area.[7] The plant he opened was the first factory in the world completely powered by electricity.[8]

With the opening of the cement plant, Cement City grew rapidly. By 1908 there were approximately 500 people living in the village,[9] and by 1922 that number had risen to 700.[10] In the 1920s, the town contained a post office, a bank, a feed mill, two general stores, a grocer, a wagonmaker, and a hotel.[11]

Life After Cement

The plant operated for 60 years, and though it left grit and grime in the air, it provided numerous jobs to residents of Cement City.[12] When the plant finally did close, the layoffs affected over half of the village's population.[13]

You can still see the spot where the old factory was, though nothing is left except the ground on which it sat. There were plans to tear down and redevelop the plant, and though the building was razed, the redevelopment plans never came to fruition.[14]

Cement City Today

Though the closing of the cement factory was a hardship for Cement City, village residents have worked over the years to help the community survive. Today agriculture is a focus, with a handful of farms, particularly dairy farms, just minutes away from the village downtown area. There is also a plant nursery nearby.

The village itself is quiet, and in nice weather there are often numerous people out and about, either at the park in the center of the village or just in their front yards. The village has a post office, a storage center, a market, a saloon, a body shop, a powersports store, a Masonic Lodge, and a fire training center. The village recently established a museum in a building on Main Street.[15] There is a Baptist church in the village; it was established in 1848,[16] long before the village itself, and Cement City also holds an old cemetery, with some graves dating back as far as 1838. One headstone, for Abigail Every, notes that she died at 99 years of age, and was born in 1739 in New York, when it was still a British colony.[17]

The marl deposits in Cement City were dozens of feet deep, and they sometimes contained unexpected finds. A geological survey of the Cement City marl noted that elk antlers were sometimes found up to 30 feet deep in the marl.[19]

TOP: A look at the old Pacific Hotel building, built in 1904

Population: 220 **Incorporated:** 1964[1]

INSETS L to R: The Alger County Fairgrounds • The Chatham Apostolic Lutheran Church • The Michigan State University AgBioResearch station • Another view of the station

In 1907, the "Poor Farm" opened in Chatham, which often provided work to former lumberjacks.[23] The farm remained in operation until 1945.[24]

On July 30, 1904, the *L'Anse Sentinel* proudly proclaimed that Chatham was "now in telephonic communication with the outside world."[25]

Chatham

History of Chatham

CHATHAM, MICHIGAN, IS NAMED AFTER CHATHAM, ONTARIO.[2] It began as a lumber camp built by James Finn in 1896, though the camp did not last long, and when Michigan State University turned the location of the camp into a research station in 1899, little was left of the camp.[3] The Munising Railway Company first brought the railroad to the area of Chatham the same year Finn started his camp.[4] After Finn left, the railroad and local lumber company decided there should be a community at that point where the main road and the railroad intersected.[5] The organization of the resulting village was spearheaded by William G. Mather, president of an iron mining company.[6]

The early industry of Chatham was lumber, and the area produced cedar, hardwoods, and hemlock.[7] There were also limestone quarries nearby. People came from all over to work in the area near the village, and a community of people from northern Europe, particularly Swedes and Finns, grew in and around the Chatham area.[8] Between 1900 and 1920, the village's population grew from 365 to 1450.[9]

The first post office, which also served as a store, opened in 1897.[10] John H. Gatiss was the first postmaster.[11] Early businesses in the village include a livery stable, a general store, various boarding houses, a blacksmith, a clothing shop, a hotel, and a saloon, though the saloon burned down within a decade of being built.[12] The hotel, called the Pacific Hotel, was built in 1904, and the building still stands in Chatham today.[13] Over the years it has served as a rest house, a restaurant, and a café.[14] It even served a stint as an emergency hospital in the flu epidemic of 1918.[15]

As the lumber industry began to fade, Chatham shifted to become an agricultural town, and areas cleared of trees were sold to farmers for future development.[16] In addition, oil and petroleum businesses came to the Chatham area, and other types of businesses began to open as well, including a bowling alley and a youth center.[17]

The Michigan State University Research Station

The Chatham area is perhaps most well known for its long ties to Michigan State University, which opened its Upper Peninsula Research and Extension Center in 1899. The center was opened after it came to the attention of researchers and state legislators alike that the soil in the Upper Peninsula differed significantly from that found in the Lower Peninsula.[18] The land for the research station was donated by the Munising Railway Company, and the state provided $5,000 for agricultural research at the station.[19] Leo M. Geismar was the first to lead the research done at the station.[20]

In the hundred-plus years since the station opened, it has conducted leading-edge research on a variety of agricultural topics, including crop rotations, pasture-based cattle management, the use of cover crops, soil health, potato and corn varieties, and season extension.[21] Research is not the only task of the station, however; outreach and education are other key focuses. The station provides new farmers the opportunity to learn about sustainable farming in a northern climate, and the farm also grows organic produce for local businesses.[22]

Chatham Today

While the MSU research station is certainly a focal point of the town, it is not all Chatham has to offer. The Alger County Fairgrounds, home of the Alger County Fair, are just one block southwest of the village's main intersection. There is a village pub, a bank, an auto glass shop, a teledata shop, a motel, a bakery, a storage center, a car wash, a laundromat, a fitness center, a credit union, and a cooperative store. Services in the town include a library, a post office, and a township volunteer fire department. The village also has a park, and for additional outdoor activities, one end of the Coalwood Trail is just north of the downtown area, and the Eben Ice Caves are only a few miles to the north.

It's a quiet yet thriving town. And, with the research station nearby, if you're walking down the street and offer a "Go green!" you're likely to hear back a "Go white!"

William G. Mather, who played an instrumental role in Chatham's beginnings, had a steamship named for him. The ship, which served as a freight vessel on the Great Lakes, is on display at the Great Lakes Science Center in Cleveland.[26]

TOP: Clarksville Elementary School is part of Lakewood Public Schools

Population: 394[1]   **Incorporated:** 192[2]

INSETS L to R: Many of the buildings in the downtown area of Clarksville have stood in the village for some time • Clarksville's library • The main intersection in town • One of the residential streets in the village

A Clarksville resident, W. Earl Weygandt, went on to participate in the Minnesota Starvation Experiment, in which 36 volunteers agreed to undergo starvation in a year-long controlled scientific study.[23] This enabled doctors to understand the biology of starvation. All were conscientious objectors during World War II.

Clarksville

History of Clarksville

THE FIRST EUROPEAN SETTLERS in the Clarksville area were a pair of brothers from Ireland, Martin and Jeremiah Campbell, in 1840.[3] Martin Campbell's wife, Winifred, also came with the brothers.[4] Campbell Township, in which Clarksville resides, was nearly named Winifred instead, but she did not want the "notoriety."[5]

The village that grew up in that area was originally called Skipperville, but in 1875 the village received its first post office and the name of the community became Clarksville, after Clark L. Howard, who owned a store in the village.[6] His was not the only business in 1875; there was also a wagon shop, a hall, two physicians, and a second store.[7] A Wesleyan Methodist congregation also worshiped in one of the store buildings.[8]

Clarksville found early success and growth. By 1908, the village had its own bank and weekly newspaper, the *Clarksville Record*.[9] There was a hotel and a local school, and both residents and their children could receive music lessons from Mrs. D. A. Dickinson or Maud Richards.[10] Town business enterprises were varied, with everything from a stationery shop and a dentist to a milliner and a painter.[11] There were cattle breeders and a veterinarian for the local farmers, and a few people were also involved in the apple business, as the town had both an apple dryer and a cider mill.[12] Like many small towns of the era, lumber was important as well, with the Hager Lumber business in town.[13]

The population has stayed relatively stable in Clarksville, with approximately 375 recorded in 1900, 400 in 1920, and still around 400 today.[14] It seems likely that one reason for this is that Clarksville was never a town that relied only on one industry, making it more or less immune to sudden changes in industry or demand.

Annual Events Bring the Community Together

There are two main events that bring the Clarksville community together every year, and these are the annual Ox Roast and the annual Antique Tractor Show. The antique tractor show, held in the spring of each year, includes events for all ages, including live music, a flea market, a spark show, tractor games, a children's barn, a sawmill, and demonstrations.[15] Each year has a different featured tractor, and attendees are invited to bring and show off their own tractors.[16]

The Ox Roast is held in the summer, and has been running in its current incarnation for over 40 years.[17] The tradition, which dates back to the early days of Clarksville's history, was revived by Frank Reser in 1975.[18] First Frank, then his sons, continued the tradition each year, and now the event gets the whole village involved.[19] The downtown area of the village gets closed to traffic, and events take place all day, from a breakfast at the fire station to a craft show to a parade, and finally to eating the ox that cooks for around 24 hours.[20]

In addition, the village holds other events throughout the year, including a Halloween party and a Memorial Day parade.

Clarksville Today

As was true in its past, Clarksville today is a community built upon a variety of agricultural, business, and community ties. They bill themselves as "a small community with big heart," and take great pride in caring for both the village and its residents.[21]

Village businesses include a hardware store, an auto repair store, a village inn, a bank, a gas station, a family medicine practice, a grain elevator, a feed store, a pizza and ice cream parlor, a technology solutions business, a salon, and a lumber company. The Campbell Township fire department and offices are located in Clarksville, and there is also a post office, a library, a village hall, and a recycling center. There is a Bible church and a community church in the area. Clarksville is served by Lakewood Public Schools.

Though some people have wondered otherwise, the Monkees' song "Last Train to Clarksville" was written about a fictional town rather than the one in Michigan.[22]

Population: 344[1]   **Incorporated:** 1870[2]

INSETS L to R: A business in the village that deals with pallets • Clayton has its own village library • One of the tree-lined residential streets in the village • The Clayton Fire Department

In 2017, the *Detroit Free Press* selected the Lake Hudson Recreation Area in Clayton as one of the seven best places to stargaze in the state.[16] This was the only spot selected south of Michigan's thumb.

TOP: The Clayton United Methodist Church

Clayton

History of Clayton

WHEN THE LAKE SHORE AND MICHIGAN SOUTHERN RAILWAY came to Hudson Township in the mid-1830s, the village of Clayton had not yet formed.[3] Indeed, the railroad's arrival is what prompted the formation of the village in 1836.[4] Clayton received its first post office, then called East Dover, for the name of one of the two townships (the other being Hudson) Clayton spanned, in 1837.[5] The first postmaster was Levi H. Soper.[6]

The village was first platted in 1843 by Reuben E. Bird, and two years later the post office was renamed to Clayton.[7] The name came in recognition of a friendship Bird had with one Reverend Clayton in New York.[8]

Despite its size as a small town, Clayton soon developed into a town with an important business district, and one involved in a number of different trades.[9] By the early part of the twentieth century, the village had a tinsmith, a cheese manufactory, a cheese box manufacturer, a bank, a hardware store, a carpentry, two physicians, a general store, a butcher, an undertaker, and a grocer, among others.[10]

Clayton in the Civil War

Michigan, like many Midwestern states, contributed tens of thousands of soldiers to the war effort, some 90,000 in all. Many saw action in some of the most important battles in the conflict, and some were captured in the process. Many Union soldiers who were captured ended up at the infamous Andersonville Prison, which held some 45,000 prisoners of war, and where more than 12,000 died from starvation, disease, or exposure. This included a number of soldiers from Clayton and hundreds from around the area. When the surviving soldiers were released, they needed to be transported home. A steamboat, the *Sultana*, was hastily commissioned to take the soldiers up the Mississippi—a deal in which the captain agreed to take a financial kickback for each soldier transported. Some 1,900 troops boarded the ship, which usually carried fewer than 400 passengers, and as they came aboard, hasty repairs were being made to a leaky boiler. The repair was initially slated to take several days, but not wanting to lose soldiers (and therefore some of the kickback), the repair was rushed. On April 27, 1865, one of her boilers detonated, and the others followed suit. The vessel immediately lost power and burst into flame, and the explosion killed many on board or thrust the still-emaciated prisoners of war into the water where they were exposed to the cold spring meltwater. In all, 1,192 people died, including many from Michigan.[12] One of the heroes from that event eventually called Clayton home. Thomas Love was stationed aboard the *Essex*, a U.S. Navy ironclad that wasn't far from the disaster site. He personally helped rescue survivors. In an account, he said, "among those I rescued was one man so badly scalded that when I took hold of his arms to help him into the boat the skin and flesh came off his arms like a cooked beet."[11] Years later, at a reunion of survivors from the Sultana, he met the man he saved, wryly noting, "I had the pleasure of taking the above described man by the hand. It was with a grip that did not slip." Love later lived in Clayton, where he was a merchant.[13]

Pride in Education

Its status as an important center of business in the area brought many benefits to Clayton in addition to those related to business. One of those benefits was education. The school at Clayton, built sometime in the 1860s, was the first in Hudson Township to organize its students into grades. When the building was condemned sometime around 1908 or 1909, a brick replacement costing $12,000 was erected in Clayton overlooking the railroad.[14]

Churches in Clayton

Religion has deep ties in Clayton. The Presbyterian Church Society has been active in Clayton since 1860. The first Baptist Church group in the town was formed around the same time, perhaps even in the same year, as the Clayton Bible Church, which classifies itself as an "Independent Fundamental Bible Believing Baptistic Church," and lists its date of establishment as 1860.[15] In addition to the Clayton Bible Church, Clayton also has a Rollin Center United Methodist Church, which holds its church services in an old brick building first built in the late 1870s.

Clayton Today

Clayton today is a small and peaceful town. In addition to the two churches in town, Clayton also has a boxing club, a fence contractor, a lumber business, and a food mart. The Dover/Hudson-Clayton Fire Department is also located in the village, and there is the Lake Hudson Recreation Area just outside of the village. In addition, there is also a public library, open four days per week. The Clayton Public Library is part of the Lenawee District Library system and hosts a variety of events and activities for the whole family.

Clayton's history date backs to before the Civil War. Its first church was active by 1860, and its first school was built in the same year.

TOP: The old grain elevator in Clifford has been renovated and restored in recent years

Population: 324[1]   **Incorporated:** 1891[2]

INSETS L to R: A combined laundry and car wash called Suds Row • Many businesses in Clifford still have their original fronts • One of the older buildings in the area • The library in Clifford

One notorious Clifford resident was Charles E. Coughlin, who preached at St. Patrick Chapel from 1924 to 1925.[21] He went on to be a radio priest, and during the Great Depression, he preached the evils of a variety of subjects, including labor unions and Wall Street.[22] At one point his radio show had an audience of 90 million.[23] However, his show turned anti-Semitic and his name was used at pro-Nazi rallies, and after the United States entered World War II, the Catholic Church and U.S. government combined to silence him.[24]

Clifford

History of Clifford

THE VILLAGE OF CLIFFORD can trace its start back to the early 1860s when Arden W. Lyman built the first structure there.[3] Lyman lived in the building and ran a post office and store out of it as well, serving as the town's first postmaster.[4] He named the town Clifford after his son.[5] In addition to working as a postmaster and shopkeeper, Lyman also went on to build a sawmill in 1875, thought it burned down eight years later.

The road running north and south through Clifford became a main road in the area not long after the village began, and in the early 1870s, Moses Middaugh built a hotel there. What really brought life to the town though was the arrival of the Pontiac, Oxford, & Port Austin Railroad to Clifford in 1882.[6] Within a dozen years of the arrival of the railroad, the town had grown to have over 60 buildings, including two new sawmills, four general stores, three blacksmiths, two drugstores, two shoe stores, two elevators, a furniture store, and a meat shop.[7] The community incorporated as a village officially in 1891.[8]

In terms of population, Clifford peaked as a village in the first few decades of the twentieth century, and now more residents work outside of Clifford than inside the village.[9] The school in Clifford, which served over time as both an elementary and a high school, closed in the 1960s, though in the 1970s it underwent renovations and now serves as the Clifford Library, with additional space set aside for rent and some historical schoolhouse items on display.[10]

Historic St. Patrick Chapel in Clifford

In 1879, St. Patrick Chapel, which still exists, began, though at the time there was no church building for the parishioners to hold mass in.[11] The community began when Father Crebs from Gagetown began to visit Clifford.[12] The church was constructed in 1886, and the first wedding was held in the church before construction had completed.[13] Recently the church has restored the original Stations of the Cross from 1886 as part of their 125th anniversary celebrations.[14] The building is recognized as a historical site in Michigan.

As you might guess from the name, the church's original founders were Irish, and each year the church and Catholic community celebrate this heritage with St. Patrick's Heritage Day.[15] This event, which has been running for nearly 30 years, includes historical displays, a flea market, games for kids, and a bingo game.[16]

Clifford Today

Like most small towns, it is the people that make Clifford, and the village focuses on building and maintaining "neighborly cooperation."[17] In addition to the Catholic chapel, Clifford is also home to a Baptist church. Clifford Park is near the site of the old school building, now the library, and has playground equipment, a pavilion, a basketball court, and horseshoe pits. There is a skate park as well. Businesses in the village include the Rosebud Café, an exercise facility, a laundromat, a machine company, a car wash, a post office, and village offices.

Since the turn of the century, Habitat for Humanity has worked on two houses in Clifford, including a renovation of a house that was more than 100 years old.[18] Clifford was also the site of an air disaster. In 1975, a C-130 Hercules carrying six members of the Air Force Reserve crashed in Lapeer County.[19] Pieces of the engine were found in fields in Clifford.[20]

TOP: An old church in the village

Population: 194[1]   **Incorporated:** 1891

INSETS L to R: A playground area with picnic tables and a pavilion • The Copemish post office and a local shop • Solar panels near CBS Solar in Copemish • The Copemish village hall

The Copemish area is located quite close to some prime trout fishing. The Bear Creek watershed is home to a blue-ribbon trout stream (the highest ranking) and First Creek to the southwest of the village, was once dammed, and the resulting pond was stocked with trout.[22] That dam partially collapsed in the 1980s, and it was then removed, returning the river to a free-flowing condition.[23]

Copemish

The "Polar Bears" from Copemish

WORLD WAR I ENDED IN 1918, but for some troops the peace agreement did not mark the end of their military engagement. One group of soldiers trained for World War I was instead sent to Northern Russia for an intervention mission.[2] This group contained many soldiers from Michigan, including John Bigelow from Copemish[3] who, to his mother, looked "like a boy with his dad's boots on."[4] The Polar Bear Expedition, as it was called, had a mission to simply defend military supplies in northern Russia, near Archangel, but specific details of their mission, which extended nine months, were never supplied.[5] In addition, the troops, trained for the trench warfare of World War I, were unprepared for the freezing temperatures, wild terrain, and harsh living

conditions, including the need to sometimes get their water from local swamps.[6] And though it was supposed to be a guard mission only, fighting soon broke out between the Polar Bears and the Bolsheviks, even as the soldiers in Europe celebrated the end of the war.[7] Approximately 300 Americans died in Russia, including Bigelow.[8] He was only 22.

History of Copemish

In the early 1880s, the Buckley & Douglas Lumber Company came to the Copemish area and set up a lumber camp.[9] A few years later, in 1889, two railway companies, the Toledo, Ann Arbor, & Northern Michigan Railway and the Manistee & Northeastern Railroad, selected a location near the camp for their two lines to intersect, and within no time Copemish grew up in that area.[10] The village was platted that same year, and the first post office opened in 1890.[11] One year after that, in January of 1891, the village was officially incorporated.[12] C. B. Caniff was elected as the first village president.[13]

The community built up so fast with the arrival of the railroad that, for a time, the village could not support the needs of its residents, and residents had to travel some distance for supplies and services.[14] By the time the village held its first elections in February 1891, the town's population was already approximately 400.

Archangel Ancient Tree Archive

Copemish may be a small town, but one of its local organizations has made a big name for itself. A small nonprofit in the heart of Copemish, the Ancient Tree Archive aims to "propagate the world's most important old growth trees before they are gone," "reforest the earth," and "archive the genetics of ancient trees."[15] Each tree they choose to work with is chosen for a specific purpose and placed in a specific area based on the ecological system of the location.[16] One project they have taken on is the loss of the Redwood forests on the United States' West Coast. They take live growth from some of the largest, oldest, and most successful trees, clone them, then replant them in a grove in Oregon.[17] The group looks to preserve existing genes rather than to modify and create new ones.[18] It may be too early to tell what the group's long-term impact will be, but the future looks promising for them, and the nonprofit has received national attention with their work featured on NPR,[19] in the *New York Times*,[20] and a number of other national news outlets.

Copemish Today

Today, Copemish is a quiet town with fewer than two hundred residents. In addition to the Archangel Ancient Tree Archive, the village also has a Catholic church, a secondhand store, a post office, a hardware store, a family market, and a café. Mr. Chain, a business on the west side of town, is the only business in the U.S. that makes plastic chains.[21] There is also a solar energy equipment provider in town.

For outdoor activities in Copemish, there is a pond in the southwest area of the village, and the Betsie Valley Trailway runs through the town as well. During the summer, there is a weekend flea market.

Each summer Copemish holds an event called Copemish Heritage Days. There is a parade, food, games, a silent auction, a cakewalk, fire truck rides, and a variety of other entertainment options for the whole family.[24]

TOP: The veterans' memorial in Copemish

Population: 190[1]   **Incorporated:** 1917[2]

INSETS L to R: One of the buildings at a mine near Copper City • The Copper City Community Hall • An old grocery market in the village • A general store in the village

According to one calculation, the Calumet & Hecla company paid out $99 million in dividends from 1871 to 1907.[18] That's the equivalent of perhaps $2.4 billion today.

Copper City

History of Copper City

NEAR THE TURN OF THE TWENTIETH CENTURY, much of Houghton County was busy with mining. As more and more copper was found, more and more workers came to Copper Country, and in 1907, J. T. Finnegan determined to do something to meet the needs of the workers.[3] He bought 80 acres in the area where Copper City is now located—a prime location due to the fact that there were six mine shafts all within a few miles.[4]

Within a few years, the town had grown considerably. In 1910, Copper City received a post office, and Frank W. Clark was chosen as the first postmaster.[5] By 1922, the town had 900 residents, a saloon, a grocery, a hotel, a department store, a lumber and gas company, and a school.[6] It was also a stop on the Keweenaw Central Railroad.[7]

One of the big mining companies in the Upper Peninsula was Calumet & Hecla, and the last mine they opened was the Kingston Mine, right in Copper City.[8] They cut one shaft into the Kearsarge Conglomerate in 1964 and mined up to twelve levels deep, finding copper, silver, cuprite, and epidote.[9] A strike in 1968, however, resulted in the permanent closure of the mine,[10] though you can still see some of the old mine buildings just outside of town.

Calumet Township, where Copper City is located, has historically been home to many families who emigrated from Finland and Sweden. Dennis Harju, who took a break from his daily walk to talk to me about Copper City, is Finnish, and it was his great-grandparents who first came to the United States.[11]

Frank Stubenrauch, a Calumet Township Legend

Frank Stubenrauch, who passed away in 2014,[12] was something of a legend in Calumet Township, and in Copper City itself. He was a constable in nearby Allouez Township, but in Copper City he was known for his role in education.[13] He was superintendent at the Copper City and Centennial Schools,[14] and he saw his role as being to help local children get a full education.[15] He went above and beyond in this role, working to expand the view of the world for his students. One thing he did, for instance, was take them on a field trip to see the opera.[16]

Copper City Today

With the end of the mining in the area, the population of Copper City dwindled, and today it is a much smaller town that it was at its peak. One reason for that, however, is that the town wants to keep much of the historical architecture, and this desire limits business interest in the town.[17] However, not everything is kept as it once was. In the summer of 2017, there was construction on a new road coming into town, and another relatively recent addition is an extensive veterans memorial near the town park. When I visited the town, they were performing repairs on the memorial, which lists local veterans and honors those who died in action by placing a star by their name.

In addition to the park and veterans memorial, Copper City also has a general store, a post office, and village offices. Fulton Creek and Slaughterhouse Creek lie to the west and north of town, and the village is also home to Queen Anne's Falls, a waterfall of about 30 feet on Slaughterhouse Creek.

A popular winter pastime in and around Copper City is cross-country skiing. Unfortunately, the old Copper City ice rink, where residents used to play pickup hockey in the 1950s and 1960s, is no longer in existence.[19]

TOP: This iconic cow head adorns the side of the building that used to hold Bonser's Market

Population: 284[1]   **Incorporated:** 1895[2]

INSETS L to R: Some of the businesses along US Route 10 • A
beauty salon occupies a building formerly used as a bank • More
businesses along Route 10 • St. Mary's Church

Custer was named for General George Custer, who is
best remembered for Custer's Last Stand.[26]

Custer

Women with the Custer Post Office

THE POST OFFICE IN CUSTER has had a long history of employing women, dating back to 1915 when the village selected Sarah (Sadie) J. McDonald as the village's postmistress.[3] She served in the role until 1946, both at the village's post office and then, later, out of her own home. In 1948, Lillian E. Porter served in the role alongside Eseler J. Hanna.[4] In addition, Eileen Melson and Clara Hissong have also served as rural mail route carriers in Custer, both prior to 1980.[5]

History of Custer

As with many early settlements in Michigan, European settlers were drawn to the area by the abundant forests.[6] In the late 1840s, pioneers in the area named their settlement Black Creek, for the town's first resident, a Mr. Black.[7] In 1878, the village moved to a new location—its current location—and was renamed for George Armstrong Custer, who died in 1876 at the Battle of Little Bighorn.[8]

The first hotel in the village was built in 1875, and the Pere Marquette Railroad came to Custer in 1874.[9] Charles E. Resseguie platted the new village location in 1878 and built a few buildings in the new town, including a store.[10] The first sawmill was also built in 1878, by the Wicks Brothers.[11] In 1880 a wooden bowl factory opened,[12] and in 1881, the town got a cheese box factory, which was later replaced by a pickle business.[13] A year later, in 1882, Custer got its first tannery.[14]

Placed on the site of the old general store, Custer's depot was built in the first few years of the twentieth century.[15] Within a few more years, the town's population had grown to approximately 375 people, and there were a variety of thriving businesses, including three general stores, two physicians, a saloon, a livery stable, a blacksmith, a barber, a hotel, a stationery, a justice of the peace, a shoemaker, a milliner, a hardware store, and a mason.[16] There was also a school and two churches.[17] Electricity came to Custer in 1911.[18]

Custer was not only about business, however. In the first few decades of the twentieth century, there was also a pool hall, a dance hall, and a roller skating rink.[19] The circus also sometimes came to town.[20]

When U.S. Highway 10 came to Custer at the beginning of the twentieth century, the business geography of the town changed, with the business district largely moving three blocks to the north of where it had been.[21] Much of the old business area on Main Street, however, was taken over by a meatpacking plant owned by the Sanders family.[22] Sanders Meats still has a presence in Custer today.

Custer Village Looks to Expand

In the fall of 2017, the Village of Custer made an official request of Mason County to extend its land by annexing part of what is now Custer Township.[23] Part of Marlins Wildlife Safari, which has a petting zoo, camel rides, parakeets, and a corn maze,[24] occupies the land the village is looking to expand into, and the goal of the annexation is to have the entire wildlife park located within the official village limits.

Custer Today

Today Custer has a hardware store, an auto glass center, an engine repair center, an auto sales business, a wood furniture company, a laundromat, a hair and tanning salon, a skate center, a car-detailing business, and self-storage units. There is also a VFW hall and a village hall, and Custer is home to the Mason County Eastern school district. St. Mary's Catholic Church serves the Custer area.

Perhaps the most well-known fixture of Custer today, however, is the large cow's head adorning the side of the old Bonser's Meat Market, which may have been the last large independent grocery store in the county.[24] The market is closed, but the cow head is still there, serving as a landmark in the area.

Custer's mail was carried by Ralph Tower from 1936 to 1947, and he was best known for singing songs when his vehicle had problems rather than expressing anger or frustration as others might have done.[27]

TOP: The Daggett Moravian Church is one of only three Moravian churches in Michigan

Population: 258[1] **Incorporated:** 1902[2]

INSETS L to R: The Daggett Township Hall • Fran's Rink and Park • Buildings near the railroad tracks on 24 Mile Road • Heidenreich Park, home to Three Angels Field

Before the village was named for Clara Daggett's father, the area had been called simply Section 25, because it was located a distance of 25 miles from Menominee.[26]

Daggett is located on U.S. Highway 41, which runs from Miami, Florida, to Copper Harbor, Michigan, right at the northern tip of the Upper Peninsula.

Daggett

History of Daggett

THE FIRST EUROPEAN SETTLERS in the area that would eventually become the village of Daggett came to the area because of the lumber industry.[3] The village of Daggett was founded by Thomas Faulkner in 1876.[4] He was in the area working on a farm for the Holmes & Son Lumber Company when he founded the village.[5] His wife, who ran the first post office in the village, was a woman by the name of Clara whose maiden name was Daggett.[6] Originally from Elmira, New York, Clara was only in the area to visit her brother in nearby Marinette, Wisconsin, but she stayed when she married Thomas.[7] The village was named in honor of her father.[8]

The Chicago & North Western Railway made Daggett a flag stop in 1880 (passengers could flag the train down to be picked up), and in 1883 the village received a depot.[9, 10] Early buildings in Daggett included a small handful of stores, a few sawmills, a planing mill, a shingle mill, a post mill, a hotel, and a theater.[11] A Moravian church—one of the oldest Protestant denominations—opened in Daggett in 1911, and it was known for its handbell choirs.[12] The congregation still practices in Daggett to this day, and it is one of only three Moravian churches in the state of Michigan.

Once the trees had all been cut in the Daggett area, the village shifted its industry to agriculture, though in truth there had been farming in the area from the time Thomas Faulkner first came to the area.

The main crops grown around the village were hay, cabbage, and a variety of root crops, including potatoes and turnips.[13] Some fruit trees, such as apple, plum, and cherry, were also grown in the area, but these were primarily for an individual family's use rather than as a market crop.[14] Many families in the area also owned dairy cows, and the Daggett area supported three dairy factories.[15]

George H. Westmon

George Westmon was head of the Westmon Lumber Company in Daggett, but the path he followed to get there was not an easy or a straight one. He was born in Norway in 1847 and came to the United States with his family at the age of 7.[16] He lived for a time in Wisconsin where he earned his first job as a clerk before moving to Iowa to attend college.[17] After college he returned to Wisconsin and took a job on a trading ship.[18] After three years he was able to purchase the ship and its entire stock, which he ran for three more years before leaving the sea and working in a variety of positions, including as a grocer, a traveling salesman, and a general store owner.[19] In 1888 he sold his business interests in Wisconsin and the Chicago area and moved to Daggett, where he took over the general store there.[20] He also developed the lumber company, and served as its vice president and then as its president.[21]

Agritourism in Daggett

Today, Daggett maintains its role as an agricultural community, and one new endeavor tried by a local farm is agritourism—tourism based around agriculture. For Elmcrest Acres, owned by the Buechler family, a Daggett farm that has grown Christmas trees since the 1940s and raised lambs and Haflinger horses since the 1990s, agritourism comes in the form of a folk school at the farm.[22] The school invites people to come to the farm for special events and classes, and visitors have enjoyed a variety of "simple life" classes on topics such as quilting and scrapbooking.[23] In addition, you can stay at the farm's vacation rental.[24]

However you come to the farm, though, you are sure to enjoy time getting to know the Buechler family and the work they do on the farm.[25]

Daggett Today

With the focus on agriculture in the Daggett area, it can be easy to overlook the village itself, but to do so would be a mistake. The railroad still passes through town, and some of the buildings still have the original architecture, but there are new elements to the town mixed in with those that are older. In addition to the Moravian church, there is also an Evangelical Lutheran church.

Businesses include a health supplies store, a convenience store, a dentist, a storage center, an auto body shop, a collision center, a vehicle restoration business, a woodworking studio, and a medical marijuana dispensary. The Little Cedar River runs on the south side of town, and Hays Creek is to the east of the village. There are two parks in Daggett, plus a ballfield and a sledding hill.

IN HONOR OF ALL WHO WERE MEMBERS OF MENOMINEE MID-COUNTY VFW POST 5966 CHARTERED FEBRUARY 1946 SURRENDERED APRIL 2011 YOUR SERVICE IS FOREVER REMEMBERED

Just south of town on US-41, you can see a giant statue of a cow out front of an excavating business.[27] The statue is commonly called "Naughty Cow," as the cow is lifting her skirt to show her udder.

TOP: The Dansville branch of the Capital Area District Libraries

Population: 563[1]   **Incorporated:** 1867[2]

INSETS L to R: The old Dansville Fire Department • A barber shop located on Jackson Street • The building that houses the Dansville village offices also contains a food and clothing bank • A popular Dansville restaurant and bar

In 1880, the village of Dansville organized a band of cornet players.[21] The thirteen musicians ranged in experience from novices to experienced players.[22]

In 1898, an Owosso resident named Fred Robinson was in Dansville preparing for an exhibition called "Blowing up Maine." Something went wrong while he was working with a gas pipe and there was an explosion that killed him instantly.[23]

Dansville

History of Dansville

DANSVILLE WAS FIRST SETTLED IN 1836 when Samuel Crossman and his son John settled on 40 acres.[3] Samuel Crossman built the first frame house in the area in 1846 and opened the first business, a general store, the following year.[4] The area was officially platted in 1857, though a new platting in 1866 included two additions.[5] Dansville was named for two of its early prominent residents, Daniel C. Crossman, who helped plat the village, and Dr. Daniel T. Weston, its first postmaster.

By the mid-1860s, Dansville had grown to include a variety of businesses, including different types of stores, a hotel, a blacksmith, multiple cabinetmakers, a sawmill, and a grist mill.[6] There was also a carriage factory and various places that would perform repairs on carriages. As Dansville was on a stagecoach route, these businesses likely saw many customers.

The first school in Dansville began in 1846.[7] Though the village residents built a log schoolhouse, the first meeting, with eight children, was at a local wagon shop.[8,9] The first teacher was thirteen-year-old Catherine E. Hill.[10] The school was successful, and a few years later the log schoolhouse was replaced with a wood-frame building.[11] In the late 1860s, this was replaced by a two-story brick building called the Union school building, which was in turn replaced in 1920.[12] The Dansville school district still operates today, with classes for students from kindergarten through twelfth grade.[13]

Fire in Dansville

The first fire in Dansville took place in the mid-1800s and resulted in the loss of one log building in the town.[14] Though it was only one building, at the time it was the only building in the village that served in a public capacity.[15] A second fire took place in the late 1880s and destroyed a much larger area of the town.[16]

The Burning Bed

In 1977, Dansville resident Francine Hughes set fire to her ex-husband's house, killing him as he slept.[17] He had abused her for twelve years, and when she turned herself in for the crime, she said she'd done it because she'd feared for her life.[18] She was charged but found not guilty by reason of insanity.[19] Her story helped spark nationwide attention to issues of domestic violence, and it has been adapted into a bestselling book, *The Burning Bed*.[20] In addition, her story inspired a made-for-television movie of the same name and the song "Independence Day" by Martina McBride.

Dansville Today

Today Dansville is a thriving small community in Ingham County. There is the Wooden Nickle Saloon, Confectionately Yours Bakery, Dansville Mercantile, an embroidery shop, an antique store, a veterinary clinic, a grain elevator, a fuel service, an auto store, and a gas station. The school system has an athletic fields complex, and there is a public library. Village and township services include a community center, a food and clothing bank, a cemetery, and a fire station. Hart Farms, just outside of the downtown area of the village, has been owned by the same family for over a century, making it a Centennial Farm. The village is also served by a variety of churches, including Heritage United Brethren, Dansville Baptist Church, and Dansville Free Methodist Church.

Dansville is home to the two-story Dr. D. J. Weston Octagon House. Originally built in 1861, the house was used to hide former slaves as part of the Underground Railroad.[24]

Population: 325[1]   Incorporated: 1899[2]

INSETS L to R: Union Presbyterian Church • A sign in the village
with information about local businesses • The DeTour Village Inn
• A ship's anchor is used as a decoration in the village

TOP: The Marina at DeTour, located near the Drummond Island Ferry

DeTour was the site of the first Ford dealership in the eastern Upper Peninsula—sort of.[26] Father Theodore Bateski applied to open a Ford dealership to get a discount on a car, but once he received the car, he returned the dealership.[27]

DeTour

The Turn

DETOUR GOT ITS NAME NOT from the word *detour* as some might guess but from the French *de tour* or *the turn*.[3] The current-day village is situated on the far eastern tip of the Upper Peninsula and surrounded on three sides by water. Ships coming from Lake Huron sail through the DeTour Passage to reach St. Marys River pass and, eventually, Lake Superior. The French were not the first to recognize the importance of this place, however. The Ojibwe called this area *Giwideonaning*, variously translated as *point which we go around in a canoe* or, more simply, as *to turn*.[4,5]

History of DeTour

The area where DeTour now stands has always been important due to the proximity of the DeTour Passage. American Indians lived in the area, and early European traders passed through as well.[6] The current village finds its origins in the mid-nineteenth century, when entrepreneurs began supplying fuel and docking services to ships sailing through the passage.[7] The DeTour lighthouse opened in 1848, but due to the inferior quality of the building supplies used, the lighthouse was replaced in 1861.[8] That lighthouse lasted until 1931, at which point it was replaced with the DeTour Reef Lighthouse.[9] This lighthouse has since been preserved and now serves as a tourist attraction, with tours of the lighthouse, a volunteer-based lightkeeper program (where visitors can apply to become lighthouse keepers for a weekend), and other larger events.[10, 11]

The first post office in DeTour opened in 1856, though at the time the station was named Detour, and it closed a year later.[12] Finally in

1869, a new post office opened.[13] Nearly 100 years later, in 1953, the post office was renamed to its current spelling of DeTour then, a few years later, to DeTour Village.[14]

In addition to the shipping industry, DeTour also had successful fishing and lumbering industries near the end of the nineteenth century, and the village prospered.[15] By the turn of the century, there were nearly 700 residents of the village, a few hotels and boarding houses, a variety of stores, and a jail.[16] A local woman gave piano lessons out of her house.[17] The village schoolhouse, built in the 1850s, saw, at times, up to 100 students.[18] Sometime later a second school opened and served students up through tenth grade, and when that, too, ran out of space, the school rented rooms in a village hall, and eventually, yet another new school was built.[19]

Life in DeTour was not all work and school, however. The village had a variety of entertainment options for residents and visitors alike. There were places to play sports, such as tennis and baseball, in the summer, and in the winter there were opportunities for sleigh rides and ice skating.[20] Year-round, people would go dancing, and there was a roller skating rink in McGuire's Hall.[21]

DeTour Today

Known as "The Gateway to the North," DeTour is still an important community on the Great Lakes. All traffic headed from Lake Huron and Lake Michigan to the Soo Locks passes by DeTour, including some cruise lines.[22] There are nearby quarries that employ a number of DeTour residents,[23] and these things combined with recent gains in tourism have allowed the village to thrive. Visitors can rent lakefront cabins and visit the DeTour State Harbor, the local marina. Ferries leave DeTour once an hour for nearby Drummond Island. More than a dozen shipwrecks lie offshore in the DeTour Passage Underwater Preserve, making them a popular dive site. One abandoned barge is even partially visible above water.

In DeTour there is a building center, a concrete company, a gas station, a bank, a credit union, a grocery store, an insurance agency, a hair salon, an art gallery, and a variety of other local businesses. There are also both village and township offices, a post office, volunteer fire and ambulance services, a historical museum, and a public library.[24]

There is a strong sense of community in the village. During the summer and early fall, there is a weekly farmers market, and residents can donate to a local food bank. Seniors in the community can enjoy a senior lunch three days per week at the village hall, and once a month there is a senior potluck.[25]

Many ships—including ocean-going freighters headed to Lake Superior—pass by DeTour Village each year, making it a great place to shipwatch.

63

Population: 123[1]   **Incorporated:** 1873[2]

INSETS L to R: Trees line the drive at the Eagle Park Fairgrounds •
One of the churches in the village • The village still has a handful
of older buildings • Hunters from the surrounding area can bring
their game to this business to be processed

George McCrumb, the founder of the village,
endured many tragedies in his life. His father died
by the time George was 18, leaving George to fend
for the family. Later, when he became a father,
only three of his eight children survived, but he
persevered, becoming the owner of a sawmill that
thrived in the area.

TOP: An old railway caboose is on display at the Eagle Park Fairgrounds

Eagle

History of Eagle

THE FIRST EUROPEAN SETTLERS in the area that would eventually become Eagle Township were Anthony Niles and Stephen B. Groger in 1834.[3] Soon, a new village formed, and it was named after the township.[4] The first post office in Eagle opened in 1841, but it was actually named Waverly, changing its name to match the village the following year.[5]

It was the arrival of the Pere Marquette Railroad and the construction of a depot in the 1870s, however, that really spurred growth in the village. George W. McCrumb, the supervisor of Eagle Township, purchased land in the area, along with Jacob Schott, and in 1873, Eagle was officially platted, recorded, and incorporated as a village, though its new location was actually half a mile away from where it had first begun.[6] McCrumb also built the depot on his own land and paid for its construction in full.[7]

The first store in Eagle also opened in 1873 and was run by Loyal W. Hill, and a blacksmith and a second store soon followed suit.[8] In 1876, the first hardware store opened, and the first church opened as well. By 1880, the village had added a hotel, a grocery, a general store, a second blacksmith shop, a milliner, and a school.[9] Just outside of the village there was also a sawmill, a planing mill, a moulding mill, and a feed mill.[10]

In the late 1800s, the village had its own ladies' room, which provided social opportunities such as dancing.[11] By the early part of the twentieth century, there were two churches that sometimes hosted community events as well—a Methodist Episcopal church and a Universalist church.[12] Eddy Lala also provided music lessons to Eagle residents.[13]

The Fire of 1897

Eagle saw a major setback in 1897 when a fire that started at McCrumb's store burned down the village's entire business district and one house.[14] Even in major cities with fire brigades, fires could still prove devastating, as the Great Chicago Fire of 1871 had shown. Eagle's business district didn't stand a chance. Thankfully, the town rebuilt, picking up the pieces from the disaster.

Annual Eagle Fair Days

Every year on the weekend after Labor Day, the village of Eagle and various nearby communities gear up for the annual Eagle Fair Days Weekend. The event, which runs Thursday through Sunday, includes a cruise-in, horseshoe and ball tournaments, tractor pulls, fair exhibits, a bake sale, a flea market, food, and live entertainment.[15]

The current iteration of Fair Days has been running since 1976, when the current fairgrounds were opened, but before that the event had been on a hiatus of approximately 20 years.[16] The reason for the break in the festivities? When I-96 had come through the area, the old fairgrounds closed.[17] But by the mid-1970s, the community of Eagle was itching for a return to its old tradition, and a combination of residents and local businesses got the ball rolling again.[18] They were helped, too, by the fact that there was still money left in an account from the old Fair Days events, and the village had been told they would need to return the money if they didn't spend it soon.[19]

The first Fair Days at the new fairgrounds was small. It had one ballfield for a tournament, and there was one food stand and a beverage tent.[20] The event has grown since then, with the addition of new buildings, and, recently, new bleachers, but one key thing about the improvements is that they have largely been donated by people and businesses who want to see the event succeed.[21]

Eagle Today

When not in the midst of their annual Fair Days event, Eagle is mostly a calm and quiet town where people will stop even a stranger on the street to say hello. There is a party store, a deer processing center, a boat sales shop, an inn, a storage center, an archery shop, an auto repair shop, a township hall, and a post office. The village is served by two churches: Believers Christian Church and, just across I-96, Crossroads Community Church.

The building that now holds Swampers Party Stop has previously been used as a meat processing business and, prior to that, contained the lone village jail cell.

TOP: The Elberta Mercantile Company sells antiques

Population: 372[1]   **Incorporated:** 1911[2]

INSETS L to R: A sign at the trailhead to the Elberta Dunes South • One way of getting to Elberta is to cross the bridge over Betsie Lake • Some of the dunes at Elberta • Buildings and businesses on the west side of Frankfort Avenue

The name Elberta comes from the name of a peach that grows in the Elberta area. Elberta peaches are a good variety for canning.

The dunes in Elberta have remained undeveloped thanks to the work of Jim Thorpe, who, with the help of the Michigan Natural Resources Trust Fund, worked to ensure that the land would be protected by the work of a conservancy.[25]

Elberta

History of Elberta

THE FIRST EUROPEAN SETTLER IN THE AREA of Elberta was Joseph Oliver in the 1840s, though John and Caroline Greenwood, who came to the area in 1855, are often listed as the first instead.[3] However, it was the arrival of a different man, George M. Cartwright in 1866, which truly started the village.[4] He recorded the first plat of the village, though at the time it was recorded as Frankfort City.[5] When it was recorded, it became the first "legally correct plat" in all of Benzie County.[6] The first post office was named something different again—South Frankfort—and in 1872, George A. Douglass became the first postmaster.[7]

In 1867, Frankfort Iron Works built a blast furnace in what is now Elberta.[8] At the time it was the largest manufacturer in the entire county.[9] When the railroad came to Elberta a year later, it came because of Frankfort Iron Works.[10] However, the company's stay in Elberta would be short lived, and the furnace shut down in 1883.[11] The area the company owned, as well as some of the buildings, has been used over time as a machine shop and as land for the railroad.[12]

Elberta was not the end of the line for the railroad tracks, however. A car-ferry service, operated by the Ann Arbor Railroad, ran in and out of the village harbor, beginning in 1892.[13] The ferries moved railroad cars from Betsie Lake, which is north and east of Elberta, out into Lake Michigan and then to Wisconsin.[14] The ferry service was the first to be used across such a large and open body of water.[15] The ferry service was permanently shut down in 1982.[16]

The U.S. Life-Saving Station Saves the Crew of the Ann Arbor No. 4

Before the ferry service was shut down, the crews of the rail ferries were safeguarded by crews from the U.S. Life-Saving Service, the forerunner to the U.S. Coast Guard, which had a station in Elberta (though it was usually called the Frankfort station). The crews on site trained for all varieties of rescues, and they were involved in an especially harrowing rescue in 1923. The *Ann Arbor No. 4*, loaded with some railcars carrying coal and others full of automobiles, encountered a full-blown storm in February.[17] The wind, blowing from the west, reached speeds of hurricane-strength, and 30-foot waves ravaged the ship. This caused the railcars to break loose, the car carrying Buicks to go overboard into Lake Michigan, and the ship to begin taking on water.[18] Eventually, the ship's captain, a man by the name of Frederickson, decided to turn and attempt to make it back to port.[19] This meant turning his ship and exposing it, broadside, to the full fury of the storm. Somehow, the ship survived the maneuver, and even made it back to the Frankfort harbor entrance, but its luck ended there as the ship crashed into the south pier and became partially submerged.[20] The crew, still aboard, was now soaking wet and exposed to the elements without a way to get to shore.[21] The Life-Saving crew, already alerted to the vessel's plight, jumped into action. The ice-covered pier now resembled a storm-wracked glacier more than a manmade structure, and the Life-Saving crews were dressed to match, with ice-spurs on their boots and roped together to prevent falls.[22] Eventually, they managed to free the entire crew, albeit in separate groups, and the *Ann Arbor No. 4* was eventually raised and rebuilt.[23] The Life-Saving Station has since been restored, and it's now a popular site for weddings, events, and more.

Elberta Today

Elberta today bills itself as "the gateway to lake Michigan." Its location in between Betsie Lake and Lake Michigan makes it an ideal location for tourists to come visit, and in the summer months especially, you can see a good number of people out enjoying the village and its beautiful views. There are many local food businesses in the town, including the Cabbage Shed tavern on the Lake Betsie waterfront (which was once a storage space for cabbage), Conundrum Café, Lighthouse Café, Elberto's Taqueria, the Mayfair Tavern, and others.[24] There is also a mercantile company, a tire and auto store, and more. For services, there is a post office and a community building.

There are also a variety of outdoor options in the town. There are dunes in Elberta to explore along the Lake Michigan shoreline, and there is beach access as well. There is a waterfront park, a marina, and a boat launch on the shore of Betsie Lake. Visitors can go on a salmon charter or explore the *City of Boston* shipwreck near the town. The Betsie Valley Trail is accessible from Elberta as well.

In the 1940s, three street names in Elberta were changed in honor of soldiers from Elberta who lost their lives in the Second World War.[26] The new street names were Acre Street, Bigley Street, and Van Brocklin Street.[27]

WELCOME
ELBERTA DUNES SOUTH
NATURAL AREA

Population: 349[1]   **Incorporated:** 1938[2]

INSETS L to R: Ellsworth has its own labyrinth garden • The Banks Township Historical Society building • The Christian Reformed Church is Ellsworth was organized in 1901 • The Banks Township Fire Department has a station in Ellsworth

The first stop signs came to Ellsworth in 1943.[34] Their arrival marked the beginning of traffic enforcement in the area.[35]

TOP: Ellsworth is the seat of Banks Township and so has the Banks Township Community Hall Building

Ellsworth

History of Ellsworth

ONE OF THE EARLIEST SETTLERS in the Ellsworth area was a woman named Lois Hardy.[3] She was a homesteader who built a log cabin by what is now known as Skinner Creek and lived there with her brother and sister.[4] She named the nearby lake Hardy Lake.[5] No trace of her cabin remains, but it is believed to have been located right in the center of Ellsworth.[6]

The official settlement started in 1881 with the arrival of Augustus Davis and his nephew Erwin Dean (though some sources record that Davis was Dean's nephew).[7] The settlement was at first called Ox Box, and a second settlement to the south was originally called Needmore.[8,9] The combination of the two settlements eventually formed into one village, and that village received its first post office in 1884, with Lewis A. DeLine as the first postmaster.[10] DeLine named the post office Ellsworth, after Colonel Elmer Ephraim Ellsworth, whom he had served under in the Civil War.[11]

One early and prominent resident in Ellsworth was Falle H. Skow. Originally from Denmark, Skow was involved in the lumber, farming, retail, and real estate businesses.[12] It was not his business interests he was remembered for, though. Skow was always ready to lend a helping hand to his neighbors, even when it meant spending his own money to do so.[13] When the Chicago & West Michigan Railroad came to town in 1892, its depot was built on land he donated for the purpose.[14]

The railroad's arrival in town was a big moment for the town in terms of business and travel, but it also affected the layout of the town. Lois Hardy's log cabin was torn down to make room for the railroad, and the Ellsworth Lumber Company opened a new building by the tracks.[15]

In addition to the railroad's arrival, 1892 was also the year Ellsworth was first platted.[16] At the beginning of 1893, around 30 families lived in the town.[17] More mills opened, taking advantage of the abundance of trees in the area, and Ellsworth continued to grow.[18] Some of the mills ended up employing over 50 people.[19]

The village was officially incorporated in 1938, and Elmer H. Rood was elected the first village president.[20] The village chamber of commerce was formed eleven years later with the goal of supporting business in the town.[21]

The Story of Elmer Ephraim Ellsworth, the Village's Namesake

The village of Ellsworth is named after Elmer Ephraim Ellsworth, a Colonel in the Union Army and the first Union officer killed in the Civil War. He was friends with Abraham Lincoln, having met Lincoln while he was a clerk at Lincoln's law office in 1860.[22] When Lincoln moved to Washington after being elected president, Ellsworth, who had previously served as a colonel in the National Guard, came with him.[23] With tensions brewing between the Northern and Southern states, Ellsworth gathered a regiment back in his native New York and brought his troops back to Washington, where they were assigned to march into Alexandria, Virginia, on the day Virginia seceded from the Union.[24]

The mission went off without a hitch, which may have been what inspired Ellsworth to do what he did next. There had been a Confederate flag flying from the roof of the Marshall House, a hotel in Alexandria.[25] The flag was large enough that it could be seen from Washington, and Ellsworth decided to take it down.[26] He entered the hotel with four others, climbed to the roof, and removed the flag, all with no resistance. But as he was coming back down, the innkeeper, a man named James Jackson, shot him.[27] Francis Brownell, one of Ellsworth's men, shot Jackson in return, but it was too late; Ellsworth, twenty-four-years old, was dead.[28] His body was returned to Washington where Lincoln and the Union cause both mourned his death.[29] During the Civil War, one rallying cry was "Remember Ellsworth!" and one regiment from New York called itself Ellsworth's Avengers.[30] It was to honor this man that Lewis A. DeLine decided to name a small village in Michigan after Ellsworth.

Ellsworth Today

Today, Ellsworth is a smaller town than it was in its lumber heyday, but it is still a thriving community. The village has its own community school system, serving students from pre-kindergarten through high school, and the Ellsworth schools score highly in state rankings.[31] Ebenezer Christian School is also located in Ellsworth.

The village has a four-acre community park at the location of an old industrial site.[32] The park has playground equipment, a pavilion, a labyrinth, a boat dock, walking paths, a sledding hill, and an archery range that is the largest outdoor archery range in Michigan.[33] Businesses in the village include a bank, a resale store, a funeral home, a farmers exchange, a gas station, a garage, a historical society, a community hall, a restaurant, and a bed and breakfast, among others. Churches in Ellsworth include a Wesleyan church and a Christian Reformed church.

Every summer Ellsworth hosts a Pig Roast—a two-day event marked by a parade, a horse pull, games, archery competitions and, of course, fresh roasted pig.

BANKS Township Historical Society

TOP: The Star of the West company has elevators for a variety of crops

Population: 269[1]   **Incorporated:** 1883[2]

INSETS L to R: Some of the businesses along Main Street in town • Our Lady of Mt. Carmel Catholic Church • More of the businesses along Main Street • A decoratively carved pole on Main Street

There is a KOA campground in Emmett. From May through mid-October the campground offers tent and RV camping sites.

Emmett

History of Emmett

THE FIRST EUROPEAN SETTLERS IN THE AREA of Emmett village and Emmett Township more broadly were Patrick Kennedy, Patrick Fitzgerald, James Cogley, Dennis Gleason, David Donahue, and Henry P. McCabe, all of whom came to the area in the first half of the nineteenth century.[3] The first platting of the village was done by Thomas Crowley in 1856, though he called the village Mount Crowley.[4] The fact that the land in the area was all but flat did not seem to matter much to him in his name choice.[5] Mount Crowley received its first post office in 1869, though the post office was named Emmett, for the township.[6] A short time later, the village switched its name to match that of the post office.[7]

An early business in the town was a shoe and boot store run by John Buckley, who started the business at only 16 years of age. Buckley, along with his brother, also started a brick manufactory.[8] The village also had a sawmill beginning in 1870, and William Butler, its owner, added a grist mill to his business in 1872, both of which performed very well.[9]

With successful businesses and the ever-present demand for lumber, Emmett grew quickly. The Grand Traverse Railway passed through the village, and Emmett received its own railroad depot in 1872.[10] It was incorporated as a village in 1883.[11] By the early twentieth century, the lumber business had gone into decline in the town, and so Emmett turned its focus to agriculture. In 1908, the village shipped agricultural products, including hay, grain, butter, and eggs.[12] It had a flour mill, an apiary (beehive), a cattle shipping business, and a grain elevator.[13]

The Storm of July 6, 1879

A massive storm system swept through the Upper Midwest on July 6, 1879, causing damage from Minnesota to Michigan. Variously reported as a tornado or heavy windstorm, it dumped huge amounts of rain and had very high winds, which damaged and destroyed buildings and caused a number of fatalities, including one near Emmett.[14] Weather forecasting was decidedly primitive at the time—the Weather Bureau, the forerunner to the National Weather Service, was only founded in 1870—and there were no storm warning systems to warn inhabitants ahead of time.[15]

The Irish Influence on Emmett

The village of Emmett had a historically Irish population—as indeed did Emmett Township, for which the village is named. Both the township and the village are in reference to Robert Emmet, an Irishman who led a revolt against the British government in the early 1800s.[16] Before the name of the township and village was standardized as the American spelling of Emmett—with two Ts—the name of the village was spelled two different ways.[17] Michigan's Emmet County, also named for Robert Emmet, uses the traditional Irish spelling with only one T.[18]

The town's name, however, is not the only place Irish history and culture can be found in Emmett. In 1876, local Irishmen started a group called St. Patrick's Benevolent Society.[19] The group worked to raise money for the poor, and one way they raised money was by fining members for violating the group's rules, which included refraining from dueling, avoiding political discussions at group meetings, and even requiring that members attend the annual St. Patrick's Day parade. Irish Catholics in Emmett had their own parish, as well, and they built their first church building in 1897.[20] The church burned down in 1966, but a new one was built around 1970.[21] There is now a historical marker in Emmett marking the history of the church.

Emmett Today

Emmett today is nearly the same size as it was a hundred years ago. It still produces hay from a farm just north of town, and there is a feed store as well. Near the south branch of the Pine River, there is also a mill. A local berry farm offers visitors to the farm the chance to pick their own berries, and another local farm breeds and trains horses and also raises sheep.[22,23]

In the village itself, there is a farmstand, a VFW, a Lions Club, a hair salon, a welding company, an inn, a bank, a restaurant, a service center, a pub, and a hardware store. Services in the town include a post office, a fire department, and an elementary school.

Emmett is also home to a roadside attraction fans of the television show *The Simpsons* might recognize. Next to Waldenburg, a furniture and cabinet maker downtown, there's a huge can of Homer's favorite Duff beer, as well as a massive pack of cigarettes.[24]

Population: 375[1] **Incorporated:** 1895[2]

INSETS L to R: A church building in the village • Local newspapers are available outside some of the local businesses • An anchor is used as a decoration outside one of the local hardware store • The sign welcoming visitors to Empire, the "Gateway to the Sleeping Bear Dunes National Lakeshore"

Empire was named in 1865 after a schooner became icebound in the bay by the village. *Empire* was the name of the vessel.[22]

TOP: The Empire Area Museum

Empire

"Gateway to the Sleeping Bear Dunes National Lakeshore"

ONE OF THE MOST POPULAR TOURIST DESTINATIONS in the state is Sleeping Bear Dunes National Lakeshore. The park, which has over a million visitors annually,[3] has been named the most beautiful place in America by *Good Morning America*.[4] The park encompasses 35 miles of the Lake Michigan shoreline on the west coast of Michigan and also two islands.[5] It includes twenty-six lakes, twelve miles of rivers, nearly 250 species of birds, and nearly 1,000 species of plants.[6] Empire is the gateway to it all. It is the closest town to the park and also home of the Philip A. Hart Visitor Center for the dunes.

History of Empire

The first European settlers in the Empire area were John LaRue and his family.[7] They came to the area in 1851 and were followed shortly after by Marvin La Core and George Aylsworth (sometimes spelled Aylesworth).LaRue became the town's first postmaster in 1864.[8, 9]

In its early days, Empire was a lumber town. The first sawmill in the area was built in 1873 by Aylsworth, and a second sawmill opened around a decade later.[10] The Empire Lumber Company bought that second mill in 1887 and added to the mill until it could produce twenty million feet of lumber per year.[11]

With such a production of lumber coming from the area, planing mills were added to the village to finish the cut timber, and two docks were constructed on Lake Michigan.[12] The lumber company also built a railroad that helped bring the wood they cut to their mills, and eventually that line was connected to the Manistee & Northeastern Railroad and passenger service was added.[13]

The sawmill burned down in 1906 but was rebuilt, as there were still a number of trees growing in the area.[14] Still, with the turn of the century, the lumber industry began to slow somewhat, and farms began to spring up on the cleared land.[15] When the mill burned for the second time in 1917, it was not rebuilt, and the local economy became one of agriculture.[16] The area grew mainly potatoes and fruit.[17] Cherries were so prominent that in 1909 there were 16,000 cherry trees in Leelanau County.

Now, the economy in Empire has shifted again. While there are still many farms in the Empire area, tourism has been a big business since the Sleeping Bear Dunes National Lakeshore first opened in 1970.

Empire Air Force Station

Empire is home to the Empire Air Force Station, an early warning radar system from the Cold War era.[18] Starting in 1950, the 752nd Aircraft Control and Warning Squadron called Empire their home as the radar station kept a lookout for any Russian bombers approaching from the Canadian Arctic or ICBMs approaching the United States.[19] It was a top-secret operation with exceedingly strict security measures until it finally closed in 1978.[20] At that point, the FAA started using the station for air traffic radar, though nowadays the site is largely operated by computers rather than human personnel.[21]

Empire Today

Despite its small population, Empire can be a busy town, especially in the summer. The visitor center for Sleeping Bear Dunes is in the village, and there are places to rent bikes, surfboards, and kayaks. There are numerous inns and vacation rentals in the village. For food, there is the Shipwreck Café, Joe's Friendly Tavern, the Empire Village Inn, Little Finger Eatery, and Tiffany's Café. Grocer's Daughter Chocolate is a local chocolate confectioner.

Shopping options are also available in the village, with stores selling everything from art and antiques to clothing and souvenirs. For the locals, there is a hair salon, a gas station, a bank, an insurance company, a self-storage center, an engineering consultant, and a hardware store. For services, there are village offices and a fire department. The village also has a historical museum. Churches in the area include a United Methodist church and a Catholic church.

In the fall, Empire has a Hops and Harvest Festival that brings together local food and beer for a day of live music and celebration.

TOP: The view from Lakeshore Drive, which runs along the peninsula

Population: 418[1]   **Incorporated:** 1925[2]

INSETS L to R: : A tank on display at the Veterans' War Memorial, which is located near the village hall • The village has a large green space that includes playground equipment, benches, and picnic tables • The area where Swan Creek meets Lake Erie • Nautical items serve as decorations for the Sovey Street Bar and Grill

It is said that Estral Beach is named because of its similarity to *estrella*, the Spanish word for star.

Estral Beach

History of Estral Beach

ESTRAL BEACH HAS A HISTORY as a resort community. Water is the community's biggest feature; it sits on the shores of Lake Erie and Swan Creek and is nearly surrounded by water. The southern end of the village sits on a long and narrow peninsula, and many of the houses are right on the water.

Not much is known about the early days of Estral Beach's history. It incorporated as a community in 1925, and it has spent much of its time since then as a quiet and private community. It is the smallest municipality in all of Monroe County.[3]

The Flood of 1952

Resort communities are for getting away and enjoying a quiet life amidst nature. With Lake Erie to the east and Swan Creek to the south, the residents of Estral Beach have access to an abundance of nature. But nature can turn on humans suddenly, and in the spring of 1952, a storm hit Lake Erie.[4] Rather than coming out of the west, the winds in that storm came from the northeast and created "sea-like" waves.[5] The end result was that the entire village ended up three feet underwater, and to get around, residents had to travel the streets in their boats.[6] Engineers came to the village to survey the damage, and their recommendation to the residents was that the people should pack up, leave, and not come back.[7]

Two families did leave, but the large majority of residents decided not to give up on their homes and community—even when difficulties came from every side.[8] A second storm hit not long after the first, and when the village president tried to borrow money to help with repair costs, he was told his village wasn't worth the cost.[9] So the residents took boats to their houses and began repairs themselves, without any help except that which came from their fellow community members.[10] Finally, in the fall, the army came in to repair the old and outdated dikes in the village.[11] In the end, they were able to get nearly $200,000 in federal aid and built a new dike that completely surrounded the village.[12] Finally, more than two years after the storm hit, the village was back to normal.

Estral Beach Today

Estral Beach still deals with flood problems today, but nothing as catastrophic as in 1952. The community is ready to take and deal with what comes, but it is also not waiting for the next problem. They have worked with FEMA to raise the elevation of some houses and have also been awarded grants for other improvement projects. The village replaced the community building after the 1952 flood, funding the construction largely with village fundraisers. The new building contains the village hall and fire department, and there is a park alongside that has playground equipment and a war memorial. The war memorial includes a tank from World War II.

The community today is still very private. There is no public beach access in the town, and the only true business is the Sovey Street Bar and Grill.

From Estral Beach, it's easy to spot the cooling towers of Enrico Fermi Nuclear Generating Station, a nuclear power station, which is located not that far away.

INSETS L to R: This building contains two local businesses • A view looking south on Fife Lake • Fife Lake's historical walk • Railroad tracks still pass through the village

Fife Lake itself covers over 600 acres and contains two islands. It is a good spot for fishing, and contains bluegill and pumpkinseed sunfish, pike, walleye, and various types of bass.[31]

TOP: This school was built in 1878 in Fife Lake

Fife Lake

History of Fife Lake

FIFE LAKE CAN TRACE ITS HISTORY as a settlement back to the mid-1800s when a team of surveyors set out to determine the best way to connect Traverse City and Midland by road.[3] They passed the lake now known as Fife Lake, naming it after one of their team members, William Fife.[4] When in the early 1870s railroad workers came through the area while building the Grand Rapids & Indiana Railroad, they decided that Fife Lake would be a good place for a town.[5] The village was founded in 1872.[6]

The early industry in Fife Lake primarily focused on lumber, especially pine.[7] The first sawmill was built in the village in 1872, at a lumber camp owned by W. W. Bailey.[8] A hotel, some stores, and frame houses followed quickly.[9] The first school was built in 1876.[10] Until the first church was finished in 1884, religious services were held in the schoolhouse.[11] A new schoolhouse replaced the first in 1884, and at that time the original schoolhouse was moved to a new location and became the town's firebarn.[12] When the town was incorporated in 1889, it had more than 700 residents.[13]

Lumber was not the only business in Fife Lake near the turn of the century. There was an ice plant started in 1890, and by the early 1900s, the town had half a dozen grocers, nearly as many dry goods stores, a shoemaker, a baker, a barber, a hardware store, a painter, a carpenter, and its own newspaper.[14, 15] The town also had a bandstand and a lodge for the Independent Order of Odd Fellows and its female auxiliary, the Rebekahs.[16]

As with many lumber towns, the economy shifted to become more agricultural as the trees were cleared, but unfortunately, the soil in the Fife Lake area was not good for farming.[17] That, coupled with the end of the lumber boom, caused the village's population to drop drastically, and by 1920, the population in the town had shrunk to a number less than half of what it had been in 1889.[18]

It was in the 1920s that Fife Lake's prospects began to change, when people starting building cottages on the lake.[19] The town began to grow again, but this time as a resort community, with tourism as its new main business interest.[20]

Fife Lake Historic Walk

Downtown Fife Lake is home to the Fife Lake Historic Walk. The Historic Walk has 27 stops, and the plaque at each stop contains a photograph of historic Fife Lake and accompanying text explaining the photograph. On the walk, you can learn about the old auto sales store from 1920 or see what the depot looked like before it was torn down in 1959.

The photos on the Historic Walk are what truly make the experience of reliving Fife Lake's history special. Many of the photos were taken by Fife Lake resident Willis Brower from approximately 1890 to 1920.[21] What is remarkable about the photos is that so many of them are candid rather than posed shots, giving modern viewers a glimpse into what life was like around the turn of the twentieth century.[22] In 1967, Brower's daughter Nina donated the photos to the museum, and now they are on display for all to see.[23]

True Crime in Fife Lake

Mary McKnight is among the most infamous figures in Michigan history. A serial killer whose weapon of choice was the poison strychnine, she was responsible for perhaps a dozen murders, though the three that eventually landed her in jail for life occurred in the Fife Lake area.[24]

McKnight was babysitting a three-month-old baby when the child's mother returned to find that her baby had died.[25] Soon, the mother, Gertrude, started having seizures and also died.[26] Her husband died not long thereafter. Soon, however, the bodies of the child and the mother were exhumed, and rat poison was detected in their systems.[27] McKnight confessed and was sentenced to life in prison, and investigators soon tied her to other deaths, many in her own family.[28] The story became national news; the *New York Times* referred to her as the "Michigan Murderess."[29] Incredibly, she was paroled and released after 18 years in prison.[30]

A Growing Town Once Again

Since reimagining itself as a tourist town, Fife Lake has once again begun to grow. The downtown has a number of restaurants and shops, a quilting store, and there are lodging options by the lake. There is a laundromat, a hardware store, a hair salon, a barbershop, a veterinary clinic, and an ice cream parlor. Many of the town's older buildings still stand, including the original schoolhouse-turned-firebarn, a second school building, the hardware store, and the building for the museum.

Three churches serve the Fife Lake area populace: St. Aloysius Catholic Church, the Fife Lake Baptist Church, and the Fife Lake United Methodist Church. The town also has a park, a village hall, a library, township offices, an elementary school, and a post office. There is a private marina as well as a public beach and boat launch.

Fife Lake is located along the North Country Trail, a hiking trail that runs over 4,500 miles from New York, through both Michigan peninsulas, and finally to North Dakota.[32]

TOP: Looking east onto Lake Huron

Population: 136[1]   **Incorporated:** 1895[2]

INSETS L to R: A playground area • St. John Chrysostom Catholic Church • A view down one of the main streets in the town • The Forestville Post Office

Early roads in Forestville were difficult to traverse, even with oxen or horses. The first cars came to the area around 1908, but almost a decade later it was not uncommon for drivers to have to push their cars through deep sand.[20]

Forestville

History of Forestville

FORESTVILLE CAN TRACE ITS ROOTS back to 1853 when Alva Kelly first bought land in the area.[3] The area was heavily forested, and a sawmill, the village's first frame structure, was built a year later by Captain E. B. Ward.[4] Captain Ward's wife briefly ran a school out of her house, but the pair left the village less than a year later, before the town had even received its name.[5] A true schoolhouse was built in the area around 1859, but it was not right in Forestville.[6]

When Ward left, he sold the mill, but the new owners were forced out of business only two years later when the "Great Panic" of 1857 struck the village. However, with the start of the Civil War, the demand for lumber increased, and the mill reopened, this time with different owners.

Harvesting the Forest, and the Fire of 1871

Forestville received its name from the abundance of forested land in the area, and this allowed the newly revived sawmill business to find ample success. In the late 1860s, the combined mills of the village produced nearly one million feet of lumber every week.[7] The profitable times were not to last, though, and a fire swept through the area in 1871, burning down most of the pine and also destroying the mills and most of the town.[8] Forestville wasn't the only town that suffered from that fire; much of Michigan burned in October of that year, though the Michigan fires were largely overshadowed by the Great Fire of Chicago, which struck around the same time.[9] A second fire struck the area a decade later, but thankfully this time it was stopped before reaching Forestville.[10]

After the Fire

The fire left many in the village unemployed, and many families decided they could not stay. Though there had already been businesses in Forestville, including a post office and a hotel, they had all burned in the fire.[11] The first years after the fire were hard; everyone needed to help rebuild, and the post office closed in 1872, though it was restored a year later.[12] The village had been growing rapidly before the fire, but it took time for the businesses to come back. By the mid-1880s, the village had two general goods stores, a drugstore, a warehouse, a hotel, and a shoe store.[13] The village was not incorporated until 1895.[14]

Religion in Forestville

Forestville was a rare settlement in its early days as it went some time without any type of church building. The reason? One of the prominent men in the village, Isaac Green, disliked religion and was opposed to churches.[15] When the village proposed building a church in its early days, he used his considerable influence in the town to ensure that no money was available for a church's construction.[16] The result was that for many years, those who wished to practice religion in Forestville and the surrounding area had to meet at the school building.[17]

Finally, in 1881, the township was able to build its first religious building, a Methodist church, and once there was one, others soon followed.[18] By the early days of the twentieth century, Forestville had a Catholic, Lutheran, and Methodist church serving a population of around 250 people.[19]

Today, churches in the area include a Catholic church and a Lutheran church.

Forestville Today

Forestville, on Lake Huron in Sanilac County, is a quiet town despite the fact that US-25 runs north and south through the town.

There is no harbor on Lake Huron, but there are docks and a public beach, as well as a park area with playground equipment and a pavilion. The area is primarily residential, though there is a bar and grill, an antique store, a post office, and village offices.

Unlike other Michigan town sites, Forestville did not have any churches in its early days thanks to Isaac Green, a local iconoclast who disliked religion. Today, it has two churches.

Great Lakes RESTORATION

Funded by U.S. Environmental Protection Agency in collaboration with MI Dept. of Natural Resources & Environment.

Population: 193[1]   **Incorporated:** 1913[2]

INSETS L to R: American flags line Main Street • A stylized building in the downtown area • This sign welcomes visitors to the village • The Fountain Area Community Center, built in 1909

In the mid-1900s, Fountain had a baseball team known as the Fountain Bearcats. Paul Schoenherr, the lumber baron, managed the team.[23]

TOP: This sculpture, called "Out of the Forest," is part of the Mason County Lumber Heritage Trail

Fountain

History of Fountain

THE SETTLEMENT AT FOUNTAIN came about due to the nearby Flint and Pere Marquette Railroad and the nearby North Branch of the Lincoln River.[3] It was at the place where the railroad and the river were planned to meet that the first sawmill in the area was built by a man named Frank Young.[4] It was 1881, and Young was not the only one who came to the area. A pump house was started in the area, and a couple with the last name of Boomer built a boarding house.[5]

Nicholas J. Bockstanz started a store on the other side of the tracks, and he was instrumental in founding the village of Fountain.[6] The name Fountain was chosen because those who settled there all got their water at a nearby spring they called the Fountain Head.[7] The village was named after that spring. In 1882, Bockstanz's request for a post office was granted, and he became the town's first postmaster.[8]

In 1883 William Rogers became the town's second postmaster.[9] That was also the year the village built its first school.[10] Soon a handful of stores and a hotel opened. Other businesses in the first few decades of Fountain's history included a bank, a meat market, a casket factory, a jeweler, a watchmaker, and a saloon.[11]

As the trees were cut down, clear land opened up, and the official place for the settlement's growth was chosen, in an area near the river that the railroad traversed diagonally.[12] As more people came to Fountain, the logging pioneers set up in the original location while the town proper was built up at the nearby location.[13] The original location started to separate more clearly from the first and was first called Poff's Crossing then later Paxton's Crossing.[14]

The lumber industry in Fountain had something of a slow start. Sawmills were small and often changed ownership in the early days.[15] But sometimes patience and hard work is better than a sudden windfall. Two brothers by the name of Foster had a sawmill that they sold in 1907 and that again changed hands twice more in the next ten years.[16] Finally it ended up in Paul Schoenherr's hands, and over the course of three and a half decades, he built the business into a large and successful lumber company.[17] Today, the Fountain Lumber Company is still present in Fountain.

Entertainment in Early Fountain

The citizens of Fountain were not a group that liked to simply sit around all day. Entertainment options in the town were numerous, even as far back as the 1930s.[18] An old building was redesigned to be a theater and also had room for dancing.[19] A lodge hall was built for community events, and traveling shows came to Fountain to perform.[20] The Independent Order of Odd Fellows had their own hall, and the first floor was often used for dancing and other social events.[21] Fairs came to the village, and movies were screened outdoors for free.[22]

Fountain Today

The village today has a variety of local businesses, including a child development center, an insurance company, a storage center, a gas station, a hardware store, a market, and a tavern. It has a post office, a fire department, and is home to the Sherman Township hall. Fountain has a park with a baseball field, and it is only a short distance away from the Huron-Manistee National Forests. For over 50 years, the village has hosted a horse pull over Memorial Day weekend. The event draws people from hundreds of miles and also includes family-friendly events. They event ends with the Fountain Area Fire Department's Fireman's Ball.

There is sculpture from the Mason County Lumber Heritage Trail in Fountain. The sculpture, located in Heritage Park, depicts two horses pulling lumber.[24]

TOP: This former school building was completed in 1913

Population: 144[1]   **Incorporated:** 1913[2]

INSETS L to R: Playground equipment in town • The Free Soil Community Gymnasium • The fire department in the village spells its name Freesoil, without the space • One of the churches in Free Soil

Free Soil has had three different bands over the years, each with their own leader or conductor. One band, organized by L. F. Peterson, included students and local businessmen in its numbers.

Free Soil

History of Free Soil

FREE SOIL WAS ANOTHER EARLY LUMBER TOWN in Mason County, though its first European settlers were the homesteading Ritter family in the 1860s.[3] The loggers came second, mostly in the 1870s and later. The first mill belonged to a man named Rothchild and the second to J. W. Bennett.[4] As the lumber business picked up, the need grew for more residences for the workers, and a row of houses, called Smoky Row, was built for the workers.[5]

The growing logging business was not the only thing happening in Free Soil. The first school was built in 1870 on the Ritter family farm.[6] The downtown area gained businesses and board sidewalks, and the first church in Free Soil, a Methodist church, was built in 1880.[7] A village

hall followed a year later.[8] By 1908, the town had a lumber and shingles company, general merchandise dealers, a drugstore, a notary, a milliner, a blacksmith, a physician, a harness maker, a grocer, a meat market, a general store, and a shoemaker.[9] Other early businesses in Free Soil included a furniture store and a potato warehouse.

Two more churches were added as well. The Reorganized Latter Day Saints church was built in 1901 and the Catholic church in approximately 1900.[10] In 1913, a new school building was built that served all students from elementary through high school.[11]

As the lumber industry waxed and waned in the area, some former lumber workers found themselves out of work. They congregated together in camps north of town and offered their services for tasks around the town.[12] One project such men worked on was the construction of the new schoolhouse in 1913.[13]

As the supply of lumber diminished, the mills in the area also began to shut down. One mill was turned into a canning factory, which itself was later turned into a planing mill.[14] Later still the same building was used as an apple warehouse and shop.[15]

Politics Comes to Free Soil

Free Soil is the name of a former antislavery political party. First organized in Buffalo, New York, in 1848, the party's slogan was "Free soil, free speech, free labor, and free men."[16] However, the party might not have been as forward thinking as it seems; one motivator of the party was the fear of the competition caused by "black-labor," whether free or slave.[17] In the short years of the political party's existence (they seem to have tapered off in the mid-1850s), they nominated former president Martin Van Buren for president and also gained a handful of seats in Congress.[18]

Free Soil Village was settled after the decline of the Free Soil Party, but politics were still important in the village. After the village hall was built in 1881, it became a focal point for political activity. For instance, before one national election, the Republicans in the town built a pole right in front of the village hall and "topped it with a large silver-colored globe."[19] The Democrats responded by erecting a second pole across the street.[20] They topped theirs with a broom to symbolize how the Democrats would "sweep the nation."[21]

Free Soil Today

Free Soil is a small community, but its surrounding farmland gives it an important role to play in Mason County. Local farms produce apples, cherries, pumpkins, and a variety of other fruits and vegetables. Dairy farms are also plentiful in the surrounding areas.

Free Soil itself has a community garden, a gas station, a fire department, a community hall, a self-storage center, a repair center, a community center, and a post office. The village is served by a United Methodist church and a Catholic church. The village is located within the Huron-Manistee National Forests.

Free Soil Village is located in Free Soil Township, and over the years, there have been different spellings, including FreeSoil and Freesoil.

TOP: A memorial honoring those from the area who served in U.S. wars

Population: 347[1]   **Incorporated:** 1919[2]

INSETS L to R: One of the older buildings in Gaastra • A view of the Gaastra water tower • Some of the businesses, current and former, on Main Street • A view down Main Street

Officers with the Gaastra Police Department have, in the past, participated in the Cone with a Cop event, where residents were invited to come talk to the officers in an informal environment (an ice cream shop).[33]

Gaastra

History of Gaastra

THE FIRST EUROPEANS TO BUY LAND in the area of Iron County that is now Gaastra came to the area in the late 1870s.[3] Alfred Kidder was the first, and he selected the land for the larger area the village would eventually grow up on.[4] He, and those who came after him, were looking for land that would be favorable for mining, lumber, or both.[5] In 1908, the patent for the tract of land was passed to a building contractor and real estate speculator named Douwe Gaastra.[6] It was Gaastra who finally platted the settlement and named it after himself.[7]

Within five years of the village's platting, it had grown to include a grocery, a dry goods store, and two saloons. In 1914, Gaastra received its first post office, and Olaf Olson became the village's first postmaster.[8] An electric street railway line came to the village at around the same time but ended up being a failure and was shut down only a few years later.[9]

Gaastra did keep growing, though. The village was incorporated in 1919, largely due to the efforts of Edward Peterson, Louis Kotler, and Albin Olson.[10] John E. Looney was elected as the village's first president.[11] The village council got right to work after the election. They began renovating the water system in the town, built a village hall, laid cement sidewalks, and planned for ways to improve fire protection in the area.[12] By the early 1920s there was a blacksmith, three groceries, a dry goods store, a general goods store, and a confectionery.[13] Early school classes were held in the village hall, but in the mid-1920s, a school was built.[14]

Located on the Menominee Iron Range, Gaastra was also a mining town for generations. The industry survived in Gaastra through the early 1960s, when the Buck Mine finally closed.[15]

A Tragic Mine Collapse

While the iron mines have closed, their legacy is still obvious in the community, and in 1960, one of the mines made a sudden reappearance. The Smuggler Mine, a long-abandoned and forgotten mine located just west of town, ran beneath County Road 424.[16] When the road was built, no one remembered the mine, or how it came to within 20 feet of the surface.[17] On a foggy night, the road gave way, creating a cave 40 feet deep.[18] Unfortunately, the foggy conditions made it impossible for the occupants of two cars to notice in time, and they plummeted into the mine.[19] One person was killed and two others were hurt.[20] The road has since been rerouted, and the cave-in site is now a lake, visible from the road.[21] This is the only known example of a cave-in causing a death in Iron County.[22]

Indian Village Historical Marker

In 1851, a surveyor by the name of Guy H. Carleton recorded an Ojibwe village and burial site near the area where Gaastra now sits.[23] The chief of the village was named *Meshkawaanagonebi*, though Europeans in the area would end up calling him Chief John Edwards.[24] *Meshkawaanagonebi* received a patent for his village's land in 1884, but as mining grew as a business in the area, many of the Ojibwe were forced to move elsewhere.[25] *Meshkawaanagonebi* sold the land in 1891, though a nearby park retained the name of his wife, *Biindige*, which the Europeans mispronounced as *Pentoga*.[26]

The land sat mostly idle for the next years, but in the early 1900s, Herbert Larson Sr., an engineer in Iron County, persuaded the county to purchase the land and turn it into a historical park in honor of those who had once lived there.[27] The site was dedicated as "Indian Village"

in 1922, and a historical marker was placed at the site in 1980.[28] But that was not all that was left behind in the area: descendants of *Meshkawaanagonebi* and *Biindige* still live in the Stambaugh Township area.[29]

Gaastra Today

Today, Gaastra is home to a variety of local businesses, including a tile company, a hair salon, a collision center, a wood products store, a taxidermy shop, and a logging business. The city has a post office, a water tower, a public works building, and a city hall. It also has a veterans memorial. It borders Caspian to the northwest, and shares some public services with its neighbor, including police and fire and rescue.[30]

For leisure, there are soccer fields and a playground. In addition, the Apple Blossom Trail, a part of the Heritage Trail system, provides residents of and visitors to Iron County with opportunities for walking and biking.[31] The trail is near the Iron River, and it follows a route similar to the rail line on which trains once carried ore from Upper Peninsula mines to larger cities.[32]

Gaastra has the honor of being the third-smallest city in Michigan.

TOP: A bar and grill on State Street in the downtown Gagetown area

Population: 388[1]   **Incorporated:** 1869[2]

INSETS L to R: The Gagetown Center is used for local events • The elevator in Gagetown is part of the Cooperative Elevator Co., which is owned by over one thousand farmers in the thumb region • The Thumb Octagon Barn • The Catholic church in Gagetown

In 1879, Father Clement Krebs established the first church in all of Tuscola County. That church, St. Agatha, is located in Gagetown.[24]

Gagetown

History of Gagetown

THE FIRST CONSTRUCTION IN THE VILLAGE of Gagetown was a mill and a store built by Joseph Gage in 1869.[3] Two years later, he platted the village, though shortly after he did so William Cleaver platted an addition to the town.[4] In the early 1870s, Gage added a hotel to the village, and shortly after, a grist mill, though that burned down in 1876.[5] A new grist mill was built in 1881, but the town's start was relatively slow until the railroad came to the area in 1882.[6] At that time there was a sash, door, and blind company, a shoe store, one wagon shop, two blacksmiths, a livery stable, a planing mill, four general stores, a drugstore, a hardware store and tin shop, and a shingle mill, in addition to the businesses already mentioned.[7] The town had a Roman Catholic church and was planning on building an Episcopalian one as well.[8]

With the arrival of the railroad, Gagetown's growth increased. Within another year, the village had gained nearly twenty buildings, including a meat market, a brewery, and a harness-making shop.[9] A fifth general store, a second physician, a second drugstore, a second planing mill, and another hotel were added as well.[10] And as the lumber was cleared in the area, the town turned to more agricultural pursuits, as the soil was fertile for growing crops. Products from the Gagetown area included hay, apples, cherries, pears, and peaches, among others.[11]

More additions followed in the town. The State Savings Bank of Gagetown opened in 1890, and an opera house was added in 1907.[12] St. Agatha erected a new church in 1917, and that building is still used by the church today.[13]

The Thumb Octagon Barn

Gagetown is home to the Thumb Octagon Barn, an eight-sided barn built for James Purdy from 1923 to 1924.[14] Purdy had first seen an octagon barn in Iowa and, drawn by the shape, determined to build one for himself one day.[15] It was not only Purdy who was taken with the idea of an eight-sided barn; the octagon-shaped barn was being promoted in agricultural communities as a more accessible building for farmers to use.[16] This turned out to not be the case, however, and the added cost of building such a barn made them fall out of favor before too long.[17]

But having been popular only for a short time has made octagon barns unique structures today, and the building in Gagetown has been turned into an agricultural museum. Purdy and his wife, Cora, sold the barn and its corresponding property in 1942, and after passing through the hands of a few private owners, the property was eventually acquired by the Michigan Department of Natural Resources in 1991.[18] Their original plan was to demolish the barn and all other structures on the land, but the barn was on a list of historical places in the state.[19] It was not that easy to save the barn, though. It was four more years before the Friends of the Octagon Barn were given control of ten acres of land and the barn.[20]

The barn has been restored over the past two decades and now serves as an agricultural museum with a focus on "agricultural heritage and rural living."[21] It is open to visitors from May through October.[22]

Gagetown Today

The Thumb Octagon Barn is not the only spot of interest in Gagetown and the surrounding area. The village is home to the Sherwood on the Hill Golf Course, and just north of the village you can find Noah's Ark Family Fun Center, with go-karts, miniature golf, a carousel, a wooden maze, and other family-friendly activities.[23] In the farming country beyond the downtown village area, there are also a variety of farms, including one with alpacas.

In the village itself you can find a community center, a municipal building, an elevator, a feed plant, a gas station, a market, a salon, a bar and grill, and a post office. The village is served by a United Methodist church, a Church of the Nazarene, and St. Agatha Catholic Church.

In 2015, the village of Gagetown was recognized as a historical site. The two-sided plaque can be found in the village near St. Agatha Church.

Population: 380[1]   **Incorporated:** 1875[2]

INSETS L to R: A monument in honor of those who have served in the U.S. armed forces • The former depot in Gaines currently serves the village as a library • The view down Genesee Avenue • A patriotic sign in the village

TOP: The Gaines Veterans Memorial Park

Until recently, the police department in Gaines was staffed by a single officer: Tim Bradshaw.[23] When he retired in the summer of 2016, there was no one to take his place, and so Gaines disbanded its police department.[24]

Gaines

History of Gaines

IT WAS THE COMBINATION of the abundant forests and the nearby creek that first brought European settlers to the area where Gaines now lies.[3] Hartford Cargill, in 1836, became the first settler in the area, and three years later a man named Joshua Dart came as well.[4] It was Dart who organized and named the township in 1842, choosing the name of his friend General E. P. Gaines.[5]

The Gaines area got its first post office in 1852, and it was run out of Bergan C. Covert's nearby farm.[6] It moved to the town when the Detroit & Milwaukee Railroad came to the area in 1856, and the depot and post office both took the name of Gaines, after the township.[7] The depot was built slightly before the post office, though, and so has the honor of being the first building built in the village.[8] The first true home in the village was built in 1856, shortly after the arrival of the railroad.[9] The village was platted in 1859 by Henry Walker and became officially incorporated in 1875.[10]

Despite the area forests, early industry in Gaines largely centered around agriculture, as the trees were hardwood trees and set closely together, making working in the area difficult.[11] When the railroad came, Gaines shipped out wheat and oats in addition to wood products, including barrel staves and broom handles.[12] Within a few years of being incorporated as a village, Gaines had a wagonmaker, three general stores, a drugstore, a hardware store, two hotels, a grocery, a millinery, a meat market, a broom handle maker, two physicians, a shoemaker, a blacksmith, a harness maker, and a livery stable.[13]

Within 30 years, the population of the village had more than tripled.[14] The village had a school and three churches.[15] It had added a grain elevator, a clothing store, two barbers, a mason, and a veterinarian, among others.[16] The town continued to grow through the early part of the twentieth century, though eventually business in the town slowed.

The Life of a Depot

In 1881, the original wooden depot in Gaines was removed, and it was replaced with a brick building in 1884.[17] The new building, built by the Detroit, Grand Haven, and Milwaukee Railroad, features a yellowish brick from the Owosso area and served as the depot until the railroad ended service to Gaines in 1957.[18] The station sat vacant for a while, until a stained-glass business bought and used the place, but after a few years, that closed as well, and the station was once again left empty and soon fell into disrepair.[19]

In 1991, a local organization called Gaines Station, Inc., began restoring the station.[20] One of their focuses in the restoration process was to ensure that the building could remain as close to its historical origins as possible, and the building has since been listed on the National Register of Historic Places.[21] The building now serves as a library, but visitors to the library can still see the cabinets, doors, window frames, and ticket windows that were part of the building's original construction in the 1880s.[22]

Gaines Today

In addition to the Station Library, Gaines today is home to other local services, including a post office, a fire department, a village office, and a village park, named Peace Park. The park, by the library, hosts outdoor events, such as concerts, Easter egg hunts, and ice cream socials. Gaines also has a veterans memorial at Veterans Memorial Park.

There are two churches in Gaines: Gaines United Methodist Church and Faith Church. There is an elementary school in the village, Gaines Elementary School, and it serves students beyond the village as well as part of Swartz Creek Community Schools. Businesses in the village include a superette, a motorcycle club, a bar, and a tractor store.

The streets in Gaines run on diagonals rather than on north-south or east-west compass bearings. When the village was platted, the streets were put at angles to match the railroad line that came through town.

TOP: This building includes a vacation rental for visitors to the village

Population: 221[1]   Incorporated: 1886[2]

INSETS L to R: A small creek runs through the town and out to Garden Bay • The Marygrove Catholic Retreat Center • The Garden Veterans Memorial • The Garden Area Historical Museum

The annual Independence Day festivities in Garden include a parade, games, a petting zoo, bingo, a raffle, a lumberjack competition, and many other family-friendly activities. The event is sponsored by the Garden Old Timers and the Garden American Legion Post 545.[32]

Garden

History of Garden

THE VILLAGE OF GARDEN is a small settlement on Lake Michigan's Garden Peninsula, and it is directly on the water of Garden Bay. The whole area got its name due to the fertility of the soil on the peninsula.[3] The early European settlers in Garden and the surrounding areas were primarily French.[4] One of the first settlers in the area was a man by the name of Philomen Thompson.[5] He was a homesteader who built a cabin near the site of Garden in 1850.[6]

Early on in Garden's history, the settlement was called Garden Bay or Haley's Bay.[7] The name did not officially change to Garden until 1865, when a post office named Garden was opened in the village.[8] Even after the name change, however, the area was still sometimes referred to by these older names.[9] The first postmaster was Asel Y. Bailey, though the job of postmaster was not to last long.[10] The post office was shut down in January of 1871. It did reopen, but not until nearly a year and a half had passed without postal service in the village, and even then the mail came twice per week by stagecoach.[11]

Garden was originally a logging and agricultural settlement. Pine, hemlock, and a variety of hardwoods were all amply available on the Garden Peninsula.[12] Potatoes were one of the main crops in the area.[13] Despite this, however, Garden got off to something of a slow start and didn't truly take off until the 1880s. By 1888, the town had an estimated 1,000 inhabitants, nearly 10 times what it had had only a little over a decade before.[14] In the nonwinter months, a weekly steamboat came to

Garden from Escanaba, and another from Green Bay came twice per week.[15] There was also a stagecoach line that came daily to Garden from Manistique, and that cost travelers $2.[16]

Life After Lumber

Near the turn of the century, the lumber industry in the area began to go into decline, and a mine in nearby Fayette had also shut down some years before.[17] The population in Garden fell as a result of these changes. By 1908, there were only approximately 500 people still living in the town.[18] People who stayed in Garden focused more on living off of the land, especially fish and apples.[19] You can still see wild apple trees growing in various places in and around the Garden area.[20] In the 1970s, the State of Michigan began requiring permits for many activities the residents of Garden had been doing their whole lives without issue, and that resulted in clashes between the residents and the Michigan Department of Natural Resources.[21]

Politicians from Garden

Two politicians have been born in Garden, and both were born there in 1904. The first was James D. Dotsch, a Democrat.[22] At age twenty, Dotsch was elected president of Garden, and nine years after that he was again elected to the village council as supervisor.[23] He served in the Michigan State Senate from 1937 to 1940.[24]

The second was John B. Bennett, a Republican.[25] He attended Marquette University Law School, graduating in 1925.[26] He passed the bar exam in both Wisconsin and Michigan but ultimately ended up practicing law in Ontonagon, Michigan.[27] He was first elected to Congress in 1942 and served until 1945.[28] After being elected a second time in 1947, he continued to be reelected to his post until his death in 1964.[29]

Garden Today

Garden today is a quiet town that is slowly transitioning to a tourism-centered economy. There is a bed and breakfast in the village, a motel, a selection of restaurants, and a golf course. There is a historical museum and a shop that showcases and sells art by local artisans. The village also has a bank, a post office, a coffee shop, a hair salon, a storage center, and a gas station with a mini-mart. There is a pavilion in the town that is used for both village and township events. The local American Legion maintains the Garden veterans memorial.

There are two churches in the village: Garden Area Catholic Churches and Garden Congregational Church. Garden is also home to the Marygrove Retreat Center, a Catholic retreat center.

There is a wind farm in Garden and Garden Township that generates enough energy to power approximately 7,000 homes, which is roughly half of the households in the entirety of Delta County.[30] However, not all of the village residents support the project; some are particularly concerned with noise, health, and safety issues for Garden residents.[31]

The maximum pay rate for a schoolteacher in Garden during the 1937 to 1938 school year was $80 per month.[33]

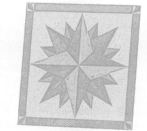

Population: 272[1]   **Incorporated:** 1934[2]

INSETS L to R: This arch is iconic in the Grand Beach area • One of the tree-lined, quiet streets in the village • An area park • A view of the golf course in Grand Beach

Grand Beach is known for the "stately white gates" that grace its entrance. The gates have been in place for over a century.

TOP: Grand Beach is located on the southeast shore of Lake Michigan and boasts stunning lake views

Grand Beach

History of Grand Beach

GRAND BEACH WAS FOUNDED IN THE EARLY 1900s when Floyd R. Perkins came to the area and purchased 600 acres on the west side of Berrien County.[3] He had originally intended the land to serve as a "shooting preserve," but then opted to build a resort community instead, deciding that would be a more profitable use of the land.[4] He started the Grand Beach Company with George Ely, and the pair added beach property to their existing purchase and began building a community that would draw tourists and residents alike.[5]

The first cottages in Grand Beach were purchased from Sears and Roebuck in 1907, and that number more than doubled by 1911, the year the community's golf course was built.[6] People flocked to Grand Beach,

particularly Chicagoans, as they could take one of three daily trains to the village.[7]

One of the famous early buildings in Grand Beach was the Golf-more Hotel, which opened in the early 1920s.[8] The hotel had 175 rooms and offered visitors access to concerts, movies, and even a ski jump.[9] Unfortunately, the hotel is no longer in Grand Beach today, having burned down in 1939.[10] Instead, the village had to make do with the Pinewood Lodge, which is now called the Grand Beach Inn.[11]

Famous Visitors and Residents of Grand Beach

Grand Beach has attracted an illustrious list of residents and visitors over the years. These have included the following: Father Andrew Greeley, a Catholic priest who was known as much for his work in theology and sociology as he was for his nearly seventy novels, many of which were described as "racy";[12] and Richard J. and Richard M. Daley, a father-son pair of mayors from Chicago, the latter having served from 1955 to 1976, when he died in office,[13] and the younger having served from 1989 to 2011.[14] Frank Lloyd Wright also built a few homes in Grand Beach, two of which are still standing.[15]

Another prominent member of the Grand Beach community, if only temporarily, was James Braddock, who spent two months training at the Pinewood Lodge as he readied himself for a prizefight with Joe Louis in 1937.[16] Riding on the wave of excitement over the fight, the nearby Golfmore Hotel set up a training ring and invited the public to watch.[17] The training setup at the hotel ran until right before Braddock's fight and was called the "Camp of Champions."[18] Despite his training, however, Braddock went on to lose the fight, making Joe Louis Heavyweight Champion.[19]

Grand Beach Today

Today, Grand Beach is made up of a mix of permanent residents and those who have vacation homes in the village. Many of the houses in Grand Beach are both large and old, and the golf course is still in use. The village also has a park with playground equipment and tennis courts. Each summer, a social club runs in the village and provides members with a variety of entertainment and social options, including a book club, bingo, golf dinners, and children's parties, among others.[20]

Grand Beach also has village offices, which provide services to the village's residents. These include a village attorney, maintenance, and police.

Grand Beach, in the Eastern Time Zone, is about a mile away from the northwest corner of Indiana, where people are on Central Time.

Population: 441[1]   **Incorporated:** 1885[2]

INSETS L to R: Heritage Park includes Halloween decorations and a corn maze in the fall • The Conklin Reed Organ Museum • Heritage Park, established in 2002 • Hanover High School closed in 1962 but was turned into a museum by the Hanover-Horton Area Historical society in 1977

One way the historical society has funded all of their projects has been through their ownership of 42 acres of farmland in Hanover, which they farm.[25] They also sell maple syrup and sweet sorghum molasses.[26]

TOP: Part of the historical museum in Hanover contains this schoolroom setup

Hanover

History of Hanover

HENRY WICKMAN CAME TO THE HANOVER AREA in the 1830s and named the area after his hometown of Hanover, Germany.[3] A year after Wickman arrived, Hanover received a post office, and John Cruttenden was appointed as postmaster.[4] For a time the village of Hanover was mainly cultivated farmland, and in those days, life in Hanover was difficult.[5] The closest mill was a few dozen miles away, and sometimes the pioneers in the area would have to wait over a day to grind their flour.[6] They were also the victims of a bad-currency scheme that resulted in the state legislature being called in, though the banks supplying the currency were able to fool the investigators.[7]

Once the Fort Wayne, Jackson, & Saginaw Railroad arrived in 1870, the village began to grow rapidly.[8] George O. Bibbins platted the town that same year, and the first store, a grocery, opened as well.[9] A brick schoolhouse, built to replace the original log structure first erected in 1839, and a Methodist church were both added in 1873 for a total cost of $16,000.[10] Another church was added the next year, and a third in 1876.[11] Other businesses in the town in the early years after it had been platted included two blacksmiths, multiple general stores, a lumber mill, a planing mill, a furniture dealer, a drugstore, a painter, three physicians, a milliner, a hardware store, a harness maker, a hotel, a meat market, and a cigar store. The town also had its own flour mill.

As the village grew, there came a need to expand their school services. A new school was built in 1911, and a Depression-era relief fund was awarded to Hanover to add a gym to the school in 1934.[12] In 1940, the school in Hanover consolidated school services with ten other local schools to form the Hanover-Horton School District.[13] The village added an elementary school in 1954 and a new high school in 1958, finally phasing out classes at the 1911 building in the mid-1960s.[14]

The Hanover-Horton Area Historical Society

The historical society in Hanover, which also encompasses the history of nearby Horton, is very active in the local area. In Hanover, they have a museum in the old 1911 school building and the town's Heritage Park is just next door to the building.

The museum in Hanover has two main parts. The first part is made up of a series of rooms, each with its own historical theme. One room shows what a classroom might have looked like in the school; another houses items used by various businesses in the early 1900s while still another shows how a family might have set up their living space at around the same time. The true gem of the museum, though, is the second part, which has nearly 100 functional and historical reed organs. In fact, it's the largest collection of working reed organs in the country.[15] The organs on the floor of the museum are not the only ones there, however; there are a few dozen others undergoing repairs and restoration at any given time. To keep up with the maintenance on the organs, volunteers come to the museum from all over to assist with the work.[16]

A Trip Back in Time

Heritage Park, opened in 2002, has a variety of historical artifacts for the whole family to visit and try out. There is a functioning sawmill from the early 1900s that was donated to the park in 2008, and a planing mill and a drying shed.[17] Next to the sawmill is a sugar shack, with components donated to the society in 2013.[18] To build the shack itself,

volunteers used wood they cut on the sawmill.[19] During late winter or early spring, you can visit the shack and see how maple syrup is made, maybe even trying it out yourself.[20] If you visit the park in October, you might also see volunteers making sweet sorghum molasses, an early American substitute for true molasses, which is made from sugarcane.[21]

The latest addition to the park is an antique farm equipment barn, which was added in 2016, but the society is getting ready to add two new buildings as well.[22] In the meantime, visitors can try to find their way out of the corn maze in the fall, see the plowing in the spring, or attend the annual Rust 'n' Dust Antique Tractor and Farm Show in the summer.[23]

Hanover Today

Hanover today is a proud town that both looks to its past and its future. In addition to the park and museum, the village has an elementary school, a library, a bank, a pizza parlor, an auto store, a bar and grill, a feed store, a funeral parlor, and a market. Natural Environmental Reclamation Concepts, Inc., a business focused on "mass seeding and erosion control," makes its home in Hanover.[24] There is also a post office, a fire department, and a Baptist church.

In Hanover, you can visit Bibbins Lake Park, named after George Bibbins, who first platted the town.

THE SAWMILL
This sawmill was built by the A.B. Farquar Co. of York, Penn. in the early 1900s. Its husk has a dual friction carriage drive. The blade is 46" in dia. with the drive on babbitt bearings. The carriage long with three knee block is on 45 of steel

TOP: Joe Videc Memorial Park includes a pavilion and playground equipment

Population: 143[1]   **Incorporated:** 1891[2]

INSETS L to R: The Harrietta United Methodist Church • Slagle Township has a fire department in Harrietta • Slagle Creek, which passes through the southern portion of the village • The Harrietta State Fish Hatchery

Various international flags fly in the village of Harrietta today. They were put in place by the Ladies Civic Club as part of a village beautification project.[21]

Harrietta

History of Harrietta

THE VILLAGE THAT IS NOW KNOWN AS HARRIETTA started with a post office called Springdale, first built in the area in 1874.[3] The Ann Arbor Railroad came to the village in 1889, and the village was platted in that year by a few railroad workers, who called the town Ashley.[4] James Ashley named the village Harriette, by combining the names of his father, Harry, and his fiancée, Henrietta.[5] The next year, two parcels of land were added to the town, one by a man named Gaston, who subsequently renamed the village in his own honor.[6]

The workers at the station in the village did not like the change, and they threatened to close the station unless the name was changed back.[7] In 1892, the station became Harriette once again, and an act of the Legislature in 1893 made the change official.[8] The change of spelling to Harrietta was made in 1923.[9]

The village experienced several setbacks in its early years. Gaston and Campbell, who added the other addition to the village in 1890, built a sawmill and began manufacturing "novelties" from the hardwood in the area.[10] Their business was ultimately not successful, however.[11] A chemical plant and several charcoal kilns were built near the railroad station in the early 1890s, though these were moved to another settlement a few years later.[12] The town had its own shingle mill, but after only a few years, all the available trees had been cut down, and that business ended as well.[13]

The village started its own newspaper in 1891, though it was shut down two years later.[14] Over the next few years, other attempts to start a newspaper were made, but few lasted long.[15]

The business that finally stuck in Harrietta was fish farming. The nearby creek, named Slagle Creek, had an abundance of trout. Near the turn of the twentieth century, state officials decided to build a fish hatchery in the area and supplied a few thousand dollars for the necessary work in developing the project.[16] Finally things started to look up for the village.

Harrietta State Fish Hatchery

The fish hatchery in Harrietta is the oldest in the state, opening in 1901.[17] The hatchery raises brown trout and rainbow trout that are then released into Michigan's inland lakes and the Great Lakes.[18] The hatchery has public displays about fish, hatcheries, and Michigan watersheds, and it also has different interactive exhibits for visitors to try out. The website for the hatchery even has recipes for different ways of cooking trout.[19]

Harrietta Today

Today, Harrietta does not have any open businesses in its downtown area, but don't take that to mean that the community is somehow failing. Residents of Harrietta feel a connection with their town and have worked hard to see that it continues to overcome the hurdles that have so often been placed before it. The nearby fish hatchery employs many members of the Harrietta community, and the village also has a post office, fire department, and a local airport. Church services in the area include a Catholic church and a United Methodist church.

Each summer the village of Harrietta hosts a blueberry festival, which includes a parade, tours through a local blueberry farm, a car show, a quilt show, and a variety of other activities geared toward the whole family. Plus, you can sample a variety of blueberry products, from pancakes to ice cream.[20]

In 1913, Harrietta was the site of a dramatic bank robbery.[22] Its safe was blown open in a well-planned robbery, and about two months later, the robbers struck again, this time in neighboring Falmouth, Michigan.

TOP: This shop, called Moose Tales, has a variety of colorful moose decorations out front

Population: 493[1]   **Incorporated:** 1905[2]

INSETS L to R: The sign for the Harrisville Township Recreation Area. • Harrisville is on the coast of Lake Huron • A few of the businesses in the downtown area of the city • Flags fly over the harbor in Harrisville

Harrisville is home to the *Alcona County Review*, a weekly newspaper founded in Harrisville over 140 years ago.

Harrisville

History of Harrisville

HARRISVILLE CAN TRACE ITS ROOTS BACK TO 1854, when Simeon Holden and Crosier Davison first bought some land in the area and called it Davison's Mill.[3] They were fishermen and purchased land near Mill Creek.[4] They also acquired rights to water power privilege in the area.[5] A short time later, they sold their holdings to Benjamin Harris and his two sons, Levi and Henry.[6] In 1860, when Harrisville township was first organized, it was named for the three men.[7] The village itself was also named for the Harris family and received its first post office in 1857 under the name of Harrisville.[8] Levi O. Harris was the village's first postmaster.[9] Less than a decade later, the village was sold again, this time to Weston, Colwell, & Company, who first founded the settlement in 1866 then had it officially platted in 1870.[10]

Harrisville grew quickly and was named the seat of Alcona County in the 1870s, an honor which it still holds today.[11] By 1877, the village had around 800 residents, and lumbering was its primary—but not only—industry. Farmers worked the land near the village, growing wheat, hay, oats, potatoes, and other vegetables.[12] Businesses in the town included three groceries, three general stores, a saloon, a hotel, a farm implements store, and two sawmills.[13] The local creek generated water power.[14]

Eventually the Detroit & Mackinac Railway came to Harrisville, and a depot was built in the village in 1901.[15] The harbor on Lake Huron had already been a point of trade for lumber and goods, but the railroad added another avenue for the businesses to use in selling their goods. By 1903, the village had fallen to approximately 550 residents, but the number of businesses in the village had swelled.[16] It had three churches, a courthouse, a jail, a library, and a variety of public and community halls.[17] Businesses in the town included three apiaries, a boarding house, a saloon, a dressmaker, a surveyor, a coroner, a laundry, a confectionery, and a bicycle shop, among many others. In 1905, the community was reincorporated, this time as a city,[18] and within another fifteen to twenty years, Harrisville had added a high school, an opera house, and an electric light plant.[19]

As the lumber industry slowed in the Harrisville area, the community shifted its focus to farming. Without the lumber, however, and with the rise in automobile owners, the railroad found its service to be less and less needed. Passenger service ended in Harrisville in 1951, and all service was suspended in the 1960s.[20] In 1961, the harbor in Harrisville was designated a harbor of refuge.[21]

Hazen Shirley Cuyler, One of Baseball's Greats

Hazen Shirley Cuyler, better remembered by his nickname Kiki (which rhymes with sky-sky), was one of baseball's great hitters—and he was born in Harrisville in 1898.[22] He played for eighteen years in the major leagues, primarily for the Pittsburgh Pirates and the Chicago Cubs.[23]

Though Cuyler's father had played minor league baseball and Cuyler enjoyed the sport as a youth, his path to professional baseball wasn't clearcut. He served in the army during World War I, but was not sent to Europe.[24] After the war, he moved back home, got married, and took a job at a Buick factory.[25] It was while he was employed by Buick that he found his way back to baseball, playing in industrial leagues in both Flint and Detroit.[26] In 1920 he joined the minor leagues, playing for the Bay City Wolves, and after two seasons, he moved up to the big leagues.[27] The Detroit Tigers didn't want him, so he ended up in Pittsburgh.[28] After a few years during which he struggled, something finally clicked into place for Cuyler. In 1925, he won the World Series for the

Pirates with his game-winning hit in the seventh game of the series. Four times in his career he led the MLB in stolen bases, and he ended his career with a .321 batting average.[29]

Cuyler died of complications from a heart attack in 1951, 17 years before he was inducted into the Baseball Hall of Fame.[30]

Harrisville Today

Harrisville is a thriving lake town, and the harbor is still a focal point of the town. Its relatively small size (there are approximately 100 slips) allows the facility to offer a wide range of amenities for boaters.[31]

As the seat of Alcona County, Harrisville has a wide variety of local services for city, township, and county residents. There is a county sheriff's office in town, as well as a library, a Secretary of State branch, a county health department, an airport, a county jail, and, of course, a courthouse. Other businesses in the town include a gas station, a few craft and gift shops, a credit union, a bowling alley, a restaurant, a pizza place, a coffee shop, a hardware store, a pharmacy, an art gallery, and a hair salon. There are three parks in Harrisville as well: Mill Pond Park, Harbor Park, and Harrisville State Park.

In 2012, a team of divers discovered a shipwreck in Lake Huron, just 25 miles northwest of Harrisville.[32] The *New York*, a nearly 300-foot-long steam vessel, was lost in a storm in 1910.[33] Thankfully, her crew was rescued by a passing freighter.[34]

Population: 350[1]   **Incorporated:** 1875[2]

INSETS L to R: The Hersey River passes through the village • The Hersey Village Mosaic Park • The Hersey Roller Mills Store • A shady area serves as a spot for a playground and pavilion

In Hersey you can find Blodgett Landing Campground, a campground named for Hersey's first settler and postmaster.

TOP: A restaurant and bar along Main Street

Hersey

History of Hersey

THE FIRST EUROPEAN SETTLER in the Hersey area was Delos A. Blodgett, who came to the area around 1851.[3] A few other settlers came over the next fifteen years, and when Alcona County was officially organized in 1867, Hersey was chosen as the county seat.[4] The settlement might have been small at the time, but the recognition by the county helped it grow. In 1868, the first post office in all of Alcona County was established in Hersey, and Blodgett was named postmaster.[5] A year later, after the Pere Marquette's plan for the railroad in the area became clear, Blodgett platted and recorded the village, much of which was on his farmland.[6]

Early industry in Hersey centered around logging, and the nearby Hersey and Muskegon Rivers made the site of the settlement especially well-suited for the industry.[7] A sawmill, a grist mill, and a roller flour mill were quickly constructed at the place where the two rivers came together.[8] The first store in the village opened in 1869, and the next year marked the first holding of the circuit court.[9] 1870 was also the year the railroad arrived in town.[10]

The village was incorporated in 1875, and Josiah K. Heartt was elected as the first president.[11] For a time, Hersey was the most successful settlement in Alcona County, though as lumber interests in the area waned, the lumber companies left for other communities in northern Michigan.[12] Still, Hersey not only would survive, it would thrive. By the early 1900s, the village had three churches, electric lights, a power plant, a bank, a creamery, a telephone company, the Hersey House Hotel, a bowling alley, two livery stables, and a variety of other businesses, not to mention numerous county officials, such as judges, attorneys, and clerks.[13] In 1927, however, Hersey's days as the county seat came to an end, when that recognition was given to nearby Reed City instead.[14]

Hersey Heritage Days

Every summer, the village of Hersey gets together to celebrate its past. For three days, the village gets together for yard sales, a classic car show, tours of local buildings and businesses, a parade, games, music, and food. If the weather is nice, the village will screen a movie at Mosaic Park, and on Sunday morning the local Congregational church holds their service outdoors.

A Revitalized Industry in Hersey?

In all of Michigan, there is only one source of potash (a potassium-based fertilizer), and that is found in Hersey.[15] The mine, which first began operations in 1989, shut down in 2013, resulting in the layoff of local workers, but it may soon reopen.[16] The company that has owned the mine is now proposing new mining methods to extract the potash, which is richer in potassium than the potash found at similar mines in Canada and Russia.[17] It is unclear when work may begin at the site, but it's possible that the operations in Hersey could prove to be profitable for both local workers and farmers.[18]

Hersey Today

Hersey today is home to a variety of local businesses, including a plant store, a Michigan-made gift shop, a restaurant and bar, and an auto repair shop. There are many outdoor recreational opportunities available to residents and visitors to the town, including Mosaic Park, Blodgett Landing Campground, outdoor athletic fields, and a place to

rent tubes and canoes. Hersey also has a trailway that is part of the Rails to Trails program in Michigan. The trail in the village runs on the old Pere Marquette Railroad line. The village also has a village hall, a fire department, a post office, a cemetery, and two churches.

The United Methodist Church in Hersey was the first religious organization in the village. It formed in 1867 and celebrated its sesquicentennial in 2017.[19]

TOP: The Cherry Bowl Drive-In Theatre opened on July 4, 1953

Population: 328[1] **Incorporated:** 1914[2]

INSETS L to R: A view down Main Street • This colorful building contains an art store • Banners and American flags line some of the streets in the village • The Honor Congregational Church

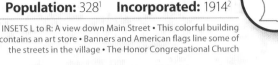

After the Civil War, Honor was, for many years, home to a large gathering of Civil War veterans, including the last large gathering of the Grand Army of the Republic, an organization for Union veterans of the Civil War.[22]

Honor

History of Honor

AFTER THE CIVIL WAR ENDED, many veterans made their way to Honor.[3] The area around Honor was good logging country, filled with pine and various hardwood trees, and once the trees had been cut, the land proved to be good for farming as well.[4] Honor was established in 1895 when the Guelph Patent Cask Company came to the area.[5] The manager of the company, J. A. Gifford, named the town after his infant daughter.[6]

The first post office in Honor opened the same year the village was established, and Leslie C. Hart was the town's first postmaster. Within just two years of being established, the town had grown to 300 residents.[7] In addition to the cask company, Honor had a grocery, two general stores, a blacksmith, a clothing and dry goods store, a drugstore, a hardware store, a lawyer, and a barber.[8] By 1903, the population had climbed to around 500, and the number of businesses had more than tripled.[9]

Legendary Fourth of July Celebrations

For a time, Honor was the place to be for local celebrations. Its Fourth of July celebrations in particular were local legends. On one occasion, a hot-air balloon "ascension" took place, with a daring stuntperson dangling from it via a rope ladder.[10]

After Lumber

The population in Honor fell between 1910 and 1920 as the lumber in the area was exhausted.[11] Those who stayed, however, still found plenty of life left in their town. It had a station on the Chicago & West Michigan Railroad, a Congregational church, a bank, and its own newspaper.[12] The burgeoning automobile industry benefited Honor as well, and in 1953, the Cherry Bowl Drive-In Theatre opened in the village.[13] The theater, still open today, is the only drive-in theater still in use in all of northern Michigan.[14]

Another longtime industry still active in Honor is the nearby Platte River State Fish Hatchery, which first opened in 1928.[15] The hatchery raises coho and chinook salmon and has been a main force in successfully introducing Atlantic salmon to the Great Lakes.[16] In 1967, the village held its first annual National Coho Salmon Festival.[17]

What's in a Name?

Though the village was named for a person, residents in Honor today feel a deeper connection with the name, and the idea of honor is now essentially part of their identity.[18] Recent revitalization and restoration plans have centered around this idea, and the local Honor Area Restoration Project would like to further strengthen the connection between the community and its name.[19]

No doubt thinking back to past gatherings of Civil War Veterans in the area, the Honor Area Restoration Project has considered reaching out to veterans and public service organizations about the possibility of partnering with the community for commemorative events.[20] The goal is not only to bring people to the community, but also to share their own identity with others who feel honor is an important part of who they are.

Honor Today

Today, Honor is experiencing something of a reawakening. Rather than regretting the lack of modernization, residents of the village are finding pride in their past. They see their community as a type of "time capsule" that offers visitors a look into a historic past.[21]

That is not to say, however, that the town is without its contemporary comforts. The village, on U.S. Highway 31, has many businesses, including a gas station, two pizza places, a car wash, a dollar store, a family market, a pharmacy, a senior center, an auto sales business, a building supplies store, a self-storage center, a hair salon, a wellness center, and a gift shop.

Sports Afield, a hunting magazine, has given Honor the recognition of being the number one outdoor sports town in Michigan.[23]

Population: 512[1]   **Unincorporated**

INSETS L to R: The village's United Methodist Church • The general store in Horton Bay was established in 1876 • The historic school in Horton Bay • This historical marker discusses the village's history and connections with Ernest Hemingway

In its more than 140 years of operation, the Horton Bay General Store has had 27 different owners.[24] Many of these owners helped maintain and restore the physical building to ensure that it continued to stand proudly in the village.[25]

TOP: The Red Fox Inn and Bookstore in Horton Bay specializes in Michigan and Hemingway merchandise

Horton Bay

History of Horton Bay

BOTH THE COMMUNITY of Horton Bay and nearby Horton Creek are named for Samuel Horton, who came to the area in the mid- to late-1800s and founded the village in 1876.[2] The settlement was a lumbering community, and early structures included a sawmill, a boarding house, and a blacksmith shop.[3] The first store in the village was the Horton Bay General Store, which opened in 1876 and still operates there today.[4]

The settlement received its first post office in 1879 and Alonzo J. Stroud was appointed as the first postmaster, though at the time the post office was named Horton's Bay rather than Horton Bay.[5] The name was changed to the present spelling in 1894.[6]

Despite the early buildings in the town, Horton Bay got off to a bit of a slow start. In 1903 there were only 60 people in the town, and five years later that number had only increased by 15, though a feed mill had also been built in the intervening period.[7,8] In 1910, the post office in the village closed, and mail came by way of rural delivery from Boyne City, over five miles away.[9]

The community stayed small in the first decades of the twentieth century, though it did have both a Methodist Episcopal church and an Evangelical church.[10] The Red Fox Inn, which originally served the community as a boarding house for lumberjacks, turned into a family-style restaurant with the end of the logging business in the town.[11] Two other restaurants also opened around the same time: Dilworth's and the Waffle Shop.[12]

Relaxing at the General Store

The early industry in Horton Bay was logging, and the general store served as a community center.[13] In addition to purchasing supplies at the store, nearby farmers could weigh their beans at the store and then ship them, and those with dairy cows could separate their milk at the store.[14] In addition, the store served as a social center, and it was not uncommon to find people relaxing there in the evening, women knitting, men talking about matters of the day, and children playing, sometimes being rewarded with a piece of penny candy.[15]

The community of Horton Bay has grown since its early days, though it is still an unincorporated community. Today there are over 500 people in Horton Bay.

Ernest Hemingway in Horton Bay

As a boy and young man, the author Ernest Hemingway spent many of his summers in Horton Bay.[16] In his youth, he fished on the lake (now called Lake Charlevoix) and in Horton Creek, and visited a variety of the sites around the town, many of which still stand today.[17] In 1921, Hemingway married his first wife, Elizabeth Hadley Richardson, in the village.[18]

What really connects Hemingway to Horton Bay, however, is that it is where he set many of his Nick Adams stories—24 short stories featuring a character named Nick Adams and set in northern Michigan.[19] The stories, written over a period of approximately ten years, are said to represent a younger alternate ego of Hemingway himself.[20]

But Hemingway did not only draw on his own life; many residents of Horton Bay and other local areas have said they recognized themselves and others in the stories—and not in positive ways.[21] As time has passed, however, some of the old wounds have begun to fade, and many in the town today celebrate his connection to the community.[22] The Red Fox Inn is currently a bookstore themed around Hemingway, with works by and about Hemingway, as well as Hemingway-themed memorabilia.[23]

Horton Bay Today

Today, Horton Bay is best known for its connection to Hemingway, but even if you don't have an interest in the author, the town is still a fascinating place. Multiple buildings in the town were built over 100 years ago, including the general store, the Red Fox Inn, a school, and a church. The town also has a landscaping company, an antique store, a wedding venue, a Bay Township hall, and a United Methodist church. To the northwest of the community, there is the Nick Adams Nature Preserve.

Both the Horton Bay General Store and the Red Fox Inn have been designated as historical sites. They are both housed in structures that are over 100 years old.

TOP: The Hubbardston Community Center puts out seasonal decorations

Population: 395[1]   **Incorporated:** 1867[2]

INSETS L to R: Dugan Field is named for William Patrick "Dugan" McGinn, a longtime Little League coach in Hubbardston • The Hubbardston Fire Department • A pavilion in Mill Pond Park • The Hubbardston Hydro Dam shut down in 2010 but returned to producing power in 2015

Shiels Tavern, in downtown Hubbardston, is the oldest continuously operating bar in the state of Michigan.[22]

Hubbardston

History of Hubbardston

AN EARLY EUROPEAN SETTLER IN HUBBARDSTON was Joseph Brown, who came to the area in 1851 and purchased 240 acres of land.[3] The land he bought included water power on Fish Creek, and over the next two years, he built a dam, a sawmill, and a boarding house.[4] In 1853, the village's namesake, Thomas Hubbard, came to the area, along with a few other men, and bought the land and mill owned by Brown.[5] They made improvements to the sawmill over the next few years, enlarging it and installing a steam engine.[6]

A year or so later, the second frame building was built in the village, the first having been the sawmill.[7] This building was used as a store.[8] The Howard House hotel was added in 1856, and soon a number of other buildings appeared as well, including homes, shops, and a flour mill.[9] The early village was so successful that the residents knew they would soon need a railroad line in the town, and they decided to organize their own: the Westphalia, Hubbardston, and Northern Railroad Company.[10] That railroad never did come to fruition in the town, but additional negotiations at the township level finally brought the arrival of the Marshall and Coldwater Railroad to Hubbardston in the early 1870s.[11]

Around the same time the village was trying to bring the railroad to Hubbardston, the Catholic community in the town erected St. John's Catholic Church, which was, at the time, believed to be the largest church in the county.[12] The Methodist church was built around the same time, and a Congregation church was added some years later.[13] A school was another addition in those years.[14]

In 1903, the village had approximately 500 residents and its own bank.[15] Business enterprises in the town included an insurance business, a weaver, multiple people involved in raising and breeding livestock, a hotel, a fruit evaporator, a cider mill, a flour mill, and a variety of general, dry goods, and grocery stores.[16]

The Hubbardston Irish Dance Troupe

Many of the residents in Hubbardston over the years have been able to trace their roots back to Ireland. The community celebrates this heritage, particularly around St. Patrick's Day, and one way it does so is with the Hubbardston Irish Dance Troupe. The troupe, consisting of children from age three to age eighteen, performs traditional Irish dances.[17] Patricia McCormick Baese started the group in 1995 with the goals of both teaching Irish dance and helping the youth of the area embrace aspects of Irish culture.[18] The program also helps children practice their own creativity by inviting them to, at times, design their own choreography.[19]

The troupe has around 70 members and is well loved in the Hubbardston area, but they don't only display their skill in their hometown.[20] They have traveled all over the mid-Michigan area and have even gone farther away from home to perform on Mackinac Island and at Disney World.[21]

Hubbardston Today

Hubbardston today is much like its earlier self in that it is a town full of community. The village finds reason to bring people together all throughout the year, from St. Patrick's Day in the spring to the annual MSU-UM football game in the fall. The Masonic Lodge hosts events as well, including an annual chicken dinner. There is a community center in the town, which contains a historical society, and village offices. For outdoor gatherings, there is a village park and a butterfly garden.

In addition, Hubbardston is home to Shiels Tavern, a nursery, a market, a hardware store, and an American Legion post. There is a gallery of art where people can also buy Irish gifts. For services, Hubbardston has a post office and a fire department. There are two churches in Hubbardston, Mount Hope Church and St. John the Baptist.

The dam in Hubbardston, first built in the 1850s when Joseph Brown came to town. In the 1920s, a hydropower plant was added, operating until 2010.[23] After spending more than $100,000 on refurbishments to the power station, bringing it up to code, it reopened in late 2015.[24]

TOP: Colorful chairs are set out back of the Landing Restaurant

Population: 140[1]   **Unincorporated**

INSETS L to R: The Landing Restaurant is set on Lake Charlevoix, right next to the Ironton Ferry • The Ironton Ferry takes cars across a narrow point of the south arm of Lake Charlevoix • A nature trail waiting to be explored • Looking down on one area of Ironton and the lake

After the closure of the Pine Lake Iron Company in 1893, the population declined for some time in Ironton. In recent years, however, the community has been on the rise. The U.S. Census Bureau estimates that the population in Ironton has gone up nearly 15 percent since the 2010 census.[21]

Ironton

History of Ironton

THE PINE LAKE IRON COMPANY spurred the settlement of Ironton. Robert Cherry, the president of the company, came to the area in 1879 to start an iron plant.[2] In operation by 1881, the plant turned iron ore into pig iron, a semifinished form of iron that is later further refined into specific products, including steel.[3] The company employed between 200 and 300 workers, and many of those workers made the area of Ironton their home.[4]

Even before the iron plant began operations, the Pine Lake Iron Company was developing the area that would become the village of Ironton. They opened a company store in 1879, and a year later a post office opened, with Leslie E. Hildreth as the first postmaster.[5] In 1882,

Ironton received a school and its first church, built by the Methodist Society.[6] The settlement was platted in 1884 by E. K. Robinson, and a second church was built the same year.[7]

The company was successful for those first few years, processing 30,000 tons of iron ore.[8] This was good not only for the residents of Ironton, but also for the rest of Charlevoix County, which had a market for the wood they produced, as the iron company used around 36,000 cords of wood each year.[9] However, the company failed in 1893 and ceased all production.[10]

Within ten years, the population of the village fell to around 150 people, and many, though certainly not all, of the businesses closed or moved elsewhere.[11] Farming in the area was profitable, though, and that no doubt helped the community. In 1903, there were two general stores, a hotel, two carpenters, a mason, a sewing machine agent, a clerk, and two blacksmiths.[12] There was also someone in charge of supporting the community's poor.[13]

The Ironton Ferry

One good change did come to Ironton in those years immediately following the closure of the iron plant. Ironton, on the south side of the south arm of Lake Charlevoix (originally called Pine Lake), was the perfect place for a ferry, allowing travelers to cross the south arm of the lake rather than go around, saving ferry-goers a distance of about twenty miles.[14] The first ferry was built in 1883 and was a wooden scow and required a ferry worker to pull the vessel along by hand.[15] Early prices for the ferry ranged from five cents for a footman, to ten cents for a "beast except sheep," to a full dollar for a threshing machine.[16]

In 1927, the older ferry was replaced by a newer one, called the *Vessel Charlevoix*, which cost $12,000.[17] For a time, the ferry was mostly known only to people in and around Lake Charlevoix, but in 1936, *Ripley's Believe It or Not!* featured the ferry. The story they chose to tell was about Sam Alexander, the ferry operator: "Sam Alexander, ferry boat operator, has traveled 15,000 miles and was never farther than 1,000 feet from home."[18]

Today, the vessel *Charlevoix* is still the ferry in use, though today it is more likely to carry cars than livestock, though passengers on foot or bicycle are still welcome to ride. The ferry operates from mid-April through mid-November, with the first ferry departing at 6:30 a.m. and the last at 10:30 p.m.[19] The ride, which takes approximately ten minutes, is repeated by the ferry roughly 100 times per day, usually carrying four cars at the rate of $3 each.

Ironton Today

The Ironton Ferry is today the center of the community, and most of the local businesses and organizations are clustered around it. Next to the ferry is the Landing Restaurant, which has seating set up so diners can watch the ferry. There is also public beach access, a marina, and a rental shop, where visitors and residents alike can rent boats, jet skis, and even water trampolines.[20]

The Ironton Ferry features a sign advertising its 1884 rates for ferriage. At the time, ferry riders with a double team of oxen owed 30 cents, and sheep cost 10 cents apiece, with a discount if you had more than six.

TOP: The old Lake Angelus school building was constructed in 1917

Population: 290[1]   **Incorporated:** 1930[2]

INSETS L to R: Tree-lined dirt streets keep the neighborhood quiet and peaceful • A sign for Lake Angelus Shores • A pedestrian path in Lake Angelus • The streets in the small city are mostly private roads

It's unclear why Lake Angelus was ever called Three Mile Lake, as none of its dimensions are equal to three miles, and it is also not three miles from any significant place.[21]

Lake Angelus

History of Lake Angelus

LAKE ANGELUS IS A COMMUNITY in Oakland County that surrounds a lake with the same name. The current town was founded around the turn of the twentieth century by a group of men that included Charles Staff, Neil C. McMath, Elmer E. Gallogly, Fenn J. Holden, Hiram L. Walton, and Charles Roehm, though at the time the lake was called Three Mile Lake.[3] It did not change to its current name of Lake Angelus until the 1920s, when Mrs. Sollace B. Collidge led the effort to change the name of the lake.[4] The exact motivations for the change are unclear, but most believe it had something to do with religion. "The Angelus" is the name of a Catholic prayer.

The early history of Lake Angelus was connected to the city of Detroit. People from Detroit, particularly those in the auto industry, would come to the area of Lake Angelus, usually for relaxation in the summer.[5] Their similar lives, circumstances, and business interests resulted in the formation of a community around the lake. They determined to make their own rules, regulations, and restrictions for governing themselves as a community separate from those around them.[6] They were particularly interested in how the community would use both the lake and the land around it.[7]

Things were not so simple, however. The budding town at Lake Angelus was in a less-developed state than those around it, and more than one already-established local government tried to make the lake and its surrounding territory part of their own communities.[8] Finally, in 1929, the State Legislature stepped in and granted the Lake Angelus community homerule. A year later, Lake Angelus was officially incorporated as a village.[9]

Just 55 years later, in 1984, Lake Angelus changed from a village to a city, allowing it to collect taxes and hold statewide elections.[10,11] The switch from village to city put Lake Angelus on the list of smallest cities in Michigan, and as of the 2010 census, it has the title of smallest city in Michigan.[12]

The McMath Hulbert Observatory

Neil C. McMath was one of the founders of Lake Angelus, and in 1930, his father, Francis C. McMath, and brother, Robert R. McMath, teamed up with Henry S. Hulbert to build a new observatory in the Lake Angelus area.[13] One of their interests was in taking celestial motion pictures, both for entertainment and scientific purposes.[14]

As his brother and father's work with the telescope and observatory advanced, Neil found himself drawn in, and in 1933 joined them at the observatory.[15] Over the next few years, they added a tower with a spectrograph well and a new telescope drive, which was used to move the telescope along with the motions of the celestial bodies it was tracking.[16] The new equipment helped the McMaths and Hulbert disprove a then-popular theory about how solar prominences—large bright features that extend from the sun's surface—form.[17]

More improvements followed over the next few years, but in the late 1930s Francis McMath died. His son Neil took his place on the board and as Honorary Curator of the Observatories of the University of Michigan.[18] Robert became director of the observatory itself.[19] Research continued at the telescope until 1979, when the University of Michigan's support for the project ended.[20]

Lake Angelus Today

Today, Lake Angelus is primarily a residential community. The streets in the community are wooded and private, and the area feels peaceful. The lake itself is private and open only to people in the community. There is a walking path in the area as well.

The remnants of the observatory are still standing, and attempts have been made to restart some astronomical research in the city, but it's unclear if they will pan out or not.

Population: 268[1]   **Incorporated:** 1892[2]

INSETS L to R: The Lake Ann Grocery sells both grocery and hardware items • Lake Ann village sits on the north side of the lake of the same name • The Lake Ann Brewing Company • The sign for S. S. Burnett Park, which is named for Sam Burnett, who an early Lake Ann businessman

During Prohibition, some Chicago "gangster" families operated whiskey distilleries in Lake Ann Village, at the place where the Baptist camp now stands.[17]

TOP: S.S. Burnett Park has playground equipment, a volleyball court, and a basketball court

Lake Ann

History of Lake Ann

THE FIRST EUROPEAN SETTLERS in the Lake Ann area were A. P. Wheelock and his family, who came to the lake in 1862.[3] He named the lake for his wife, Ann, though originally it was called Ann Lake instead of Lake Ann.[4] When the village began to grow up, it was named for her as well.[5] Wheelock was an influential man in the area, and when Almira Township was organized in 1864, his house served as the site of the first meeting.[6]

In its early days, Lake Ann was a lumber town. The Manistee & Northeastern Railroad built a depot in Lake Ann in 1888, allowing for easy transportation of the lumber out of the village.[7] Three years later, the first post office opened in 1891, with Elijah Ransom as the first postmaster.[8] By 1897 the population of the village was near 700.[9]

A Series of Tragic Fires

However, disaster struck the village that same year, on Independence Day, in the form of a fire that destroyed much of the village.[10] Though there were fire brigades in Lake Ann, they were not enough to stop the fire, and nearly an hour passed before help arrived from Traverse City.[11] The town suffered $100,000 in damages, the equivalent of more than $3 million today. The town was rebuilt, but it never again reached the size it had been before the fire, especially when a second fire tore through the town in 1914 and another in 1918.[12]

The village pressed on, though, refusing to give up. In the early 1920s, its population had rebounded to a respectable 150 people, and it housed a school organized by grades, a Congregational church, and a variety of businesses, including a blacksmith, a hotel, several real estate agents, a milliner and dressmaker, a garage, a physician, and two general stores.[13] This included one building, a general store, that had been built around 1892,[14] and though additions have been added to the space, now the grocery store, the core building still stands in Lake Ann today.

The town began to grow again over the coming years, as the community became a resort community and began to focus more on the tourism industry.

Harmony Park, the Harm Farm

Harmony Park, part of which is known as the Harm Farm, is a historic nature preserve in Lake Ann that was founded in 1966.[15] More than that, however, it's a place where residents of Lake Ann and the surrounding area can come together for both personal and community events, from weddings to music festivals.

One event is the now-annual Dunesville Music Festival, which celebrated its fourth year in 2017. The event is a weekend "bluegrass, folk and roots music festival,"[16] and everything from the music, which is all local bands, to the food and drink vendors is designed to evoke a sense of Michigan.

The summer festival isn't the only time the Dunesville Music Festival and the Harm Farm team up, however. In 2017 they joined forces to host a one-night event called the Great Pumpkin Jamboree. The event included a showing of the *Rocky Horror Picture Show*, a costume contest, a haunted forest, and more live music.

Lake Ann Today

Today Lake Ann is a resort community that is also welcoming to visitors. There are many cottages, both on and near the lake, and the downtown area of the village includes a bed and breakfast, a restaurant, a coffee shop, an ice cream store, and a local brewery. The grocery store now provides a variety of grocery items, hardware, and general merchandise. There is also a party store, a party rides business that provides transportation for events such as weddings, and three different village parks. For a more serious nature experience, the Lake Ann State Forest Campground is located just on the west side of the lake.

Services in the village include a library, a historical society, a township hall, and a web design company. Lake Ann has Lutheran, United Methodist, and Wesleyan churches and is also the home of a Baptist retreat and camp.

One of the early inhabitants of the town was one Ned Farr, who was renowned both for his pronounced stutter and the delight he had in telling funny stories, during which he often removed his hat while gesticulating, sometimes even removing his own wig, revealing a "head as innocent of hair as an ostrich's egg."[18]

TOP: The village of Leonard is right on the Polly Ann Trail

Population: 403[1]   **Incorporated:** 1887

INSETS L to R: The barber shop in Leonard • The village has worked in conjunction with Oakland County to restore and preserve the old Leonard Mill • The main intersection in Leonard is often called the four corners • A plaque thanking a local foundation for "supporting the development of The Polly Ann Trail"

Today, the community of Leonard is trying to save its historic grain elevator, and the current plan is to refurbish the building and make it a point of interest on the Polly Ann Trail.[14]

Built in Leonard in 1898, Rowland Hall was donated to the village by its founder, Leonard Rowland, and still stands proudly today.[15]

Leonard

History of Leonard

LEONARD WAS FOUNDED IN 1882 when Leonard Rowland came to the area.[2] That same year, the Pontiac, Oxford, and Northern Railroad came to that area.[3] The village was initially called Trombley[4] but was renamed for Rowland in 1884 when a post office called Leonard opened.[5]

The village got off to a bit of a slow start. In 1888, only one year after incorporating as a village, the population was 20, and in addition to the depot, which was then named Dryden, there was a general store and a justice of the peace.[6] It did not stay that small, though. Shortly after the turn of the twentieth century, the population had climbed to 300 people and more businesses, including a sawmill, a dressmaker, a drayman (a brewer's delivery person), a hardware store, a drugstore, a meat market, a grocery, and a hotel had opened.[7]

A grain elevator had also come to the village in that time, opening in 1889.[8] The Leonard Grain Elevator and Beanery, built right next to the railroad tracks, allowed farmers in the area to both process and ship their farm products.[9] This was good for the town, especially as the lumber supply in the area diminished, and by 1912, Leonard had gained a fruit evaporator, and agriculture had surpassed lumber as the primary industry of the area.[10]

With the decline of the lumber industry and the coming of automobiles, the railroad eventually decreased its service to Leonard, first removing passenger service in 1955 and then ending all service in 1984.[11]

This in turn caused the grain elevator to lose business, and after first attempting a switch to a dry goods store, the facility closed in 2004.[12]

Leonard's Annual Strawberry Festival

The summer of 2017 marked the 65th annual Addison Township Firefighters Strawberry Festival. The festival, which is held in Leonard, dates back to 1952, when the Addison Township Firefighters, who worked out of the station in Leonard, first served strawberry sundaes to the public.[13] That tradition still carries to today, but the festival has also expanded to include a cook-off contest, a car show, a parade, a talent show, arts and crafts, live music, and dancing in the streets.

Leonard Today

Leonard today is home to a variety of businesses, including a market, a storage center, a design studio, a gas station, and a well drilling company, among others. There is an elementary school which is part of Oxford Community Schools. *The Village Crier*, a message board for area businesses and residents, is located at the main intersection in Leonard.

The Polly Ann Trail, part of the Rails to Trails program in Michigan, runs through Leonard, right alongside the grain elevator, following the line of the old railroad. The Polly Ann Trail Management Council is also located in Leonard. Other services in the village include the township fire department and a post office. The area is served by a United Methodist church, a Brethren in Christ church, and a Community church.

August 4, 2007
In Grateful Appreciation to
THE CHRYSLER FOUNDATION
for their generous contribution
supporting the development of
The Polly Ann Trail

The author Trey Hamburger lives in Leonard. His work includes the humor novel *Ghosts/Aliens* and *REAL Ultimate Power: The Official Ninja Book*.

TOP: Horse-drawn buggies are not an uncommon sight in LeRoy

Population: 256[1]   **Incorporated:** 1883[2]

INSETS L to R: LeRoy has its own museum for the village and the surrounding area • The hardware store in LeRoy • A quilt square can be seen on the side of the post office in the village • The community library in LeRoy

Each year, LeRoy holds Razzasque Days, a two-day festival that includes a golf tournament, carnival games, food and drink tents, two parades, a 5k run and walk, a car show, and other family-friendly events. The event is a re-creation of a merchant promotion that ran in LeRoy early in the town's history.

LeRoy

History of LeRoy

LEROY BEGAN FIRST AS A TOWNSHIP. Around 1871, a group of businessmen in LeRoy Township decided that the township would benefit from having a village.[3] They picked a spot on the Grand Rapids & Indiana Railroad, which was being constructed in the area, and in the summer of 1871, some of those men, including James E. Bevins, relocated to the area where LeRoy Village now stands.[4] Bevins, who is credited as the founder of the village, became LeRoy's first postmaster in 1871 and also platted the village in 1872.[5] When LeRoy became incorporated as a village in 1883, Bevins was elected as its first president.[6]

Almost as soon as the railroad was completed in LeRoy and the first trains began to come to the area, the village began to grow. Lumber was its primary business, and by 1877 LeRoy, then sometimes spelled Le Roy, had three sawmills and a grist mill, and the population was around 150.[7]

As the trees in the area were cut, farms were started where forest had once been, and for a time, the village had success in both the lumber and farming industries. Near the turn of the twentieth century, LeRoy shipped lumber, tanbark, grain, and potatoes and was quickly growing in the area of fruit farming.[8] The town also had a meat market, an apiarist (beekeeper), a surgeon, a photographer, multiple general and dry goods stores, a barber, a lawyer, a bank, a school, a hotel, four churches, and a weekly newspaper.[9]

Forest Ray Moulton, American Astronomer

One of America's well-known astronomers was born in LeRoy in 1872.[10] From a young age, Forest Ray Moulton was drawn to knowledge. His parents valued education and were involved in opening a school in the LeRoy area, and Forest himself was the first person from LeRoy to attend college, graduating from Albion College in 1894, and then earning a PhD in mathematics and astronomy from the University of Chicago in 1899.[11] He was later awarded honorary degrees by a number of other colleges and universities.

Moulton made a wide variety of contributions to the fields of mathematics and astronomy. Along with geologist T. C. Chamberlin, he developed the planetesimal hypothesis to explain planetary orbital patterns, and while much of the hypothesis was later discarded, the idea of planetesimals is still alive and well in modern theory.[12] He also wrote a variety of textbooks, including *Descriptive Astronomy, Celestial Mechanics, and Differential Equations.*[13] He also was a regular contributor to the magazine *Popular Astronomy.*[14]

As a major in the army during World War I, Moulton headed the Ballistics Branch of the Ordnance Department where he worked on projectile motion.[15] After the war, he turned his attention to the meteorite that made Meteor Crater in Arizona and attempted to calculate its size and mass.[16] His work here has held up well and his findings were very close to those calculated by scientists years later.[17]

Moulton did not only work in the sciences; he also continued his interest in education more generally. He formed the first Parent-Teacher Association in Chicago, started a journal focused on visual education, and was a longtime member in the American Association for the Advancement of Sciences.[18]

LeRoy Today

The railroad left its mark on LeRoy in many ways, and two examples that are still visible today can be found in the layout of the streets and in the White Pine Trail. While many of the streets in LeRoy run along the cardinal directions of the compass, others run at diagonals that were, at one time, either parallel or perpendicular to the railroad. Now, however, they match the angle of the Fred Meijer White Pine Trail rather than any railroad tracks. The trail, which is 93 miles long, is part of the Rails to Trails program in Michigan and passes right through downtown LeRoy.

Businesses in LeRoy today include an auto repair shop, a self-storage center, a bait and tackle shop, a tire center, a VFW post, a milling company, two sawmills, two salons, a garden store, and a handful of construction and manufacturing companies. Services in the village include a post office, a bank, a community library, a community park, a historical museum, a fire department, and four churches. The village also has a farmers market that runs from May to October.

LeRoy's native son Forest Ray Moulton is memorialized in both astronomy and mathematics. The lunar crater Moulton is named for him, as are several terms in mathematics.

Population: 337[1]   **Incorporated:** 1907[2]

INSETS L to R: Lincoln is located on two lakes, so many of the residents have property on or near the water • The Alcona County fair is held in Lincoln • The county fair is held every August and includes a variety of events, including the showing of livestock • A view down one of the main streets in the village

TOP: The depot this railway car is in front of stood in Lincoln when it was called West Harrisville

Lincoln recently received a grant from the Michigan Economic Development Corporation to help the community build new sidewalks, gutters, curbs, benches, and lighting in the village.[28]

Lincoln

Private Josiah M. Donaldson

IN 1864, AT THE AGE OF FOURTEEN, Josiah M. Donaldson enlisted in the Union Army, giving his age as eighteen.[3] He served as a flag holder in the same regiment as his father Joel did, the 4th Pennsylvania Cavalry.[4] The father-son pair fought in over a dozen battles, and though Josiah was wounded more than once, both survived the war and were present in Appomattox for General Robert E. Lee's surrender.[5] There, they served as part of a special guard for General Ulysses S. Grant.[6]

After the war, Josiah moved to Michigan, where he was eventually married and became a father.[7] He lived part of that time in the Lincoln area, and when he died in 1937, at age 89, he was buried in Lincoln's Twin Lakes Cemetery.[8] Both his parents and his wife were also buried in Lincoln.[9]

For some reason, however, Josiah's grave was left unmarked when he was buried.[10] His burial place remained without a headstone for decades, until, in 2011, two residents from Alcona County were able to get his burial place marked with a Civil War military headstone.[11] Donaldson was the last Civil War veteran from Alcona County to die, and now his sacrifices for our country have been acknowledged and honored, both with the headstone and with a historic marker at the cemetery's entrance.[12]

History of Lincoln

Like many settlements in Michigan, Lincoln began as a lumber town.[13] It was settled in 1885, and in its first years, it was known as West Harrisville, as it was located just over seven miles west of the existing

118

settlement of Harrisville, between Brownlee Lake and Lincoln Lake.[14] The village's location between the two lakes was vital to the success of its early lumbering industry. Lincoln Lake was the more essential of the two, as it made it easier to move the lumber to the village's depot, where it was loaded onto trains.[15]

The Detroit & Mackinac Railway came to the area in 1886, and the village depot was opened.[16] Also in 1886 was surveyor A. J. Freer's platting of the village, though the plat was not recorded until the following year.[17] When the village was platted, it spanned parts of two separate townships, and to this day the north part of the village lies in Hawes Township while the south part of the village is in Gustin Township.[18]

The village received its first post office in 1887, and William C. Reynolds was selected as the first postmaster.[19] The post office still bore the name West Harrisville until 1899, when it was officially changed to Lincoln, and the rest of the village followed suit.[20] It was under the name Lincoln that the village was incorporated in 1907.[21] The first elections were held in March of 1908, and W. G. Anderson was elected as the first president.[22]

By that time the village had grown to approximately 200 people, and the village had begun to expand its businesses ventures.[23] It had two general stores, three grocers, a meat market, a physician, a livery stable, a flour mill, and a hotel.[24] There were also two churches.[25] Within another fifteen years it had added a bank, a drugstore, a pool hall, a veterinarian, a watchmaker, and businesses that included a garage, hardware, and auto store.[26] The village also received service from a stagecoach line.[27]

Lincoln Today

The population has grown since the early lumber days, and today Lincoln is home to over 300 people and a number of local businesses. The village has an animal clinic, an insurance agency, a ceramics shop, a gift shop, a restaurant, a bistro, a dog grooming salon, and a car wash,

among others. There is a Masonic temple, a funeral home, and a senior center. The area has a United Methodist church, a Baptist church, and a Lutheran church.

In addition, Lincoln also has a variety of township and county services. It is home to the Alcona County Humane Society, a branch of the county library, and a post office. Alcona Community Schools are located south of the main village area and provide education services to students from kindergarten through twelfth grade. The Alcona County Recreation Area is just to the east of the village area, and that is the site of the Alcona County Fair, which runs each August.

The Lost Lake Woods Club, begun in 1926, is partially located in Lincoln.[29] It is a "private, member-owned" club that covers more than 10,000 acres and encompasses five lakes.[30]

TOP: Luther Grocery is located on State Street

Population: 318[1]   Incorporated: 1893[2]

INSETS L to R: The Luther Area Museum • Burnett Park • The Newkirk Township Municipal Hall • The bell from the old Luther school house

William A. Luther, after whom the village was named, owned one of the first houses in the village.[21] The house is still standing in present-day Luther and now serves as the Fellowship Baptist Church.[22]

Luther's Valley Cemetery is the final resting place of a Medal of Honor recipient. Alonzo Woodruff was a Sergeant in the 1st U.S. Sharpshooters Infantry during the Civil War.[23] During the Battle of Hatcher's Run, in Virginia, Woodruff rescued one of his comrades from the rebels.[24] To do so, he resorted to hand-to-hand combat, capturing the would-be Confederate captor in the process.[25] He repeated the feat later in the battle, suffering serious wounds.[26]

Luther

The G. H. Gordon Biological Station

LUTHER IS HOME to Hillsdale College's G. H. Gordon Biological Station. Covering nearly 700 acres, the station is Michigan's largest biological research station operated by a private college.[3] The research station was begun in 1999 and provides students and faculty with research opportunities and off-campus course options.[4]

At the station there is also the Rockwell Lake Lodge and the Plym Village Cabins. Both provide accommodations for visitors to the area, whether those visitors are coming for a vacation or for a work-related event.[5] While staying at the center, visitors can hike nature trails, spend time fishing, or go swimming. If you're lucky, you might even spot the pair of bald eagles that live at the station.[6]

History of Luther

First settled in 1880, Luther was originally called Wilson after Luther and Wilson Lumber, the local sawmill business.[7] It was renamed to Luther, after the other partner in the lumber business, in 1881, after the village learned that there was already another town named Wilson.[8] That same year, the Grand Rapids & Indiana Railroad came to Luther.[9]

Over the next few years, the village of Luther grew quickly. The first post office opened in 1882 with Thomas Crebbin as the first postmaster, and the village was incorporated in 1893.[10] Within five more years, the village had over 1,000 people and was shipping not only lumber, but also charcoal, shingles, and bark.[11] There were dozens of businesses in the town, a few of which included a tinsmith, a millwright, a jeweler, and a dressmaker.[12] There were multiple restaurants, saloons, grocers, general stores, blacksmiths, and real estate businesses, and there was even an opera house.[13]

Over the next few decades, the population in Luther slowly tapered off, though this village itself remained a thriving place. A second railroad had come to the village near the end of the nineteenth century.[14] By 1912, the village had electricity and was a larger community than the Lake County seat.[15] It had a school organized by grades and five different churches, making it a prime place to live in Lake County.[16]

Luther Today

Today, the residents of Luther want to be known more for their close-knit community than for any particular business or industry in and around the Luther area. Though there are businesses in the town, including a restaurant, a gift shop, a grocery store, and others, Luther resident Julie Morgan says it is the strong sense of community that truly sets their town apart.[17] Residents of Luther support each other through the good times and the bad, and everyone works together to strengthen both the community and the village itself.[18]

One recent project in the village has been the improvement of Mill Pond Park.[19] The park, which used to be the site of a mill, has had numerous updates over the past few years, including a trail system, a garden, and a dam.[20]

Other community-centered locations and services in the village include a library, a township hall, a museum, department of public works buildings, a post office, a senior citizen center, and a Lions Club. Churches in Luther include a Catholic church, a Baptist church, a United Methodist church, a Wesleyan church, and a Church of Christ.

Each Fourth of July weekend, Luther holds its annual Luther Logging Days. The event features games, dancing, a lumberjack competition, a horse pull, parades, and a fireworks show recognized for being one of the best in all of northern Michigan.[27]

TOP: During the tourist season, Main Street is crowded with tourists but there are no motorized vehicles

Population: 492[1]   **Incorporated:** 1899[2,3]

INSETS L to R: The Grand Hotel is one of the island's most famous sites • There are many historic sites on the island, including this Missionary Bark Chapel • This church is a historical site and is commonly called the "Little Stone Church" • Fort Mackinac is home to the oldest building in Michigan

Mackinac Island City is one of the few Michigan cities that has been able to celebrate its bicentennial, which it did in the summer of 2017.[24]

Mackinac Island City

History of Mackinac Island

MACKINAC ISLAND, located in the Straits of Mackinac between Michigan's Upper and Lower Peninsulas, has been a location of importance for hundreds of years. When Europeans first came to that area of Michigan in the seventeenth century, American Indians, particularly the Ojibwe and the Odawa, had already inhabited the island for centuries, and the early white explorers and fur traders soon followed suit. Early Europeans in the area included Father Jacques Marquette (Pere Marquette), a prominent figure in early Michigan history.

Sometime in the early eighteenth century, around 1715, the French built a fort on the south side of the Straits of Mackinac and called it Michilimackinac.[4] The name comes from the American Indian term for the area, which many interpret to mean "Great Turtle."[5] In the 1770s, the English took over the fort as the result of the Treaty of 1773, and a few years later they moved the fort from its location near the present day Mackinaw City to the island and renamed it Fort Mackinac.[6]

Control of the fort passed to the Americans in 1795.[7] The British won the fort back in the War of 1812 but only maintained control of it for three years, at which time it returned to the United States.[8] Two years later, in 1817, the city, now being called by the shorter *Mackinac* rather than *Michilimackinac*, received a civil and local government.[9]

Though the fort and the island were often used by military forces in the eighteenth and nineteenth centuries, the majority of the population on the island was American Indian.[10] This made for an often-contentious situation, as the U.S. government wanted to remove the American Indians from their land.[11] Recently, the city has been trying to bring this portion of the island's history to the forefront.[12]

In the mid- to late-1800s, the island became known as a resort destination, and businesses in the community included a number of hotels and stores.[13] The fort still held a garrison of soldiers but was not otherwise much in use.[14] The Mackinac National Park was created to preserve the island's scenic and historic sites in 1875, and, 20 years later, control of the park changed over to the state of Michigan, and the park was renamed as Mackinac Island State Park.[15] In 1899, the community was officially incorporated as the city of Mackinac Island, removing its previous designation as a village.[16]

An Island Without Cars

Mackinac Island City is a city without cars and has been that way since 1898, when the island passed an ordinance banning all private automobiles.[17] Highway M-185, which runs for about eight miles along the outside of the island, is the only "Motorless State Highway" in the nation.[18] The island does have emergency vehicles, including a fire truck, a police car, and an ambulance, but residents and tourists alike walk, bike, ride horses, or ride in horse-drawn carriages to get from place to place.

There have been a few exceptions to the no-cars rule over the years. Detroit auto manufacturers have sometimes used Mackinac Island as a location for photographing and filming car ads.[19] In these instances, the cars generally are taken to the island on a ferry and then hauled to the appropriate location by a horse-drawn cart.[20] Another exception occurred in 1979, when the movie *Somewhere in Time*, starring Christopher Reeve and Jane Seymour, was filmed on the island; for the movie, two cars were allowed to drive short distances on the island as film props.[21]

Mackinac Island Today

Though Mackinac Island has only a few hundred year-round residents, during the summer months it can bring in over 10,000 tourists per day. In the summer, people generally get to the island by ferry (service is provided to and from both Mackinaw City and St. Ignace), private boat, or airplane.

The island is home to the famous Grand Hotel, which boasts a 660-foot-long porch and which has hosted such figures as Mark Twain, Thomas Edison (whose phonograph was debuted on site), and many U.S. presidents.[22] There are also a number of other hotels, inns, bed and breakfasts, and cottages to stay at. You won't find any chain hotels or franchises on the island though; every place is family owned and unique.[23] There are dozens of dining options on the island, from upscale dining to more-casual diners and coffee shops, and ample opportunities for shopping.

Fudge is one of the premier products on Mackinac Island, and there are seven different fudgemakers on the island, some of which have been making fudge for over 100 years. The fudge is made fresh daily, and visitors can often stop and watch the process and maybe also try a sample.

There are many ways to interact with history on the island, too. Visitors can tour Fort Mackinac and Fort Holmes or visit one of the museums on the island. While simply walking or biking around the main area of the city, people can encounter various historical signs and plaques.

As with the tourists who come to Mackinac Island in the summer, many of the horses on the island are also seasonal. Each May, around five hundred horses come to the island by ferry, then leave again in the fall and winter.[25] Only a small number of horses live on the island year-round.

TOP: This steam engine, built in 1890, is on display in Marenisco

Population: 254[1]   **Unincorporated**

INSETS L to R: The Roosevelt School building, constructed in 1922 • Despite being an unincorporated community, Marenisco has its own library • Earla's restaurant serves the community • The veterans' memorial in Marenisco

During the Great Depression, workers at one of the lumber camps near Marenisco were paid in aluminum tokens.[26] The tokens could be exchanged for merchandise at the local company store, though the local tavern would also accept them.[27] The tokens were discontinued in 1936.[28]

Marenisco

History of Marenisco

THE SETTLEMENT THAT WOULD EVENTUALLY become Marenisco started with an 1884 land donation from Emmet H. Scott, who had a large ownership in lumber holdings.[2] To name the village, he took the first three letters from his wife's first, middle, and last name—Mary Enid Scott—to form the name Marenisco.[3]

That same year, the Milwaukee, Lake Shore, and Western Railway Company platted the town, and the lumber industry in Marenisco began.[4] Despite that, the town traces its roots to 1886 and lists that as its date of establishment on village signs. For the first 20 years of the town's existence, there was little there except for lumber businesses, a general merchandise store, a jail, and lodging accommodations.[5] Many of the row houses built by the Charcoal Iron Company still stand in the village today.[6] There had been mining operations to the north of the village as well, but that venture ended around the turn of the century.[7]

Marenisco erected a town hall in 1912, and the first school in the village, the Roosevelt School, which still stands in Marenisco today, was built in 1922.[8] Even as the village added more buildings and businesses, however, the lumber industry continued strongly, mostly cutting pine.[9] A new lumber company opened in the town in the late 1920s, and lumber operations continued in the town through the Great Depression, and into the 1940s and 1950s.[10, 11]

Eventually the lumber supply in the area did run out, and with it came the decline and then closure of the railroad. The village's depot was closed and then replaced by a trailer office near the end of the 1960s.[12] A little more than two decades later, the trailer office was removed and all rail service to the village ended.[13] Today, there is a trail that follows the path of the old railway line.

The End of Stagecoach Robberies in the United States

The last stagecoach robbery in Michigan—and possibly the whole of the United States at the time—occurred in 1889 by a man from Marenisco just ten miles from the village.[14] In August of that year, Reimund Holzhey of Marenisco pulled out two revolvers and stopped a stagecoach that was traveling along the Gogebic Stage Coach Road.[15] The stagecoach held two bankers, Adolph Fleischbein and Donald Macarcher, who were staying at a resort on the south side of Lake Gogebic, east of the village.[16] The previous day, Fleischbein had gone fishing, taking with him a guide employed by the resort.[17] That guide had been Holzhey.[18]

This was not Holzhey's first robbery. Since spring, he had been robbing trains and coaches in northern Wisconsin and in Michigan's Upper Peninsula.[19] This robbery turned violent however, and Holzhey shot Fleischbein, who died the following day.[20] Holzhey was captured a few days later when he was recognized at a hotel in Republic.[21] He was arrested and taken to Marquette for trial, where he was found guilty and given two life sentences.[22] His sentence was commuted to forty years by Governor Fred Warner in 1911.[23] He was paroled in 1914.[24]

Marenisco Today

Marenisco bills itself as a "town for all seasons," and that is true of both the Marenisco Village and Marenisco Township alike. There are snowmobile and ski trails in the area, and there are opportunities for camping, fishing, and hiking.[25] Lake Gogebic is to the northeast, and Presque Isle River is just to the east of the downtown area of Marenisco. The State Line Trail, part of the Rails to Trails program, runs north and south through the town.

The village itself has two restaurants, a bar, and a gas station with a mini-mart, a place to rent U-Hauls, a skate park, a medical clinic, and a public library. There are also police and fire services and a post office. In the middle of the town, near the village green area, there is a veterans' memorial and, on display, a steam engine built in 1890.

Marenisco is in a Michigan Tax Free Renaissance Zone—an area designed to promote business and resident growth by significantly reducing or altogether eliminating taxes in the area.[29]

Population: 410[1]   **Incorporated:** 1946[2]

INSETS L to R: The US-131 Motorsports Park • School and town pride are demonstrated here, on the entrance to the football field • Looking down 10th Street in Martin • This carving, on the tall stump of an old tree, honors America's armed forces

In addition to the Grand Rapids & Indiana Railroad, Martin also eventually gained a depot for the interurban railway.[25] This line was often used by rum runners in the 1920s.[26]

Martin is home to the US-131 Motorsports Park, a top-tier drag racing park that bills itself as the fastest track in Michigan.

TOP: A unique carved wooden statue in town

Martin

Stop and Pay the Toll

IN THE 1850S, A PLANK ROAD was built from Grand Rapids to Kalamazoo, and it passed right through the village of Martin.[3] The road created a good route for travelers but it also benefited its owners, as those who would use the road were charged a toll.[4] When the toll went into effect in 1855, the rate was "one penny per horse per mile."[5] The road, which was built with oak and elm, was eight feet wide and the per-mile cost of building the road was approximately $1,400.[6]

Unfortunately, the building technology did not match the plans for the road, and within only a few years, the once-easy-to-travel route began to deteriorate. The planks used to build the road began to warp and suffered from rot.[7] The result was that plank roads quickly became syn-onymous with difficult travel; Mark Twain, after journeying along the plank road on his way to Kalamazoo said, "The road would have been very good if some unconscionable fellow had not now and then dropped a plank across it."[8] The plank road shut down in the fall of 1869.[9] Today, US-131 runs along the same general path.[10]

History of Martin

Martin was founded in 1836 when Mumford and Jane Eldred came to the area and purchased land.[11] In December of that same year, Jane gave birth to a son named Samuel, who was the first European child born in the area.[12] A month later, Michigan became the twenty-sixth state to join the Union.

Other settlers soon joined the Eldreds in the area, including Calvin White, the Monteith family, and Cotton Kimball.[13] There were also a number of families of Scottish descent who came to Martin up until around 1850.[14]

Jane Eldred was asked to name the village, but the first name she chose, Albion, was already in use.[15] George Barnes, a representative for the State of Michigan, suggested the name Martin for Martin Van Buren who had recently been elected the eighth president of the United States, and the local community agreed with the choice.[16]

Martin grew quickly as a community. The first post office in the town opened in 1844, and Abraham Shellman was selected as its first postmaster. By the mid-1860s, there were over 700 people living in the town and surrounding area.[17] There was a hotel, two shoe merchants, two blacksmiths, two general stores, two physicians, and a handful of other businesses.[18] The Grand Rapids & Indiana Railroad came to Martin in 1870, and the village and township both only continued to grow, reaching over 1,000 combined residents in the mid-1870s.[19, 20]

By 1888, the businesses in Martin had expanded, and there had been added a meat market, a flour mill, a tinsmith, and a church[21] Also in 1888, Martin built its first high school.[22] The building served Martin until 1908, when it burned down.[23] The next year a new high school was built, and that one held classes until it was replaced with a newer structure in 1965.[24]

Martin Today

Martin is home to a variety of businesses, including a pizzeria, a hair salon, a daycare, a café, a gas station, a dollar store, an insurance company, a storage center, a hardware store, a computer repair center, a commercial fueling station, and a plastics manufacturer, among others. The mascot of Martin schools is a Clipper ship, and it is referenced in many of the locally owned businesses in the village.

Agriculture is also prevalent in the village. There are a variety of farms in the area, and the village itself has a grain elevator, a feed center, and a business that provides dehydrated proteins for use in animal feeds.

Services in the village include a library, a post office, a department of public works, and a fire department. The area is served by a United Methodist church and a Reformed church.

Martin schools are currently at work on a plan to provide 99 percent of the school's energy through the installation of solar panels on school buildings.[27]

Population: 205[1]   **Incorporated:** 1883[2]

INSETS L to R: The McBride post office • A walking path and park bench in a park on the northwest side of town • The McBride Church of Christ • Robert Lee Davis Memorial Park

In 1995, McBride's Depot was moved from McBride to Montcalm Heritage Village.[25] The building underwent restoration and now contains a variety of historical artifacts for visitors to see.[26]

TOP: Playground equipment in town

McBride

History of McBride

THE FIRST BUSINESS in what is now the McBride area was a sawmill built in 1873 by Emery Mallet.[3] The next year Alexander McBride came to the area and purchased the sawmill.[4] It burned down in 1875, but McBride quickly rebuilt it, and the spot where it stood became known as McBride's Mill.[5] This name was used for some time, and when the Pere Marquette Railroad came to the area, the station was also called McBride's Mill.[6] It's unclear when the name was switched to simply McBride.

The first business in the village was a store opened by a man named Chillson.[7] His business was successful, and records indicate that the business earned over $8,000 in sales in just its first six months.[8]

A second store soon opened, selling clothing.[9] The village was platted in 1877 by D. J. Jacobs, only six weeks after nearby Custer was platted.[10] Custer, which soon became a part of McBride, added a blacksmith and a wagon-making shop to McBride's existing businesses.[11]

The Fire of 1885

The early growth and prosperity of McBride was interrupted in May of 1885, when high winds caused a fire that started in a stovepipe to spread to other areas of the village.[12] Fifty-seven buildings were destroyed in the fire, which caused $57,000 in damages and left 24 families without their homes.[13] Many of the buildings were not insured, leaving less than $15,000 total to help with rebuilding and repairs.[14]

The village did not let the fire stop its progress. It continued to grow, both in terms of population and businesses present. Its growth was such that another early settlement in the area, Westville, could not keep pace and eventually dwindled from a prosperous town to a mere handful of residents.[15] The railroad helped with this success, as did the fact that the area produced quality produce from the local farms.[16] Benjamin Caldwell owned and operated a grain elevator—the only one in McBride—and sold large amounts of grain and animal feed.[17]

By 1916, McBride had a few hundred residents.[18] Businesses in the town included two general stores, two hardware stores, a drugstore, a hotel, a candy store, and a bank, among others.[19] McBride also had its own newspaper.[20]

A Town with Two Names

While this book is choosing to use the spelling McBride, there's actually some debate over whether the village is called McBride or McBrides. The confusion is twofold. First, in official governmental documents, the spelling changes based on who is doing the writing. For instance, the post office is called McBrides, and all documentation at the post office uses that spelling,[21] while the United States census data favors McBride.[22]

The second point of confusion is the fact that residents of the village and of Day Township use both spellings, both in speech and writing. Some people insist on one spelling or the other while others feel that the two can be used interchangeably.[23]

The confusion, however, only surrounds the correct spelling. Residents of the village and township know what you mean whichever you use, and mail makes it to the correct address whether the envelope says McBride or McBrides.[24]

McBride Today

Today, McBride is home to a gas station, a combination pawn shop and used auto sales center, a telephone company, an irrigation company, a post office, and a township fire department. There is also a Church of Christ in the village.

The Fred Meijer Heartland Trail runs through parallel to Depot Street in McBride, giving residents and visitors opportunities for walking and biking. The village is also home to the Robert Davis Memorial Park, which includes ballfields, a campground, playground equipment, a pavilion, shuffleboard, and a trail. The village also uses the park for local events, such as Easter egg hunts or family movie showings in the park.

In 2016, McBride started an annual tractor show. The event includes arts and crafts, a raffle, homemade ice cream, and, of course, lots of different tractors.

TOP: The Hog Town Tavern in Melvin sponsors the annual Hog Town Run

Born in Melvin, Frank D. Beadle was a major player in Michigan politics in the 1950s, eventually serving as the majority leader of the Michigan Senate.[19] He was also a decorated World War I veteran, having served in the Marines.[20]

Melvin

History of Melvin

IN 1862, MELVIN SAW THE CONSTRUCTION of its first building, a saloon.[3] The first post office in Melvin went into operation in 1874 with Charles Dewey as its postmaster.[4] Dewey was a prominent man in the growing village, and he also opened a general store in the village, which he owned for over fifteen years.[5]

By the mid- to late-1880s, the village had grown to include a sawmill, a grist mill, two general stores, two blacksmiths, a cabinetmaker, two carpenters, a shoemaker, a cattle dealer, a physician, and a hotel.[6] By this time, it also was a station on the Port Huron and Northwestern Railway.[7]

Shortly after the start of the twentieth century, Melvin had a residential population of approximately 250 people.[8] The village had added a second hotel, two livery stables, a wagonmaker, a dressmaker, a drugstore, a grocery, a bicycle repair person, and a hardware store.[9] There was also a money-order office, a bank, three different churches, and a cemetery.[10]

As with many towns that had an early interest in lumber, once the forests were felled, Melvin turned to agriculture. Farming became more prevalent in the area, and Melvin farmers produced hay, livestock feed, and cider.[11] There was also a creamery.[12]

The Annual Hog Town Run

Melvin may be a small community, but it is making a big difference in the world. Each summer, the Melvin "Hog Town" Tavern hosts the annual Hog Town Run. The event, which brings in motorcyclists from across the state, is a fundraiser for United Hospice Service at the hospital in nearby Marlette.[13]

The motorcycle run starts in Melvin at the local park, and registration for the event includes a raffle ticket, participation in the run, bike games, and food.[14] For the run itself, motorcyclists ride to the Hospice Residence at Marlette Regional Hospital.[15] Once at the Hospice Residence, riders participate in the "blessing of the bikes."[16]

The event, which has been running for more than ten years, attracts hundreds of motorcyclists and has brought in well over $100,000 for the Hospice Residence.[17] All proceeds from the event go to the residence and are used to support hospice patients and their families.[18]

Melvin Today

Melvin is a part of the local motorcycle community, and not just once a year for the annual Hog Town Run. It's not unusual to see a line of motorcycles at the Hog Town Tavern in the mornings, particularly on the weekend. When the weather is nice, residents of the village and visitors alike can often be seen outside, talking with their friends and neighbors.

In addition to the tavern, Melvin is home to a party store, a post office, a Baptist church, a United Methodist church, and the Speaker Township Fire Department. The Melvin Village Park has a basketball court, playground equipment, a pavilion, and bathrooms. The park sometimes hosts outdoor events such as concerts.

If you're a motorcyclist, Melvin should be on your radar, as it has the unofficial nickname of "Hog Town" and hosts the "Hog Town Run" followed by a "blessing of the bikes" each year.

Population: 394[1]   Incorporated: 1902[2]

INSETS L to R: Part of the Mesick Consolidated Schools campus
• This building houses the village offices and a village garage •
Looking east down West Mesick Avenue • A ballfield in town

The Hodenpyl Dam is still an active generating station, and the lake it produced is a popular fishing locale. More than a dozen fish from the lake have qualified for Michigan's master angler list, including a 22-pound, 6-ounce northern pike caught back in 1995.[21]

TOP: This building, located on North Eugene Street, holds the Mesick Public Library

Mesick

The Mushroom Capital of the United States

MESICK IS KNOWN as the mushroom capital of the United States, and for good reason. Every May since 1959, hundreds of people have come to Mesick to join in the celebrations at their annual Mushroom Festival.[3] The festival, which is hosted by the local Lions Club and takes place Mother's Day weekend, includes a flea market, a carnival, arts and crafts, a pastie sale, a parade, games, music, food, dancing, and other events for the whole family.[4] Through it all, there is a mushroom contest to see who can find the most mushrooms, generally morels. People who want to participate in the contest—mushroomers, as they call them—can buy mushroom picking kits right at the festival office and then head out into the forested area around the village to see what they can find.[5]

The History of Mesick

The community at Mesick started from a former homesteading plot of 160 acres.[6] It received its first post office in the early 1880s. Henry N. Brooks served as Mesick's first postmaster.[7]

The village of Mesick was first platted in 1890 by Howard Mesick, a sawmill owner after whom the village is named.[8] Mesick also founded the village in the same year.[9] The village was incorporated in 1902, and the first village election was held in March of that year.[10] R. M. Harry was elected as the first village president.[11]

Within a year of the time Mesick had been incorporated, it had grown to a settlement of over 500 people.[12] Its population was enough that it was able to support a variety of local businesses, a library, and four different churches.[13]

Sherman's Loss, Mesick's Gain

Problems at a nearby settlement helped Mesick. There was an issue with bonds in nearby Sherman and the result was that a planned railroad connection at Sherman was never built.[14] This resulted in the growth of Mesick as a trading town, as most of the rail business that would have been done at Sherman was carried out in Mesick instead.[15] This also created a division of businesses between two settlements rather than concentrating them all at one location.[16]

Mesick continued to thrive through the early 1920s. It had its own newspaper, a bank, a carpet weaver, a restaurant, a bookstore, and a jeweler, among others.[17] Despite the presence of the railroad and the steady rise of the automobile, the village also was still able to support a daily stagecoach line.[18] Even during the Great Depression, the town still saw some positive changes, such as the construction of the Hodenpyl Hydroelectric Dam, which created a new lake to the southwest of the village.[19] The lake brought new business to the area from lake sports and tourism.[20]

Mesick Today

Mesick bills itself as a "small town, with a big heart," and welcomes visitors to town. In addition to the Mushroom Festival and the Blessing of the Jeeps, Mesick hosts a number of community events each year, including movie nights and a Halloween Extravaganza. But even when there isn't a community-wide event taking place, there is a variety of activities available in the Mesick area. There are two campgrounds to the west of town, just across where the Manistee River flows into Hodenpyl Dam Lake, and the Huron-Manistee National Forests are located about a mile south of the village. To the east of the village is a golf course, and there is also a village park in Mesick itself.

Businesses in Mesick include two motels, two bars, a pharmacy, a coffee stand, a hair salon, a dollar store, a car wash, a gas station, a U-Haul rental center, an insurance company, two markets, and a few businesses specializing in auto service. Some of the businesses have embraced Mesick's reputation as the mushroom capital of the United States, such as the Mushroom Sports Bar and Grill and the Mushroom Cap Motel.

Services in the town include a library, a fire and ambulance station, a bank, and a post office. A second fire station, belonging to Springville Township, is located just east of town. The Floyd M. Jewett Elementary School, part of the Mesick Consolidated School District, is located in the village. In addition, there is a United Methodist church, a Free Methodist church, and a Bible Believers church.

Each year on the Saturday before Mother's Day, the village of Mesick celebrates its annual Jeep Blessing at the start of the off-road season.[22] The blessing is for the safety of those participating in off-road events and also for the well-being of the community more generally.[23] More than 1,000 Jeeps typically attend the event.[24]

Population: 182[1]   **Incorporated:** 1945[2]

INSETS L to R: The park in Michiana is named in honor of Forest McCance, who was a long-time village worker • This sign is a hand-painted map of the village • Michiana lies on the southeastern shore of Lake Michigan, near the border with Indiana • Forest McCance park includes tennis courts and playground equipment

Many of the street names in the village have been named to honor American Indians, who were, of course, the first true residents of the area.[18]

TOP: This sign, near the village offices, welcomes visitors to the village

Michiana

History of Michiana

MICHIANA IS A RESORT COMMUNITY on the southeast side of Lake Michigan, near the Indiana-Michigan border. The land that Michiana now sits on used to be difficult to access due to its marshy nature, which resulted in the community being one of the more recent resort communities to develop in its area of the state.[3]

The original Michiana area was located in both Michigan and Indiana and was given the name Michigan Shores or Michiana Shores.[4] Because the area had the same developer in both states, the Long Beach Development Company, the community largely thought of itself as one.[5] When a realtor began selling cottages in the area at an alarmingly fast rate, the community association decided to incorporate as a village to retain more control over the land use.[6]

As the community had land in two different states, the area was essentially split in the eyes of the two state governments, and the area on the Michigan side of the state line incorporated as a village prior to the Indiana community's official recognition.[7] The people in the village, however, did not like the idea of being separate from their neighbors in Indiana, and so they chose to name their community by combining the words *Michigan* and *Indiana* and settled on the name Michiana.[8]

The Women's Club and the Village Community Center

When the village began, village business was run out of Rita and Leroy Cole's house, and village meetings were sometimes held at the Cohen family house.[9] Right away, residents realized they needed something more permanent and autonomous. The Women's Club began to raise money to fund the construction of a community center.[10] During the building process, the Women's Club and the village entered into a rental agreement for the building, with the Women's Club agreeing to lease the main space of the building to the village for the cost of $1 per year.[11]

The Michiana Signal Oak

One early landmark in the community was a tree residents referred to as the Signal Oak. The oak was located at the corner of Powhatan Drive and Michiana Drive and was used by early surveyors to mark the boundary between Michigan and Indiana.[12] When the Long Beach Development Company began developing the area, they built an amphitheater around the oak and brought prospective buyers there for talk and entertainment.[13] Later still, the site was used by the Michiana Community Association for meetings.[14]

Michiana Today

Today, Michiana is a quiet residential and resort town along Lake Michigan near the border with Indiana. Many of Chicago's more prominent and well-known families come to the village in the summer months, but there are also a number of year-long residents. There are no places available in the village for commercial or industrial development, and that is exactly as planned.[15] The development is strictly residential. Indeed, one of the two parts of the village's mission statement is to "discourage industry from ever entering the village."

Michiana does have some public beach space, but there is no parking for the public, meaning that there are rarely public beachgoers there.[16] Because of the relative lack of streetlights near the beaches, they are said to be excellent places for stargazing.[17]

Michiana does provide services for residents in the village. There is the village community center, a police force, and fire protection services. The public works department handles a variety of public service tasks in the village, including general maintenance, landscaping, snow removal, and road maintenance.

Some residents of Michiana refer to locations around the village based on the old bus stations that used to exist in the town.[19] For instance, someone might say they live by "stop forty."

Population: 271[1]   **Unincorporated**

INSETS L to R: This sign and display of colorful bikes welcomes visitors to the village • This organ is on display in the Dompierre House • The Dompierre House, built in the 1800s, is now part of the Michigamme Historical Museum • Some of the older buildings in the village

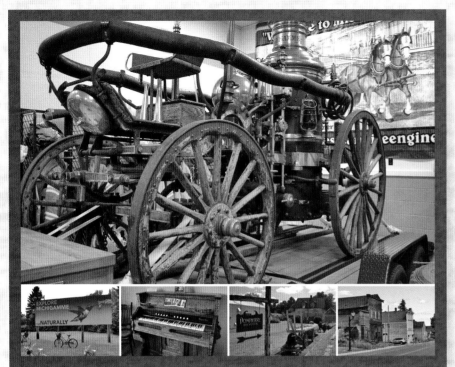

TOP: This steam fire engine was used in the village in the early 1900s

The Michigamme Mine is part of the Marquette Iron Range. The mine is no longer open, but in the days it was, workers mined minerals such as iron ore and some quartz.[35]

Michigamme

Michigamme's 1900 American Metropolitan Steam Fire Engine

SHORTLY AFTER THE START OF THE TWENTIETH CENTURY, the village purchased a 1900 American Metropolitan steam fire engine.[2] At the time, the steamer was cutting edge technology.[3] The steamer arrived by train and, brand new, cost the village $3,500.[4] When the village's volunteer fire department began using the steam engine, it was pulled behind a team of horses, though they were replaced with a Ford Model AA in the late 1920s.[5] The steam engine was used into the 1950s.[6]

It then sat idle for a time, then in 1962, the township sold the engine to a collector for $1,000.[7] For many years, the community at Michigamme thought the engine lost, though members of the fire department tried to locate it.[8] Finally, in 2000, the community found the location of the engine, but when the engine went up for auction four years later, the citizens of Michigamme were outbid.[9]

Luck finally graced the village in 2007 when the engine went up for bid on eBay, and when there were no bids, the owner agreed to sell the steam engine to the village.[10] The township lent the village the $150,000 needed to buy the engine, and the village has started a massive fundraising campaign.

The steamer is believed to be the only steam engine of its kind left in the world—and what's more, the steamer is believed to be operable even though it has not needed to be restored.[11] Currently, the engine is housed in the fire hall, though the village plans to build a special building to house and display the engine to the public.[12]

History of Michigamme

The village of Michigamme can trace its roots back to the surveyor Jacob Houghton's discovery of iron ore nearby in 1872.[13] The deposit, which was first called Mt. Shasta before coming to be called the Michigamme Mine, played a sizeable role in the village's early history. The first building, built alongside Lake Michigamme, was a log cabin for the engineers of the Michigamme Mining Company, and it was the company that platted the town the same year the mine was found.[14]

Because of the availability of work in the area, the settlement grew quickly. Workers and even entire families came to the settlement in covered wagons, and a full community began to form.[15] In less than a year, the village gained a sawmill and a post office and became officially incorporated.[16] However, a few problems made the town's early development uneven and unpredictable. In the summer of 1873, a forest fire destroyed all but four or five buildings in the village.[17] By September most of the destroyed buildings had been rebuilt, but in October, the village was hit with a financial scare that resulted in the mine's workforce being reduced from approximately 300 workers to fewer than 20.[18]

The village refused to give up, even after the recession in the early- and mid-1880s. Other mines were opened in the area, and by 1903, Michigamme had approximately 1,000 residents, two railway depots, a sawmill, a bank, a school, and three churches, including a Swedish Lutheran church.[19] Other businesses include a watchmaker, a confectioner, a road commissioner, a hotel, a milliner, and more than one saloon.[20]

The Dompierre House

Behind the historical museum in Michigamme is the Dompierre House, a log house from the late 1800s that was originally owned by the Michigamme Mining Company.[21] The house passed from the mining company to the Beauvais family, and it is said that Napoleon Beauvais Jr. killed his stepmother in the house.[22] Eusebe Dompierre eventually bought the house some years later, paying $200.[23] He and his family lived in the house for some time, and in 1914, his granddaughter Della was born in the house.[24] Eventually, though, the house was abandoned and fell into disrepair, until in 2001, when it was moved to the property of the Michigamme Historical Museum.[25] It took nearly three years to restore the cabin, and Della, who was born in the house and still lived in Michigamme, lived to see the restoration completed.[26] The house is now a museum of its own and is open to the public in the summer months.

Moose in Michigamme

Though moose are native to Michigan's Upper Peninsula, development in the early twentieth century wiped out the population.[27] In the 1960s, however, a biologist with the Department of Natural Resources determined that the circumstances had shifted enough to reintroduce moose to Michigan's Upper Peninsula.[28] It took twenty years, but in 1985, moose from a park in Ontario were captured and flown to Michigan—more specifically, to Michigamme.[29] A second moose lift, Moose Lift II, was completed two years later.[30] All in all, the moose drops, as they are called in Michigamme, reintroduced 59 moose to the area, and even today, it's not uncommon to see moose in the area.[31]

Michigamme Today

Today, the community is friendly and welcoming. Resident Mike Hosey recalled a restaurant in the town that, when a breakfast order came in, would send a worker down the street to buy the eggs fresh.[32] And now, he says, the general feel of life in the village is the same, even though years have passed and no one needs to run down the street to buy eggs to serve a restaurant order.[33]

In addition to the museum and Dompierre House, the village itself has a market, an inn, a gift shop, an art gallery, and cabins for rent on the lake. There is a post office, a township hall, and a fire department.

The name Michigamme comes from an old Ojibwe term used to reference the area that is now Michigan.[34]
Some of the scenes in the movie *Anatomy of a Murder*, starring Jimmy Stewart, were filmed in Michigamme.

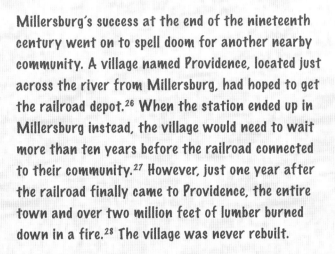

Population: 206[1]   **Incorporated:** 1901[2]

INSETS L to R: This pavilion area is along the North Eastern State Trail • Millersburg Historic Park and Trailhead • This depot, built in 1917, was in use until 1980 • Along the North Eastern State Trail

Millersburg's success at the end of the nineteenth century went on to spell doom for another nearby community. A village named Providence, located just across the river from Millersburg, had hoped to get the railroad depot.[26] When the station ended up in Millersburg instead, the village would need to wait more than ten years before the railroad connected to their community.[27] However, just one year after the railroad finally came to Providence, the entire town and over two million feet of lumber burned down in a fire.[28] The village was never rebuilt.

The fire station in Millersburg has an old fire steam engine on display in a special case out front.

TOP: This corner area has been transformed into a small park

Millersburg

History of Millersburg

THREE EVENTS WITHIN TWO SHORT YEARS near the turn of the twentieth century can be said to have spurred the start of the village of Millersburg. First, C. R. Miller came to the area in 1897 and surveyed, platted, and founded the village.[3] Then, in 1899, men by the names of Gardner and Peterman came to the area and built a sawmill and, in the same year, the Detroit & Mackinac Railway came to Millersburg, and the first depot was built.[4]

The site was particularly good for a railroad station, as it was in Millersburg that the extended railroad would cross the Ocqueoc River, but it was the sudden boom of the lumber industry in the area that brought people to the area.[5] Within a few years of becoming incorporated, the village had a population of over 800 people.[6]

Lumber was not the only business interest in Millersburg, however. The village was also involved in the mining and the railroad shipping industries.[7] Shipping was primarily accomplished through the railroad, but the village was also built up right alongside the Ocqueoc River, which runs through the southeast corner of the town. In addition to lumber, the village also shipped out finished products such as posts and railroad ties, and farm products, including hay.[8]

With the success in business came other growth in the town. In 1903, a second platting was done in the village.[9] By 1907 Millersburg had a bank, three different denominations of churches, its own newspaper, and a school that organized the students into grades.[10] There were a few dozen businesses in the town, including general and dry goods stores, a painter, a baker, a milliner, a restaurant, a lawyer, a hotel, and others.[11]

Not everything in those early years was easy, though, despite businesses success in the town. A fire burned the train depot down in 1914.[12] A new structure, made of concrete blocks rather than wood, was built, but not until 1917.[13] By 1922, the lumber boom in the town had ended, and though there were people still involved in the business, the area's resources could no longer support the same population, with the result that the population had fallen to around 300 people.[14]

The last train to Millersburg came in 1980 and marked the end of the railroad era in the village.[15] For a time the depot sat idle, but it has since been renovated for use by the local historical society.[16]

Home to the Presque Isle County Fair—Again

The first Presque Isle County Fair was held in Millersburg in September of 1901.[17] It was a traditional county fair at the time, focused on farming and all related activities.[18] In 1932 the fair was moved out of Millersburg and found a home in Onaway instead, where it remained for over 50 years.[19] Toward the end of the twentieth century the fair moved again, first to Posen and then to Moltke Township.[20]

Finally, in 2000, the fair returned to its original home in Millersburg, where it has remained ever since.[21] But the fair's return to its original location wasn't the only change to recognize its past. In 2012, the fair board made the decision to make the fair itself feel more like it had in its early days.[22] The changes included removing the carnival rides in favor of "energetic" activities for the whole family, putting the focus back on agriculture, and changing the date so it could be held in September once again.[23]

Millersburg Today

Though the lumber industry has not disappeared from Millersburg, the village has largely remade itself since its early days as a lumber town. Today, business, leisure, and community are on display. The North Eastern State Trail passes through the village, running all the way to Alpena in the southeast and Cheboygan in the northwest. Foot, bike, horse, ski, and snowmobile traffic are all welcome on the trail. The village is also home to Millersburg Historic Park and Trailhead, which contains the depot that was built in 1917 and a pavilion for events and gatherings. Finally, there is a village square with a gazebo, an old fashioned clock, benches, and a sculpture.

Businesses in the town include a gas station and mini-mart, a resale store, a diner, a restaurant, a photography and video business, more than one lumber company, and a conveyor systems manufacturer, among others. Services in the village include a post office, a community center, a fire station, and a library. Churches in the village area include two Baptist churches and a United Methodist church.

Each winter from 1888 to 1914 workers known as "river men" would shepherd the timber harvest along the Ocqueoc River.[24] A series of dams along the river made this journey possible, as the water would gather at the dam then be released all at once, providing the power to continue moving the lumber downstream.[25]

TOP: The City Hall building in Minden City, which is actually a village

Population: 197[1]   **Incorporated:** 1882[2]

INSETS L to R: Horseshoe pits in town • Minden City has its own fire department • This park area includes playground equipment and a pavilion • A view down Main Street

Minden City had its own community band around the end of the nineteenth century.[24] The first conductor of the band was R. A. Puschinsky, and the band was primarily made up of brass players, though there were saxophones, percussion, and a drum major.[25]

Minden City

The Home of the Last Known Michigan Wolverine

MICHIGAN IS KNOWN AS THE WOLVERINE STATE, but for centuries, no wolverines (which prefer colder climates) have actually been spotted in the state.[3] That changed in 2005, when hunters spotted one near Bad Axe, Michigan, about 20 miles from Minden City.[4] Eight years later, that wolverine was found dead in Minden City State Game Area, just five miles southwest from town.[5]

History of Minden City

Despite its name, Minden City is actually a village. It was founded in 1855 when Philip Link named the settlement Minden, after his hometown of Minden, Germany.[6] Other early settlers in the area included Michael Brady and his family as well as Gottlieb Volz and his family.[7]

Volz, who came to Minden in 1857, built a sawmill just north of where the town now sits.[8] In the same year, Norman Wait opened the settlement's first grist mill.[9] This was the only mill in the area, and people would come from miles around to grind their flour at the mill.[10]

The first store in the village was opened by Alfred Gunning in 1859, and three years later, Minden received a post office.[11] William Donner, who had bought Gunning's store around 1861, was selected as the first postmaster.[12] In 1880, a Methodist church was built in the village, the first religious building in Minden.[13] Four years later, a Congregational church was added to the town.[14]

Things began to pick up in the village when the Pere Marquette Railroad opened a station in Minden in August of 1880.[15] Even the huge

Thumb Fire of 1881, which damaged or destroyed much of the village and ravaged much of Michigan's Thumb Region, could only provide a temporary slowdown to the village's growth.[16] The railroad, which provided avenues for travel and commerce in the village, was no doubt a big part of the village's continued growth even when faced with adversity. The trains brought supplies to the village and took away grain and produce, among other village goods, but they were also popular among the everyday citizens of the village and surrounding areas.[17] By 1892, rail service to the village included three trains per day for passenger travel.[18]

The village was incorporated in 1882, and the following year it was renamed to its current Minden City.[19] Martin Diamond was elected as the first village president.[20] Within a few years of being incorporated, the village had its own bank, a jeweler, a dressmaker, a milliner, a drugstore, an auctioneer, a wool mill, a brickyard, a foundry, a grain elevator, a public school, three hotels, and a local newspaper.[21]

The Minden City Tractor Pull

Each summer, the village of Minden City celebrates an annual homecoming as part of its Tractor Pull weekend. The event, put on by the combined efforts of the local Lions Club and fire department, begins with a two-day tractor pull competition but also includes food tents, live music, and a variety of other activities that can vary from year to year, including a mud volleyball tournament, a bicycle rodeo, a 5K, and a parade.[22] The event draws people from all over the area and all proceeds go to help fund projects for the entire community.[23]

Minden City Today

The downtown area of Minden City is, in a sense, actually two smaller downtown areas, which are separated from each other by a few blocks and some houses. The village doesn't feel split, though, and there is a definite sense of connection and camaraderie in the community. There is a community park that contains a variety of activities for residents of the village, including volleyball courts, horseshoe pits, playground equipment, a baseball field, and two separate pavilions.

The community also has a number of local businesses, including an inn, a market, a pizzeria, a meatpacking company, a printing company, a farm supply store, a home décor business, a boutique, a holistic center, a taxidermist, and a funeral home. There is also a grain elevator, a fire department, a post office, and, just outside of the village proper, a Lutheran church.

Fires hit Minden City in 1871 and 1881, both times causing significant amounts of damage. After one fire, a woman recalled eating baked potatoes that had been baked in the ground from the heat of the fire.[26] The Thumb Fire of 1881 had an effect on the rest of the country, too. So much smoke and ash were thrown into the air that the sky appeared yellow on the East Coast, earning it the nicknames "Yellow Tuesday" and "Yellow Day."[27]

TOP: The grain elevator near the edge of town

Population: 342[1]   **Incorporated:** 1906[2]

INSETS L to R: A view down one of the side streets in the village • This Methodist Church dates back to 1882 • The post office in the village is located on West Hakes Street • This sign welcomes visitors to Montgomery, which is sometimes known as "Frogeye"

In Montgomery, Halloween involves more than trick-or-treating. That still happens, but afterward, the village puts on a parade and then has games and a cakewalk for the local children.[24]

Montgomery

What's In a Name?

BEFORE IT WAS NAMED MONTGOMERY by William R. Montgomery, the register of the county, the village went through a few informal names. Some of the earliest residents in the settlement simply called the town "The Station," after the railroad station that prompted its beginning.[3] Others in the town referred to it as Frogeye after all of the ponds and, no doubt, frogs in the area.[4]

However, it was those earliest residents who took on the task of registering the settlement and its platting, and they told the county register the place was called "The Station."[5] The registrar declined to record the plat under that name, saying it wasn't truly a name for a community.[6] At this point, the residents of the village decided on a compromise. They would allow the registrar, a man named William Montgomery, to put his own name on the town, and in return he would record the plat at no expense.[7]

Over time, the name "The Station" has faded from the town's collective identity, but it still embraces the name "Frogeye." Each summer they hold a three-day Frogeye Days festival, which includes a soapbox derby, a bake sale, an auction, children's games, a pony pull, a horseshoe tournament, fireworks, a frog jump, and a variety of other community-based activities designed for the whole family.[8]

History of Montgomery

The land where Montgomery now sits was once considered rather undesirable. Unlike other parts of Michigan, it didn't have access to towering pines. Instead, it consisted of an oak opening—a combination savanna- and forest-like area with only intermittent trees, primarily oaks.[9] There were no plans to settle the area until the Fort Wayne, Jackson, & Saginaw Railroad came to the area, around 1869, and needed a place for a station that would be convenient for a number of farmers.[10] The site was chosen and Montgomery was effectively founded.[11]

With the railroad station, both businesses and families came to the new village, and the settlement developed quickly.[12] A. P. Kellogg was the first person to open a store in the village, and his business sold hardware, implements, and groceries.[13] Shortly after Kellogg's store opened, O. M. Hayward opened a second store, a combination dry goods and grocery, and Joshua Dobbs opened a general goods store as well.[14] 1870 saw the village's first hotel, and the first sawmill opened two years later.[15]

In 1874, Charles L. Ballard became the village's first postmaster.[16] In the same year, a company making window blinds opened in the village, but it closed only two years after opening and the space was taken over by a hardware store.[17]

A Growing Town

Montgomery grew quickly. Within a decade of its founding, the population had climbed to 300 people, who lived and worked in approximately 100 different buildings.[18] There was a hotel, a school, two meat markets, three blacksmith shops, and half a dozen stores.[19] In addition, the village became one of the more-important shipping points in the area, sending off farm products and livestock, including approximately 200,000 bushels of wheat.[20]

The village continued to flourish into the early twentieth century. The railroad in the village had changed to the Lake Shore and Michigan Southern Railway, but other than that, life stayed largely the same, even while the community itself moved into the twentieth century. Montgomery had a weekly newspaper, three churches, and a number of businesses, including a cheese company and a cement block manufacturer.[21]

By the early 1920s, the town had grown to approximately 500 residents, but as the automobile became more prominent in the state and across the country, rail travel diminished in importance.[22] As the railroad fell into decline, so did Montgomery, but it was not destined to be a village that faded away into obscurity.[23]

Montgomery Today

Today, Montgomery is primarily a residential community with over 300 residents. It's a quiet but friendly community where, on a nice day, you're likely to see a good number of people out in the village, either walking or biking on the streets, working in their yards, or enjoying Montgomery Park. The park, which was first established in 1916, has large green spaces, a pavilion, a baseball field, and other community-focused features. There is an American Legion post in Montgomery, which also has both New Beginning Church and a United Methodist church, and both are active in the local community.

Businesses in the town include an animal clinic, a sporting goods store, a restaurant, a tavern, a thrift shop, and a business that helps kids learn how to show livestock. The village also has its own post office.

In 2017, Jerald Keegan from Montgomery set a record at the National Lightweight Horse Pull competition by pulling 4,225 pounds with his two-horse team.[25]

Population: 553[1]   **Incorporated:** 1903[2]

INSETS L to R: This old grain elevator can be found along the railroad tracks • A town park • A view down one of the village's residential streets • The Roxand Township Fire Department

TOP: These railroad tracks run east and west through the village

Michigan author Amy Mayhew published a 2017 supernatural thriller that takes place in mid-Michigan, including in Mulliken.[14]

Mulliken

A Mulliken Tie to Thomas Merton

IN 1967, COLLEGE STUDENT LEILANI BENTLEY was at work on a college paper about Thomas Merton, the famous Trappist monk who was well known for his essays, poetry, and writing about world religions.[3] Still widely read today, Merton is also well known for his famous outreach to other religious leaders, including the Dalai Lama, Martin Luther King Jr., and Thich Nhat Hanh.[4] Bentley wrote Merton for advice, and he was kind enough to send back a long letter, which is now preserved in his collected letters.[5]

Rallying Around the Flag

During the First World War, German-American citizens were viewed with deep suspicion, and those in Michigan were no exception to this. Just 60 miles from Mulliken, the town formerly known as "Berlin, Michigan" changed its name to "Marne" (after the site of several famous battles from World War 1).[6] Elsewhere, German Measles were dubbed "Liberty Measles," and all over the country German-Americans were forced (sometimes at the threat of violence) to kiss the flag or undergo loyalty pledges.[7] One such occurrence happened in Mulliken. According to the *Belding Banner* for April 11, 1917, a man entered a blacksmith's shop and tore down the flag that was hanging there.[8] The blacksmith threw a hammer at the man, killing him.[9] The paper readily supported this: "Certainly there is not a jury that would convict the man for protecting Old Glory."[10]

The History of Mulliken

Theodore E. Potter founded the village of Mulliken in 1888.[11] The first post office opened in the same year, with Albert Lawrence as the first postmaster.[12] The village was named for the contractor who built the railroad through the village.[13] Over its history, it has been home to a hotel (which burned in 1909), a stagecoach stop, a railroad depot, and a number of shops and agricultural pursuits, including an apple dryer. In 1908, the town was also the site of a railroad mishap, when a Pere Marquette train ran into an open switch and derailed, causing the engine to topple into the mud. The engineer was seriously hurt, and nearly a dozen others were injured.

Mulliken Today

The village contains a taxidermy business, a thrift store, an auto repair shop, an auto salvage center, a funeral home, a Masonic temple, a tavern, a restaurant, a bar and grill, a heating and refrigeration company, and a business that produces outdoor furnishings made from recycled material. The railroad tracks still run through the town, and there is a grain elevator right alongside the tracks. Services in the town include a bank, a library, a post office, a township fire department, and a village office. There is also a village park, which includes playground equipment and a pavilion.

North of Mulliken is Cryderman Lake, and the Parker Extension waterway passes west and south of the village.

In August of each year, Mulliken hosts the annual Hot Rods and Harleys motorcycle event, which includes a car and motorcycle show, live music, food and drink, and a variety of bike-related events.[15]

Population: 97[1]   **Unincorporated**

INSETS L to R: Most of the side roads in Nessen City are dirt • This sign welcomes visitors to Nessen City • A view down one of the streets in the community • Looking toward the main intersection in the town

The bell on the Nessen City Schoolhouse originally came from the nearby Griner School and was donated to Nessen City by Roger Griner.[25]

TOP: The old Nessen City Schoolhouse, which recently was extensively renovated, was built in 1892

Nessen City

History of Nessen City

THE COMMUNITY OF NESSEN CITY, which isn't actually a city, was founded in 1889 by John and Edith Nessen, who had come to the area from Manistee.[2] Within their first year of residence at the town, John, a Swede who was also one of the only remaining lumber barons in the area, had opened a store, built a sawmill on Peppermint Creek, and gained the position of postmaster, all of which were firsts for the town.[3]

The Manistee & Northeastern Railroad had a depot in Nessen City, and this connection to the railroad helped make the village a thriving community at the end of the nineteenth century.[4] The town primarily was home to the families of lumber workers, but the village store also attracted farmers from other parts of the township and surrounding area.[5]

Other businesses in the village included a boarding house, a livery stable, a hall, a saloon, and a hostelry, and there was also a schoolhouse and a Catholic church—one of only two in all of Benzie County at the time.[6]

From One Type of Wood to the Next

As the twentieth century dawned, Nessen City was still a thriving albeit small town of fewer than 200 people.[7] Manufacturing was a new industry in the town, and there was a shingle mill, a broom handle manufacturer, and a business that sold both cigars and confectionery products.[8] By 1908, the village had begun to produce a significant amount of farm products as well, particularly potatoes but also butter, eggs, poultry, and various fruits.[9]

Often, as the lumber industry exhausted timber of one type in the area, a new owner would take over a mill, focusing on a different type of lumber.[10] For instance, when the pines in the area had all been cut, the focus shifted to using "rock elm" that would be sent to another location for use in harness making.[11]

Nessen City had come late to the lumber boom in Michigan, and while the mills supplied enough work to support the village, they could not last forever. The mill closed in 1914, and a number of fires in the village in the two decades preceding the mill's closure also took their toll.[12] Of perhaps greater significance, though, was a competing railroad junction only a few miles away from the village.[13] For a brief period, the mill was repurposed as a "pickle station," producing pickles from cucumbers, a fairly common crop in the Upper Midwest.[14] Another fire in the village destroyed the church sometime in either the 1920s or the 1930s, and it was not rebuilt.[15] The population began decreasing in the town, and in 1922, there was a general store, a produce company, a grain elevator, and little else in the way of businesses.[16] The village's post office closed in 1933.[17]

The Nessen City Schoolhouse Renovation

The community at Nessen City today may be smaller than it once was—small enough that some refer to it as a ghost town—but it's not letting go of its past or identity. One recent project in the town has been the restoration of its schoolhouse, which was built in 1892.[18] The local residents who spearheaded the project not only want to keep one of only four original buildings from the town for the next generation, they also want to help keep a piece of history alive.[19] Many of those involved in the project had parents or grandparents who attended the school before it shut down in the 1950s.[20]

After closing as a school, the building was used for a time as a town hall, serving as a place for local events, or even just for organizing a few games of cards among friends.[21] In 1985, however, the one-time school was changed to a storage building, and over the next thirty years it fell into disrepair.[22]

Finally, in 2015, the building received new life. The Nessen City Schoolhouse Renovation Project acquired the building and set to fixing up the building.[23] It received new windows, a new coat of paint, and many other touches of renovation, both big and small. The community rallied around the product, donating much of the money for the materials, all with the goal of making the building once again an integral part of the village.[24]

Nessen City Today

Some people call Nessen City a ghost town, and it certainly is tiny and may not even show up on some GPS systems, but it's still its own community—and also a census designated place. Some communities might give up once they get so small, but there are signs in Nessen City that the people here are not ready to do so. There is a sign painted red, white, and blue welcoming visitors to the town, and the refurbished schoolhouse gleams with a fresh coat of paint and small red, white, and blue decorations over two of the entranceways. The aura of new community-life seems to spread out from the school, with carefully cropped grass and a few newer planted trees.

Early in the twentieth century, Nessen City had its own civic band, which had around a dozen musicians.[26]

Population: 290[1]   **Incorporated:** 1887[2]

INSETS L to R: The village of Oakley is surrounded by farmland,
much of which produces corn and soybeans • The view down
Main Street • The park in Oakley • The railroad tracks run alongside this grain elevator

The author of this book has family that came from
Oakley, and one of her great-grandfathers, Omer
Hemond, is buried in the cemetery there.

TOP: One of the residential streets in the village

Oakley

History of Oakley

BEFORE IT WAS GIVEN ITS CURRENT NAME, the village of
Oakley was known as Mickleville, after Philip Mickle, who opened a tavern in the area in 1842.[3] The land surrounding where the village now sits
was covered in trees, including walnut, oak, beech, ash, and elm.[4] There
were also a number of maples in the area, making maple sugar popular.[5]

In 1856, 14 years after coming to the area, Mickle was appointed
as the first postmaster of Mickleville.[6] Four years later, the post office
was moved to Havana, a small settlement a few miles to the northeast.[7]
The post office was renamed Havana at that time, but in 1860, it was
moved back and this time given the name Oakley.[8]

Mickleville was also home to the only railroad station in the area.
The Jackson, Lansing & Saginaw Railroad came to the town in 1867

and was used, among other things, to ship lumber and farm products,
including wheat, corn, and oats.[9] Andrew Huggins officially platted and
recorded the village in 1868, one year after the railroad came to the
community.[10] At this time, the name of the settlement officially switched
to Oakley.[11]

Business in the village grew through the end of the nineteenth
century, and for a period of a few decades the village maintained a
population of somewhere between 200 and 300 people.[12] Businesses in
Oakley over that time included general stores, blacksmiths, a brickmak-
er, a carpet weaver, a wood engraver, stone crushers, a confectionery, a
mason, and manufactories for staves and hoops.[13]

The Beginnings of a Nondenominational Church

The Reverend Horatio Allen Baker visited the village in the late 1870s.[14] He had spent nearly 30 years preaching in Baptist churches around mid-Michigan and, for a period of four years, in New York State.[15] As part of his work, he had even helped found both a congregation and a church in Lansing.[16] In 1876, however, growing frustrated with the sectarian organization of the Christian religion and believing it actually worked against God's goals, he retired from the ministry.[17]

On his visit to Oakley, some of the villagers asked if Baker would preach to their community.[18] He was hesitant to agree to their request, explaining his views on denominations within Christianity.[19] He would, he said, only stay to preach if the church that grew from that choice would be a nondenominational one, welcoming all Christians.[20] Those in Oakley agreed, and a short time later, Baker moved to the village, where he first preached to the people in a space above a saloon in the village.[21] Finally, in 1879, a building was built for the congregation.[22]

The spirit of Baker's work is still present in Oakley today, and can be seen in the nondenominational Oakley Community Church. The Community Church values accessibility and invites anyone to participate in their services, which draw on a wide variety of Christian styles, from Southern to contemporary to classic.[23]

Oakley Today

While the population of the village of Oakley is about the same size as it was 100 years ago, other things in the village have changed. The primary industry in and around the village today is agriculture, particularly soybeans, corn, and wheat. Businesses in the village include a gas station, a tavern, a bar, a family diner, a restaurant, a thrift store, a beauty shop, and a party store, among others. Services in the town include a post office and a village hall. There is also a Catholic church and a Catholic cemetery.

For those who prefer the outdoors, the Shiawassee River passes through the southeast corner of the village, and Mickles Creek is to the south of the town while Deer Creek is to the north. In addition, the village also has a park.

The name Oakley was chosen in honor of one of the early settlers' uncles who was a judge in New York State.[24]

TOP: This building looks like a church building but is actually the old Omer Masonic Hall

Population: 313[1] **Incorporated:** 1903[2]

INSETS L to R: A park in the village • A view of the Rifle River in Omer • A brick structure in the village • A sign welcoming guests to the Riverbend Campground in Omer

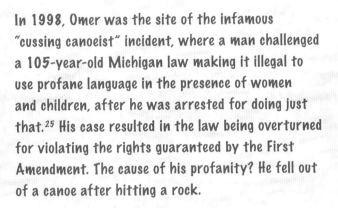

In 1998, Omer was the site of the infamous "cussing canoeist" incident, where a man challenged a 105-year-old Michigan law making it illegal to use profane language in the presence of women and children, after he was arrested for doing just that.[25] His case resulted in the law being overturned for violating the rights guaranteed by the First Amendment. The cause of his profanity? He fell out of a canoe after hitting a rock.

Omer is the second-smallest city in Michigan, behind only Lake Angelus.

Omer

History of Omer

THE CITY OF OMER WAS FOUNDED IN 1866 when George L. Gorie and George Carscallen built a sawmill in the area.[3] Together, the two men ran a sizeable lumber business—the sawmill could process 25,000 feet of lumber per day—and they were also involved in grinding flour.[4] Carscallen suggested the name of Homer for the settlement, but they called it Rifle River Mills instead, as the mill was built on Rifle River.[5] When the first post office opened in 1872, the postmaster, Carscallen, once again suggested the name Homer but learned there was already a post office of that name in Michigan.[6] He solved this problem by removing the *H* and simply calling it Omer.[7]

The same year the post office opened, the town was officially platted as a part of Bay County.[8] Eleven years later, however, Omer was one of the towns that made up the newly organized Arenac County.[9]

The Only Woman in Town

There were very few women in the settlement during its early days as a lumber town. When Carscallen was married in 1877 to a woman named Ann from Scotland, his wife moved to Omer, and for a period of approximately two years, she was the only woman who resided in the community.[10] Some of the other early women in Omer also came from Scotland with the intention to marry businessmen in the village as well.[11]

By the early 1880s, Omer had grown to include more families, with the result that there were two general stores, a hardware store, a drugstore, a schoolhouse, and an assortment of other everyday shops.[12] The first church building was not built until closer to the turn of the century, and so early Methodist church services were held in the school instead.[13]

With the town's saw and grist mills, the population grew to be approximately 600.[14] Even as the lumber industry slowed, Omer continued to thrive due to the success of the farmland that sprang up where trees had once been, and that in turn allowed for the continued success and increased diversity of town businesses. By 1908, the city had businesses that included a cheese manufacturer, a restaurant, a veterinarian, a photographer, two saloons, and more than half a dozen carpenters.[15] Fifteen years later, there would also be a roller rink, a creamery, an elevator, a pool hall, and two stock dealers.[16]

A Few Decades of Struggle

Not everything was easy for the community, however. Between 1897 and 1916, Omer experienced a tornado that took a house away, a forest fire, two village fires, including one that nearly destroyed the entire village in 1914, and a flood that destroyed its dam.[17]

Haunted Omer: The Witchy Wolves

There is an old Ojibwe legend in the Omer area that says a spirit that is half-wolf and half-dog protects and defends the graves of Ojibwe warriors by attacking anyone who disturbs them.[18] The legend has been associated with the Omer Plains, an area near the city of Omer that is heavily forested and that has an old graveyard.[19]

The legend was maintained over the years through informal retellings, such as from parent to child, but particularly through stories told by teenagers in the area.[20] Eventually, the story gained enough traction that a paranormal group came to Omer to investigate.[21] The group,

a Michigan-based paranormal investigation team and an entertainment group, came to Omer in 2009 and, as part of their investigation, they explored the area and talked with local residents, many of whom reported their own strange encounters in the area.[22]

Whether you believe the story or not, it has attached itself to Omer, and in many ways the community has decided to embrace that fact. Most residents in the area have an opinion on the story, and the tale has also inspired a race that takes place in the Omer Plains each year.[23]

Omer Today

The city of Omer is where US-23 crosses the Rifle River, and this meeting of river and road is nearly in the exact center of the city. The river in particular, though, helps define the community. There are two campgrounds in Omer, as well as a canoe and kayak rental business. Each year in the spring, people come to the river from all over for sucker season, which takes place in March and April.

There are a variety of community services located or available in Omer, including a library, a city hall, a county road commission, a fire department, a post office, and a township hall. There is also a Masonic Hall, which was built in 1890 to serve as a courthouse then sold to the Grand Lodge of Free and Accepted Masons three years later.[24]

Businesses in the town include two markets, a café, an early childhood center, a party rentals business, an auto repair shop, an ice cream parlor, a refrigeration and heating company, and a company that specializes in motor repair.

In 2002, both Omer and Arenac Township held an election to decide whether six city residents could secede from the city and join Arenac Township instead, as they did not want to pay the city water tax.[26] Though the measure did not pass in the city, there were enough votes in favor from the township, with the result that the residents in question were no longer part of Omer.[27]

Population: 411[1]   **Incorporated:** 1891[2]

INSETS L to R: A souvenir store in Onekama, across from the lake •
A propeller is used as a historic decoration near the lake • A view
along Main Street in the village • The public beach area along
Portage Lake includes playground equipment

Due to non-locals frequently mispronouncing the village name as "one comma," the locals will sometimes refer to Onekama as "1."[29] You can even find this mispronounced spelling on their community Facebook page! The correct pronunciation is "Oh-NECK-uh-ma."

TOP: Onekama sits on Portage Lake, which today connects to Lake Michigan

Onekama

History of Onekama

WHEN SURVEYORS FIRST CAME to the area where Onekama now sits in the early- to mid-1800s, they had little that was positive to say about the area.[3] An early surveyor remarked, "Little can be said in favor of this township. It is almost entirely composed of high and steep hills, unfit for the purposes of cultivation. They will scarcely answer for sheep farms."[4]

In a way, the surveyor was right—though there were trees for logging, the land was not ideal when it came to the agricultural pursuits that usually drew in settlers. On the other hand, however, the surveyor overlooked the township and the town's greatest asset: the water.

An early settler in the Onekama area was Joseph Stronach, who built a sawmill and a dam in 1840 at Portage Stream, the natural outlet

of water from Portage Lake.[5] A village built up around the mill and the lumber industry in the area, taking the name Onekama, as their first choice of a name, Portage, was already taken.[6] It is unclear where the name Onekama comes from, but two prevailing theories both relate to Portage Lake. One theory says that it was named based on the Ojibwe word for *portage*, which is *onigam*.[7] The second theory says it was named after the Ojibwe word for *arm*, which is *onikama*, as Portage Lake is an arm of Lake Michigan.[8]

The first postmaster of the town was Augustine W. Farr.[9] Farr was a prominent resident of the town and also played a role in making the area a tourist destination.[10] He discovered that a spring near his house contained traces of minerals and set to developing a mineral spring in

Onekama to attract people to the spring's healing waters.[11] At the time, some believed the spring at Onekama would grow to be one of the most famous springs anywhere.[12] This obviously did not come to pass, but for a time there was a resort near the spring and people would come from across both the state and Lake Michigan to visit the spring.[13] The main hotel at the resort burned down in 1892, and in 1916, Farr's nephew gave the land with the springs to Onekama Township.[14, 15] You can visit the springs at Glen Park, which is just off of 4th Avenue in Onekama.

Of course, in the end the true tourist draw of Onekama and its surrounding area was the presence of the two lakes, with Portage Lake directly to the village's west and Lake Michigan just beyond that. Even today, these lakes create the main draw for the area, bringing a large number of tourists, particularly in the summer, each year.[16]

Connecting Portage Lake and Lake Michigan

Before European settlers came to Michigan, Portage Lake and Lake Michigan were only connected by a small stream.[17] In the 1860s, a mill owner in the area decided to dam the creek in order to provide the water necessary to power his lumber mill.[18] This caused the water level of the lake to rise by about six feet as well.[19] This flooded the area directly around the lake each year, and the people whose lands were flooded eventually went to court in an attempt to end the flooding.[20] They won their case, but only on paper—the mill continued as it had before and the flooding remained a problem.[21]

At this point those affected decided to take the matter into their own hands. They found a place about one mile south of the dam and dug a four-foot-wide ditch from Portage Lake to Lake Michigan, a distance of about one thousand feet.[22] But this, too, had unintended consequences, and when the water in the lake breached the coffer dam on Portage Lake, the sudden influx of water turned the small ditch into 500-foot wide channel.[23] The water continued to flow until the water level in the two lakes equalized one another, draining Portage Lake of at least four feet of water.[24] To this day, this accidental channel connects Portage Lake with Lake Michigan, though the creek connecting the two no longer exists.[25]

Onekama Today

Onekama remains a thriving tourist town today, though the town still maintains a strong identity of its own. One resident who takes on the role of both visitor and resident is Jane Mueller, who has spent part of the last eighteen years in Onekama and who also owns a business in the town. "What I like is the people, the lake, the boats, and being on the water," she says when asked about what draws her to Onekama.[26]

The summer is the tourist season, and from Memorial Day to Labor Day, especially, the town is full of tourists and "cottagers," and the town's unofficial population can swell to between 2,000 and 3,000 people.[27] In addition to the opportunities afforded by both Portage Lake and Lake Michigan, the village has a number of shops and stores, including souvenir shops, restaurants and cafés, an ice cream parlor, a mini-mart, and a gas station. There are several places to stay in the town and on the lake, including motels and multiple places with cottages.

During the winter, the town is much quieter, as that time of year tends to see more residents than visitors in the town. Some of the businesses shut down or reduce their hours.[28]

For over 40 years, the village of Onekama has been celebrating Onekama Days. The 2017 iteration of this event started Thursday evening with bingo and ended Monday with an outdoor concert. In between, festivalgoers enjoyed arts and crafts, a parade, a scavenger hunt, a demo derby, a car show, a dance party, and other family-friendly events.

TOP: This picnic area is near the public beach swimming area on Otter Lake

Population: 389[1]   **Incorporated:** 1883[2]

INSETS L to R: The Otter Lake Fire Department • Painted murals decorate the fronts of some of the buildings along Detroit Street • A large brick building in town still bears a painted sign for its former business • Some of the buildings in town have recently undergone renovations, including this one on Detroit Street

In the mid-1880s, the forests around Otter Lake were said to produce some of the highest-quality pine in all of Michigan.[31]

Otter Lake

History of Otter Lake

ONE OF THE FIRST EUROPEANS IN THE AREA of Otter Lake was Andrew McArthur, who had come to the lake in 1838 in order to hunt.[3] He named the lake Otter Lake because of a number of otters he'd seen in it.[4] However, it would still be some time before a true settlement would grow up in the area.

The land that now holds the village of Otter Lake was originally part of a 6,000-acre purchase made by Gerritt Smith.[5] Sometime later the land was sold to C. B. Benson, who was from New York and who started a lumber company called Page & Benson.[6] Company operations started in late 1871, and a sawmill opened the following summer.[7]

By 1873, the village of Otter Lake was on the Flint River Railroad, and though the settlement at that time was at the very end of the line, it was also where the railroad met with the Detroit & Bay City Railway.[8] The presence of the railroad was a boon not only for the lumber company, but also for the new settlement, and sometime in 1873 or 1874, Page & Benson lumber company unofficially platted the village.[9]

The original platting of the village organized the village into 25 blocks, with 100-foot-wide, compass-oriented streets.[10] The original lots were each an area of 100 square feet, and there were eight lots per block.[11] When the lots went up for sale, the village already had a sawmill, a boarding house, and shops, and many of the company's workers already had houses as well.[12]

Page & Benson found success in Otter Lake. By the mid-1870s, they still owned over 5,000 acres of land that had yet to be cleared for the mills and were also able to employ 250 workers.[13] With their success, the owners of the lumber company made a number of changes in the village. They performed an official plat of the village and had that plat recorded in 1874.[14] They also rebuilt the sawmill, making it two stories high rather than one, and started work on a village school.[15]

Despite its success, Page & Benson began to remove its interests from Otter Lake in the late 1870s and early 1880s, first selling the company store in 1876 and then the mill in 1880.[16] All remaining company interests in the town were sold to S. O. Sherman, the manager in the area.[17] A new lumber mill had been opened in the village the previous year by a man named W. C. Cummings, and he eventually acquired the Page & Benson sawmill and converted it to a planing mill.[18]

Larger changes were coming to the village, though. As the available timber declined and the automobile rose in prominence, train stations all over Michigan began to close, and Otter Lake was no exception. The first railroad ended service to Otter Lake in 1933, and the second line shut down as well in the 1970s.[19]

Otter Lake Medical and Surgical Sanitarium

In the early 1900s, Otter Lake was home to a sanitarium, which, despite its name, was actually a home for children who had lost their fathers in warfare.[20] The sanitarium, which was run by the American Legion, had the goal of giving children something as much like a home as possible.[21] There was a "supervising mother" who prepared food for the children based on health needs and a doctor who looked after the children's health.[22, 23] The program was a success, and a second center was built in Kansas.[24] The sanitarium, which would go on to hold over 500 children, continued to operate until the 1970s.

Otter Lake's First Church

In the 1880s, there was no religious building in which the village residents could worship, and so instead they met in the dining hall of the village's boarding house each week.[25] This situation was not ideal for the residents of Otter Lake, and so they decided to build a church.[26] The town held three denominations of Christians at that time—Presbyterian, Baptist, and Episcopal—and since it was not practical for three churches to be built, the community held a meeting at which they decided to vote on which denomination they would affiliate with, with the majority of votes carrying the impromptu election.[27] The vote was close, and in the end, the Episcopalians defeated the Baptists by a margin of only one vote.[28] In consideration for the large number of Baptists in the town, it was decided to call the new church, which was constructed in 1885, St. John the Baptist.[29]

Otter Lake Today

Otter Lake may be a small body of water, but it is still enough to be a point of interest for tourists. The village today takes advantage of this and has a waterside campground that includes a park, a small beach, basketball courts, two pavilions, and a boat launch. The lake is clean, and on an average summer day you can see people out swimming, boating, or fishing.

The village itself is home to a number of businesses and organizations. There is a literary club, a historical society, a car club, a VFW, an American Legion Post, and a club responsible for running the village's annual Otter Lake Days event.[30]

Otter Lake is home to three churches: the St. John the Baptist Episcopal Church, the Otter Lake Church of the Nazarene, and the Otter Lake Seventh Day Adventist Church. Other services in the village include a post office, a library, an elementary school, and a fire station.

For a small lake (just 68 acres), Otter Lake is quite deep, reaching more than 100 feet at its deepest point.

TOP: The view down Main Street, toward the village water tower

Population: 241[1]   **Incorporated:** 1905[2]

INSETS L to R: This community building serves both the village of Owendale and Brookfield Township more broadly • Owendale is home to a grain elevator and a few wind turbines • One of the older buildings in the village • The United Methodist Church in Owendale

There are two barns in Owendale that are part of the Thumb Quilt Trail, which features barns that are adorned with quilt "block" patterns on them. First is the Bernhardt Barn, which has a quilt block called Old Maid's Puzzle Block.[18] The second is the Murphy Barn, which has a quilt block called Propeller Pinwheel.[19]

Owendale

History of Owendale

THE VILLAGE OF OWENDALE is named for a pair of cousins, John G. and John S. Owen.[3] Together, they came to where Owendale now is and purchased land in an area known as the Columbia Swamp.[4] The following year they opened a sawmill.[5] The primary wood in the area at the time was oak.[6] In 1877, another pair of relatives, named Edward and James Erskine, bought land in the area as well.[7]

The village was first surveyed in 1887 by civil engineer Quincy Thomas.[8] When the plan was complete, it was decided that the streets and parks would be "dedicated" to the town's general populace to ensure that the village residents would always be able to use them without being beholden to a private company.[9]

The same year the village was surveyed by Thomas, Owendale also got its first post office.[10] One year after that, the Pontiac, Oxford, and Northern Railroad came to town, allowing for a quick and easy way to transport lumber from the village.[11] Unfortunately for the village residents and the lumber workers, the lumber industry would not remain long in Owendale. A fire destroyed the sawmill in 1896, and after that time, the primary business enterprise in the village was agriculture.[12]

The Silver Bullet Speedway

Owendale is also home to the Silver Bullet Speedway, previously called the Owendale Speedway, which lies just east of the village on Sebewaing Road. The Silver Bullet Speedway, built in 1955, is Michigan's oldest still-operating dirt track.[13] The track holds races every Saturday night in the summer, and each day has its own event theme.[14] During the track's history, it has seen a number of racers not only from the Thumb area of Michigan, but from across the country. A. J. Foyt, who won the Indianapolis 500 in 1961, 1964, 1967, and 1977,[15] and Parnelli Jones, who won in 1963,[16] both have raced at the speedway.[17]

Owendale Today

The switch Owendale made to agriculture at the end of the nineteenth century is still evident in the town today. Owendale is surrounded by farms, and the village itself is home to a grain elevator and a crop production company. There are other ways, too, that Owendale is a mix of the old and new. Some of the buildings retain a late-nineteenth-century style of architecture while others, such as the community building, have a more modern feel.

Businesses in Owendale include a gas station, a construction company, a market, and a restaurant. There is a village park in the center of town with playground equipment, a grill and a pavilion that was built by the Lions Club. Services in the town include a school, a post office, and a community building. There is also a United Methodist church.

The school district in Owendale has been merged with that of Gagetown, and the resulting district is called Owendale-Gagetown Area Schools. Their mascot is a bulldog.

TOP: The veterans' memorial honors local service members

Population: 406[1]   **Incorporated:** 1891[2]

INSETS L to R: Perrinton Park • This building houses the Perrinton village office • The post office in Perrinton • The park with the baseball field is named in memory of Mark Daniels

The village was originally called Perrin, after the man who headed a law firm that had interests in the area, but when the first post office opened in 1887, the name switched to Perrinton, as there was already an office called Perrin in the state.[19]

Perrinton

History of Perrinton

IN 1886, the Toledo, Saginaw and Muskegon Railway built a station in the area where Perrinton now stands, and that event prompted the beginning of the village.[3] When Ansel H. Phinney heard about the railroad coming to the area, he decided to purchase land near where the station would be.[4] Phinney had founded the village of Ashley, and, with Warren W. Baker, decided to use the land he bought to plat a new village, which he did in 1887.[5] Three years later, an addition was made to the plat, and in 1891, the village became officially incorporated, with David H. Brown being elected as the first village president.[6]

Two main things contributed to Perrinton's growth in its first years as a village. First, the land in and around Perrinton was well suited for agriculture.[7] The town had a sawmill and a planing mill, but agriculture was the true industry of the town, which supported a grain elevator, a flour mill, an apiarist (beekeeper), a farm implements store, and farms dedicated to livestock, sheep breeding, and poultry, eggs, and butter.[8] The prevalence of agriculture no doubt played a role in the second main benefit in the town, the railroad, which made Perrinton a noted shipping point.[9]

Perrinton developed fairly quickly as a town, both in terms of residence and population. A two-story public school was built in Perrinton in 1888, and in 1889, the Perrinton Bank was founded.[10] In the early 1900s, the town had 450 residents, two churches, a hotel, and a number of other smaller businesses, including those involved in wallpaper, men's hats, coal, and cement.[11]

A Well-Known Son

He would become famous as a well-known sociologist and the chancellor of the University of Wisconsin-Madison, but William Sewell's story began in Perrinton, where he was born in 1909.[12] His father was a pharmacist in the town, and Sewell, who wanted to be a doctor, began his science career as a pharmacist.[13] He attended university at Michigan State where he earned an undergraduate and a master's degree in sociology, then went on to earn a PhD at the University of Minnesota.[14]

In 1946, Sewell was hired as a faculty member at the University of Wisconsin, first as a professor, then as the chair of the sociology department, and finally as the chancellor.[15] While at the university he performed extensive research, including a major longitudinal study of 1957 high school graduates, the findings of which are still regularly consulted today, and developed a vision for the sociology department that is still used today—one of "decency, excellence, and diversity."[16]

Beyond the university, he was an active member of the sociological community, serving as president of the Sociological Research Association, president of the American Sociological Association, and chair of the National Commission on Research.[17] He is credited with helping bring recognition and respect to sociology as a scientific discipline.[18]

Perrinton Today

Agriculture is still important in Perrinton. The village still has a grain elevator, and much of the surrounding land is used for farming. The village's economy itself is more diverse, however, being home to a number of businesses, including a salon, a CPA business, an inn, an auto service center, a party store, and a company that works with golf carts.

In addition to the businesses listed above, Perrinton also has a number of services for community members, including a post office, a fire department, a community senior center, a Catholic church, a village office, and, just outside of the official village limit, the township offices for Fulton Township. There are two outdoor areas in the village. The first is a community park with playground equipment, a grill, and a pavilion that is located toward the center of town. The second is on the west side of the village and is primarily a baseball field in memory of Mark Daniels, a sergeant from Perrinton who was killed in the Vietnam War.

Until the early 1920s, there was a Grand Army of the Republic Post in Perrinton.[20] Rather like the VFW and American Legion of today, its members consisted of Union Civil War veterans. The Perrinton Post was #405 and named for Charles A. Price, a volunteer with the 3rd Michigan Infantry.[21] He was awarded the Kearny Cross, a medal decorating extreme bravery.[22]

TOP: This building is a replica of the Pewamo Depot

Population: 469[1]   **Incorporated:** 1871[2]

INSETS L to R: A sign welcoming visitors to Pewamo • This piece of old railroad equipment is on display at the Pewamo Trailhead Welcome Center • Blossom Time Park • A mural in town

Each year, Pewamo hosts an annual Block Party and Fall Fest the weekend after Labor Day. The event, designed to bring the community closer together, includes food, music, games, and even a talent show. "I think we were made for community," says Wolniakowski. "You just have to give people a reason to get out of the house, visit, and get to know their neighbors."[23]

Pewamo celebrated its sesquicentennial in 2009 and commemorated the occasion by dedicating Sesquicentennial Park. The park, which is next to the post office, has trees, benches, and a fountain.

Pewamo

The Pewamo Daredevil

IN THE LATE 1930s AND EARLY 1940s, Pewamo daredevil Joe Winkler performed a series of stunts in and around the Pewamo area. He performed stunts on his motorcycle, often riding through walls, and would hang from a trapeze beneath a hot air balloon. With the goal of creating bigger and more impressive stunts, Winkler began planning to perform stunts with other people, in which they would each parachute from a hot air balloon. On his first team stunt, however, his younger brother and partner, Peter, was killed, and in the future, Joe refused to allow anyone to perform with him.[3]

History of Pewamo

Pewamo began as a depot along the Detroit & Milwaukee Railroad, which was slowly expanding westward through the state during the late 1850s.[4] John C. Blanchard, along with his father, Dr. Washington Z. Blanchard, and a few others, purchased land for the station and the village.[5] Pewamo was first surveyed in 1857, but it was another two years before the village plat was recorded,[6] and more than a decade before the village became officially incorporated and elected Amos W. Sherwood as its first president.[7] It is the 1859 date, however, that the village recognizes as its founding.

At first, Pewamo consisted of only a few log houses, but in 1857, Hiram Blanchard opened the first village store,[8] and, later that year when a post office was established, he was also named postmaster;[9] a second store, a tavern, and a blacksmith shop soon opened as well.[10] Toward the end of 1857, six families lived in Pewamo, but it was some time before the village saw real improvements or growth.[11] At the time, Pewamo's primary purpose was to supply firewood to the trains that stopped at the depot,[12] but the village's location was far from ideal for people arriving by road. The village was surrounded by woods and sat on a low tract of land, which resulted in the roads to and from the village often being impassable. Upon his arrival in Pewamo, Hiram Blanchard is said to have remarked that the village "looked as if it had ought to be given over to the control of the frogs."[13]

The railroad, however, ensured the village's survival. It was in a key location for shipping, and many trains delivered their goods to the village depot.[14] When the township turned its attention to the state of the roads, the village began to thrive, and by the early 1870s, Pewamo had a collection of churches, dry goods stores, groceries, drugstores, shops, and hotels. It also held a mill, a factory, a money-order office, and a school that employed two teachers.[15] Later, in 1941, Pewamo schools joined with five other districts to create the Pewamo Rural Agricultural School District, which merged again in 1959 to form the Pewamo-Westphalia school district, which is still in existence today.[16]

Honoring an American Indian Chief

When it came time to name the village, John Blanchard suggested the name *Pewamo*, after an Ottawa chief he had met some years previous. The two had spent time fishing and hunting together, and Blanchard thought highly of Pewamo, whose name meant "trail diverges."[17] The others involved in the purchase of the village agreed with Blanchard's choice, and the village was officially named.[18]

It was some time later, however, that Pewamo first learned of his namesake village. In the 1870s, while in Canada, Blanchard finally met again with Pewamo, and it was during this meeting that the Ottawa chief learned of the village named in his honor.[19] Pewamo was delighted with the news, especially since the village sat in the Grand River watershed, the area he called home.[20] He is remembered to this day in the town, and is commemorated in a mural in Sesquicentennial Park.

Pewamo Today

Today Pewamo is focused on celebrating both its current identity and its past. "There's a great appreciation for where we came from," says Sandy Wolniakowski, the Pewamo Village Clerk. "We aren't in a hurry to forget. We wouldn't even be here if not for the railroad."[21] Though there is no longer a rail line running through Pewamo, the Fred Meijer Clinton-Ionia-Shiawassee Trail runs along the old railroad corridor. The trail, which is over 40 miles long, runs east and west through the village and passes right by the Pewamo Trailhead Welcome Center. The Welcome Center, which was modeled on the original depot built in the 1850s, contains restrooms, a drinking fountain, shaded picnic tables, and displays of old railroading tools. It is a place for people to come together and appreciate the region's history.

In addition to the trailhead, the village is home to a post office, a fire department, and two churches: Bible Believers Grace Church (now housed in the building that formerly served as a Methodist church), and St. Joseph's Church and School, which celebrated 100 years of service in 2003.[22] At the downtown intersection of State and Main Streets, there is a deli, a lounge, a bar and grill, and a salon. The village office is on Main Street, right next to Sesquicentennial Park. In addition, the village contains Blossom Time Park, which covers nine acres and includes pavilions, playground equipment, baseball fields, tennis courts, horseshoe pits, and a sand volleyball court.

Pewamo made the news in 2016 when four seven-year-olds, all survivors of severe medical issues from heart problems to leukemia, ended up in the same first-grade classroom.[24] The children, who are all doing well after their various treatments, are part of what the Pewamo community calls "The Miracle Class."[25]

TOP: The Pierson Bible Church is located on Grand Street

Population: 172[1]   **Incorporated:** 1873

INSETS L to R: The Village Inn is a restaurant and bar in the village • Pierson is on the Fred Meijer White Pine Trail • This building has the village's veterans' memorial out front • This sign welcomes visitors to the village

In August of 1900, an error led to a southbound train from Howard City and a northbound train from Sand Lake ending up on the same set of tracks.[19] The two trains collided near Pierson, and all crew members aboard the two trains died.[20]

Pierson

History of Pierson

IN THE EARLY 1850s, four members of the Pierson family from New York, three brothers and their father, came to Pierson Township.[2] At the time, Pierson Township covered a larger area than it does now, as it included area that came to be Maple Valley, Reynolds, and Winfield Townships.[3] For much of the first few years they spent in the township, the Pierson men, their families, and some other settlers to the area—which in the end totaled eighteen people—lived in one cabin together.[4]

Despite the less than ideal living conditions at the beginning, the Pierson family found success in the township. They made shingles that they sold in Rockford, and the woods in the area provided ample game.[5]

They also had success in farming, particularly with corn and potatoes, though they lost seven hogs to a bear that lived nearby.[6]

In 1856, David Pierson, one of the brothers, bought forty acres in the area where Pierson is now located.[7] The following year, he and two other men, Dexter Clark and John Shar, founded the village, likely as a result of the Grand Rapids & Indiana Railroad's plan to come to the area.[8] The first post office in Pierson also opened in 1857 and was run out of David Pierson's house, with Pierson himself as the first postmaster.[9]

Even with the railroad and the beginning of the lumbering business in the town, Pierson got off to something of a slow start. The first store opened in 1867, the first hotel was built in 1868, and the first physician came to the town in 1869.[10] Over the next dozen years, the village went on to add a second hotel, a flour mill, two general stores, a drugstore, a confectionery, a school, and two churches, and the town's population climbed to over 400 people.[11]

However, in the early- to mid-1880s, the lumber in the area was exhausted, and while the village did switch its focus to other types of industry, the population began to fall, with the result that by the early 1900s there were only approximately 250 people in Pierson.[12]

A Dam Difficult Environmental Case

In 1997, Pierson landowner Stephen Tvedten got an unexpected letter from the Michigan Department of Environmental Quality.[13] It referenced two "debris dams" on his property, which the state alleged were illegally constructed and maintained, flooding a neighbor's property.[14] In a tongue-in-cheek response that has since gone viral on the internet, Tvedten informed the state they were beaver dams, and that he had never made any changes to the dams.[15] His hilarious letter questioned whether all beavers, or just his, had to apply for permits before building dams, defended the beavers' Miranda rights, and, of course, included copious use of the word "dam."[16] The state later dropped its case, but Tvedten's fame continues.[17]

Pierson Today

Pierson today is a quiet town, despite its proximity to US-131, and is primarily residential. It is home to a restaurant and bar, a self-storage center, and a combination gas station, convenience store, meat shop, and pizzeria. During the summer months, there is also often a produce stand open. There is also a municipal building, a township hall, a post office, and a church.

The village has several outdoor opportunities for people who prefer to spend time outside. There is a playground, a baseball diamond, a golf course, and the Fred Meijer White Pine Trail State Park runs right through the middle of Pierson. The trail, which follows the line of the old railroad, runs parallel to US-131 and is 93 miles long.[18]

The first decade of the twentieth century saw aviation and automobiles in their infancy; it also saw the first motorboats reaching the wider market. Pierson was home to an early adopter. According to *Motor Boat* magazine, one W. S. Bloomer ordered a 22-foot Pope Special motorboat with a six-horsepower engine.[21] Bloomer was from Chicago but bought the boat for use in Pierson.[22]

TOP: The Port Hope Hotel is known for its Leroy Burger, an 18-ounce burger

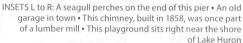

Population: 267[1]   **Incorporated:** 1887[2]

INSETS L to R: A seagull perches on the end of this pier • An old garage in town • This chimney, built in 1858, was once part of a lumber mill • This playground sits right near the shore of Lake Huron

All that remains of the lumber mill in Port Hope today is its chimney, built by John Geltz in 1858.[33] It is the last lumber mill-era chimney left standing in Michigan.[34]

Port Hope

Naming Port Hope

THE VILLAGE AT PORT HOPE got its name after two men found themselves alone on Lake Huron and desperately needing to make it to shore. The two men, Southerd (sometimes spelled Southard) and Witcher, had been on a steamboat on the lake and, in a skiff the two took from the boat, tried to row their way to shore.[3] They were on the water all night without finding shore and, as their worry increased, Southerd said that if the two men did make it successfully to shore, they would declare their point of landing a "port of hope."[4] When they did finally reach the shore, they upheld the declaration and named the site Port Hope.[5]

A Treacherous Coast

Southerd wasn't the only sailor who encountered trouble on the waters of Lake Huron. Wrecks are littered along the bottom of Lake Huron, and many are now preserved in the Thumb Area Bottomland Preserve.[6] Some are just a few miles from Port Hope. One such wreck, the *Dunderburg*, sank in a collision in 1868.[7] The ship is in pristine condition, though covered in invasive mussels, and is accessible to divers, but only those with a good deal of experience.[8]

History of Port Hope

The first land bought in the area that is now known as Port Hope was purchased by Reuben Dimond in the mid-1850s.[9] In 1857, businessman William R. Stafford came to the area and purchased the land from

Dimond and other landowners in the area.[10] He built a sawmill the following year, and the settlement grew up around the industry created by the mill.[11] The sawmill burned down in 1871 but was rebuilt.[12]

Despite the sawmill's demise, 1871 was not an entirely bad year for the village. That same year, though before the fire, an editor from the *Detroit Tribune* visited the village and wrote that Port Hope was "the handsomest village in general appearance above Lexington."[13] The article goes on to paint the village, which at that time had a population of 400 people, as a prosperous place with neat houses, a park, and one of the best harbors of refuge in the state.[14] Around the time the article was written, the town also had two schools—one with instruction in English and one in German.[15]

As the timber in the area was exhausted by logging, the area around Port Hope turned to farmland, some of which was inhabited and worked by squatters.[16] Two forest fires had burned in and around Port Hope, in 1871 and 1881, and after the second fire, farming fully replaced the lumber business in the town.[17] Stafford responded to the changes by building a flour mill and a grain elevator rather than choosing to rebuild the sawmill a second time.[18] The temperate climate in the area was also particularly well-suited for growing fruit.[19]

Another early industry in the village was salt, and the first two salt wells created in the village each produced an average of over one hundred barrels of salt per day.[20] The town also had a general store, a hardware store, a millinery, a hotel, and one merchant who specialized in both books and shoes.

The Railroad in Port Hope

Around 1870 there was talk of extending the railroad to Port Hope, but after the forest fires of 1871, which destroyed parts of the town and much of the surrounding forest, there was no longer a reason for trains to visit Port Hope.[21] As the village still had success with shipping over the water, the lack of railroad did not create too much of a problem. As the village grew, however, the community eventually began to feel the lack of overland shipping, and once again talk turned to bringing the railroad to the village.[22]

The prime obstacle was the cost.[23] The Pere Marquette Railroad had an interest in a Port Hope station, but interest was not enough.[24] Stafford and a group of other business owners in the village decided to make the decision easier for the railroad and offered to hire the Pere Marquette Railroad Company as contractors to build a "Harbor Beach and Port Hope" Railroad.[25] Upon completion of the project, they said, the village would sell the railroad back to the company.[26]

Construction began in 1902, and in 1904, the railroad officially began operation.[27] The wooden Port Hope depot was built using a modern design, with a divided waiting area that separated passengers from freight.[28]

The railroad didn't last all that long, however. Automobile traffic soon overtook the railroad as a means of transit, and beginning in the 1920s, the Port Hope railroad began to transport passengers at a monetary loss.[29] When the Depression hit, the railroad could no longer maintain this arrangement, and the last passenger train left Port Hope in 1936.[30] Freight service continued until the early 1970s.[31] In 2010, after decades of various uses, the depot was restored and moved to a new location in the village.[32]

Port Hope Today

Visitors to Port Hope have a lot to make them feel at home, including a hotel, cabins, and options for RV and tent camping. There is also a township hall, a village hall, a gas station, a café, an antique shop, a hardware store, a bank, a mercantile, and a medical clinic. Port Hope also has its own post office and police department, and there is both a United Methodist church and a Lutheran church.

In 1987, at the village's centennial, the residents of Port Hope decided to celebrate by burying a time capsule. Residents spent the next two years collecting items to put in the capsule and finally buried it in 1989. The capsule will be opened on the village's 200th birthday in 2087.

Population: 234[1]   **Incorporated:** 1907[2]

INSETS L to R: Posen Consolidated Schools includes both a high
school and an elementary school • This veterans' memorial was
dedicated by the South Presque Isle VFW Post • One of the farms
in the Posen area • This fire and rescue display is out front of the
Posen Fire Department

In 2001, Posen erected a marker to recognize the
heritage of many of the villagers. This marker
seeks to help the people both in Posen, Michigan,
and in the Poznań area of Poland remember the
ancestors that they have in common.

TOP: A monument to the Preseque Isle Electric Cooperative, which brought electricity to the town

Posen

History of Posen

MANY OF THE EUROPEAN SETTLERS in Posen came from Po-
land, traveling to Presque Isle County in groups.[3] In 1870, a large group
of immigrants from Poland came to the area where Posen would eventually be built up, brought by lumber companies who needed workers to
cut trees and work in their mills.[4] Because a large number of these immigrants had come from a part of Poland that was occupied by Prussia,
and later Germany, many of them knew both Polish and German, and
some of the town and township business was recorded in German.[5]

As the trees in the area were cut and processed at the sawmills, the
once-forested land became farmland. Many of the villagers had worked
as farmers in Poland, and rather than leave to look for more-lucrative
lumber work, many chose to stay.[6] They chose the name Posen for their
town, as it was the German spelling for Poznań, the province in Poland
from which many of the villagers had come.[7]

By 1912, the village had a bank and a handful of mills and did
considerable shipping business, particularly in the surrounding area.[8]

A New Deal Program Comes to Posen

Roosevelt's New Deal program during the Great Depression
brought aid and progress to many communities in Michigan, including Posen. Established in 1935, the Rural Electrification Administra-
tion—or REA—was designed to help bring electric power to rural areas
at a low cost, and in 1937, the REA came to Presque Isle County.[9] In
September of that year, the Presque Isle Electric Cooperative erected

its first-ever utility pole in Posen, which was also the first Rural Electric Cooperative utility pole in the State of Michigan.[10] Exactly three months later, the electricity was turned on.[11]

The Annual Posen Potato Festival

Posen holds an annual Potato Festival in September of each year. The festival runs for three days and includes activities inspired by the village's Polish heritage, such as polka dancing and a kielbasa-eating contest. The festival begins on Friday evening with an opening ceremony held at the flagpole in the village, and then the fun begins.[12] The weekend features a flea market, a 5K, an arts and crafts show, a parade, and a demo derby. But it wouldn't be a potato festival without, well, potatoes. The event includes a potato pancake dinner and contests for potato dishes and displays. The festival also includes the presence of Miss Posen, who takes part in the parade with her parents.

Posen Today

The residents at Posen were close knit when the village first started, and that sense of community is still present in Posen today. Because of the town's Polish ancestry, the Catholic church in Posen has a particularly active community, and the village also has a community center, a library, and a farmers market that runs in the summer months. The town is also home to Posen Consolidated Schools.

Posen has also remained focused on agriculture. The land around the village is primarily used for farming—including potatoes—and the town itself has an elevator. In addition, Posen has other opportunities for its residents and visitors to get outdoors, including at a baseball field just south of the village limit and the North Eastern State Trail, which runs diagonally through the village.

Businesses in the town include a gift shop, an auto parts store, a logging business, a dollar store, a gas station with a mini-mart, a credit union, a party store, and a diner and lounge. There are also family apartments, a fire and rescue, a post office, and a village hall.

The Elowsky Mill in Posen was built by Michael Elowsky after he moved to Presque Isle County in 1870.[13] The mill eventually included a variety of milling operations.[14] The mill still stands in Posen today, and tours are available.

TOP: This building is located near the medical center in Powers

Population: 422[1]   **Incorporated:** 1915[2]

INSETS L to R: A view down toward the railroad tracks in town •
The Pinecrest Medical Care Facility • Solar panels at the medical
complex • Grace Evangelical Lutheran Church

Most of Michigan is in the Eastern Time Zone, but part of the southwest portion of the Upper Peninsula, including Powers, is actually on Central Time.

Despite its tiny size, Powers is something of an athletic powerhouse when it comes to basketball. Powers North Central, which takes in students from around the area, went more than three seasons without losing a game, making for the longest winning streak in Michigan history.[18] At the time, it was also the longest running winning streak in the entire country.[19] The winning streak finally ended at 84 games on December 14, 2017.[20]

Powers

History of Powers

POWERS CAN TRACE ITS BEGINNING BACK TO 1872, when the community was founded.[3] The town seems to have been named after a man whose last name was Powers.[4] When the railroad came to Powers in 1873, the village found itself at an important point of the railroad in the western Upper Peninsula, as it was located at a junction of the Chicago & North Western Railway's main line and the branch that led out to the Menominee Iron Range.[5,6] This meant that many of the male residents of Powers found work in the iron mines, and that the village profited from the shipments of iron ore and lumber that passed through the village.[7] The station at Powers was for a time also referred to as Forty-Two, as it was placed at a distance of 42 miles from Menominee.[8]

Many men in Powers worked at the nearby Breen Mine, and by the late 1870s, the town had truly started to come alive.[9] A post office opened in 1877, and Carrie Brook became Powers' first postmistress.[10] The population climbed to 500 people by the beginning of the twentieth century, and the population supported four separate churches.[11]

A Diversified Economy

While Powers was primarily a mining town, it did business in lumber and in agriculture, and the village grew to contain a wide range of businesses. In the first two decades of the twentieth century, business ventures in the town included an insurance company, a dentist, a hotel, an optometrist, the First State Bank of Powers, and the Powers Opera House.[12]

The Dangers of the Railroad

While the presence of the railroad brought work, profit, and convenience to Powers, it also came with risks. For instance, in one month alone in 1877 at least two men from the Powers area were injured or killed while attempting to jump from a moving train.[13] In both instances the men attempted to exit a moving train, struck an obstacle, and were thrown back into the train's path.[14]

The Fire of 1914

With its proximity to Iron Mountain and location on US-2, Powers is a thriving community, though according to the residents of Spalding Township, it encountered quite the setback when a fire tore through town in 1914.[15] The fire, which one newspaper said was started by a couple of homeless individuals in an abandoned building, wiped out most of the town's business district.[16]

An Explosive Way to Celebrate

To mark the country's 101st birthday, the residents of 1877 Powers had a celebration that not only included traditional fireworks but also incorporated two other dynamic outpourings of festivity that are much less seen today. One thing they did was fire an anvil, which involves using gunpowder to launch an anvil up into the air.[17] In addition, they also had a dynamite explosion as part of the celebration.

Powers Today

The village has a variety of businesses, including a gas station, a motel, an auto sales center, an insurance agency, a realty office, a diner, a sports bar, and even a chain fast food restaurant—a rarity in smaller towns.

Powers is also home to a health clinic, Great Northern Home Care, and the Pinecrest Medical Care Facility. Other services in the village include a branch of the First National Bank of Norway, a fire department, a state police office, and a village hall.

Carrie Brook has not been the only female postmaster, or postmistress, in Powers' history. Other women who have served in the role include Marie Prince and Alberta Montpas at the beginning of the twentieth century,[21] and Doreen Bellmore and Elizabeth Shannon in more recent years.[22]

Population: 266[1]   **Incorporated:** 1947[2]

INSETS L to R: Harper's Barbershop in town • The view down
Harrison Road • Prescott's ballpark • The park in Prescott includes
playground equipment and a pavilion

TOP: This painted canoe sits outside one of the buildings in the village

The Whittemore-Prescott boys track and field team won the Division IV state championship in 2017.[24] The school district has also won state titles in wrestling and football.[25]

Prescott

The Prescott Family

CHARLES PRESCOTT IS REMEMBERED in Ogemaw County as the lumber businessman for whom the village of Prescott was named, but his personal history goes beyond that. He was an ordained minister in the Baptist Church, and before coming to Michigan he lived in Maine and Pennsylvania.[3] He came to Michigan to harvest pine, became involved in the railroad business in 1880, lent his name to Prescott village, then used the land he owned in Ogemaw County for agricultural purposes, particularly related to livestock.[4] His ranch, which was the largest in the state at the time, had beef cattle, dairy cows, sheep, and horses.[5]

Charles was married to a woman named Sarah, and in 1862, while still living in Pennsylvania, Sarah gave birth to a son that the couple named George.[6] George A. Prescott went on to be a force in Michigan, not just in Prescott and Ogemaw County. He was elected to serve as a state senator for Michigan's 28th district, serving from 1895 to 1898.[7] Then, in 1905 he became Governor Fred Warner's Secretary of State.[8]

George's sons, George Prescott Jr. and Charles T. Prescott, also went on to be involved in Michigan politics, with George Jr. serving as a delegate to the Republican National Convention of 1928 and Charles serving Michigan's 28th district from 1947 to 1961.[9] In addition, George Jr.'s son George Prescott III was a representative in the Michigan House from 1967 to 1978.[10] Even while representing different districts across Michigan, the Prescott family kept its connections to the village of

Prescott by continuing to run and manage the Prescott Ranch, which the Prescott family finally sold in 1958.[11]

History of Prescott

The village of Prescott began with lumbering ventures. A pair of brothers named Hale, who cleared timber in the area, owned a portion of railroad in Ogemaw County.[12] In 1880, they decided to move their business interests elsewhere, at which point they sold the railroad to Charles Prescott.[13] The settlement at Prescott is named in honor of him.[14]

Prescott already owned over 8,000 acres of land in Ogemaw County, including land where the village of Prescott is now found.[15] In the early 1880s, he extended the railroad to the eventual village location, allowing for a thriving lumber trade to be built up in the area.[16] Julia A. Davison became the first postmistress of the town when the post office was opened in 1882.[17]

A few years later, after Prescott had sold the railroad to a new owner, the railroad was extended again, this time to the site where the village of Alger would form.[18]

Because Prescott was a lumbering town, much of the village's early growth tied to the lumber industry in the area.[19] By the late 1880s, in addition to the sawmill, the village had a hotel, a general store, a blacksmith, and a combination drug and grocery store.[20] Within the next few years, the village also gained a millinery, a hardware store, a meat market, a saloon, a livery stable, and both a flour and a planing mill.[21] The town also had a music teacher.[22]

As the timber in the area was exhausted and the land turned to being used for agricultural purposes, sheep and cattle farming became important ventures in the Prescott area. At its peak, the farmers in the area combined to own around 9,000 sheep, and this supported both a wool carding mill and a wool business in Prescott.[23]

Prescott Today

Prescott is a quiet village that lies to the southeast of Johnson Lake, with Johnson Creek running east and west through the village itself. The village has a physical therapy office, a family medical practice, a pawnshop, a party store, a barber shop, a laundromat, a market, a funeral home, and a café. Services in the village include a department of public works, a county library, a post office, a baseball diamond, and a park that includes playground equipment, picnic tables, and a pavilion. There are three churches in the Prescott area: God's Covenant Church, Faith Lutheran Church, and Judson Baptist Church.

The schools of Prescott and nearby Whittemore were merged in 1957 after voters in the two districts agreed to the creation of Whittemore-Prescott Area Schools.[26]

TOP: This sign welcomes visitors to the village and includes information about local churches

Population: 368[1]   **Incorporated:** 1968[2]

INSETS L to R: The Rosebush Village Hall • The Rosebush Farm Market • The main intersection in the village • The United Methodist Church in the village

The Rosebush area, like much of Middle Michigan, is home to a thriving Amish community. Contrary to popular belief, not all Amish people spurn modern technology entirely; some make use of cars and cell phones, whereas others only depend on them in emergencies.[18]

Rosebush

History of Rosebush

THE FIRST EUROPEAN SETTLERS of Rosebush came to the area in the early 1840s, including Cornelius Bogan who owned and operated a general store.[3] The store was called Halfway, as it was located approximately halfway between Clare and Mount Pleasant on the area stagecoach line.[4] In 1868, James Bush came to the store and used its location to plat a new village.[5] Five years later, Bush opened a hotel in the young village, calling it the Half Way House.[6]

A post office opened in the settlement around the same time Bush started the hotel, and the post office was called Calkinsville.[7] However, when the Ann Arbor Railroad opened a depot in the town, the depot would take a different name than the post office at the request of Bush,

who donated the land for the depot to the railroad but did so with the request that the depot be named after his wife, Rose.[8]

For a time, this meant that mail to the settlement came to Calkinsville, while railroad passengers disembarked at Rosebush. In 1889, the post office changed names to match the railroad depot, but the change did not last long.[9] The following year it changed back to Calkinsville.[10] Not until 1903 did the names once again match, and this time, the name Rosebush remained.[11]

Even with the name changes, the village fared well. At the time the name changed for the final time, the village had a confectionery, a general store, a business selling farm implements, a flour mill, a barber, a dressmaker, a blacksmith, a photographer, a veterinarian, a physician, and a teacher.[12] There were also a number of people involved in livestock, grain, or other areas of agriculture.[13]

The Rosebush Bank Building

A bank opened in Rosebush in 1908 after a group of bankers from Mt. Pleasant started the Rosebush banking company.[14] For years, the bank was a center of the community, and the brick corner building was a landmark in the town. The bank was eventually sold to Chemical Bank and the business was moved to a new building, which itself eventually closed in 2016, 108 years after first opening.[15] The bank building itself, however, would outlast the business. After sitting vacant for some years, it was purchased by Chris Bair, who opened a diner in the space, naming it Roz's Diner after his late mother.[16] Bair's goal for the space is to have the building once again be a focal point of the community.[17]

Rosebush Today

Rosebush is sandwiched, in a sense, by two larger towns, with Mount Pleasant seven miles to the south and Clare eight miles to the north. US-127 marks the village's east border. Yet, even with all of this, it remains a small and even quiet community. It retains much of its agricultural roots, with a grain elevator, a feed and grain store, a fertilizer company, a tractor store, a farm supply company, and a farmers market. The village also has a library, an IGA grocery, an inn, a diner, an automotive store, a plumbing company, a fuel distribution company, and an American Legion post. The township park on the west side of town contains baseball diamonds, playground equipment, a pavilion, and a walking path. There is also a United Methodist church, a Presbyterian church, and an Ojibwe Baptist church.

Rosebush has been holding a Fourth of July celebration for over 75 years. The event, which features a parade, a car show, a softball tournament, and, of course, fireworks, brings over 500 people to the village each July.[19]

INSETS L to R: One of the side streets on the west side of the village • This flagpole and patriotic banner can be seen out front of the post office • Rothbury has its own Little Free Library • This baseball field is located at Czarny Park

TOP: Looking down Michigan Avenue

While digging a pond in 1963, Adrian "Ed" Huls found a partial skeleton of a young female mastodon.[22] You can see the find, which included a jaw, teeth, and tusks at the Lakeshore Museum Center in Muskegon.[23]

Rothbury

Electric Forest Festival

EACH SUMMER AT THE END OF JUNE, the Electric Forest Festival brings tens of thousands of music lovers to tiny Rothbury. The festival, which began in 2011, is held at the Double JJ Ranch in the village, but a bit outside the village limits.[2] The air of the festival is one of friendliness and kindness, and festivalgoers say that is one of the things that makes the festival unique.[3]

Still, not all of the residents in Rothbury can truly be said to be in full support of the festival.[4] They recognize that it brings business and recognition to their town,[5] but it also can bring mess and noise—things the residents of the village would sometimes prefer to do without when the rest of the year the village remains mostly small and quiet.[6]

History of Rothbury

When Rothbury was first settled by Europeans in the 1850s, it was originally called Malta.[7] One prominent early resident was Nelson Green, who came to the settlement in the mid-1860s and bought a section of land.[8] When the Chicago & North Western Railway came to the village in 1875, Green allowed his property to be used for the location of the depot, which was subsequently named Greenwood Station.[9]

The post office, which opened one year after the railroad came to the village, was called Malta, though it closed in 1877.[10] Still, having a town that used a different name for the post office and railroad depot could be awkward, and when the post office was set to reopen in 1879, the community decided to use the same name for both institutions.[11]

As there was already a post office named Greenwood in Michigan, the name Rothbury was suggested after one man's hometown in England.[12] Charles D. Arnold was selected as the new postmaster.[13]

A Diversified Economy

Unlike some other nineteenth century towns in Michigan, the population in Rothbury did not experience a sudden spike in population with the coming of the railroad. Toward the end of the 1880s, the population in the town was about 60 people, and there was a painter, a hoop manufacturer, a jeweler, a general store, a blacksmith, a manufacturer of concrete blocks, and a violin maker.[14] Produce, particularly fruit, was a focus of agricultural production toward the beginning of the twentieth century.[15]

As the population in the town grew, the community gained religious and school buildings. A school called the Mears School, originally built in the 1870s, was replaced in 1888, and within a few years of the start of the twentieth century, the school was renamed the Lawson School after Philip Lawson, who had purchased the land where the school stood.[16] The town also had three different churches.[17]

Like many towns, Rothbury experienced setbacks during the Great Depression, though a decent number of businesses in the town survived the difficult years, including a pickle canning factory, a lumber yard, and a feed store.[18] There were also warehouses for potatoes and beans grown in the surrounding countryside.[19]

But businesses were not the only things damaged by the years of poor economy; churches could suffer as well. The Methodist church in Rothbury burned down and wasn't rebuilt, and the town's Seventh Day Adventist church lost so many parishioners that they gave up their building, though it was soon taken over by a new religious group in the village that would go on to become the Rothbury Community Church.[20]

Rothbury Today

One thing the village of Rothbury values today is its community. The village has a community center in town, a village hall, a baseball field, and a village park with basketball and tennis courts, a pavilion, and playground equipment, all of which are designed to bring people together.

The Huron-Manistee National Forests have some land in the village, right along Carlton Creek. Within a mile of the village there are six different small lakes and a few opportunities for camping. Double JJ Ranch, the site of the Electric Forest Festival, is to the town's northwest, and the space also includes a resort and a golf course, with a restaurant and a waterpark nearby. The village itself also has a bike and walking trail.

Business in the town include a hardware and farm supply store that first opened in 1955, a steel foundry, a gas station, a dollar store, an auto service shop, a tavern, a barbeque eatery, and a place where you can get tamales.[21] Services in Rothbury include a post office, a police department, a township fire department, and a township hall.

Fishing is another industry that has been important to Rothbury, which is only a few miles from the Lake Michigan shoreline. Several families in the Rothbury area have had long-term involvement in the fishing industry.

Population: 500[1]   **Incorporated:** 1879[2]

INSETS L to R: The Nelson Township Sand Lake Library • This display at the Sand Lake Trading Company contains a menu from the old Steer Haus Restaurant • The Sand Lake Trading Company is an antique store on East Lake Street • The Fred Meijer White Pine Trail

TOP: The village of Sand Lake is on the south shore of the lake of the same name

One of Sand Lake's early residents, A. H. Farnum, enlisted in the Nineteenth Ohio Volunteer Infantry in 1861.[24] He served three months, reenlisting when that tour was up, and then reenlisting again, serving until 1865.[25] In all, he saw action in some 90 engagements, including 40 battles, and was never wounded or captured.[26] After the war, he lived in Sand Lake for several years, running a shingle company before moving on to the Upper Peninsula.[27]

Sand Lake

Remembering the Civil War in Sand Lake

FOUNDED BY FOUR CIVIL WAR VETERANS, Sand Lake has long held events memorializing the Civil War and those who fought and died in it. In the first few decades of the twentieth century, there were often reunions and encampments in the village for those who had fought in the Civil War.[3] These reunions were held in Old Settlers Park, which is now known in the village as Salisbury Park.[4]

In addition to the reunions, sometime around 1906 or 1907 the community decided to build a Civil War monument and to place it in the cemetery.[5] In September of 1907, the monument was erected and dedicated "by the M. H. Whitney Post No. 350 of the G. A. R. and the M. H. Whitney Corps No. 144 of the Woman's Relief Corps," which had worked together to raise the money needed for the monument.[6] Neither of these organizations exists today, but new organizations in Sand Lake and the surrounding area have stepped up to continue to support the remembrance of those who fought in our nation's civil war.[7] In 2001, the monument was cleaned and rededicated at the community's Fourth of July celebrations.[8]

History of Sand Lake

The village at Sand Lake, which was named for the nearby shoal lake of the same name, was started in 1869 by four veterans of the Civil War.[9] It began as a lumber community that predominantly worked with white pine.[10] Because of the lumber production in the village, the Grand Rapids & Indiana Railroad brought its services to the settlement in 1869.[11]

The first post office opened the following year, with Robert Salisbury as the first postmaster.[12] In 1871, the village was platted and recorded.[13] Two additions to the plat were made in 1872 and 1876, and the village became officially incorporated in 1879.[14] Peter Haifley was elected as Sand Lake's first president.

With the prime lumber available in the area and the presence of the railroad, the population climbed quickly.[15] In 1880 there were approximately 700 people living in the village, which had five sawmills and several shingle mills, and a planing mill.[16] There was also a milliner, a carpenter, a jeweler, a barber, a grocer, a harness maker, a drugstore, a hardware store, and a hotel.[17] The village also had its own newspaper.[18]

Lumber and Agriculture

Sand Lake village was not destined to be only a lumber town. By the early 1900s, agriculture and tourism became the dominant industries, and the town was home to a summer resort, a hotel, a real estate company, a theater, and a bank.[19] Agricultural interests in the town included hay, grain, honey, fruit, potatoes, dairy products, and meat.[20]

Fourth of July in Sand Lake

Sand Lake's annual Fourth of July celebration lasts more than just one day, or even one weekend. The 2017 festivities started the Thursday before the Fourth with a book sale and a parade, and ended Tuesday the Fourth with a demolition derby, another parade, and fireworks.[21] In between, the celebration included a midway, a children's parade, a book sale, die-cast car races, a petting zoo, a tractor pull, a rodeo, a car and tractor show, and many other family-friendly events.[22]

Sand Lake Today

Today Sand Lake is a seasonal resort community that still feels like a small town. It has a close-knit group of residents who are friendly and welcoming to outsiders. The village has a large number of businesses, including two pizza parlors, a tavern, an ice cream parlor, a family dining restaurant, a salon, an auto supplies store, a gas station, a dollar store, a bank, a resale shop, and a veterinarian. There is also a library, which was just refinished in the past few years,[23] a village park with a gazebo and tennis courts, a VFW hall, an elementary school, a chamber of commerce, and a police department. The village is also one of the stops in Fred Meijer White Pine Trail State Park.

A 2010 move to dissolve the village of Sand Lake due to taxes was put before the village's voters, who ultimately defeated the proposal.[28]

TOP: This old gas station has been left intact on the corner of Main and Division Streets

Population: 309[1] **Incorporated:** 1887[2]

INSETS L to R: Fall foliage lines Division Street • The Masonic Lodge in Sherwood • The sign out front of the Sherwood Free Methodist Church building • One of the buildings near the main intersection in town

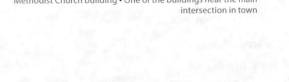

Sherwood is currently home to the oldest Free Methodist church in the entire state of Michigan.[21] The Free Methodist Society in Sherwood was first organized in 1867.[22]

Sherwood

Sherwood's Stanton Farm

ONE OF THE FIRST FARMS FOUNDED in Sherwood was the Stanton family's farm, which began in 1835.[3] Since then, the farm, which is 500 acres, has seen eight generations of the Stanton family work the farm.[4] In addition to its longevity, the farm is also well known for a practice race track that has been used by Jeff Stanton, a U.S. motocross legend.[5] He has not only used the farm for racing practice—he has a history of spending his off time helping work his family's farm and embarking on many new business ventures.

History of Sherwood and Its Many Names

Sherwood was founded in the 1830s, after Alexander Tomlinson came to the area and named it after his home of Sherwood Forest in England.[6] The name did not stick at that time, however, and when E. F. Hazen started a farm in the area, it was called Hazenville.[7] The name changed again the following year, when the first post office opened and was named Durham, and again in 1839 when the name Sherwood had its first official use.[8]

The village had a slow start, but with the arrival of the Air Line division of the Michigan Central Railroad in 1870, the pace of its development increased.[9] That same year the village was platted by Hazen and Manton E. Sawin, and the plat was called Hazenville.[10]

The first store in the village was a grocery owned by Frank M. Warner who opened for business in 1870.[11] Only a year after opening the store, he sold it to Jerome J. Studley who in turn sold it to Isaac Maltby not long after.[12] In the mid-1870s the building was converted into a hotel. In those years, a few more stores were built as well, but the main business in the town centered around a sawmill, a grist mill, and a planing mill.[13]

The town's original post office had closed in 1866, but a few years later, the post office from Newstead was moved to Sherwood and Jerome J. Studley became the new postmaster.[14] It seems that sometime in the mid- to late-1870s, the name of the settlement, post office, and depot all finally became known as Sherwood, as sources from around that time refer to the village as Sherwood.[15]

The village experienced steady growth in the 1870s and 1880s. A brick schoolhouse was built in 1876, and by the time the village was incorporated in 1887 and Robert Fraser was elected as the first village president, the town had grown to have a bank, an opera house, two churches, a newspaper, and a variety of small businesses, including a millinery, a shoe and harness maker, a meat market, a physician, a blacksmith, a clothing store, a saloon, a barber, and a dressmaker.[16] By the early 1900s, the village also had its own pickle factory.[17]

Cartoons from Sherwood

Jonny Hawkins is a Sherwood resident who has found success by combining two things he loves: agriculture and humor.[18] Hawkins, who has been drawing cartoons since he was a small child, has created over 40,000 cartoons, and with many major credits to his name, he's had success placing his work in publications across the country.[19]

Sherwood Today

Today Sherwood is a quiet town with tree-lined streets. It has a woodcrafter's shop, an auto repair shop, a used furniture store, a grill and pizzeria, a party store, a post office, and a library. There is a Free Methodist church and, at the north end of the village, a cemetery. The brick schoolhouse built in 1876 is still standing in the village today and is used as a Masonic Lodge.[20] An old gas station sits at the main intersection in the town, with the old pump and building kept up as a small piece of history. In fact, many of the village's commercial buildings are older, and whether in use or not, the effect can make you forget we're now in the twenty-first century.

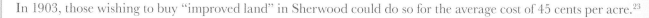
In 1903, those wishing to buy "improved land" in Sherwood could do so for the average cost of 45 cents per acre.[23]

TOP: The post office in Stanwood is located on South State Street

Population: 211[1]   **Incorporated:** 1907[2]

INSETS L to R: This road, heading away from the village, has a sign warning drivers to watch out for horse-drawn buggies • Businesses at the intersection of Front Street and Jefferson Street SE include a feed store and a café • Near the Copper Top Convenience Store • Looking to the northeast down Front Street

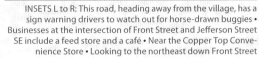

The Stanwood area is home to a large Amish community. There are over 80 Amish families living in or around the village.[24]

Stanwood may be a quiet village, but in recent years it has also been at the fringes of controversy, as the Nestle water-bottling plant in Stanwood has raised environmental concerns around the state.

Stanwood

History of Stanwood

EUROPEAN SETTLERS FIRST CAME to the Stanwood area in 1870, and that year saw a flurry of activity in the soon-to-be village.[3] The Grand Rapids & Indiana Railroad arrived and built a depot, and a post office that had previously been in Big Creek was moved to the village and given the name of Stanwood.[4] It is said the name was chosen because the village area contained a "splendid" stand of trees.[5]

Stanwood started out as a lumber town.[6] There was a sawmill and a grist mill, and many of the town's early businesses supported the industry, particularly the sawmill.[7] Early stores in the village included general stores, carpenters, and a hotel.[8]

By 1903, Stanwood had reached a population of 300 and the village had multiple stores, a telephone connection, a cider mill, and even an opera house.[9] By the 1920s, the village had gained the Stanwood State Savings Bank and the Stanwood Electric Light and Power Company.[10] There was also a large number of village residents involved in agriculture, and significant variety in terms of crops and agricultural pursuits. There were many threshers in the village, for instance, but there were also people involved in general produce and in selling agricultural implements.[11]

George W. Reed

George W. Reed came to Stanwood in 1863 at age 19 and took winter work as a laborer in the lumber business.[12] Within 20 years he had defined himself not only as one of Stanwood's well-known residents, but also as someone of importance to all of Mecosta County.[13] When a county history was published in 1883, he was listed as someone who should be admired in the county due to his "energy, industry and economy."[14]

Reed came to Stanwood from Livingston County after two years spent fighting in the 16th Michigan Volunteer Infantry during the Civil War.[15] After being honorably discharged, he spent two years working in the forests at Stanwood and gained his first property of 80 acres through the Homestead Act of 1865.[16] A decade later he moved out of the log cabin he had built for himself on the land and opened a mercantile in the village itself.[17] The following year he was selected as postmaster for Stanwood.[18] His business was successful, and in 1880, he was able to add a partner to his business.[19]

During this time he also took on larger work for the village and township. He served two terms as township supervisor, spent a year serving on the Highway Commission, and was a Justice of the Peace for nearly a decade.[20]

Stanwood Today

The Morley Stanwood Community Schools elementary school is located in Stanwood and serves students from preschool through fifth grade. The school has a parents' group that works to create and run events for the children of the district, including movie nights and roller skating outings.[21] In addition, the group raises money to help improve the school's playground.[22]

Businesses in Stanwood include a convenience store, a pub, a gas station, a party store, a gift shop, a feed store, a sporting goods shop, an archery center, a vintage shop, a barber, and a café. Stanwood has the extremes in business size and culture, from the Ice Mountain bottling plant just outside of the village that is run by a large corporation and employs more than 200 people, to a number of Amish shops in the area that sell handmade goods.[23] Services in the village include a Greyhound bus stop, a post office, a Church of Christ, and a Free Methodist church. The Fred Meijer White Pine Trail runs parallel to Stanwood Drive, following the path of the old railroad. An easy way to access the trail in the village is through the village's park.

In 1883, a large structure meant to serve as a poorhouse and an "insane asylum" was built in Stanwood.[25] However, in the fall of that same year, the structure burned down as the result of suspected arson.[26]

TOP: The Turner Bean and Grain Elevator

Population: 114[1]   **Incorporated:** 1915[2]

INSETS L to R: Some of the farming equipment at the local elevator • Much of the area surrounding Turner is used for farming •
Main Street in Turner is lined with American flags • One of the
main roads leading into Turner

A prime cow sold at auction in Turner in 1919 could
fetch over $150.[27]

Turner

History of Turner

AROUND 1870, JOSEPH TURNER, for whom the village is named,
came to the area and purchased a few large tracts of land to be used
for lumbering.[3] He started a lumber company, which he called Turner,
Miller and Lewis, and invited two of his brothers-in-law to join him.[4] He
hired them on as general foremen for the company.[5] That done, one of
Turner's first tasks was to select a line for the necessary railroad.[6]

The railroad, which was about ten miles long, started at the Rifle
River and extended to a spot just to the east of Turner's modern location.[7] This terminus is where Joseph Turner built his first lumber camp.[8]
He went on to build two more branches, which serviced two more
camps.[9] One of those camps was located approximately one mile north
of Twining's eventual location.[10]

The railroad in Turner was not only for moving lumber. Turner's
lines hooked up to the main line in the area, the Detroit & Mackinac
Railway, which allowed for the village to ship its products, lumber
and otherwise.[11]

An Infamous Accident

In 1911, Turner was the site of a case that became a footnote in
Michigan legal history. On a misty summer night in June 1911, schoolteacher Edith Barhite was waiting for a passenger train at the town
depot.[12] Standing close to the track, she was accidentally struck by a
different train that was traveling—backwards—through the town.[13]
The unfortunate Miss Barhite was pulled into the train machinery, and
her surviving family (whom she supported financially), sued.[14] Initially,

they were awarded financial damages, but that result was later overturned by the Michigan Supreme Court in 1914.[15]

Progress and Then, a Major Fire

By the dawn of the twentieth century, Turner had established itself as more than a lumber town. In addition to the town's sawmill, it was home to a variety of stores, a bank, and a weekly newspaper.[16] The town's population had climbed to 600 people, though over the next 20 years it would begin to fall as the trees in the area were cleared.[17]

In 1918, a fire in the village destroyed several businesses and caused $50,000 in damages.[18] Though the fire luckily did not destroy the entire village, several businesses were still consumed, including a hardware store, a pool hall, and the bank.[19] Most of the buildings were rebuilt.

In 1926, the residents of Turner voted to spend community funds on the construction of a new community center.[20] The center was constructed the same year and contained, among other features, a basketball court and a stage.[21]

Progress Comes to Turner

The years between 1917 and 1937 contained many changes for the residents of Turner as new technologies and programs became available. Electricity was turned on in Turner in 1917, though it would still be a few years before the town made extensive use of the power.[22] The first radio came to the village a few years later, in 1922, when F. M. Hunt installed one in his pool hall.[23] The radio was able to pick up stations from both Detroit and Pittsburgh.[24] Paved streets came in 1937 as part of the New Deal during the Great Depression.[25]

Turner Today

As of the 2010 census, Turner had the honor of being the smallest incorporated village in Michigan.[26] Some people might see this as nothing more than a sad decline, but many towns in the state have faced hardships when the industries that birthed them died out. Turner is a community that has been through this, moving from a lumber town to a shipping point to a residential community, but through it all it has maintained its own identity and pride. One example of community pride is the American flags that fly from the utility poles on Main Street.

The countryside surrounding Turner is used for agriculture. The village is home to the Turner Bean & Grain elevator, and the farms surrounding the village grow a variety of crops, including soybeans.

One early business in Turner was Fred Whitehouse's grocery store, which was opened in 1897.[28] He would go on to operate the store until 1954.[29]

TOP: Looking west down Church Street toward Neilson Street

Population: 230[1]　**Incorporated:** 1893[2]

INSETS L to R: Powell's Grocery • The sign out front of the community center and library announces the village's annual Tustin Daze Festival • Tustin is home to the Pine River Area Museum • At Powell's Grocery, residents and visitors alike can try the various flavors of homemade jerky

Tustin is home to the Kettunen Center, which is a conference and retreat center run by the Michigan 4-H Foundation. When it opened in 1961, it was the "first 4-H volunteer and youth training center in the nation."[25]

Tustin

How the Swedish Settled Tustin

SETTLEMENT IN SOME WESTERN AREAS of Michigan was slow in the 1870s, after an ill-informed government official reported that the land there was mostly unusable.[3] At the same time, railroad companies in Michigan were moving west across the state and were in need or workers.[4] To solve the labor shortage, a group of railroads jointed together to create and support programs that helped immigrants.[5] For instance, immigrants who came to the United States to work on these railroads might find free transportation on the railway they were to be employed with.[6]

In Europe, this call to work was particularly well received in Sweden, where a famine in the late 1860s had caused widespread starvation, even among farmers.[7] When the coalition of railways sent the Episcopalian minister Josiah Tustin to Sweden in 1870, he was able to find a number of families willing to give up life in their home country and move to the United States.[8] When Tustin returned to Sweden a year later, even more families were willing to travel to Michigan to work for the railroads.[9] It was this second group of immigrants that largely found its way to Osceola County and the eventual village of Tustin, where the railroad donated 80 acres to the developing town.[10]

With such a large population of a common heritage living in one place, it is no surprise then that the community that built up had many Swedish influences—including, at first, its name. For the first few years after the immigrants from Sweden had come to Osceloa County, the settlement at Tustin was named New Bleking (after a province in Sweden) possibly to help encourage the immigration of more workers from Sweden to the village.[11] Sometime in 1872 or 1873, the name was officially changed to Tustin in honor of Josiah Tustin, though it is unclear whether the railroad company or the residents of the village prompted this change.[12]

A Growing Town

Around the same time the railroad came to Tustin, W. J. Townsend moved to the area and started the first lumbering work in the area.[13] In the spring of that year, the first store, a general store, was opened by Daniel McGovern, and the village received a post office.[14] With the construction of the railroad now complete, the business focus in the town changed to lumber and agriculture.[15]

By 1877, Tustin had begun to come into prominence. It produced potatoes, hay, and grain, and shipped a variety of products out of the village, including lumber, shingles, railroad ties, and hemlock bark.[16] Within another decade, the population had more than doubled, climbing to 400 people, and a school, a bank, a newspaper, and several mills having been added to the village.[17]

A World War I Hero

Tustin, like many towns in Michigan both big and small, saw many of its young men serve overseas in World War I. One Tustin soldier, Robert Bigelow, saw more than his share of action. A member of the First Expeditionary Division (later called the 1st Infantry Division), Bigelow belonged to the 18th Infantry Regiment.[18] Bigelow, along with the rest of the First Expeditionary Division, were the first U.S. troops to see combat.[19] And did they ever. One of their first battles was the Battle of Cantigny, where U.S. troops successfully took their objective and then defended a number of counterattacks.[20] Bigelow was injured in the course of the battle, but continued bringing food and water to his fellow soldiers.[21] He survived, only to endure the German Spring Offensive of 1918 and later, the horrifying Battle of the Argonne Forest, where more than 26,000 Americans died.[22]

Tustin Today

Today, Tustin is a quiet yet welcoming village. A sign arranged with white stones welcomes you to the town, and in the town itself there are people who will stop and invite you to experience their community, whether you'll be there for a few minutes or a few days. Many of the businesses in the village have been owned and operated by the same family for many years, and the workers are always willing to stop and share the history they and their businesses have seen.

The grocery store in town is one of those family-owned businesses, and within it customers can also get specialty meats, including homemade jerky that comes in a variety of flavors.[23] Then there is the hardware store, which was opened in 1941 and has remained in the same family for all the years since.[24]

Visitors to Tustin often remark that they feel at home. The village has an ice cream store, a restaurant, a gift shop, a hair salon, a library, a museum, a bank, and a family practice lab. There is also a post office and a fire department.

The Fred Meijer White Pine Trail runs north and south through the village, which also has two parks. Religious buildings in the village include Lutheran, Baptist, and Presbyterian churches.

The Little Creek Park along Rose Edgett Creek in the village was named in 2001 by the local fifth-grade class.[26]

TOP: The intersection of Main and State Streets

Population: 181[1]   **Incorporated:** 1903[2]

INSETS L to R: : The Twining Food Market • The Twining Mason Turner Fire Department • The now-closed Arenac Eastern Elementary School • Just outside Twining

Twining was home to several newspapers in its early days. The first was the *Twining Siftings*, established in 1905 and run by Ruby Robinson, who was just 19 at the time.[26] She later went on to work on its successor, the *Twining Herald*.

The price for beans harvested in Twining in 1914 was a little under $2 per bushel.[27]

In 1925, a married couple in Twining started a fox farm just outside of the main area of the village.[28]

Until 2017, students in town were a part of the Arenac Eastern School District. In April of 2017 they joined Standish-Sterling Community Schools.[29]

Twining

History of Twining

LIKE NEARBY TURNER, Twining had its start in lumbering when Joseph Turner came to the area in 1870 and started the Turner, Miller and Lewis lumber company.[3] When Turner built the railroad for his company, allowing the lumber to be transported from where it was cut to locations for processing or shipping, one of the rail branches passed about a mile north of where Twining is currently located and a lumber camp was started there.[4]

Twining was named for Frederick L. Twining, a lumberman who bought the first store built in the township from its original owner.[5] Because of this, the depot was named for him when the Detroit & Mackinac Railway came to the area in 1894.[6] Then, three years later when the

first post office in the village opened, Twining became the first postmaster at the office that bore his name.[7]

In 1896, John McCready built a combined saw and shingle mill in Twining.[8] He discontinued work at the shingle portion of the mill in 1898 and established a planing mill instead.[9] His business was both large and successful, and the sawmill alone could process 25,000 feet of lumber per day.[10] Another development in Twining in the late 1890s was the construction of a schoolhouse, which was built by Chauncey D. Brooks.[11]

Within a decade of the railroad's arrival in Twining, the town grew to have 500 people, many of whom were involved with one of the village's mills. Frederick Twining still did business in the town, both at his store and with his own lumber company, but he also had become involved in agriculture and owned an elevator and feed mill.[12]

The lumber industry in Twining continued into the 1920s, even if it did slow somewhat, with the result that the town's population fell.[13] Still, the town continued to be successful. Twining expanded his business interests to include a creamery, and the village also gained its own bank.[14] Electricity came to the village in 1917.[15]

Dr. Richard H. Wood, Doctor and Agriculturist

In the early years of the twentieth century, the physician in Twining was a man named Richard Wood. Born in Flint in 1853, Wood began studying medicine as soon as he finished his education in Flint.[16] He began practicing in his mid-twenties, first in South Dakota and Iowa and then back in his home state of Michigan.[17] Upon his return, he first worked in Clio for four years, then spent another six in Montrose, before spending a year with the department of instruction in Lansing and another year with the State Industrial School.[18]

In his work, Wood was successful and well known, both respected by his peers and well liked by his patients.[19] But he was not only successful in the field of medicine; he was also involved in agriculture, particularly livestock, and met with success in that industry as well.[20] He performed experimental agricultural work for the government and also wrote in several farm journals.[21]

Twining Soldiers in World War I

One of the first soldiers from Arenac County to be drafted during the First World War was James Moore of Twining.[22] Another village resident, Andrew Clyde Thompson, also fought in World War I.[23, 24] On his draft card, he indicated he was 21 years of age, tall, with a medium build and blue eyes and black hair. He attempted to get exempted from service on account of a ruptured eardrum, but this was apparently unsuccessful. He died of disease in 1918, presumably from the Spanish Flu or pneumonia, which killed more U.S. troops than enemy weapons did.[25]

Twining Today

The shift to agriculture that Frederick Twining undertook around the end of the nineteenth century and into the twentieth has continued up to this day. The village is home to farm equipment suppliers, a grain elevator, and a greenhouse, and the land surrounding the village is dotted with farms. There are still railroad tracks that pass through the village, though they are certainly less busy than they were one hundred years ago.

Twining is split between two townships, Turner and Mason, and is the location of the Mason Township Hall. Other businesses in the town include a counseling center, a market, an insurance agency, and a bar. The village also has a fire department, a post office, a United Methodist church, and a Baptist church.

The first paved roads came to Twining in 1937 as a result of a New Deal program.[30] Curbs and gutters were added to the town in 1948.[31] With the widespread arrival of automobile, the railroad declined; the depot in Twining was sold in 1953.[32]

Population: 301[1] **Incorporated:** 1875[2]

INSETS L to R: This stone is carved with information about a family who sent six sons and sons-in-law to fight in World War II • Wat Lao Buddha Temple is located on Mill Street • Milo Barnes Park is at the location of a former Underground Railroad site • The post office in Vandalia can be found on Mill Street

Vandalia and Cass County remember their history with the Underground Railroad by celebrating Underground Railroad Days each summer. The festival includes historical events, including tours and presentations.

TOP: The bell on display out front of the fire station is from the old Vandalia school

Vandalia

History of Vandalia

THE FIRST MILL BUILT IN VANDALIA was a grist mill built by Charles Ball and Stephen Bogue sometime toward the end of the 1840s.[3] A few years later, the pair platted the village, and the first person to come to their new settlement was Abraham Sigerfoos, who became the village blacksmith.[4] Soon afterward, Sigerfoos was joined by Asa Kingsbury, who was a merchant, and T. J. Wilcox, who became the first postmaster.[5]

The Michigan Central Railroad came to Vandalia in 1871 and built a depot in the village.[6] By 1877 the village had grown to include a grist mill, a sawmill, a handle factory, and a foundry.[7] There was also a school, a bank, and a hotel.[8] In addition to lumber and lumber products, Vandalia shipped hogs, cattle, poultry, wheat, and apples from its station.[9]

The Underground Railroad in Vandalia

Before Vandalia was formally settled by white Europeans, the area around the eventual village site was home to a different form of railroad. In the 1800s, there were at least two lines of the Underground Railroad running through Cass County, Michigan.[10] At a place not far from the current village of Vandalia, the Illinois Line, which came north from the St. Louis Area, and the Quaker Line, from Kentucky, crossed.[11]

This point was not only a junction, however. A group of Quakers living in the area helped fugitive slaves on their journey to Canada— and also helped them stay in Michigan and make a new life, if that was what they wanted.[12] Some stayed, living in cabins and working the land, helped and protected by Quakers, abolitionists, and free black people.[13]

In 1847, despite the assistance of the surrounding community, a group of twelve runaway slaves living in Cass County found themselves the target of a raid by Kentucky slave owners.[14] Suspecting their former slaves were in Cass County, the slaveholders sent a spy to the area to find their exact location.[15] The man, who went only by "Carpenter," claimed to be a reporter who worked for an abolitionist newspaper.[16] He returned to Kentucky, and a short time later the slaveholders raided the community in Cass County, going directly to the correct farms and cabins.[17]

They kidnapped nine people in the raids, and on their way out of the county again, they were met by a group of people who were determined to not let them get away.[18] The slaveholders, once confronted, agreed to stand trial in Michigan, as the Fugitive Slave Act of 1793 allowed for slaveholders to "recover" runaway slaves.[19] The case went to court but was ultimately decided in favor of the freed slaves due to a lack of necessary paperwork.[20]

For some time at the end of the twentieth century, stories of a settlement of runaway slaves in Cass County were seen as little more than local lore.[21] Finally, in 2002, an anthropology professor at Western Michigan University led a project at a farm in Vandalia and discovered more than a thousand nineteenth century artifacts and a dozen different cabin sites.[22] Between these findings, interviews, and various records, researchers concluded that the site in Vandalia was where the community of runaway slaves and their allies had lived.[23]

Vandalia Today

With its location on M-60, only ten miles or so north of the Indiana border, Vandalia is a bit of a busier town than its size might suggest, but it still keeps its small-town feel. Businesses in the town include a gas station, an express mart, a sporting goods store, and a bar and grill.

There is a community center, a youth recreation center, a post office, a township fire department, and a township hall. The village is also home to a Buddhist temple, a Community church, and a Church of God.

There are two parks in Vandalia, both of which commemorate the Underground Railroad site in the village. Out front of Milo Barnes Park there is a landmark and a historical marker. The parks also provide a place for the community to come together and include playground equipment, a baseball field, a basketball court, and a pavilion.

The Vandalia school was open from 1873 to 1971, and the school's old bell is still on display out front of the Penn Township Fire Department in Vandalia.

TOP: The site of the former Main Street Market

Population: 562[1]   **Incorporated:** 1901[2]

INSETS L to R: A playground in town • An old building near the downtown area of the village • The North Central State Trail passes through Vanderbilt • The Vanderbilt Community Church

Vanderbilt is home to Ryse Brink, a professional MMA fighter who got involved with the sport after his father passed away in 2009.[28]

Vanderbilt

History of Vanderbilt

VANDERBILT MIGHT NEVER HAVE BEEN a community at all had the Jackson, Lansing, & Saginaw Railroad kept its original plan of building the railroad through Berryville.[3] Instead, in 1875 the railroad decided to take a different route, and Vanderbilt was founded.[4] John Gullberg made the original plat of the village.[5]

Five years later, in 1880, the surveyors from the railroad planned the actual route, and the service began running to Vanderbilt in 1881.[6] With the railroad, the village grew quickly. Several buildings, which served as stores and residences, were built within the first few years, and by 1888, Vanderbilt had a two-story schoolhouse, a Masonic Lodge, two churches, a sawmill, a planing mill, and a few boarding houses.[7] The population was approximately 800 people.[8]

The village was more than a logging town, even from its early days. While some towns of the time merely shipped the lumber they harvested, Vanderbilt had multiple businesses that turned the lumber into other products. At various times the village manufactured bowls, posts, poles, barrel staves, wagons, and furniture.[9] They also had a decent-sized broom handle manufacturer.[10]

Progress on the March

With the dawn of the twentieth century, Vanderbilt saw changes and improvements to the technology available in the village. A telephone exchange opened in the village in 1902, and in 1907 a shingle mill started being serviced by electricity.[11] Within five years, the town as a whole had electricity, and the streets were lit by electric lights at night.[12]

Educational services in the village also expanded in the twentieth century. In 1913, the school in Vanderbilt, which had previously taught 10 grades of students, expanded to all 12 grades.[13] A new school building was built in the 1950s, and twenty years later additions to the school were made, including additional classrooms and an updated gym.[14]

Cornelius Vanderbilt, the Village Namesake

The village of Vanderbilt, like Vanderbilt University, is named for Cornelius Vanderbilt, a railroad tycoon and successful businessman who was the richest person in the United States at the time.[15] Vanderbilt was an executive of the Michigan Central Railroad and owned land for logging purposes in the area of Vanderbilt village.[16] While he was not a man known for philanthropy during most of his life, he did give something to the residents of Vanderbilt village.[17] After his lumber company harvested the timber in the area around the site of the eventual village, he donated some of his land to local residents.[18]

An Unconventional Way of Fixing a Train

In 1883, one of the trains in the Vanderbilt area hit a herd of cattle that had gotten onto the tracks.[19] All of the cows except for one were killed in the collision, and the train also suffered damage when "the engine blew a hole in one of its cylinders."[20] This hole allowed the steam that powered the train to escape, and so the train's crew found a nearby sapling and used the tree's wood to create a plug to fit the hole.[21] With this improvised repair in place, the train was able to continue on to its destination.[22]

The Coldest Temperature in Michigan

The coldest temperature ever officially recorded in Michigan was in Vanderbilt in 1934.[23] On February 9 of that year, the temperature, without factoring in wind chill, fell to -51° F.[24] Nearby Pellston claims to have reached -53° in 1933, but there is no official recording of that temperature, giving Vanderbilt the honor—or perhaps infamy—of holding the record for the coldest recorded temperature in Michigan.[25]

Vanderbilt Today

Vanderbilt is the "Gateway to the Pigeon River Country State Forest,"[26] a state forest in northern Michigan that is home to Michigan's only wild elk herd of any significant size.[27] The elk are a draw for tourists in Vanderbilt and the surrounding area, and there are businesses in the village that reflect this draw in their business names, including the Elkland Senior Center and the Elkhorn Grill and Tavern.

Other businesses in the village include a pizzeria, a trading post, a storage center, an auto repair center, a village market, and a few gas stations. The village is also home to a company that manufactures brass and copper tubes.

Services in the village include a township hall, a veterans memorial, a post office, a school, a Community church, a Baptist church, and a Holy Redeemer church. The North Central State Trail passes through Vanderbilt, which also has a public baseball diamond and a park with a playground.

Fox Tower Cemetery, a small graveyard from the 1800s in Vanderbilt, is said to be haunted.[29] People have reported abnormally cold temperatures, the sound of footsteps, and gates that move on their own.[30]

TOP: Tractors line the downtown area as part of Tractor Fun Day in the summer of 2017

Population: 247[1]   **Incorporated:** 1908[2]

INSETS L to R: One of the Walkerville school buildings • This playground area is shaded by a number of mature trees • The sign welcoming people to Walkerville Village Park • One of the older buildings in the downtown area of Walkerville

In November of 2017, a Michigan Lotto 47 ticket worth a jackpot of $4.3 million was sold at the Kwik Mart in Walkerville.[23]

Walkerville

History of Walkerville

THE VILLAGE OF WALKERVILLE was first platted in 1883 by Fayette Walker.[3] The site for the village that he chose was located on land he owned, but even with this and his decision to lend his name to the town, when the village post office opened later that year, the office was named Stetson for the first postmaster, Alvin Stetson.[4]

When Walker first platted the village, the settlement's success was not a sure thing. The land near the village was swampy and there was already an established general store not far from the village site.[5]

The Mason and Oceana Railroad came to Walkerville in 1888 when the line was extended to the village's location.[6] The village had grown only slowly before that point, but after the railroad's arrival, the pace of the town's growth increased, and by 1890, the village had a sawmill, a feed mill, two hotels, two meat markets, a saloon, and a selection of shops.[7]

With the village being called one thing and the post office another, there could be some confusion over what to call the village. Finally, in 1898, the name of the post office in the town changed to Walkerville.[8]

As with many towns in Michigan in the 1800s, Walkerville dealt in lumber, though the approach to deforestation in the area was a fairly haphazard one. Trees were largely cut without a thought to the future of the industry in the area.[9] But lumber was not the lifeblood of Walkerville, which also dealt extensively in agriculture by the end of the nineteenth century.[10] Produce buyers from Milwaukee would come to

Walkerville, buy produce, then have it shipped on the railroad to another station on the line.[11] At that point the produce would be transferred to a water shipping point on Lake Michigan and delivered to Milwaukee, where it would go on sale the very next morning.[12]

Walkerville: A Stop on the Miserable and Ornery Railroad

Walkerville was on the Mason and Oceana Railroad, but the engines of the trains that ran on that line were so loud that many of the workers on the line came up with their own name for the railroad.[13] Keeping the same first letters of the railroad's name, they would often call it the "Miserable and Ornery Railroad."[14] Perhaps this is one factor that contributed to the Mason and Oceana's short life, as it shut down in 1903.[15]

The railroad was also notorious for accidents, one of which occurred when a young machinist's helper slipped on a step that was icy due to a shoddy repair.[16] One of his feet was instantly severed before he was thrown into an icy snowbank, which caused him to slide back under the train, causing major injuries to his face and head.[17] He survived, however, and eventually won a major settlement against the railroad.[18]

Walkerville Thrives

There is a new community group in Walkerville that brings together community members, businesses, and organizations to help the village, well, thrive.[19] The group's goal is to "guide positive sustainable growth in the area" to benefit all residents and visitors.[20] One way the group accomplishes this is through community events, such as the Tractor Fun event held in the summer of 2017, which had farmers bring their tractors to the newly paved road in downtown Walkerville.[21] The farmers were then available to answer questions from children and families. The event also included a parade and a kids' car show.[22]

Walkerville Today

The Huron-Manistee National Forests surround Walkerville. The village has a park with playground equipment, benches, and multiple mature shade trees.

Businesses in the village include a well drilling company, a tree service business, a tavern, a gas station, a mini-mart, a dollar store, and two banks. There is also a county road commission, a library, a post office, a museum, an elementary school, a high school, and two churches.

Each Christmas Walkerville holds a Santa Parade, after which local children can meet with him to tell him what they want for Christmas.[24]

TOP: An antique store on South Shore Drive

Population: 290[1]   **Unincorporated**

INSETS L to R: Boats tied up on the eastern shore of Walloon Lake • These shuffleboard courts can be found on the east side of South Shore Drive • A monument in honor of those from Melrose Township who fought in World War II • Looking down South Shore Drive toward Hotel Walloon

People who came frequently to visit the lake in the late 1800s were often called "Wallooners."[30]

Walloon Lake

Ernest Hemingway in Walloon Lake

IN 1899, A COUPLE NAMED CLARENCE AND GRACE HEMINGWAY came to Walloon Lake and built a summer cottage, called Windemere, on its north shore.[2] That same year, Grace gave birth to a son, whom the couple named Ernest.[3] Ernest Hemingway spent much of his youth in northern Michigan and by Walloon Lake.[4] When Hemingway later began his writing career, he would remember his time at the lake and it would inspire his Nick Adams short stories.[5]

The cottage where Hemingway once lived on Walloon Lake still stands today and is now owned by a Hemingway relative. Painstakingly restored, and with the pencil lines showing the growth of a young Hemingway still on the walls, it was designated a National Historic Landmark in 1968, though the site is not available for visits.[6,7]

History of Walloon Lake

The first record of homesteaders in the Walloon Lake area dates back to 1872 when John Jones Jr. came to the area with his two sons, Elliot and Clarence.[8] Two years later, the railroad came to the area, and the three men helped with its construction by laying ties.[9] The arrival of the railroad was what truly prompted the village's beginning.

Walloon Lake began as a resort destination in the late 1800s. As the lumber industry in Michigan began to wind down, many of the railroad companies began to consider new uses for their trains.[10] One strategy many lines employed was to build hotels and resorts that were primarily accessible by railroad.[11]

In 1891, the Grand Rapids & Indiana Railroad built a new extension that went to Walloon Lake, and the resorts here attracted visitors from across the state and the Midwest.[12] Some of the visitors to the lake stayed, however, having been drawn in by the beautiful waters and available land for sale.[13]

With the abundance of tourists to the area, the village at Walloon Lake grew quickly. By 1903, there were a few hotels, a bathhouse, a boat livery, and an ice cream manufacturer.[14] Within five more years, a boat builder, a deli, a bazaar, a flour and feed mill, a yacht club, and a handful of new hotels had been added to the village.[15] By the early 1920s, there was also an electric light plant, a telephone company, and a golf course.[16]

In the first few decades of the twentieth century, Walloon Lake also saw the railroad tracks being replaced by roads as the easiest way to get to the village and the lake.[17] Boat traffic on the lake grew, and in the 1930s, people raced on the lake in sailboats specifically built for the lake.[18]

Life on the lake was good for many years, but in the second half of the twentieth century, the town began to struggle. Businesses in town closed, and there had also been a fire.[19] At one point, all that remained was a hotel, a general store, marina buildings, and a post office.[20] A plan to add lakefront condos in the town never came to full fruition after residents objected that it would block their views of the lake.[21] Finally, in 2012, a new plan to focus on promoting new business in the town was hatched by Jonathan Borisch and his son Matt. Their vision turned some of the land originally intended for condos into a village lakefront park and also helped bring a new hotel and several smaller businesses to the village.[22]

A Village and a Lake, Both of Many Names

Both Walloon Lake and the Walloon Lake village have gone by other names over the years. American Indians called the lake *Muhqua Nebis*, which is sometimes translated as "bear water," and early European settlers called it Bear Lake.[23] The original depot in the eventual village was first named Melrose after a man named Mel Rose who had surveyed the area.[24] Residents in the village wanted the first post office to be called Bear Lake after the lake, but as there was already another Bear Lake post office in Michigan, they were told to pick something else.[25] Tolcott became the name of the post office in 1897, though it was changed to Talcott two years later and finally became Walloon Lake in 1900.[26]

The final name was decided upon when a village butcher, J. R. Hass, remembered a name he had seen for the area on an old railroad map.[27] Some of the villagers looked into where that name had come from, and they discovered that at one time a group of Walloons, a cultural group of Belgians, had lived on the north shore of the lake.[28] However, even at the time the village finally became known by its modern name, there was no trace to be found of the people who had supposedly once lived there.[29]

Walloon Lake Today

Today, Walloon Lake is once again a thriving community. The lake is still as beautiful as it was a century ago, and the marina and public park provide a wonderful view of the water. The Bear River flows on the south side of town, and there is also a river trail.

Hotels and cottages make up a large portion of the town, but there are also several local businesses, including two restaurants, a general store and deli, an antique shop, a real estate company, and a collision center. There is also an area of "pop-up shops," where small businesses can rent a covered outdoor space. Services in the village include township offices, a post office, a library, and a Community church.

The most commonly seen sailboat for racing on Walloon Lake is known as a "17."[31] The name refers to the combined size of the jib and mainsail, which is 17 square meters.[32]

TOP: The building that contains the fire department in White Pine

Population: 474[1]   **Unincorporated**

INSETS L to R: The former White Pine High School • Looking toward the electric power company and copper refinery • Konteka Black Bear Resort • Gas available for sale in a parking lot near Konteka

There is a totem pole in White Pine. Erected by sportsmen in the 1960s, it is dedicated to the memory of the Ojibwe people.[32]

One of President Lincoln's distant relatives once worked at the White Pine Mine.[33] His name, coincidentally, was also Abraham Lincoln.[34]

When the White Pine Mine was set to return to operations in the 1950s, an official at a rival mine told press he believed the White Pine Mine would be "a lemon."[35] Some stories say he offered to "eat every pound of copper White Pine would produce."[36]

White Pine

History of White Pine

THE FIRST RECORDED EUROPEAN SETTLER in the area where the village of White Pine would eventually stand was John Less, a French trapper.[2] In 1865, Less's son Edward discovered copper in the area.[3] Even with this discovery, however, it was some time before any type of sizeable mining operation began in the area. That was done by Captain Thomas Hooper from 1879 to 1881.[4] In addition to his work with local mining, Hooper also was the person who named the settlement.[5] The name came from a tall white pine tree that was on a nearby hill.[6]

A Town Rich in Hard-to-Mine Copper

After Hooper ceased his mining operation in White Pine, the residents in the village primarily worked as hunters, trappers, and lumberjacks for many years.[7] In 1908, however, Tom Wilcox found more copper nearby, in Mineral River, and decided to give mining another go.[8] He extended the depth of the original shafts from Hooper's day and also constructed a few new ones.[9]

The mine began official operations in April of 1915, and this time the mining business would fare a bit better.[10] It was successful enough that a community soon built up around the mine, and within just a handful of years, the village had two churches, a moving picture theater, a gambling den, a dance hall, and a school.[11] The success was to be short-lived, however, and the operation largely shut down after only four years.[12] One problem was the difficulty in smelting the copper, due to the nature of the specific copper ore found there.[13] It was actually copper sulfide, or chalcocite, and contained a high level of silver, but mining it economically was beyond the reach of the miners at the time.[14] Still, while the mine was in operation, there were stories of workers pocketing bits of silver, as the silver wasn't what the mining company was interested in.[15]

A Good Deal on Copper

When Edward Less found copper in Ontonagon County in 1865, he was in need of a handful of items but not in need of the location of a copper deposit. He sold the location, just a few miles from White Pine, for "a barrel of pork, a barrel of flour and some grocery items."[16] The location he sold became the Nonesuch Mine, which mined the Nonesuch Lode, named for its unique type of copper (i.e., none such copper was found anywhere in Michigan's Copper Country). Because of the odd way its copper was deposited (in a grainy fashion rather than in easily accessible chunks), the mine was a failure, yielding "only" a total of 180 tons of copper over its lifetime.[17] By comparison, more-successful mines produced that in a year.[18]

A Late Mining Boom

In 1929, the company ceased all operations and the mine was sold to a Copper Range bidder at an auction for a sum equal to the amount of back taxes owed.[19] The mine sat unused and unexplored for a little over two decades, and finally, in the 1950s, the time was right for the mine to truly flourish.[20] With the Cold War, copper had increased in importance, and Copper Range, the new mining company, was granted a $67 million loan from the Defense Production Act.[21] Of as much importance, though, was the new technology available for processing copper ore such as was found in White Pine.[22]

With the new mining operations, White Pine became a company town, one of the most recent to develop in Michigan.[23] The copper company built 150 new homes, a trailer park, apartments, a dining hall, and a hospital in the village.[24] Other workers commuted to the mine from nearby communities that used to have mines of their own.[25] Even with the commuters, the town boomed in terms of population, climbing from a few dozen at the start of the 1950s to 1,800 in the 1970s.[26]

The mine was hugely successful. It quickly became the state's premier producer of copper and produced around five percent of the copper produced worldwide.[27] It remained in operation until the mid-1990s and, during that time, provided jobs to an estimated 20,000 people.[28] Mining at the White Pine site may not be over forever; a new company began exploratory drilling at a new location near White Pine in early 2017.[29]

White Pine Today

Today, White Pine seems to be in between times, and the uncertainty of new mining operations, which have run into some environmental issues, has something to do with that. It is not the thriving town of nearly 2,000 people it was 40 years ago, but neither does it feel as if all its success is behind it.

The village is near the Mineral River, where Tom Wilcox found copper at the start of the nineteenth century, and the southwest corner of the village is in Porcupine Mountains Wilderness State Park. Lake Superior lies only a few miles to the north. It is home to the Konteka Black Bear Resort, which has a motel, a restaurant, a bar, a gift shop, and a bowling alley. The resort also has sightings of black bears just outside the windows in the dining room.[30]

The village has a post office, a fire department, a Legion Post, and two churches. Just to the east of the town is the White Pine Electric Power company. There is also a ski shop and a "plant-based pharmaceutical" company.[31]

The reopening of the White Pine Mine in the 1950s brought workers to the village from all over the country. At the local school, 42 different states were represented in a grade that consisted of only 50 total students.[37] For the general election of 1968, White Pine had 486 registered voters. All but nine of them turned out to vote that year.[38]

Population: 384[1]   **Incorporated:** 1907[2]

INSETS L to R: The building that houses the Whittemore City Hall was built in 1948 • The Whittemore Speedway is the oldest speedway in Michigan • The Whittemore branch of the Iosco-Arenac District Library • The playground area in Whittemore

Students in Whittemore attend Whittemore-Prescott Area Schools, which serve students from kindergarten through twelfth grade.[25]

TOP: A park area in the city contains a gazebo, a model of a train engine, and patriotic decorations

Whittemore

The Whittemore Speedway

THE CITY OF WHITTEMORE IS HOME to Michigan's oldest operating speedway, but the speedway might never have come into existence if not for the failure of a carnival scheduled to appear in the village in 1948.[3] When organizers learned the carnival would not be able to make it, they quickly set to making alternate plans to provide entertainment at the event.[4] In addition to greasing some pigs for the children to catch and hiring an ice cream truck, a few men set up a hastily constructed racetrack and acquired some old cars from the local auto retailer.[5] The races were met with a high degree of interest from those in the village, and the next year saw the formation of the Whittemore Racing Club.[6]

In 1950, only two years after the improvised creation of the original track, the venue underwent several major upgrades, including the addition of grandstands that sat 700 people and the installation of lights on the track.[7] Other updates have been done to the track over the years as the need arose, and races have been run weekly from Memorial Day weekend to Labor Day for nearly 70 years.[8]

History of Whittemore

The village of Whittemore was founded in 1879, the same year a railroad station for the Detroit and Mackinac Railway was built in the village.[9] The village and station were given the name Whittemore.[10] The first post office in Whittemore opened in 1880, and Robert H. Martin was appointed as its first postmaster.[11]

198

The primary industry in the area at the time was lumber, particularly pine, but Whittemore also did business related to agriculture, even back in the 1880s, shortly after the settlement had been founded.[12] The soil in the region was particularly fertile,[13] allowing both pursuits to grow up with each other. In addition, the presence of the railroad helped the town, as much of the trading in the region was done in Whittemore.[14]

By 1903, Whittemore was home to over 500 people, three churches, a business dealing in farm implements, a lumber business, a saw and planing mill, a veterinary surgeon, and numerous farmers.[15] Five years later, though the population had fallen somewhat, there was also a grain elevator, a school, and a bank.[16]

In 1907, Whittemore was incorporated as a city without ever having been incorporated as a village first.[17] The village sought incorporation as a city rather than a village for a number of reasons, but most centered around the settlement's desire to more-fully control its interactions with the township it had been a part of before.[18] This included getting the township to help pay for bridges that led to, but were outside of, the town.[19]

The Roll-Inn

Also in 1907, a combination community building and livery stable was constructed in the city.[20] Over the next five and a half decades, the building also held a roller-skating rink, a restaurant, a dance hall, a basketball court, and a tavern, and it came to be called the Roll-Inn.[21] The building served an important role of community-building in Whittemore until it burned down in 1963.[22] Today a bar and a restaurant occupy the spot where the Roll-Inn once stood.[23]

Whittemore Today

Today, Whittemore is the fourth-smallest city in Michigan, though its population today is roughly the same as it was 100 years ago.[24] While the lumber industry has disappeared from the city, agriculture is still present, and Whittemore is home to a feed store, a veterinarian who works with both pets and livestock, and a cheese company.

Other businesses in the village, which is split on a north and south axis by M-65, include a party store, a hardware store, a pizzeria, a resale shop, a tavern, a combination restaurant and bar, a used car dealer, and a business that specializes in septic systems. The city also has a fire department, a city hall, a veterans memorial, a railroad park, a post office, and apartments. Within the city limits, there are two churches—one Catholic and one Baptist—and there is also a Lutheran church a little ways south of the city.

Whittemore was home to 1st Lieutenant Leland Larson, a U.S. Army Air Forces ace in World War II.[26] Larson was credited with downing six Nazi airplanes in all, including the penultimate plane downed in the European Theater of Operations and the last by an American pilot.[27]

Population: 244[1] **Incorporated:** 1903[2]

INSETS L to R: This building, once the depot in Wolverine, was built in 1906 • The park in Wolverine • One of the older buildings in the downtown area of the village • This church is located at the corner of Pine and Main Streets

TOP: The high school building in Wolverine actually serves as a middle school as well

The Wolverine Depot, which was built along the tracks in 1906, still stands in the village today.[24]

Wolverine

History of Wolverine

JACOB SHOOK AND HIS SONS were some of the earliest European settlers in Wolverine; they came to the area in 1874 as homesteaders.[3] They were joined three years later by Emphrim Ford and his wife.[4] At the time, the closest rail service was in Gaylord, and both families had to come to the Wolverine area by different means, with the Shooks using a cart pulled by oxen and the Fords walking along an old footpath.[5]

Due to the abundance of lumber in the area, though, the railroad didn't stay away for long. The village was platted in 1881 by John N. Sanborne, though at the time it was recorded with the name Torrey rather than Wolverine.[6] The land the village was to be built on was at the time owned by Daniel McKillop.[7] That same year the village

received its first post office, and the office was given the name Wolverine. The following year the village was platted for a second time, and this time the plat was recorded as Wolverine to match the name of the post office.[8]

The Michigan Central Railroad came to Wolverine in the early 1880s, and four passenger trains per day passed through the village, as well as an unknown number of freight trains.[9] Lumber was the early industry in the area, and the business was strong enough that it supported a large population in the village. Within ten years of the first platting of the village, Wolverine was home to approximately 1,000 people.[10] By 1905, that number had climbed to 1,800, and neither number included the lumberjacks who worked in nearby camps but spent many of their weekends in the town.[11] It is said that their presence could double the number of people in the town.[12]

Moving Beyond Lumber

The lumber business could not last forever, and between the human-caused deforestation and a series of forest fires, the lumber industry in Wolverine went into decline in the 1920s.[13] By the mid-1930s, many residents had moved away and those still present switched to agricultural pursuits.[14] Fish-raising farms had sprung up at the ponds that had once held lumber mills, and in 1938, a Christmas tree farm also opened in the village.[15]

Tourism was another industry the town switched to once the lumber had been depleted, though the start of this industry in Wolverine could be said to have been at the behest of the Michigan Central Railroad, which ran a campaign to promote Northern Michigan as a "curative of hayfever, asthma, bronchial and lung infections."[16] Later tourism in the area was also increased with the arrival of highways and freeways.

Hemingway and Wolverine

In addition to his time spent at Walloon Lake (page 194) and in Horton Bay (page 104), Ernest Hemingway would also sometimes visit Wolverine.[17] He enjoyed fishing, and when he fished in the Sturgeon River, which passes right through Wolverine, Hemingway would often camp in or near the village.[18]

Wolverine's Annual Lumberjack Festival

Each summer the Wolverine Festival Committee puts on a Lumberjack Festival the last weekend in June.[19] The event's fun begins before that, however, when local students are invited to create a logo for that year's festival.[20] The winner's design is then featured on the promotional materials and turned into buttons for the event, which includes lumberjack shows, children's activities, laser tag, a kayak race, a parade, and other family-friendly activities.[21]

Wolverine Today

When you enter Wolverine, a sign in the village invites you to "enjoy our seasons," and the village has a park and a campground and is on the North Central State Trail, which is part of the Rails to Trails program in Michigan. But while the village near the northern tip of Michigan's Lower Peninsula does offer visitors four beautiful and distinct seasons to experience, there is more than that to enjoy in Wolverine. The village is currently experiencing some growth and has prime real estate available for both residential and commercial development.[22]

Current businesses in the village include a cabinet company, a bait and tackle shop, a deli, a market, a real estate office, a beauty salon, an auto care business, a restaurant, and a bar, and the village is also trying to develop additional dining, shopping, and recreational opportunities for both residents and visitors alike.[23] The town also has a township hall, a post office, a community library, an American Legion post, a credit union, an elementary school, and a high school. Churches in the village include a Free Methodist church and a Baptist church.

One of the names for the state of Michigan is the Wolverine State, though there is no record of any wolverines currently living in the state. While some people think that the wolverine is also the official state animal, that honor in fact goes to the white-tailed deer.[25]

201

TOP: This building holds the Woodland Township offices and fire department

Population: 425[1]   **Incorporated:** 1892[2]

INSETS L to R: The park in Woodland contains a wooden play structure • The Woodland Township Hall, completed in 1870 • Fall foliage can be seen on this residential street in the village • Some of the older buildings along Main Street

Students at Woodland's Lakewood Early Childhood Center were treated to a rude surprise on a March morning in 2017: high winds struck the building and the roof began caving in.[21] Happily, administrators immediately declared a tornado drill and no one was hurt despite significant damage to the building.[22]

Woodland

A Township Hall Standing for 137 Years and Counting

FOUNDED IN 1837, Woodland began to flourish a few years after the end of the Civil War, when the township's population had grown to 1,000 people, so in 1867, men on the township board decided it was time to build a town hall.[3]

The board purchased land for the hall from Woodland resident and store owner Lawrence Hilbert.[4] The hall, which was completed in 1870, cost $2,000 to build.[5] Over the years, the hall, which is still standing in Woodland today, has been used for township meetings, schooling, traveling shows, and other community events.[6] Over 130 years after it was built, it remains in its original state, with a wood stove for heat, and it is still used for township meetings.[7]

History of Woodland

The first European settlers recorded in the Woodland area were Charles Galloway, his brother Jonathan Galloway, and Samuel S. Haight in 1837. In the late 1840s, John McArthur and a man named Snyder came to the area as well and started shops—a store and a blacksmith shop respectively.[8] A post office opened in 1848 with Nehemiah Lovewell as the first postmaster.[9] Jacob Strauss opened a store of his own in the early 1850s, and Lawrence Hilbert also began trading in the area sometime in the mid- to late-1850s or early 1860s.[10]

The 1860s were when the town began to see true growth, as it was about that time that lots in the village began to be designated and sold.[11] Within a dozen years, the village had grown to a size of 150 people and had become active in the lumber industry.[12] The village had sawmills and a grist mill, a grocer, a drugstore, a gunsmith, a boarding house, a tinner, shoemakers, a milliner, a wagonmaker, and a few other small shops and businesses.[13] Within ten more years the village had also gained a bank and a store selling farm implements.[14]

Until the late 1880s, getting goods in and out of Woodland was difficult, as the nearest railroad station was nine miles to the south in Nashville.[15] Woodland received its own station on the Chicago, Kalamazoo, & Saginaw in 1889.[16] With this addition to the village, Woodland's population began to grow more quickly and within three years had climbed to 500.[17]

As the trees were cut and agriculture became more and more important in Woodland, new businesses began to open, including a cheese manufactory, a grain elevator, and a fruit evaporator in the late 1880s and early 1890s, and a ginseng grower and a creamery in the early part of the twentieth century.[18] Crops grown in the area included wheat and various fruits and vegetables.[19]

Herald E. Classic Memorial Park

Woodland is home to the Herald E. Classic Memorial Park. This park, located in the center of the town, has a ballfield and a large wooden play structure and hosts local events, such as the annual homecoming. It was named in honor of Herald Classic, who served the community for over 50 years as a druggist.[20]

Woodland Today

Despite the hundred-plus years that have passed since Woodland reached its peak population, Woodland is still a thriving small town. Located on M-43, it is home to a gas station, a propane company, an auto body shop, a hitch and RV store, a building company, an express mart, a beauty salon, a food co-op, and a bar. There is a United

Methodist church, a library, township and village offices, a garage, a fire department, and a post office. The village is also home to the Lakewood Early Childhood Center.

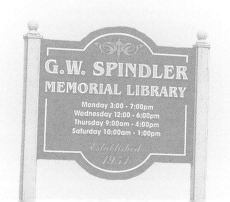

In 1888, Woodland residents were able to get to Hastings, which was 13 miles away, by taking one of the daily stagecoaches that traveled between the two places.[23] The trip cost passengers 40 cents.[24]

TOP: The Zeba Indian United Methodist Church was built in 1888

Population: 480[1]   **Unincorporated**

INSETS L to R: Zeba is situated on Lake Superior • The Whirl-I-Gig holds bowling lanes and a banquet hall • This historical marker details some of the history of the Zeba Indian United Methodist Church • One of the roads running toward the lake

Zeba got its name from a stream that passes to the southeast of the village. It is said that Zeba translates roughly to "little river."[26]

The Methodist building at the Kewawenon Mission in Zeba was the first Methodist building constructed west of Sault Ste. Marie.[27]

Zeba

History of Zeba

FUR TRADERS AND MISSIONARIES played a large role in the beginnings of Zeba. One of the first Europeans to come to the Zeba area was Peter Marksman Sr.[2] His job was to provide fur traders with government-issued supplies, and he came to the area with a few companions in the early to mid-1800s.[3]

Another early European in the area was the Reverend Frederic Baraga who came to the area in 1831 to found a mission for the American Indians in the area.[4] A Methodist minister named Daniel Meeker Chandler came to Zeba in 1834, shortly after Baraga left the area, and while Baraga had come to the area to preach Catholicism, Chandler was a Methodist.[5]

Another early person preaching Methodism in the area was *Shaw-wun-dais*, whose English name was John Sunday.[6] He was an Ojibwe man, who came in 1832, and in 1834 John Clark came to Zeba and built a Methodist mission house and a school.[7] Within a dozen years, the mission had grown to a membership of 62, all but four of whom were American Indians.[8]

With a focus other than lumber in its early days, Zeba did not grow up as a settlement focused on industry. This means that the settlement went largely unnoticed by official Michigan directories for the first 70 to 80 years of its existence, as it was not a major producer of goods or a major shipping hub. The railroad came to the area in 1874 but was not widely used; instead residents largely engaged in hunting, trapping, and farming for their own needs.[9] Still, it did offer another way of getting into or out of the area that didn't involve the use of canoes or showshoes, two common methods of travel used by those in the area prior to 1874.[10]

Beginning in 1880, camp meetings for American Indians were held in Zeba and brought people from a wide region to the village.[11] A new Methodist church was built in the settlement in 1888 and the structure, using hand-made shingles, still stands in Zeba today as the Zeba Indian United Methodist Church.[12] It is thought of as the successor to the original Methodist mission at Kewawenon.[13]

In 1910, Zeba received its first post office, and Mary E. Spruce was appointed as the town's first postmistress.[14] The post office shut down from 1912 to 1913, was restored, then shuttered again in 1933.[15]

Frederic Baraga in Zeba

When the Reverend Frederic Baraga came to the area where Zeba is now located, his goal was to bring Christianity, specifically Catholicism, to the American Indians in the area.[16] Baraga came to the United States from Slovenia on New Year's Eve, 1830, with the goal of ministering to American Indians.[17] As part of his work, he learned the languages spoken by the Ojibwe and Ottawa peoples, and in 1832, only a year after he began learning the Ottawa language, he published a prayer book written in Ottawa and intended it for use in his congregation.[18] This was the first work ever printed in the Ottawa language.[19] Known as the "Snowshoe Priest" for his habit of trekking via snowshoes to minister to the area residents, Baraga went on to become a Bishop in 1853.[20] More than a century later, he was venerated by Pope Benedict XVI in 2012.[21]

Cora Reynolds Anderson

Cora Reynolds Anderson, who both attended school and taught at the Zeba Mission in the late 1800s and early 1900s, was elected to the State Legislature in 1924.[22] Only four years after women gained the right to vote in the United States, she became both the first woman and the first American Indian to be elected to and serve in the Michigan House of Representatives.[23] She was behind only Senator Eva McCall, elected in 1920 to the Michigan Senate, as the second woman elected to public office in Michigan.[24] Anderson served one term in the House, and while there she advocated for issues such as agriculture and public health.[25]

Zeba Today

Zeba is part of the L'Anse Indian Reservation and today is primarily a settlement of American Indians. The town is on Lake Superior, and many of the houses have views of the lake. The streets are quiet and peaceful. The town is home to the Keweenaw Bay Indian Childcare Center. The Zeba Indian United Methodist Church, built in 1888, is still used in the town to this day.

Zeba is part of the L'Anse Indian Reservation, which was established by the Treaty of 1854.[28] It is the oldest and largest reservation in all of Michigan.[29]

Sources

AHMEEK

1. U.S. Census Bureau, 2010 census.
2. *Local Acts of the Legislature of the State of Michigan Passed at the Regular Session of 1909 with an Appendix* (Lansing: Wynkoop Hallenbeck Crawford Co., State Printers, 1909), 36–37.
3. "Our Story," *Sand Hills Lighthouse Inn*, accessed September 26, 2017, www.sandhillslighthouseinn.com/story.html.
4. Ibid.
5. Clarence J. Monette, *Brief History of Ahmeek, Michigan* (Lake Linden: Welden H. Curtin, 1981), 5.
6. Ibid.
7. Monette, *Brief History*, 8.
8. *Local Acts of the Legislature*, 36–37.
9. Monette, *Brief History*, 10.
10. U.S. Census Bureau, 1910 census.
11. Monette, *Brief History*, 22.
12. Arthur W. Thurner, *Rebels on the Range: The Michigan Copper Miner's Strike of 1913–1914* (Lake Linden: John H. Forster Press, 1984).
13. Ibid.
14. Ibid.
15. Ibid.
16. Ibid.
17. Ibid.
18. Ibid.
19. Monette, *Brief History*, 24–28.
20. Thurner, *Rebels on the Range*.
21. "Ahmeek Mine, Ahmeek, Keweenaw Co., Michigan, USA," *mindat.org*, accessed September 26, 2017, www.mindat.org/loc-8386.html.
22. Monette, *Brief History*.
23. *Ahmeek Streetcar Station Vacation Rental*, accessed September 26, 2017, www.ahmeekstreetcarstation.com.
24. "Photo Gallery, Ahmeek Mine, Ahmeek, Keweenaw Co., Michigan, USA," *mindat.org*, accessed September 26, 2017, www.mindat.org/sitegallery.php?loc=8386.

AKRON

25. U.S. Census Bureau, 2010 census.
26. *Local Acts of the Legislature of the State of Michigan Passed at the Regular Session of 1911* (Lansing: Wynkoop Hallenbeck Crawford Co., State Printers, 1911), 52–53.
27. "Home," *Village of Akron*, accessed June 13, 2017, www.villageofakron.org/.
28. Walter Romig, *Michigan Place Names* (Detroit: Wayne State University Press, 1986), 13.
29. Ibid.
30. Romig, *Michigan Place Names, 13; History of Tuscola and Bay Counties, Mich., with Illustrations and Biographical Sketches of Some of their Prominent Men and Pioneers* (Chicago: H. R. Page & Co., 1883), 129.
31. *History of Tuscola and Bay Counties, Mich., with Illustrations and Biographical Sketches of Some of their Prominent Men and Pioneers* (Chicago: H. R. Page & Co., 1883), 129.
32. Ibid.
33. Ibid.
34. Ibid.
35. Ibid.
36. *Michigan State Gazetteer and Business Directory for 1907–1908* (Detroit: C. F. Clarke, 1908), 300.
37. *Michigan State Gazetteer and Business Directory for 1921–1922* (Detroit: C. F. Clarke, 1922), 169.
38. Ibid.

ALLEN

1. U.S. Census Bureau, 2010 census.
2. Walter Romig, *Michigan Place Names* (Detroit: Wayne State University Press, 1986), 17–18.
3. County of Hillsdale, "History of Hillsdale County," *County of Hillsdale, Michigan*, accessed October 1, 2017, www.co.hillsdale.mi.us/index.php/county-history.
4. *History of Hillsdale County, Michigan, with Illustrations and Biographical Sketches of Some of Its Prominent Men and Pioneers* (Philadelphia: Everts & Abbott, 1879), 35.
5. Ibid.
6. Ibid.
7. County of Hillsdale, "History of Hillsdale County."
8. Ibid.
9. *History of Hillsdale County*, 260.
10. Ibid.
11. *History of Hillsdale County*, 261.
12. Ibid.
13. Ibid.
14. Ibid.
15. "Allen, MI," *Hillsdale County Historical Society*, accessed October 1, 2017, www.hillsdalehistoricalsociety.org/allen-mi.
16. Ibid.
17. "The Robert and Barbara Watkins Home – Restoration," *Hillsdale County Historical Society*, accessed October 1, 2017, www.hillsdalehistoricalsociety.org/recent-happenings/.
18. Ibid.
19. "Allen," *US 12 Heritage Trail*, accessed October 1, 2017, www.us12heritagetrail.org/collection.asp?ait=cv&cid=25.

ALPHA

1. U.S. Census Bureau, 2010 census.
2. Jack Hill, *A History of Iron County Michigan* (Iron River: The Reporter Publishing Company, 1955), 126.
3. Hill, *A History of Iron County*, 123.
4. Ibid.
5. Hill, *A History of Iron County*, 126.
6. Walter Romig, *Michigan Place Names* (Detroit: Wayne State University Press, 1986), 20.
7. Ibid.
8. Ibid.
9. "Iron County," *Western Upper Peninsula Heritage Trail Network of Michigan*, accessed October 1, 2017, www.upheritage.org/iron.htm.
10. Hill, *A History of Iron County*, 126.
11. "History," *Mastadon Township*, accessed October 1, 2017, www.mastodontownship.com/history.
12. Romig, *Michigan Place Names*, 357.
13. "Miners Smothered in Quicksand," *The Ironwood Times*, July 18, 1914, quoted at http://www.gendisasters.com/michigan/19850/alpha-mi-quicksand-smothers-miners-july-1914; village historical sign.
14. "Alpha, Michigan – Historic District," *Michigan Back Roads – Getaways*, accessed October 1, 2017, michiganbackroads.com/DayTrips/Alpha.aspx.
15. "Alpha Michigan Brewing Company," *Alpha Michigan Brewing Company*, accessed October 1, 2017, www.alphabrewingco.com.
16. "History," *Mastadon Township*.
17. Ibid.

APPLEGATE

18. U.S. Census Bureau, 2010 census.
19. Walter Romig, *Michigan Place Names* (Detroit: Wayne State University Press, 1986), 26.
20. Ibid.
21. *Portrait and Biographical Album of Sanilac County, Containing Portraits and Biographical Sketches of*

Prominent and Representative Citizens of the County, Together with Portraits and Biographies of All the Governors of Michigan and the Presidents of the United States (Chicago: Chapman Brothers, 1884), 492.

22. Ibid.

23. JoAnn Zerilli, in conversation with the author, August 6, 2017.

24. Zerilli.

25. Romig, *Michigan Place Names*, 26.

26. Zerilli.

27. Heman Conoman Smith, *History of the Church of Jesus Christ of Latter Day Saints, 1805-1890, Vol. 4.* (Lamoni: Board of Publication of Reorganized Church of Latter Day Saints), 1911.

28. Zerilli.

29. Ibid.

30. Ibid.

BANCROFT

31. U.S. Census Bureau, 2010 census.

32. Village of Bancroft, "About," Village of Bancroft, accessed August 4, 2017, www.villageofbancroftmi.org/?page_id=1082.

33. "Major Circus Families," Central Michigan University Clarke Historical Library, accessed September 27, 2017, www.cmich.edu/library/clarke/ResearchResources/Michigan_Material_Statewide/Circuses_and_Carnivals/Pages/Major-Circus-Families.aspx.

34. Ibid.

35. Ibid.

36. Ibid.

37. Ibid.

38. Village of Bancroft, "About."

39. The Past and Present of Shiawassee County, Michigan, Historically Together with Biographical Sketches of Many of its Leading and Prominent Citizens and Illustrious Dead (Lansing: The Michigan Historical Publishing Association, [1906?]), 159–160.

40. Ibid.

41. Walter Romig, Michigan Place Names (Detroit: Wayne State University Press, 1986), 41.

42. Village of Bancroft, "About."

43. Shiawassee County Historical Society, "Ghost Towns and Post Offices of Shiawassee County," The Argus Press, September 15, 2000. news.google.com/newspapers?id=9T4iAAAAIBAJ&sjid=sqwFAAAAIBAJ&pg=1568%2C1275079.

44. The Past and Present of Shiawassee County, 159–160.

45. Ibid.

46. Ibid.

47. Ibid.

48. Ibid.

49. Ibid.

50. Ibid.

51. U.S. Census Bureau, 1910 census.

52. Van Agen Sod Farm, "Van Agen Sod Family Farm History," Van Agen Sod & Tree Farm, accessed September 27, 2017, vanagensodfarm.com/about/.

BARRYTON

53. U.S. Census Bureau, 2010 census.

54. "Barryton," Michigan historical marker, Barryton, Michigan.

55. "Welcome," *MacKersie Brothers*, accessed October 8, 2017, www.mackersiemarket.com.

56. Ibid.

57. Walter Romig, *Michigan Place Names* (Detroit: Wayne State University Press, 1986), 44. "Barryton," Michigan historical marker.

58. "Barryton," Michigan historical marker.

59. Ibid.

60. Ibid.

61. Romig, Michigan Place Names; "Frank Barry," Michigan historical marker, Barryton, Michigan.

62. "Frank Barry," Michigan historical marker, Barryton, Michigan.

63. Ibid.

64. "Welcome to Barryton Elementary School," *Chippewa Hills School District*, accessed October 6, 2017, chsd.us/barryton/index.htm.

65. Michigan Economic Development Corporation, "Barryton Lilac Festival," *Pure Michigan*, accessed October 8, 2017, www.michigan.org/event/barryton-lilac-festival.

66. "Barryton Lilac Festival," *Facebook*, accessed October 8, 2017, www.facebook.com/BarrytonLilacFestival/.

67. Village of Barryton "July 19, 2017, Public Hearing Minutes," *Village of Barryton*, accessed October 6, 2017, villageofbarryton.com/?page_id=1054.

68. "Welcome to Barryton Elementary School," *Chippewa Hills School District*.

69. Michigan Economic Development Corporation, "Barryton Area Museum," *Pure Michigan*, accessed October 6, 2017, www.michigan.org/property/barryton-area-museum.

70. Ibid.

71. "Celebrate at Barryton on Wednesday, August 3," *Alma Record*, July 29, 1898, accessed through the Library of Congress website, chroniclingamerica.loc.gov.

72. Elisha Anderson, "Mich. Woman's Hobby Helps Solve Missing Person Cases," *USA Today*, February 18, 2013, www.usatoday.com/story/news/nation/2013/02/18/michigan-woman-hobby-missing-persons-cases/1927461/.

73. Ibid.

BARTON HILLS

74. U.S. Census Bureau, 2010 census.

75. Barton Hills Village, "Historical Perspectives," *Barton Hills Village*, accessed October 6, 2017, vil-bartonhills.org/about.

76. Ibid.

77. Ibid.

78. Ibid.

79. Grace Shackman and Lois Kane, "The Buried History of Barton Hills," *Ann Arbor Observer*, June 2005.

80. Ibid.

81. Ibid.

82. Ibid.

83. Ibid.

84. Ibid.

85. Shackman and Kane, "The Buried History of Barton Hills"; Barton Hills Village, "Historical Perspectives."

86. Barton Hills Village, "Historical Perspectives"; David Morris, *The Nature and Purpose of a Home Rule Charter* (Citizen's Research Council of Michigan, the Michigan Municipal League, and the Michigan Association of Municipal Attornies, 1993), www.mml.org/pdf/charter_revision/village3.pdf.

87. Ibid.

88. Barton Hills Village, "Historical Perspectives."

89. Shackman and Kane, "The Buried History of Barton Hills."

90. Ibid.

91. Ibid.

92. Barton Hills Village, "Historical Perspectives."

93. "Our History," *Barton Hills Country Club*, accessed October 6, 2017, www.bartonhillscc.com/Default.aspx?p=DynamicModule&pageid=353833&ssid=259872&vnf=1.

94. Ibid.

95. "Home," *Barton Boat Club*, accessed October 6, 2017, bartonboatclub.org/Barton%20Pond.html.

96. Shackman and Kane, "The Buried History of Barton Hills."

97. Ibid.

BEAR LAKE

98. U.S. Census Bureau, 2010 census.

99. Walter Romig, *Michigan Place Names* (Detroit: Wayne State University Press, 1986), 49.

100. *History of Manistee County, Michigan, with Illustrations and Biographical Sketches of Some of Its Prominent Men and Pioneers* (Chicago: H. R. Page & Co., 1882), 10

101. Romig, *Michigan Place Names*, 49.

102. *History of Manistee County*, 77–78.

103. *History of Manistee County*, 78.

104. bid.

105. *History of Manistee County*, 79.

106. Ibid.

107. Ibid.

108. H. R. Page, *History of Mason County, Michigan: With Illustrations and Biographical Sketches of Some of Its Prominent Men and Pioneers* (Chicago: H. R. Page, 1882), 79.

109. Ibid.

110. Ibid.

111. *History of Manistee County*, 80.

112. Ibid.

113. Bear Lake Township Planning Commission, *2002 Comprehensive Plan: Bear Lake Township*, 2002, www.lakestoland.bria2.net/wp-content/uploads/2012/08/BearLakeTownshipMasterPlan2002.pdf.

114. Ibid.

115. Michigan Department of Natural Resources, *Status of the Fishery Resource Report 2000-6, 2000*, last updated August 7, 2002, www.michigandnr.com/PUBLICATIONS/PDFS/ifr/ifrlibra/status/waterbody/00-6.htm.

116. *History of Manistee County*, 9.

117. Michigan Department of Natural Resources, *Status of the Fishery Resource Report*.

118. Ibid.

119. "Bear Lake Area Historical Society & Museum," *Facebook*, accessed October 8, 2017, www.facebook.com/blhistory/.

120. Ibid.

121. Bear Lakes Township Planning Commission, *Lakes to Land Regional Initiative: Bear Lake Township People and Land*, July 2014, www.lakestoland.bria2.net/wp-content/uploads/2014/11/Tab4_BearLakeTwp_ADOPTED_11192014_web1.pdf.

122. Ibid.

BEULAH

123. U.S. Census Bureau, 2010 census.

124. Walter Romig, *Michigan Place Names* (Detroit: Wayne State University Press, 1986), 60.

125. William L. Case, *The Tragedy of Crystal Lake*, with some Sidelights (1941), babel.hathitrust.org/cgi/pt?id=mdp.39015071291705;view=1up;seq=3.

126. Ibid.

127. Ibid.

128. Ibid.

129. Ibid.

130. Ibid.

131. Ibid.

132. Ibid.

133. Ibid.

134. Ibid.

135. "History of the CLYC," *CLYC*, accessed October 9, 2017, clyc.net/clyc-history/; Stacy L. Daniels, "Who Pulled the Plug at Crystal Lake?," The Betsie Current, August 14, 2014, betsiecurrent.com/index.php/who-pulled-the-plug-at-crystal-lake/.

136. Daniels, "Who Pulled the Plug at Crystal Lake?"

137. Romig, *Michigan Place Names*, 60.

138. Romig, *Michigan Place Names*, 60.

139. Ibid.

140. Ibid.

141. National Park Service, *Spreadsheet of NRHP Listed Properties*, updated September 2015, www.nps.gov/nr/research/data_downloads/NRHP_Links_2015.xlsx; "MICHIGAN – Benzie County – Vacant / Not In Use," *National Register of Historic Places*, accessed October 9, 2017.

142. Ibid.

143. Crystal Lake Community Business Association, "Archibald Jones Day," *Crystal Lake Community Business Association*, accessed October 9, 2017, clcba.org/event/archibald-jones-day/.

144. Stacy L. Daniels, *The "Runaway" and the "Tragedy": A Tale of Two Lakes, Having Disappeared* (Crystal Lake & Watershed Association, 2010), crystallakewatershed.org/pdfs/Tale_of_Two_Disappearing_Lakes.pdf.

BIG BAY

145. U.S. Census Bureau, 2010 census.

146. Lisa Didier, "Memories of a Murder," *Chicago Tribune*, August 20, 1989, articles.chicagotribune.com/1989-08-20/travel/8901060128_1_john-d-voelker-robert-traver-lumberjack-tavern.

147. Dennis McCann, "Marquette, Michigan Remembers 'Anatomy of a Murder,'" *Journal Sentinel*, November 7, 2008.

148. Ibid.

149. David J. Krajicek, "Killing of Michigan Bar Owner in 1952 Inspired Film 'Anatomy of a Murder,'" *NY Daily News*, January 17, 2009.

150. McCann, "Marquette, Michigan Remembers."

151. Ibid.

152. Didier, "Memories of a Murder."

153. "History," *Thunder Bay Inn*, accessed October 9, 2017, www.thunderbayinn.net/hist.php.

154. Walter Romig, *Michigan Place Names* (Detroit: Wayne State University Press, 1986), 60.

155. Big Bay Point Lighthouse," *Lighthouse Friends*, accessed December 3, 2017, www.lighthousefriends.com/light.asp?ID=574.

156. "The Tragedy and Haunting at the Big Bay Lighthouse," *Lost in Michigan*, accessed December 3, 2017, lostinmichigan.net/tragedy-haunting-big-bay-lighthouse/.

157. Ibid.

158. "History," *Thunder Bay Inn*.

159. Jay Clarke, "Rebirth of Michigan Inn Shows There's Life after the Movies," *The Baltimore Sun*, May 21, 1995, articles.baltimoresun.com/1995-05-21/features/1995141239_1_henry-ford-bay-hotel-big-bay; "Big Bay Sawmill and Surrounding Buildings from the Water at Big Bay, Michigan, circa 1930," *The Henry Ford*, accessed October 9, 2017, www.thehenryford.org/collections-and-research/digital-collections/artifact/366489/.

160. Ibid.

161. Ibid.

162. Ibid.

163. Ibid.

164. Ibid.

165. Ibid.

166. "The Inn," "The Keepers," *Big Bay Point Lighthouse Bed and Breakfast*, accessed October 9, 2017, www.bigbaylighthouse.com/home1.html.

167. Clarke, "Rebirth of Michigan Inn."

BLOOMINGDALE

168. U.S. Census Bureau, 2010 census.

169. Walter Romig, *Michigan Place Names* (Detroit: Wayne State University Press, 1986), 66.

170. Virginia Burleson, in conversation with the author, September 17, 2017.

171. Bloomingdale Area Historical Association, *Bloomingdale Oil Boom 1938*, museum pamphlet, n.d.

172. Burleson.

173. Jack R. Westbrook, in *Bloomingdale Oil Boom 1938*, a museum pamphlet by the Bloomingdale Area Historical Association, n.d.

174. Burleson; Westbrook.

175. Westbrook.

176. "History of Bloomingdale," *Van Buren County*, accessed October 10, 2017, www.vbco.org/bdale_ history.asp; Walter Romig, *Michigan Place Names* (Detroit: Wayne State University Press, 1986), 66.

177. "History of Bloomingdale," *Van Buren County*.

178. Ibid.

179. Ibid.

180. Ibid.

181. Ibid.

182. Ibid.

183. Aaron Mueller, "Deadball Era Baseball Stars Wade and Bill Killefer to Be Honored with Monuments in Paw Paw," *Kalamazoo Gazette*, July 24, 2009, www. mlive.com/sports/kalamazoo/index.ssf/2009/07/ deadball_era_baseball_stars_wa.html.

184. Ibid.

185. Ibid.

186. Ibid.

187. Ibid.

188. Ibid.

189. Ibid.

190. "Bloomingdale Telephone Company History," *Bloomingdale Communications*, accessed October 10, 2017, www.bloomingdalecom.net/?/about-us/ history/.

191. Burleson.

BOYNE FALLS

192. U.S. Census Bureau, 2010 census.

193. Walter Romig, *Michigan Place Names* (Detroit: Wayne State University Press, 1986), 73.

194. *Boyne 1839–1867: Boyne, Boyne Village & Boyne City*, http://www.boynelibrary.org/wp-content/ uploads/2016/02/BC-Time-Line-History.pdf

195. "Where the Heck is the Boyne Falls?" *Charlevoix County History Preservation Society*, accessed October 10, 2017, cchps.wordpress.com/programs-2/2011-events/where-the-heck-is-the-boyne-falls/.

196. Ibid.

197. Ibid.

198. Ibid.

199. Romig, *Michigan Place Names*, 73.

200. Edward May III, "Boyne 1892–1897," in unnamed timeline, n.d., www.boynelibrary.org/wp-content/ uploads/2016/02/BC-Time-Line-History.pdf; "A Brief History of Boyne Falls, Michigan," extracted from *A Pictoral History of the Boyne Valley Area*, accessed October 10, 2017, www.rootsweb.ancestry. com/~micharle/ccgs/ccgs15a.htm.

201. Edward May III, "1902 through 1903," in unnamed timeline, n.d., www.boynelibrary.org/wp-content/ uploads/2016/02/BC-Time-Line-History.pdf.

202. Boyne Falls, *Charlevoix County History*.

203. "A Brief History of Boyne Falls, Michigan," extracted from *A Pictoral History of the Boyne Valley Area*

204. Jeff Smith, "Boyne Ski Resorts President Steve Kircher Talks Michigan Skiing," *MyNorth*, December 4, 2013, mynorth.com/2013/12/timeline-northern-michigan-boyne-ski-resorts/.

205. Ibid.

206. "Boyne Mountain History," *Boyne Mountain*, accessed October 10, 2017, www.boyne.com/ boynemountain/media/history.

207. Ibid.

208. "Our History," *Boyne Resorts*, accessed December 3, 2017, www.boyneresorts.com/our-history.

209. Smith, "Boyne Ski Resorts President Steve Kircher Talks Michigan Skiing."

210. Romig, *Michigan Place Names*, 73.

211. *Boyne Falls Polish Festival*, accessed October 10, 2017, www.boynefallspolishfestival.com.

212. Ibid.

213. Ibid.

214. Ibid.

215. "Summer & Fall Fun," *Boyne Mountain*, accessed October 10, 2017, www.boyne.com/boynemountain/ activities/summer-fall.

216. "Home," *Avalanche Bay*, accessed October 10, 2017, www.avalanchebay.com.

217. "A Brief History of Boyne Falls, Michigan," extracted from *A Pictoral History of the Boyne Valley Area*.

BREEDSVILLE

218. U.S. Census Bureau, 2010 census.

219. "About Breedsville," *Breedsville, MI*, accessed October 10, 2017, www.breedsville.org/about.html.

220. Ibid.

221. Ibid.

222. Ibid.

223. Ibid.

224. Ibid.

225. Ibid.

226. Ibid.

227. Ibid.

228. Ibid.

229. Ibid.

230. Ibid.

231. Ibid.

232. "Human Bones Are Found in Attic," *The True Northerner*, May 19, 1916, accessed through the Library of Congress website, chroniclingamerica.loc.gov.

233. Ibid.

234. Ibid.

235. Leonard Lee, *A History of Breedsville—As I Saw It*, a transcribed oral history, n.d., www.breedsville.org/ pdf/LEE1.doc%20-%20LEE1.pdf.

236. Ibid.

237. "Photos," *Breedsville, MI*, accessed October 10, 2017, www.breedsville.org/photos.html.

238. Newschannel3, "Breedsville Bridge in Van Buren County Will Reopen Tonight," *WWMT.com*, July 28, 2017, wwmt.com/news/local/breedsville-brisdge-in-van-buren-county-will-reopen-tonight.

239. Ibid.

240. "Ribbon Cutting Planned to Mark Reopening of Breedsville Bridge," *94.9 WSJM*, July 22, 2017, www.wsjm.com/2017/07/22/ribbon-cutting-planned-to-mark-reopening-of-breedsville-bridge/.

241. "Events," *Breedsville, MI*, accessed October 11, 2017, www.breedsville.org/event.html.

242. Ibid.

243. Lee, A History of Breedsville—As I Saw It.

244. Ibid.

BURLINGTON

245. U.S. Census Bureau, 2010 census.

246. *History of Calhoun County, Michigan, with Illustrations Descriptive of Its Scenery, Palatial Residences, Public Buildings, Fine Blocks, and Important Manufactories*

from Original Sketches by Artists of the Highest Ability (Philadelphia: L. H. Everts & Co., 1877), 158.

247. Ibid.

248. Ibid.

249. Walter Romig, *Michigan Place Names* (Detroit: Wayne State University Press, 1986), 87.

250. Ibid.

251. *History of Calhoun County*, 158.

252. Ibid.

253. Ibid.

254. Ibid.

255. *History of Calhoun County*, 159.

256. Ibid.

257. "Killed Him with Gun," *Owosso Times*, September 23, 1904, accessed through the Library of Congress website, chroniclingamerica.loc.gov.

258. Ibid.

259. Natasha Blakely, "Calhoun County Farmer Takes a Gamble with Organic Yogurt," *Battle Creek Enquirer*, October 5, 2017, www.battlecreekenquirer.com/story/news/local/2017/10/05/burlington-organic-hiday-farm-yogurt-calhoun-county/717299001/.

260. Ibid.

261. Ibid.

262. Ibid.

263. Ibid.

264. Ibid.

265. "Home," *Hiday Family Farm*, accessed October 11, 2017, www.hidayfarms.com.

266. Ibid.

267. *History of Calhoun County*, 159.

268. "Short State Items," *Crawford Avalanche*, March 5, 1896, accessed through the Library of Congress website, chroniclingamerica.loc.gov.

269. Walter Romig, *Michigan Place Names* (Detroit: Wayne State University Press, 1986), 87.

CARNEY

270. U.S. Census Bureau, 2010 census.

271. Walter Romig, *Michigan Place Names* (Detroit: Wayne State University Press, 1986), 99.

272. Ibid.

273. Ibid.

274. *Michigan State Gazetteer and Business Directory for 1921–1922* (Detroit: C. F. Clarke, 1922), 310, accessed babel.hathitrust.org/cgi/pt?id=mdp.39015039495976;view=1up;seq=324.

275. Ibid.

276. Ibid.

277. Alvah L. Sawyer, *History of the Northern Peninsula of Michigan and its People,* (Chicago: Western Historical Company, 1911), files.usgwarchives.net/mi/menominee/history/h23611.txt.

278. *History of Methodism in the Upper Peninsula* (The Historical Society of The Detroit Annual Conference, 1955).

279. "Our Heritage," *Carney Evangelical Free Church*, accessed October 12, 2017, carneyfreechurch.org/history.

280. Ibid.

281. Ibid.

282. Ibid.

283. Ibid.

284. Ibid.

285. "The Election Case of William Lorimer of Illinois (1910; 1912)," *United States Senate*, accessed December 3, 2017, www.senate.gov/artandhistory/history/common/contested_elections/095William_Lorimer.htm.

286. "Newsletter," *Miller Family Farm*, accessed October 15, 2017, www.eatupmichigan.com/newsletter/.

287. "Newsletter," *Miller Family Farm*, accessed October 15, 2017, www.eatupmichigan.com/newsletter/; "What We Grow," *Miller Family Farm*, accessed October 15, 2017, www.eatupmichigan.com/what-we-grow/.

288. "Castle Cattle Company," *Facebook*, accessed October 15, 2017, www.facebook.com/pg/castlecattlecompany.

289. Jim Isleib and Monica Jean, "Pea and oat trial in Upper Peninsula completed – Part 1: Yields," *Michigan State University Extension*, September 28, 2017, msue.anr.msu.edu/news/pea_and_oat_trial_in_upper_peninsula_completed_part_1_yields.

290. Ibid.

291. "Home," "Company Profile," *Performance*, accessed October 12, 2017, performance-corp.com/company-profile/.

292. Ibid.

293. "Domestic Violence Awareness Month," *Daily Press*, October 7, 2017, www.dailypress.net/life/features/2017/10/domestic-violence-awareness-month/.

294. "Carney-Nadeau Public School – News," *Facebook*, accessed October 12, 2017, https://www.facebook.com/Carney-Nadeau-Public-School-News-221750321216642/.

295. "City of Carney," *Genealogy Trails*, accessed October 12, 2017, genealogytrails.com/mich/menominee/citycarney.html.

CARP LAKE

296. U.S. Census Bureau, 2010 census.

297. Walter Romig, *Michigan Place Names* (Detroit: Wayne State University Press, 1986), 99; "Octave Terrain," *Find a Grave*, accessed October 13, www.findagrave.com/cgi-bin/fg.cgi?page=gr&GRid=76073860.

298. "Octave Terrain," *Find a Grave*.

299. Romig, *Michigan Place Names*, 99.

300. *Michigan State Gazetteer and Business Directory for 1907–1908* (Detroit: C. F. Clarke, 1908), 520.

301. Ibid.

302. Ibid.

303. *Michigan State Gazetteer and Business Directory for 1921–1922* (Detroit: C. F. Clarke, 1922), 311–312.

304. Little Traverse Conservancy, *Leaving it Beautiful*, newsletter, 2011, landtrust.org/wp-content/uploads/2016/04/Summer2011.pdf.

305. "About Us," *Acorn Cottage*, accessed October 13, 2017, www.acorncottagerental.net/about-us.

306. Mackinaw City Chamber of Commerce, "Carp Lake"; Morgan Sherburne, "Paradise Lake Milfoil: a problem dead or alive," *Petoskey News*, August 12, 2013, www.petoskeynews.com/news/local/paradise-lake-milfoil-a-problem-dead-or-alive/article_73ac195e-6983-550f-8e3b-a32a02163231.html.

307. "PLIB News," *The Paradise Lake Improvement Board*, accessed October 13, 2017, www.paradiselakeimprovementboard.com/page/show/770566-news.

308. Mackinaw City Chamber of Commerce, "Carp Lake," *Mackinac City Chamber of Commerce*, accessed October 12, 2017, www.mackinawchamber.com/Showcase-Seasonal/carp-lake.

CASNOVIA

309. U.S. Census Bureau, 2010 census.

310. *Local Acts of the Legislature of the State of Michigan Passed at the Regular Session of 1875* (Lansing: W. S. George & Co., State Printers and Binders, 1875), 532.

311. Jackson D. Dillenback and Leavitt, comp., *History and Directory of Kent County, Michigan: Containing a History of Each Township, and the City of Grand Rapids: the Name, Occupation, Location and Postoffice Residents outside of the City; a List of Postoffices in the County; a*

Schedule of Population; and Other Valuable Statistics (Grand Rapids, MI: Daily Eagle Steam Printing House, 1870), 98.

312. Ibid.

313. Ibid.

314. Ibid.

315. *History of Muskegon County, Michigan, with Illustrations and Biographical Sketches of Some of Its Prominent Men and Pioneers* (Chicago: H. R. Page & Co., 1882), 102.

316. Walter Romig, *Michigan Place Names* (Detroit: Wayne State University Press, 1986), 102.

317. Paul Wesley Ivey, *The Pere Marquette Railroad Company: An Historical Study of the Growth and Development of one of Michigan's Most Important Railway Systems* (PhD thesis, University of Michigan, 1919), 40.

318. *History of Muskegon County*, 15.

319. *History of Muskegon County*, 102.

320. *Local Acts of the Legislature of the State of Michigan*, 532.

321. James L. Smith, ed., *An Account of Muskegon County* (National Historical Association Inc., n.d.), 92.

322. *History of Muskegon County*, 102.

323. Casnovia Old School Foundation, "About," *Facebook*, accessed October 2, 2017, www.facebook.com/pg/Casnovia-Old-School-Foundation-122680844428460/about/?ref=page_internal.

324. Ibid.

325. Ibid.

326. "Events," *Casnovia Village*, accessed October 2, 2017, www.casnoviavillage.org/.

327. Thomas Commerford Martin, "Bion Joseph Arnold," *Scientific American*, September 9, 1911, www.scientificamerican.com/article/bion-joseph-arnold/.

328. *The New York Public Library Rare Books and Manuscripts Division Accession Sheet* (New York Public Library, 1942), accessed October 2, 2017, www.nypl.org/sites/default/files/archivalcollections/pdf/arnoldb.pdf.

329. Ibid.

330. "About Us," *Caveman Pallets, LLC*, accessed September 24, 2017, www.cavemanpallets.com/about.htm.

331. *Precise*, accessed September 24, 2017, precisemanufacturing.com/.

332. Romig, *Michigan Place Names*, 102.

333. Adolphus A. Ellis, *Report of the Attorney General of the State of Michigan for the Year Ending June 30, A. D. 1894* (Lansing: Robert Smith & Co. State Printers and Binders, 1894), 192–194.

334. Ibid.

335. "Bosanko Boxed," *Telegram-Herald*, July 11, 1891, accessed from the Library of Congress website, chroniclingamerica.loc.gov.

336. Ibid.

337. Ibid.

CEMENT CITY

338. U.S. Census Bureau, 2010 census.

339. Walter Romig, *Michigan Place Names* (Detroit: Wayne State University Press, 1986), 106.

340. Ibid.

341. Romig, *Michigan Place Names*, 106; "Cement City Historical Page," Facebook, post from November 14, 2016, www.facebook.com/cementcityhistory/.

342. "Cement City Historical Page," *Facebook*, post from November 14, 2016.

343. "Cement City Historical Page," *Facebook*, post from November 14, 2016; Romig, *Michigan Places Names*, 106.

344. The Western Historical Society, *History of Lenawee County, Michigan*, (The Western Historical Society, 1909), chapter 20, www.lenaweehistory.com/lenawee-ch20.html.

345. "Cement City Historical Page," *Facebook*, post from November 14, 2016.

346. *Michigan State Gazetteer and Business Directory for 1907–1908* (Detroit: C. F. Clarke, 1908), 531.

347. *Michigan State Gazetteer and Business Directory for 1921–1922* (Detroit: C. F. Clarke, 1922), 319.

348. Ibid.

349. "Cement City Historical Page," *Facebook*, post from November 14, 2016.

350. Ibid.

351. Ibid.

352. Happenings," *Village of Cement City*, accessed October 13, 2017, www.villageofcementcity.com/happenings.php.

353. "Our History," *Cement City Baptist Church*, accessed October 13, 2017, www.ccbc-mi.org/about-us/our-history/.

354. "Abigail *Emery* Every," *Find a Grave*, accessed December 3, 2017, www.findagrave.com/memorial/19334571.

355. John Robinson, "The Abandoned Cement Factory of Cement City; Did YOU Sneak in When You Were a Kid?," *99.1 WFMK*, May 2, 2017, 99wfmk.com/cementfactory.

356. Alfred K. Lane, *Geological Survey of Michigan Lower Peninsula 1900–1903*, vol. 8, part 3 (Lansing: Robert Smith Printing Co., 1903), 34, www.michigan.gov/documents/deq/GIMDL-VOLVIIID_303213_7.PDF.

CHATHAM

357. "Chatham," *Hometown Chronicles*, accessed October 13, 2017, www.hometownchronicles.com/mi/alger/chatham.htm.

358. Walter Romig, *Michigan Place Names* (Detroit: Wayne State University Press, 1986), 112.

359. Ibid.

360. "Chatham," *Hometown Chronicles*.

361. Ibid.

362. Ibid.

363. Ibid.

364. Ibid.

365. Ibid.

366. Luke, "The Village of Chatham History," *Chatham, MI*, June 22, 2014, accessed October 13, 2017, chatham-mi.blogspot.com/2014/06/the-village-of-chatham-history_3917.html.

367. Romig, *Michigan Place Names*, 112.

368. Luke, "The Village of Chatham History"; *Michigan State Gazetteer and Business Directory for 1907–1908* (Detroit: C. F. Clarke, 1908), 546.

369. Ibid.

370. Ibid.

371. Ibid.

372. "Chatham," *Hometown Chronicles*.

373. Ibid.

374. "AgBioResearch Upper Peninsula Research and Extension Center," *Michigan State University*, accessed October 13, 2017, www.canr.msu.edu/uprc/; "Chatham," *Hometown Chronicles*.

375. "Chatham," *Hometown Chronicles*.

376. Ibid.

377. "AgBioResearch." *Michigan State University*.

378. UPREC North Farm, *Michigan State University*, accessed October 13, 2017, www.canr.msu.edu/uprc/uprec_north_farm/.

379. "Chatham," *Hometown Chronicles*.

380. Ibid.

381. "Peninsula News," *L'Anse Sentinel*, July 30, 1904, accessed through the Library of Congress website, chroniclingamerica.loc.gov.

382. "Steamship William G. Mather," *Great Lakes Science Center*, accessed December 4, 2017, greatscience.com/explore/exhibits/william-g-mather-steamship.

CLARKSVILLE

383. U.S. Census Bureau, 2010 census.

384. Walter Romig, *Michigan Place Names* (Detroit: Wayne State University Press, 1986), 119.

385. Ibid.

386. Rev. E. E. Branch, Ed., *History of Ionia County, Michigan, Her People, Industries and Institutions*, vol. 1 (Indianapolis: B. F. Bowen & Co., Inc., 1916), 97.

387. Ibid.

388. Romig, *Michigan Place Names*, 119.

389. Branch. *History of Ionia*, 97.

390. Ibid.

391. *Michigan State Gazetteer and Business Directory for 1907–1908* (Detroit: C. F. Clarke, 1908), 561.

392. Ibid.

393. Ibid.

394. Ibid.

395. Ibid.

396. *Michigan State Gazetteer and Business Directory for 1907–1908* (Detroit: C. F. Clarke, 1908), 561; *Michigan State Gazetteer and Business Directory for 1921–1922* (Detroit: C. F. Clarke, 1922), 335; U.S. Census Bureau, 2010 census.

397. "Clarksville Steam and Gas Engine Assn.," *Facebook*, accessed October 14, 2017, www.facebook.com/Clarksville-Steam-and-Gas-Engine-Assn-161424080546576/.

398. Ibid.

399. Darcy Meade, "Clarksville Ox Roast Tradition Continues," *Ionia Sentinel-Standard*, August 10, 2017, www.sentinel-standard.com/news/20170810/clarksville-ox-roast-tradition-continues.

400. Ibid.

401. Ibid.

402. Ibid.

403. "Home," *Clarksville, Michigan*, accessed October 14, 2017, www.clarksvillemi.org.

404. Bobby Hart, quoted in "Last Train to Clarksville by the Monkees," *Song Facts*, accessed October 14, 2017, www.songfacts.com/detail.php?id=2840.

405. Mary Ellen Snodgrass, *Civil Disobedience: An Encyclopedic History of Dissidence in the United States*, vol. 1 and 2 (New York: Routledge, 2015).

CLAYTON

406. U.S. Census Bureau, 2010 census.

407. Walter Romig, *Michigan Place Names* (Detroit: Wayne State University Press, 1986), 120; village sign.

408. The Western Historical Society, *History of Lenawee County, Michigan* (The Western Historical Society, 1909), chapter 22, www.lenaweehistory.com/lenawee-ch22.html.

409. Ibid.

410. Romig, *Michigan Place Names*, 119–120.

411. Ibid.

412. Romig, *Michigan Place Names*, 120.

413. Ibid.

414. The Western Historical Society, *History of Lenawee County, Michigan*, chapter 22.

415. *Michigan State Gazetteer and Business Directory for 1907–1908* (Detroit: C. F. Clarke, 1908), 562.

416. Chester D. Berry, *Loss of the Sultana and Reminiscences of Survivors: History of a Disaster where over One Thousand Five Hundred Human Beings Were Lost, Most of Them Being Exchanged Prisoners of War on Their Way Home after Privation and Suffering from One to Twenty-Three Months in Cahaba and Andersonville Prisons* (Lansing: Darius D. Thorp, 1892).

417. Ibid.

418. Ibid.

419. The Western Historical Society, *History of Lenawee County, Michigan*, (The Western Historical Society, 1909), chapter 33, www.lenaweehistory.com/lenawee-ch33.html.

420. The Western Historical Society, *History of Lenawee County, Michigan*, (The Western Historical Society, 1909), chapter 23, www.lenaweehistory.com/lenawee-ch23.html.

421. Brian Manzullo, "The 7 best spots for stargazing in Michigan," *Detroit Free Press*, March 5, 2017, www.freep.com/story/news/local/michigan/2017/03/05/where-to-go-stargazing-in-michigan/98774764/.

CLIFFORD

422. U.S. Census Bureau, 2010 census.

423. Walter Romig, *Michigan Place Names* (Detroit: Wayne State University Press, 1986), 120.

424. *History of Lapeer County, Michigan, with Illustrations and Biographies of Some of Its Prominent Men and Pioneers* (Chicago: H. R. Page & Co., 1884), 198.

425. Ibid.

426. Ibid.

427. Ibid.

428. Ibid.

429. Romig, *Michigan Place Names*, 120.

430. "About," *Village of Clifford*, http://www.villageofclifford.com/about.html.

431. "Clifford Branch," *Lapeer District Library*, accessed October 14, 2017, www.library.lapeer.org/about-us/locations-hours/clifford-branch.html.

432. "St. Patrick's Church [Clifford]," *MichMarkers*, accessed October 14, 2017, www.michmarkers.com/detail.asp?txtID=L1646; "St. Patrick Chapel," *S.S. Peter Paul ~ St. Mary's ~ St. Patrick ~ Sacred Heart*, accessed October 14, 2017, sspeterpaulnb.org/st-patrick.

433. "St. Patrick's Church [Clifford]," *MichMarkers*.

434. Ibid.

435. "St. Patrick Chapel," *S.S. Peter Paul ~ St. Mary's ~ St. Patrick ~ Sacred Heart*.

436. "St. Patrick's Church [Clifford]," *MichMarkers*, accessed October 14, 2017.

437. Phil Foley, "St. Patrick Chapel Prepares for Heritage Festival on Aug. 13," *The County Press*, July 26, 2017, thecountypress.mihomepaper.com/news/2017-07-26/News/St_Patrick_Chapel_prepares_for_Heritage_Festival_o.html.

438. "About," *Village of Clifford*.

439. "History," *Lapeer Habitat for Humanity*, accessed October 14, 2017, www.lapeerhabitat.org/history.html.

440. "Fun Facts about the County," *The County Press*, January 1, 2017, thecountypress.mihomepaper.com/news/2017-01-01/Community_View/Fun_Facts_from_around_the_county.html.

441. Ibid.

442. "Fun Facts about the County," *The County Press*, January 1, 2017; "Charles Coughlin, 30's 'Radio Priest,' obituary for Charles Coughlin, October 28, 1979, www.nytimes.com/1979/10/28/archives/charles-coughlin-30s-radio-priest-dies-fiery-sermons-stirred-furor.html.

443. "Charles Coughlin, 30's 'Radio Priest,' obituary for Charles Coughlin, October 28, 1979.

444. Ibid.

445. Ibid.

COPEMISH

446. U.S. Census Bureau, 2010 census.

447. Alexander F. Barnes and Cassandra J. Rhodes, "The Polar Bear Expedition: The U.S. Intervention in Northern Russia, 1918–1919," *Army Sustainment* (44)2, March–April 2012, www.almc.army.mil/alog/issues/MarApril12/Polar_Bear.html.

448. Leslie Stainton, "Dreaming of Home: American Soldiers in Russia, 1918–1919," in *The Michigan Alumnus* (2)101, March/April 1995, 30.

449. Mrs. C. C. Bigelow, in a letter to her son dated July 29, 1918, Polar Bear Expedition Digital Materials, quod.lib.umich.edu/p/polar/86611.0001.002?view=toc.

450. Stainton, "Dreaming of Home"; Barnes and Rhodes, "The Polar Bear Expedition."

451. Ibid.

452. Ibid.

453. Stainton, "Dreaming of Home,"; "Michigan's Polar Bears," *Midwest Guest*, January 17, 2012, www.midwestguest.com/2012/01/michigans-polar-bears.html.

454. Walter Romig, *Michigan Place Names* (Detroit: Wayne State University Press, 1986), 133.

455. Marlene R., from the Copemish Area Historical Society, "1991 Newspaper Article," July 3, 2006, lakeswimmer.blogspot.com. **Note:** This source quotes an unnamed, undated newspaper article written in 1991. However, the person who posted the article is a member of the local historical society.

456. Romig, *Michigan Places Names*, 133.

457. Romig, *Michigan Places Names*, 133; Marlene R., from the Copemish Area Historical Society, "1991 Newspaper Article."

458. Marlene R., from the Copemish Area Historical Society, "1991 Newspaper Article."

459. Marlene R., from the Copemish Area Historical Society, "1991 Newspaper Article."

460. "Mission," *Archangel Ancient Tree Archive*, accessed October 14, 2017, www.ancienttreearchive.org.

461. *Our Ancient Future: The Archangel Ancient Tree Archive Story*, video on www.ancienttreearchive.org/aata-news/our-videos/.

462. "Reforest," *Archangel Ancient Tree Archive*, accessed October 14, 2017, www.ancienttreearchive.org/our-work/reforest/.

463. Our Ancient Future, www.ancienttreearchive.org.

464. David Milarch, in conversation with Scott Simon, on NPR, December 8, 2012.

465. Jesse McKinley, "From Ancient Giants, Finding New Life to Help the Planet," *New York Times*, April 9, 2011, www.nytimes.com/2011/04/10/us/10trees.html.

466. "Home," *Mr. Chain*, accessed October 14, 2017, www.mrchain.com.

467. Michigan Department of Natural Resources, "Bear Creek," *Status of the Fishery Resource Report*, (2014), 6.

468. Ibid.

COPPER CITY

1. U.S. Census Bureau, 2010 census.

2. Walter Romig, *Michigan Place Names* (Detroit: Wayne State University Press, 1986), 133.

3. Mike Forgrave, "A City Built for Copper," *Copper Country Explorer*, October 27, 2009, www.coppercountryexplorer.com/2009/10/a-city-built-for-copper/.

4. Ibid.

5. Romig, *Michigan Place Names*, 133.

6. Forgrave, "A City Built for Copper"; *Michigan State Gazetteer and Business Directory for 1921–1922* (Detroit: C. F. Clarke, 1922), 348.

7. Romig, *Michigan Place Names*, 133.

8. "Kingston Mine, Copper City, Keweenaw Co., Michigan, USA," *Mindat*, accessed October 15, 2017, www.mindat.org/loc-13861.html.

9. Ibid.

10. Ibid.

11. Dennis Harju, in conversation with the author, August 16, 2017.

12. "Obituary for Frank Stubenrauch," *Erickson-Crowley-Peterson Funeral Home*, accessed October 15, 2017, www.ericksoncrowleypeterson.com/book-of-memories/1933332/Stubenrauch-Frank/obituary.php.

13. Harju, 2017.

14. "Obituary for Frank Stubenrauch," 2017.

15. Harju, 2017.

16. Ibid.

17. Ibid.

18. "CALUMET & HECLA 990.; Copper Stock Has Paid Over $99,000,000 in Dividends Since 1871," *New York Times*, February 17, 1907.

19. "Rinks," *Copper Country Hockey History*, accessed October 15, 2017, www.cchockeyhistory.org/CCIceRinks.htm.

CUSTER

20. U.S. Census Bureau, 2010 census.

21. *Michigan State Gazetteer and Business Directory for 1907–1908* (Detroit: C. F. Clarke, 1908), 592.

22. Mason County Historical Society, *Historic Mason County*, (Dallas: Taylor Publishing Company, 1980), 156.

23. Ibid.

24. Ibid.

25. Mason County Historical Society, *Historic Mason County*, 155.

26. Mason County Historical Society, *Historic Mason County*, 156.

27. Mason County Historical Society, *Historic Mason County*, 156; *History of Mason County, Michigan, with Illustrations and Biographical Sketches of Some of Its Prominent Men and Pioneers* (Chicago: H. R. Page & Co., 1882).

28. "Custer Township," *Genealogy Trails*, accessed October 15, 2017, genealogytrails.com/mich/mason/custertwp.html.

29. Ibid.

30. Ibid.

31. Ibid.

32. Mason County Historical Society, *Historic Mason County*, 156.

33. Ibid.

34. Mason County Historical Society, *Historic Mason County*, 156; "History," *Village of Custer*, accessed October 15, 2017, www.villageofcuster.org/history.html.

35. *Michigan State Gazetteer and Business Directory for 1907–1908*, 592.

36. Ibid.

37. Mason County Historical Society, *Historic Mason County*, 156.

38. Ibid.

39. Ibid.

40. Ibid.

41. Ibid.

42. "Custer Village Asking to Annex Portion of Township for Safari Park," *Mason County Press*, September 11, 2017, masoncountypress.com/2017/09/11/custer-village-asking-to-annex-portion-of-township-for-safari-park/.

43. "About," *Marlins Wildlife Safari*, accessed October 15, 2017, marlinswildlifesafari.com/about/.

44. Justine McGuire, "Iconic Meat Market with Signature Cow Head Closes after 61 years in Business," *mlive*, September 29, 2016, www.mlive.com/news/muskegon/index.ssf/2016/09/iconic_west_michigan_meat_mark.html.

45. Walter Romig, *Michigan Place Names* (Detroit: Wayne State University Press, 1986), 144.

46. Mason County Historical Society, *Historic Mason County*, 157.

DAGGETT

47. U.S. Census Bureau, 2010 census.

48. "Village of Daggett," *Menominee County*, accessed October 15, 2017, www.menomineecounty.com/municipalities/?i=b0a5791222e2.

49. Ibid.

50. Walter Romig, *Michigan Place Names* (Detroit: Wayne State University Press, 1986), 145.

51. Ibid.

52. Ibid.

53. Ethel Schuyler, *Menominee County Book for Schools* (Menominee, Michigan: Office of County School Commissioner, 1941), quoted in "Daggett Township," *Menominee GenWeb*, accessed October 15, 2017, menominee.genwebsite.net/documents/A87F981639897E482D5E15E270CBDF8F2DE855B.html.

54. Ibid.

55. Romig, *Michigan Place Names*, 145.

56. Ethel Schuyler, *Menominee County Book for Schools*.

57. Ibid.

58. "Daggett Moravian 'Saddles Up' for Cowboy Church Celebration," *Moravian Church in North America*, accessed October 15, 2017, www.moravian.org/moravian-church-northern-province/daggett-moravian-saddles-up-for-cowboy-church-celebration-2-2/.

59. Ethel Schuyler, *Menominee County Book for Schools*.

60. Ibid.

61. Ethel Schuyler, *Menominee County Book for Schools*.

62. *Memorial Record of the Northern Peninsula of Michigan* (Chicago: Lewis Publishing Company, 1895), 579–580.

63. Ibid.

64. Ibid.

65. Ibid.

66. Ibid.

67. Ibid.

68. "Home," *Elmcrest Acres*, accessed October 15, 2017, www.elmcrestacres.com.

69. Ibid.

70. "Vacation Rental," *Elmcrest Acres*, accessed October 15, 2017, www.elmcrestacres.com/vacation-rental.html.

71. "Home," *Elmcrest Acres*, accessed October 15, 2017, www.elmcrestacres.com.

72. "Daggett Township," *Menominee GenWeb*, accessed October 15, 2017, menominee.genwebsite.net/documents/A87F981639897E482D5E15E270CBDF8F2DDE855B.html.

73. Jerome Pohlen, *Oddball Michigan: A Guide to 450 Really Strange Places* (Chicago: Chicago Review Press, 2014), 8–9.

DANSVILLE

74. U.S. Census Bureau, 2010 census.

75. Samuel W. Durant, *History of Ingham and Eaton Counties Michigan, with Illustrations and Biographical Sketches of their Prominent Men and Pioneers* (Philadelphia: D. W. Ensign & Co., 1880), 249.

76. Durant, *History of Ingham and Eaton Counties*, 248.

77. Ibid.

78. Durant, *History of Ingham and Eaton Counties*, 248–249.

79. Durant, *History of Ingham and Eaton Counties*, 249; D. L. Crossman, "Dansville Reminiscences," a letter written in 1889, in *Michigan State Gazetteer, in Pioneer History of Ingham County*, Mrs. Franc L. Adams (Lansing: Wynkoop Hallenbeck Crawford Company, 1923), 404.

80. Durant, *History of Ingham and Eaton Counties*, 248.

81. Ibid.

82. "Dansville in 1863," *Michigan State Gazetteer, in Pioneer History of Ingham County*, Mrs. Franc L. Adams (Lansing: Wynkoop Hallenbeck Crawford Company, 1923), 399–401.

83. Durant, *History of Ingham and Eaton Counties*, 248.

84. Ibid.

85. Ibid.

86. "Welcome to Dansville Schools," *Dansville Schools*, accessed September 30, 2017, www.dansville.org/.

87. Crossman, "Dansville Reminiscences," 403.

88. Ibid.

89. Ibid.

90. Vicki Dozier, "Francine Hughes Wilson, Who Inspired 'The Burning Bed,' Dies at 69," *Lansing State Journal*, March 30, 2017, www.lansingstatejournal.com/story/news/local/2017/03/30/francine-hughes-wilson-who-inspired-burning-bed-dies-69/99834400/.

91. Ibid.

92. Ibid.

93. Ibid.

94. Durant, *History of Ingham and Eaton Counties*, 249.

95. Ibid.

96. "Owosso Boy's Sudden Death," *Owosso Times*, July 29, 1898, accessed through the Library of Congress website, chroniclingamerica.loc.gov.

97. Dorn Diehl, *Dansville, Ingham Township: Then & Now* (1984).

DETOUR

98. U.S. Census Bureau, 2010 census.

99. Charles A. Homberg, *DeTour Village, Michigan: A History to 1960* (DeTour, Michigan: DeTour Passage Historical Museum, 2008), 11.

100. Homberg, *DeTour Village*, 1.

101. DeTour Village, Michigan, *Village of DeTour and DeTour Township*, accessed September 30, 2017, www.detourvillage.org/history.html,

102. Homberg, *DeTour Village*, 1.

103. Homberg, *DeTour Village*, 4.

104. Homberg, *DeTour Village*, 5.

105. Homberg, *DeTour Village*, 5–6.

106. Homberg, *DeTour Village*, 6.

107. Ibid.

108. DeTour Reef Light Preservation Society, "DeTour Reef Light Preservation Society," DRLPS, accessed September 30, 2017, www.drlps.com.

109. Homberg, *DeTour Village*, 7.

110. Ibid.

111. Ibid.

112. Ibid.

113. Homberg, *DeTour Village*, 11–12.

114. Homberg, *DeTour Village*, 9.

115. Homberg, *DeTour Village*, 12.

116. Homberg, *DeTour Village*, 12–14.

117. Homberg, *DeTour Village*, 23.

118. Homberg, *DeTour Village*, 24.

119. Judy Jones, in discussion with the author, August 17, 2017.

120. Ibid.

121. "Our Emergency Services," *Village of DeTour and DeTour Township*, accessed September 30, 2017, www.detourvillage.org/fire-and-ambulance.html.

122. "Senior Programs," *Village of DeTour and DeTour Township*, accessed September 30, 2017, www.detourvillage.org/senior-programs.html.

123. Homberg, *DeTour Village*, 23.

124. Ibid.

EAGLE

125. U.S. Census Bureau, 2010 census.

126. Walter Romig, *Michigan Place Names* (Detroit: Wayne State University Press, 1986), 167.

127. Ibid.

128. Ibid.

129. Ibid.

130. *History of Shiawassee and Clinton Counties, Michigan, with Illustrations and Biographical Sketches of their Prominent Men and Pioneers* (Philadelphia: D. W. Ensign & Co., 1880), 441–442; Romig, *Michigan Place Names*, 167.

131. *History of Shiawassee and Clinton Counties*, 442.

132. Ibid.

133. Ibid.

134. Ibid.

135. Jerry Micdermid, in conversation with the author, May 15, 2017.

136. *Michigan State Gazetteer and Business Directory for 1907–1908* (Detroit: C. F. Clarke, 1908), 908.

137. Ibid.

138. "Business Portion of Eagle Burned," *Yale Expositor*, January 1, 1897, accessed through the Library of Congress website, chroniclingamerica.loc.gov.

139. *Eagle Fair Days Sept. 7–10 Schedule*, event flyer, www.eagleparkmichigan.org/wp-content/uploads/2016/07/Small_Poster-updated-2017_JPG-683x1024.jpg.

140. Don Volk and Missy Leonard, undated radio interview with Q106 in Lansing, www.eagleparkmichigan.org.

141. Ibid.

142. Ibid.

143. Ibid.

144. Ibid.

145. Ibid.

ELBERTA

146. U.S. Census Bureau, 2010 census.

147. Walter Romig, Michigan Place Names (Detroit: Wayne State University Press, 1986), 178.

148. Romig, Michigan Place Names, 178; Andy Bolander, "Who Were Elberta's First Settlers?," Elberta the Alert, July 3, 2015, elberta-alert.org/2015/07/03/who-were-elbertas-first-settlers/.

149. "History," Village of Elberta, accessed October 15, 2017, villageofelberta.com/about-us/history/.

150. Romig, Michigan Place Names, 178.

151. "History," Village of Elberta.

152. Romig, Michigan Place Names, 178.

153. Allen B. Blacklock, "History of Elberta," excerpted on "History," Village of Elberta, accessed October 15, 2017, villageofelberta.com/about-us/history/.

154. Ibid.

155. Ibid.

156. Ibid.

157. Ibid.

158. "Car Ferries on Lake Michigan," MichMarkers, accessed October 15, 2017, www.michmarkers.com/startup.asp?startpage=S0122.htm.

159. Ibid.

160. Ibid.

161. Blacklock, "History of Elberta"

162. Grant Brown Jr., Ninety Years Crossing Lake Michigan: The History of the Ann Arbor Car Ferries (Ann Arbor: The University of Michigan Press, 2008), 113–125; Les Bagley, "Autos Across Mackinac: Resilient Ann Arbor No. 4 Survived Many Tragedies," St. Ignace News, May 24, 2007, www.stignacenews.com/news/2007-05-24/columns/034.html.

163. Ibid.

164. Ibid.

165. Ibid.

166. Ibid.

167. Ibid.

168. Ibid.

169. Benzie County Chamber of Commerce "Life in Benzie," Benzie County, 2017.

170. Grand Traverse Regional Land Conservancy, Love the Land: Pass It On, chapter 10, www.gtrlc.org/uploads/2015/10/ElbertaDunes.pdf.

171. Village of Albert. "History." http://villageofelberta.com/about-us/history/

172. Ibid.

ELLSWORTH

173. U.S. Census Bureau, 2010 census.

174. Walter Romig, Michigan Place Names (Detroit: Wayne State University Press, 1986), 180.

175. Elsie Timmer, Gleanings from Ellsworth's Yesteryears: A History of Ellsworth's First 100 Years, 1866–1966, 1967, www.bankstownship.net/gleanings.html.

176. Ibid.

177. Ibid.

178. Ibid.

179. Romig, Michigan Place Names, 180.

180. Timmer, Gleanings from Ellsworth's Yesteryears, 1967.

181. Timmer, Gleanings from Ellsworth's Yesteryears, 1967; "Banks Township History," Banks Township, accessed October 15, 2017, www.bankstownship.net/history.html.

182. Romig, Michigan Place Names, 180.

183. Ibid.

184. Timmer, Gleanings from Ellsworth's Yesteryears, 1967.

185. Ibid.

186. Ibid.

187. Ibid.

188. Ibid.

189. Ibid.

190. Ibid.

191. Ibid.

192. Ibid.

193. Ibid.

194. Owen Edwards, "The Death of Colonel Ellsworth," Smithsonian Magazine, April 2011, www.smithsonianmag.com/history/the-death-of-colonel-ellsworth-878695/.

195. Ibid.

196. Ibid.

197. Ibid

198. Ibid.

199. Ibid.

200. Ibid.

201. Ibid.

202. Ibid.

203. Ellsworth Community School, accessed October 16, 2017, www.ellsworth.k12.mi.us/.

204. "Parks and Beaches," Village of Ellsworth, accessed October 16, 2017, villageofellsworth.com/content/parks-beaches.

205. Ibid.

206. Timmer, Gleanings from Ellsworth's Yesteryears, 1967.

207. Ibid.

EMMETT

208. U.S. Census Bureau, 2010 census.

209. Walter Romig, *Michigan Place Names* (Detroit: Wayne State University Press, 1986), 183–184.

210. Ibid.

211. Ibid.

212. Ibid.

213. Ibid.

214. Ibid.

215. *History of St. Clair County, Michigan, Containing an Account of Its Settlement, Growth, Development and Resources; an Extensive Sketch of Its Cities, Towns and Villages—Their Improvements, Industries, Manufactories, Churches, Schools and Societies; Its War Record, Biographical Sketches, Portraits of Prominent Men and*

Early Settlers; the Whole Preceded by a History of Michigan, and Statistics of the State (Chicago: A. T. Andreas & Co., 1883), 760.

216. Ibid.

217. Ibid.

218. Romig, *Michigan Place Names*, 184.

219. *Michigan State Gazetteer and Business Directory for 1907–1908* (Detroit: C. F. Clarke, 1908), 929.

220. Ibid.

221. *History of St. Clair County*, 165–167.

222. Gary K. Grice, ed., The Beginning of the National Weather Service: The Signal Years (1870–1891) as Viewed by Early Weather Pioneers, *NOAA's National Weather Service Public Affairs Office*, accessed December 4, 2017, www.nws.noaa.gov/pa/history/signal.php.

223. Romig, *Michigan Place Names*, 183; Eric Meier, "The Revolutionary Story of the Namesake of Battle Creek's Emmett Township – Robert Emmet," *K102.5*, k1025.com/robert-emmet/.

224. Eric Meier, "The Revolutionary Story of the Namesake of Battle Creek's Emmett Township – Robert Emmet," *K102.5*, k1025.com/robert-emmet/.

225. Ibid.

226. "Our Lady of Mount Carmel," Michigan historical marker in Emmett, Michigan, 2003.

227. Ibid.

228. Ibid.

229. "Zwiernik's Berry Farm," *The Blueways of St. Clair*, accessed October 16, 2017, www.bluewaysofstclair.org/natureag.asp?ait=av&aid=772.

230. *Shimmering Moon Farm*, accessed October 16, 2017, www.shimmeringmoonfarm.com/index.html.

231. Jerone Pohlen, *Oddball Michigan: A Guide to 450 Really Strange Places* (Chicago: Chicago Review Press, 2014), 197–198.

EMPIRE

232. U.S. Census Bureau, 2010 census.

233. "Statistics," *Village of Empire*, accessed October 16, 2017, www.leelanau.cc/empirevlgstats.asp.

234. "Park Statistics," *National Park Service*, accessed } October 17, 2017, www.nps.gov/slbe/learn/management/statistics.htm.

235. Alberto Orso and Sabrina Parise, "Sleeping Bear Dunes Voted 'Most Beautiful Place in America,'" *ABC News*, August 17, 2011, abcnews.go.com/Travel/best_places_USA/sleeping-bear-dunes-michigan-voted-good-morning-americas/story?id=14319616.

236. "Park Statistics," *National Park Service*.

237. Ibid.

238. Walter Romig, *Michigan Place Names* (Detroit: Wayne State University Press, 1986), 184.

239. Romig, *Michigan Place Names*, 184; Elvin L. Sprague, Esq., and Mrs. George N. Smith, eds., *Sprague's History of Grand Traverse and Leelanaw Counties, Michigan Embracing a Concise Review of Their Early Settlement, Industrial Development and Present Conditions Together with Interesting Reminiscences* (Indianapolis: B. F. Bowen, 1903), 351.

240. Romig, *Michigan Place Names*, 184.

241. Empire Lumber Company," historical marker in Empire, Michigan, 1979.

242. Ibid.

243. Frank Fradd, "Empire Known as a Lumber Town; Here's How It Started," 1973, reprinted in the *Leelanau Enterprise*, September 22, 2016, www.leelanaunews.com/news/2016-09-22/Life_in_Leelanau/Empire_known_as_a_lumber_town_heres_how_it_started.html.

244. Elvin L. Sprague, Esq., and Mrs. George N. Smith, eds., *Sprague's history of Grand Traverse and Leelanaw counties*, 351.

245. "Empire Lumber Company," historical marker in Empire, Michigan, 1979.

246. "Empire, Michigan History," *Leelanau.com*, accessed October 17, 2017, leelanau.com/dunes/sleeping-bear-history/empire-history/.

247. Ibid.

248. Ibid.

249. Codi Yeager, "When the World Came to Empire," *Glen Arbor Sun*, November 10, 2005, glenarborsun.com/when-the-world-came-to-empire/.

250. Ibid.

251. Ibid.

252. Ibid.

253. "Empire Lumber Company," historical marker in Empire, Michigan, 1979.

ESTRAL BEACH

254. U.S. Census Bureau, 2010 census.

255. Walter Romig, *Michigan Place Names* (Detroit: Wayne State University Press, 1986), 187.

256. *Resolution to Recognize the Monroe County Bicentennial Alliance*, n.d., www.estralbeachvillage.org/assets/resolutions/R%20Recognize%20Monroe%20County%20Bicentenial%20Alliance.pdf.

257. Robert J. Murphy, "Estral Beach Normal Now," unmarked newspaper clipping, July 11, 1954, www.estralbeachvillage.org/assets/FloodRecovery1954.pdf.

258. Ibid.

259. Ibid.

260. Ibid.

261. Ibid.

262. Ibid.

263. Ibid.

264. Ibid.

265. Ibid.

FIFE LAKE

266. U.S. Census Bureau, 2010 census.

267. "About," Village of Fife Lake, accessed October 18, 2017, villageoffifelake.weebly.com/about.html.

268. Ibid.

269. Ibid.

270. Ibid.

271. Ibid.

272. Elvin L. Sprague, Esq., and Mrs. George N. Smith, eds., Grand Traverse and Leelanau Counties Michigan Embracing a Concise Review of their Early Settlement, Industrial Development, and Present Conditions, Together with Interesting Reminiscences (Indianapolis: B. F. Bowen & Co., 1903), 307.

273. "About," Village of Fife Lake.

274. Ibid.

275. Fife Lake Historical Society, "Firebarn," "Schoolhouse," Fife Lake Historical Society, accessed October 18, 2017, fifelakehistoricalsociety.com.

276. Ibid.

277. Fife Lake Historical Society, "Firebarn," "Schoolhouse," Fife Lake Historical Society, accessed October 18, 2017, fifelakehistoricalsociety.com/firebarn.htm.

278. Sprague and Smith, Grand Traverse and Leelanau Counties, 307; "About," Village of Fife Lake.

279. "Ice Plant 1890," Fife Lake Historical Walk plaque, n.d.

280. Michigan State Gazetteer and Business Directory for 1907–1908 (Detroit: C. F. Clarke, 1908), 953–954.

281. Fife Lake Historical Walk plaques, n.d.

282. Fife Lake Historical Society, "Home," Fife Lake Historical Society, accessed October 18, 2017, fifelakehistoricalsociety.com/.

283. Ibid.

284. Ibid.

285. Ibid.

286. Fife Lake Historical Society, "Fife Lake Historic Walk," accessed October 18, 2017, fifelakehistoricalsociety.com/historicwalk.html.

287. Ibid.

288. Ibid.

289. Garret Ellison, "The Strychnine Saint: Jenison Author's Latest Book Details 1903 Michigan Poisonings," mlive, www.mlive.com/news/grand-rapids/index.ssf/2014/07/mary_mcknight_strychnine_saint.html

290. Ibid.

291. Ibid.

292. Ibid.

293. Ellison, "The Strychnine Saint"; "Woman Confesses to Killing Three Persons," New York Times, June 11, 1903.

294. "Woman Confesses to Killing Three Persons."

295. Tobin T. Buhk, Michigan's Strychnine Saint: The Curious Case of Mrs. Mary McKnight (Charleston: The History Press, 2014).

296. Michigan Department of Natural Resources, Status of the Fishery Resources Report: Fife Lake, 2014, villageoffifelake.weebly.com/uploads/2/7/3/2/27326905/fishing_report.pdf.

297. North Country Trail Association, "The Trail," North Country Trail Association, accessed October 18, 2017, northcountrytrail.org/trail/.

FORESTVILLE

298. U.S. Census Bureau, 2010 census.

299. "Home," *Village of Forestville*, accessed October 19, 2017, forestvillemichigan.com/.

300. Ibid.

301. "Home," *Village of Forestville; Portrait and Biographical Album of Sanilac County, Containing Portraits and Biographical Sketches of Prominent and Representative Citizens of the County, Together with Portraits and Biographies of all the Governors of Michigan and of the Presidents of the United States* (Chicago: Chapman Brothers, 1884), 497.

302. "Forestville Bicentennial History Page 2," *Michigan History and Genealogy of Sanilac County*, accessed October 19, 2017, www.usgennet.org/usa/mi/county/sanilac/forestville_bicentennial_history2.htm.

303. *Portrait and Biographical Album of Sanilac County*, 496–497.

304. *Portrait and Biographical Album of Sanilac County*, 497.

305. Ibid.

306. "Michigan History Series: Fires Ravaged Michigan's Thumb in 1871, 1881," *Michigan News*, January 8, 2007, ns.umich.edu/new/releases/1245-fires-ravaged-michigans-thumb-in-1871-1881.

307. "Forestville Bicentennial History Page 2," *Michigan History and Genealogy of Sanilac County*.

308. *Portrait and Biographical Album of Sanilac County*, 414.

309. Walter Romig, *Michigan Place Names* (Detroit: Wayne State University Press, 1986), 203.

310. *Portrait and Biographical Album of Sanilac County*, 414.

311. Ibid.

312. Ibid.

313. Ibid.

314. Ibid.

315. Ibid.

316. *Michigan State Gazetteer and Business Directory for 1907–1908* (Detroit: C. F. Clarke, 1908), 970.

317. "Forestville Bicentennial History Page 5," *Michigan History and Genealogy of Sanilac County*, accessed October 19, 2017, www.usgennet.org/usa/mi/county/sanilac/forestville_bicentennial_history5.htm.

FOUNTAIN

318. U.S. Census Bureau.

319. Mason County Historical Society, *Historic Mason County, Michigan* (Dallas: Taylor Publishing Company, 1980), 428.

320. Mason County Historical Society, *Historic Mason County, Michigan*, 427.

321. Ibid.

322. Mason County Historical Society, *Historic Mason County, Michigan*, 427–428.

323. Mason County Historical Society, *Historic Mason County, Michigan*, 428.

324. Ibid.

325. Ibid.

326. Ibid.

327. Ibid.

328. Mason County Historical Society, *Historic Mason County, Michigan*, 428–429; *Michigan State Gazetteer and Business Directory for 1907–1908* (Detroit: C. F. Clarke, 1908), 972.

329. Ibid.

330. Ibid.

331. Ibid.

332. Ibid.

333. Ibid.

334. Ibid.

335. Mason County Historical Society, *Historic Mason County, Michigan*, 429.

336. Ibid.

337. Ibid.

338. Ibid.

339. Ibid.

340. Ibid.

341. "The Mason County Sculpture Trail," *Visit Ludington*, accessed October 19, 2017, www.visitludington.com/stories/mason_county_sculpture_trail.

FREE SOIL

342. U.S. Census Bureau, 2010 Census.

343. Walter Romig, Michigan Place Names (Detroit: Wayne State University Press, 1986), 212.

344. Mason County Historical Society, Historic Mason County, Michigan (Dallas: Taylor Publishing Company, 1980), 215.

345. Ibid.

346. Ibid.

347. Ibid.

348. Ibid.

349. Ibid.

350. Michigan State Gazetteer and Business Directory for 1907–1908 (Detroit: C. F. Clarke, 1908), 980.

351. Mason County Historical Society, Historic Mason County, Michigan, 215.

352. Ibid.

353. Ibid.

354. Ibid.

355. Ibid.

356. Ibid.

357. "Free Soil Party," Encyclopædia Britannica, accessed October 19, 2017, www.britannica.com/topic/Free-Soil-Party.

358. Ibid.

359. Ibid.

360. Mason County Historical Society, Historic Mason County, Michigan, 215

361. Ibid.

362. Ibid.

GAASTRA

363. U.S. Census Bureau, 2010 census.

364. Walter Romig, *Michigan Place Names* (Detroit: Wayne State University Press, 1986), 215.

365. Jack Hill, *A History of Iron County Michigan* (Iron River: Reporter Publishing Company, 1955), 108–109.

366. Romig, *Michigan Place Names*, 215.

367. Hill, *A History of Iron County Michigan*, 108–109.

368. Romig, *Michigan Place Names*, 215.

369. Ibid.

370. Hill, *A History of Iron County Michigan*, 109.

371. Hill, *A History of Iron County Michigan*, 109; "A Rich History," *Iron County Michigan*.

372. Hill, *A History of Iron County Michigan*, 109.

373. Hill, *A History of Iron County Michigan*, 109–110.

374. Hill, *A History of Iron County Michigan*, 110.

375. *Michigan State Gazetteer and Business Directory for 1921–1922* (Detroit: C. F. Clarke, 1922), 913; Romig, *Michigan Place Names*, 215.

376. Hill, *A History of Iron County Michigan*, 110.

377. "Buck Mine, Buck Group, Gaastra, Menominee Iron Range, Iron Co., Michigan, USA," *Mindat*, accessed October 20, 2017, www.mindat.org/loc-8947.html.

378. Allan M. Johnson, *Institute on Lake Superior Geology, Proceedings, Part 5, Houghton, Michigan, May 11–14, 1994* (Houghton: Michigan Technological University).

379. Ibid.

380. Ibid.

381. Ibid.

382. Ibid.

383. Ibid.

384. Ibid.

385. "Indian Village," Michigan historical marker, 1980, accessed www.michmarkers.com/Pages/L0342.htm.

386. "Indian Village," *The Historical Marker Database*, accessed October 20, 2017, www.hmdb.org/Marker.asp?Marker=103462.

387. "Pentoga Park," *The Historical Marker Database*, accessed October 20, 2017, www.hmdb.org/marker.asp?marker=103463.

388. Ibid.

389. "Indian Village," *The Historical Marker Database*.

390. Ibid.

391. "Pentoga Park," *The Historical Marker Database*.

392. "Government," *City of Caspian*, accessed September 29, 2017, www.caspiancity.org/government.htm.

393. "Iron County Attractions," *Iron County, Michigan*, accessed September 29, 2017, ironcountylodging.com/iron-county-attractions-things-to-do/.

394. Ibid.

395. Nicole Walton, "Eat Ice Cream with Officers in Iron River," *Public Radio 90*, July 30, 2015, wnmufm.org/post/eat-ice-cream-officers-iron-river#stream/0.

GAGETOWN

396. U.S. Census Bureau, 2010 census.

397. Walter Romig, *Michigan Place Names* (Detroit: Wayne State University Press, 1986), 211.

398. *History of Tuscola and Bay Counties, Mich., with Illustrations and Biographical Sketches of Some of Their Prominent Men and Pioneers* (Chicago: H. R. Page & Co., 1883), 199.

399. Ibid.

400. Ibid.

401. Ibid.

402. Ibid.

403. Ibid.

404. *History of Tuscola and Bay Counties*, Mich., 200.

405. Ibid.

406. Ibid.

407. "Gagetown," Michigan historical marker located in Gagetown, 2015.

408. Ibid.

409. "Octagon Barn Narrative," *Thumb Octagon Barn Agricultural Museum*, accessed October 21, 2017, thumboctagonbarn.org/narrative.html.

410. Ibid.

411. Ibid.

412. Ibid.

413. Ibid.

414. Ibid.

415. Ibid.

416. Ibid.

417. Ibid.

418. "Home," *Noah's Ark Family Fun Center*, accessed October 21, 2017, noahsarkfamilyfuncenter.com.

419. "Gagetown," Historical Marker.

GAINES

420. U.S. Census Bureau, 2010 census.

421. Edwin O. Wood, *History of Genesee County, Michigan: Her People, Industries and Institutions, with Biographical Sketches of Representative Citizens and Genealogical Records of Many of the Old Families, vol. 1* (Indianapolis: Federal Publishing Company, 1916), 234.

422. Ibid.

423. Ibid.

424. Ibid.

425. Walter Romig, *Michigan Place Names* (Detroit: Wayne State University Press, 1986), 215.

426. Romig, *Michigan Place Names*, 215; Wood, *History of Genesee County*, 234.

427. "Gaines Depot," Michigan Historical Marker in Gaines, Michigan, 2017.

428. Wood, *History of Genesee County*, 234

429. Wood, *History of Genesee County*, 234 and 721.

430. *Michigan State Gazetteer and Business Directory for 1877* (Detroit: C. F. Clark, 1877), 430; Alan Teelander, "The Story of Gaines Township, Michigan," *Images of Michigan*, accessed October 21, 2017, www.imagesofmichigan.com/the-story-of-gaines-township-michigan.

431. "Village of Gaines," Michigan Historical Marker in Gaines, Michigan, 2017.

432. *Michigan State Gazetteer*, 430.

433. *Michigan State Gazetteer*, 520.

434. Ibid.

435. Ibid.

436. "Gaines Depot," Michigan Historical Marker in Gaines, Michigan, 2017; "Gaines Station Library," *Genesee District Library*, accessed October 21, 2017, www.thegdl.org/gaines-station-library.

437. "Gaines Station Library," *Genesee District Library*, accessed October 21, 2017, www.thegdl.org/gaines-station-library.

438. Ibid.

439. Ibid.

440. "Gaines Depot," Michigan Historical Marker.

441. "Gaines Station Library," *Genesee District Library*.

442. Eric Dresden, "Fate of One-Man Police Department up in the Air in Village of Gaines," *mlive*, April 20, 2014, www.mlive.com/news/flint/index.ssf/2014/04/decision_could_come_by_end_of.html.

443. "Twp. Buys Village Police Cruiser," *Swartz Creek View*, March 9, 2017, swartzcreekview.mihomepaper.com/news/2017-03-09/News_Briefs/Twp_buys_village_police_cruiser.html.

GARDEN

444. U.S. Census Bureau, 2010 census.

445. Walter Romig, *Michigan Place Names* (Detroit: Wayne State University Press, 1986), 217.

446. Ibid.

447. Ibid.

448. Ibid.

449. Ibid.

450. Ibid.

451. Ibid.

452. *Michigan State Gazetteer and Business Directory for 1877* (Detroit: C. F. Clark, 1877), 432.

453. Romig, *Michigan Place Names*, 217.

454. Romig, *Michigan Place Names*, 217; *Michigan State Gazetteer and Business Directory for 1879* (Detroit: C. F. Clark, 1879), 575.

455. *Michigan State Gazetteer and Business Directory for 1877*, 432.

456. Ibid.

457. *Michigan State Gazetteer and Business Directory for 1877*, 432; *Michigan State Gazetteer and Business Directory for 1887–1888* (Detroit: C. F. Clark, 1888), 834.

458. *Michigan State Gazetteer and Business Directory for 1887–1888*, 834.

459. Ibid.

460. Walter Romig, *Michigan Place Names* (Detroit: Wayne State University Press, 1986), 193; Cathryn Fitz-Jung, in conversation with the author, August 14, 2017.

461. *Michigan State Gazetteer and Business Directory for 1907–1908* (Detroit: C. F. Clarke, 1908), 986.

462. Fitz-Jung.

463. Ibid.

464. Ibid.

465. "James D. Dotsch," *Newspapers.com*, accessed October 21, 2017.

466. "James Dotsch Seeks Office," *Escanaba Daily Press*, July 24, 1934, accessed at www.newspapers.com/ clip/2402028/james_d_dotsch_19041986/.

467. "Cemeteries and Memorial Sites of Politicians in Delta County," *Political Graveyard*, accessed October 21, 2017, politicalgraveyard.com/geo/MI/DE-buried.html.

468. "John B. Bennet Papers," *Bentley Historical Library*, accessed October 21, 2017, deepblue.lib.umich.edu/ handle/2027.42/107659.

469. Ibid.

470. Ibid.

471. Ibid.

472. Ibid.

473. "Garden Wind Farm," *Heritage*, accessed October 21, 2017, heritagewindenergy.com/garden-wind-farm/.

474. "Concerned Citizens of Delta County," *Facebook*, accessed October 21, 2017, www.facebook.com/ pg/Concerned-Citizens-of-Delta-County-1442192416061467/about.

475. "Fourth of July Festivities," *Escanaba*, accessed October 21, 2017, blog.visitescanaba.com/ fourthofjuly/.

476. Eric Follo, "Teaching on the Garden Peninsula," *Michigan History Magazine, 90.5* (September–October 2006), accessed through Gale General OneFile.

GRAND BEACH

477. U.S. Census Bureau, 2010 census.

478. "Home," *The Village of Grand Beach Homepage*, accessed October 21, 2017, www.grandbeach.org.

479. Ibid.

480. Ibid.

481. Ibid.

482. "Home," *The Village of Grand Beach Homepage*; "The Village of Grand Beach, Michigan 49117," *Harbor Country*, accessed October 21, 2017, www.harborcountry.org/about-harbor-country/ grand-beach/.

483. "The Village of Grand Beach, Michigan 49117," *Harbor Country*.

484. "Home," *The Village of Grand Beach Homepage*.

485. "The Village of Grand Beach, Michigan 49117," *Harbor Country*.

486. Ibid.

487. Ibid.

488. "Father Andrew Greeley Obituary," *The Guardian*, June 6, 2013, www.theguardian.com/world/2013/ jun/06/father-andrew-greeley.

489. Paul Delaney, "Mayor Richard Daley of Chicago Dies at 74," *New York Times*, December 21, 1976, accessed October 21, 2017 , www.nytimes.com/ learning/general/onthisday/bday/0515.html.

490. "Richard M. Daley," *Chicago Tribune*, n.d., www.chicagotribune.com/topic/politics-government/government/richard-m.-daley-PEPLT007475-topic.html.

491. "The Village of Grand Beach, Michigan 49117," *Harbor Country*.

492. Jennifer Kenny, "Grand Beach, MI: Not Just for Golf Champions. Welcomed Jimmy Braddock in 1937," *Local Chicago Architecture*, July 1, 2017, www.localarchitecturechicago.com/grand-beach-mi-not-just-for-golf-champions/.

493. Ibid.

494. Ibid.

495. Ibid.

496. *Grand Beach Social Club*, information and registration packet, 2017, www.grandbeach.org/2017_|SocialClub.pdf.

HANOVER

497. U.S Census Bureau, 2010 census.

498. Walter Romig, *Michigan Place Names* (Detroit: Wayne State University Press, 1986), 250.

499. Ibid.

500. Ibid.

501. *History of Jackson County, Michigan; Together with Sketches of its Cities, Villages and Townships, Educational, Religious, Civil, Military, and Political History; Portraits of Prominent Persons, and Biographies of Representative Citizens* (Chicago: Inter-State Publishing, 1881), 881.

502. Ibid.

503. Ibid.

504. *History of Jackson County, Michigan*, 881; Romig, *Michigan Place Names*, 250.

505. Romig, *Michigan Place Names*, 250; *History of Jackson County, Michigan*, 881.

506. *History of Jackson County, Michigan*, 881; "Hanover-Horton Schools," Historical marker in Hanover, 1999.

507. *History of Jackson County, Michigan*, 881.

508. "Hanover-Horton Schools," historical marker in Hanover, 1999; "Hanover High School," historical marker in Hanover, 1999.

509. "Hanover-Horton Schools," historical marker in Hanover, 1999.

510. "Hanover-Horton Schools," historical marker in Hanover, 1999; "Hanover High School," historical marker in Hanover, 1999.

511. Janette Weimer, in conversation with the author, October 8, 2017.

512. Ibid.

513. "Heritage Park," *Hanover-Horton Area Historical Society*, accessed October 22, 2017, conklinreedorganmuseum.org/park.htm.

514. Ibid.

515. Ibid.

516. Ibid.

517. Ibid.

518. Lynn Jordon, in conversation with the author, October 8, 2017.

519. "Heritage Park," *Hanover-Horton Area Historical Society*.

520. About Us," *NERC, Inc.*, accessed October 22, 2017, www.plantingpros.com/id1.html.

521. Jordon.

522. "Heritage Park," *Hanover-Horton Area Historical Society*.

HARRIETTA

523. U.S Census Bureau, 2010 census.

524. Walter Romig, *Michigan Place Names* (Detroit: Wayne State University Press, 1986), 253.

525. Ibid.

526. Romig, *Michigan Place Names*, 253; John H. Wheeler, comp., *History of Wexford County, Michigan, Embracing a Concise Review of Its Early Settlement, Industrial Development and Present Condition* (B. F. Bowen, 1903), 296.

527. Romig, *Michigan Places Names*, 253.

528. Romig, *Michigan Place Names*, 253; Wheeler, comp., *History of Wexford County*, 296.

529. Romig, *Michigan Place Names*, 253.

530. Wheeler, comp., *History of Wexford County*, 296.

531. Romig, *Michigan Place Names*, 253.

532. Wheeler, comp., *History of Wexford County*, 296.

533. Ibid.

534. Ibid.

535. Ibid.

536. Ibid.

537. Ibid.

538. Ibid.

539. "Harrietta State Fish Hatchery," *Michigan Department of Natural Resources*, accessed October 22, 2017, www.michigan.gov/dnr/0,4570,7-153-10364_52259_28277-22495--,00.html.

540. Ibid.

541. "Recipes," "More Recipes," *Harrietta Hills Trout Farm*, accessed October 22, 2017, www.harriettatrout.com/.

542. "Harrietta Blueberry Festival," *Cadillac, Michigan*, accessed October 22, 2017, www.cadillacmichigan.com/events/4/883/.

543. Mardi Suhs, "Lazar Trust Funds Improvements in Harrietta," *Cadillac News*, September 20, 2017, www.cadillacnews.com/news/lazar-trust-funds-improvements-in-harrietta/article_1405419e-f48e-5036-b494-2e4d37a6689c.html.

544. "Yeggs Rob Bank at Falmouth," *Clio Messenger*, November 7, 1913, accessed through the Library of Congress, chroniclingamerica.loc.gov.

HARRISVILLE

545. U.S Census Bureau, 2010 census.

546. Walter Romig, *Michigan Place Names* (Detroit: Wayne State University Press, 1986), 254.

547. Ibid.

548. Ibid.

549. Ibid.

550. Ibid.

551. Ibid.

552. Ibid.

553. Ibid.

554. *Michigan State Gazetteer and Business Directory for 1877* (Detroit: C. F. Clarke, 1877), 479.

555. Ibid.

556. Ibid.

557. Ibid.

558. Ibid.

559. "Harrisville Depot," *Discover Heritage Route 23*, accessed October 22, 2017, www.us23heritageroute.org/alcona.asp?ait=av&aid=203.

560. *Michigan State Gazetteer and Business Directory for 1903* (Detroit: C. F. Clarke, 1903), 999–100.

561. Ibid.

562. Romig, *Michigan Places Names*, 254.

563. *Michigan State Gazetteer and Business Directory for 1921–1922* (Detroit: C. F. Clarke, 1922), 1022.

564. "Harrisville Depot," *Discover Heritage Route 23*.

565. Ibid.

566. Gregory H. Wolf, "Kiki Cuyler," *Society for American Baseball Research*, accessed October 22, 2017, sabr.org/bioproj/person/7107706b.

567. Ibid.

568. Ibid.

569. Ibid.

570. Ibid.

571. Ibid.

572. Ibid.

573. Ibid.

574. Ibid.

575. Cheryl Peterson, "Harrisville Harbor Jewel of the Sunrise Side," *Alcona County Review*, n.d., www.alconareview.com/harrisville-harbor.html.

576. MacKenzie Burger, "Lake Huron Shipwreck Discovered: Dive Team Finds 133-Year-Old Steamer New York off Harrisville," *mlive*, December 4, 2012, www.mlive.com/news/bay-city/index.ssf/2012/12/steamer_new_york_lake_huron_di.html.

577. Ibid.

578. Ibid.

HERSEY

579. U.S Census Bureau, 2010 census.

580. Perry F. Powers, assisted by H. G. Cutler, *A History of Northern Michigan and Its People, vol. 1* (Chicago: The Lewis Publishing Company, 1912), 544.

581. Walter Romig, *Michigan Place Names* (Detroit: Wayne State University Press, 1986), 263.

582. Powers, *A History of Northern Michigan*, 544.

583. Romig, Michigan Place Names, 263.

584. Romig, *Michigan Place Names*, 263; *Portrait and Biographical Album of Osceola County, Containing Portraits and Biographical Sketches of Prominent and Representative Citizens of the County, Together with Portraits and Biographies of all the Governors of Michigan and the Presidents of the United States, also Containing a Complete History of the County, from Its Earliest Settlement to the Present Time* (Chicago: Chapman Brothers, 1884), 377.

585. Powers, *A History of Northern Michigan*, 544.

586. Powers, *A History of Northern Michigan*, 544.; *Portrait and Biographical Album of Osceola County*, 377–378.

587. Portrait and Biographical Album of Osceola County, 377–378.

588. Ibid.

589. Ibid.

590. Ibid.

591. *Portrait and Biographical Album of Osceola County*, 377–378; Powers, *A History of Northern Michigan*, 544.

592. *Location, History, & Individual Communities*, Osceola County fact sheet, September 2014.

593. Andrew Topf, "Michigan Potash Mine Still in Play," *Mining.com*, June 2, 2017, www.mining.com/michigan-potash-mine-still-play/.

594. Ibid.

595. Ibid.

596. Ibid.

597. "Hersey Heritage," *Facebook*, September 10, 2017, www.facebook.com/herseyheritage/posts/1316405001798944.

HONOR

598. U.S Census Bureau, 2010 census.

599. Walter Romig, *Michigan Place Names* (Detroit: Wayne State University Press, 1986), 271.

600. "About Us," *Honor Area Restoration Project*, accessed October 23, 2017, restorehonor.org/about.html.

601. "Home," *Welcome to Village of Honor*, accessed October 23, 2017, www.villageofhonor.org; "About Us," *Honor Area Restoration Project*.

602. "Home," *Welcome to Village of Honor*.

603. Ibid.

604. *Michigan State Gazetteer and Business Directory for 1897* (Detroit: C. F. Clarke, 1897), 945–946.

605. Ibid.

606. *Michigan State Gazetteer and Business Directory for 1903* (Detroit: C. F. Clarke, 1903), 1028.

607. Louis Yock for the Benzie Area Historical Society, *Images of America: Lost Benzie County* (Charleston, SC: Arcadia Publishing, 2011), 31.

608. *Michigan State Gazetteer and Business Directory for 1907–1908* (Detroit: C. F. Clarke, 1908), 1178–1179; *Michigan State Gazetteer and Business Directory for 1921–1922* (Detroit: C. F. Clarke, 1922), 1045.

609. Romig, *Michigan Place Names*, 271; *Michigan State Gazetteer and Business Directory for 1921–1922* (Detroit: C. F. Clarke, 1922), 1045.

610. "History of the Cherry Bowl Drive-in Theater," accessed October 23, 2017, www.cherrybowldrivein.com/theatre.php.

611. "History of the Cherry Bowl."

612. "Platte River State Fish Hatchery," *Michigan Department of Natural Resources*, accessed October 23, 2017, www.michigan.gov/dnr/0,4570,7-153-10364_52259_28277-22491--,00.html.

613. "About Us," *Honor Area Restoration Project*.

614. "About Us," *National Coho Salmon Festival*, accessed October 23, 2017, nationalcohosalmonfestival.org/about-us/.

615. "About Us," *Honor Area Restoration Project*.

616. Ibid.

617. Ibid.

618. "About Us," *Honor Area Restoration Project*.

619. "About Us," *Honor Area Restoration Project*.

620. Village sign on US-31.

HORTON BAY

621. U.S. Census Bureau, 2010 census.

622. Michigan Economic Development Corporation, "Horton Bay General Store," *Pure Michigan*, accessed October 23, 2017, www.michigan.org/property/horton-bay-general-store; "Horton Bay," historical marker in Horton Bay, 1977.

623. "Horton Bay," historical marker.

624. Ibid.

625. Walter Romig, *Michigan Place Names* (Detroit: Wayne State University Press, 1986), 273.

626. Ibid.

627. *Michigan State Gazetteer and Business Directory for 1903* (Detroit: C. F. Clarke, 1903), 1029.

628. *Michigan State Gazetteer and Business Directory for 1907–1908* (Detroit: C. F. Clarke, 1908), 1180.

629. *Michigan State Gazetteer and Business Directory for 1921–1922* (Detroit: C. F. Clarke, 1922), 1046; Romig, *Michigan Place Names*, 273.

630. *Michigan State Gazetteer and Business Directory for 1921–1922*, 1046.

631. Sign on the porch of the Red Fox Inn.

632. "Horton Bay," historical marker.

633. "History of Horton Bay General Store," *Horton Bay General Store*, accessed October 23, 2017, www.hortonbaygeneralstore.com/text/history.html; Michigan Economic Development Corporation, "Horton Bay General Store," *Pure Michigan*.

634. Ibid.

635. Ibid.

636. Elizabeth Edwards, "Hemingway's Horton Bay," *My North*, updated March 4, 2008, mynorth.com/2008/03/hemingways-horton-bay/.

637. Ken Marek, "Hemingway-Related Sites in the Horton Bay/Walloon Lake/Harbor Springs Area," *Michigan Hemingway Society*, accessed October 23, 2017, www.michiganhemingwaysociety.org/hemsites.html.

638. "Horton Bay," historical marker.

639. Richard L. Lingeman, "More Posthumous Hemingway," *The New York Times on the Web*, April 25, 1972, www.nytimes.com/books/99/07/04/specials/hemingway-nick.html.

640. Ibid.

641. Robyn Meredith, "Horton Bay Journal; They Remember Papa, But Not Very Lovingly," *New York Times*, July 26, 1999, www.nytimes.com/1999/07/26/us/horton-bay-journal-they-remember-papa-but-not-very-lovingly.html.

642. Ibid.

643. Ken Marek, "Hemingway-Related Sites in the Horton Bay/Walloon Lake/Harbor Springs Area," *Michigan Hemingway Society*.

644. "History of Horton Bay General Store," *Horton Bay General Store*.

645. Ibid.

HUBBARDSTON

646. U.S. Census Bureau, 2010 census.

647. J. D. Dillenback, comp., *History and Directory of Ionia County, Michigan: Containing a History of Each Township: the Name, Occupation, Location, and Post-Office Address of Every Man in the County; a List of Post-Offices in the County; a Schedule of Population; and Other Valuable Statistics* (Grand Rapids: J. D. Dillenback, 1872), 54.

648. Ibid.

649. Ibid.

650. Ibid.

651. Ibid.

652. Ibid.

653. Ibid.

654. Dillenback, *History and Directory of Ionia County*, 54–55.

655. Ibid.

656. Dillenback, *History and Directory of Ionia County*, 53–55.

657. Dillenback, *History and Directory of Ionia County*, 52.

658. Ibid.

659. Dillenback, *History and Directory of Ionia County*, 55.

660. *Michigan State Gazetteer and Business Directory for 1903* (Detroit: C. F. Clarke, 1903), 1046.

661. Ibid.

662. "Home," *Hubbardston Irish Dance Troupe*, accessed October 23, 2017, hubbardstondance.com/index.html.

663. Ibid.

664. Ibid.

665. Ibid.

666. Ibid.

667. The Daily News Staff, "Hubbardston Offers a True Irish Experience Close to Home," *The Daily News*, March 18, 2015, thedailynews.cc/articles/hubbardston-offers-a-true-irish-experience-close-to-home/.

668. The Daily News Staff, "Hubbardston Hydro Dam is Once Again Producing Power," *The Daily News*, January 5, 2016, thedailynews.cc/articles/hubbardston-hydro-dam-is-once-again-producing-power/.

669. Ibid.

IRONTON

670. U.S. Census Bureau, 2010 census.

671. Walter Romig, *Michigan Place Names* (Detroit: Wayne State University Press, 1986), 287; *The Traverse Region, Historical and Descriptive, with Illustrations of Scenery and Portraits and Biographical Sketches of Some of Its Prominent Men and Pioneers* (Chicago: H. R. Page & Co., 1884), 216–217.

672. Romig, *Michigan Place Names*, 287.

673. *The Traverse Region, Historical and Descriptive*, 217.

674. Romig, *Michigan Place Names*, 287; *The Traverse region, historical and descriptive*, 217.

675. *The Traverse Region, Historical and Descriptive*, 217.

676. Ibid.

677. Ibid.

678. Ibid.

679. Romig, *Michigan Place Names*, 287.

680. *Michigan State Gazetteer and Business Directory for 1903* (Detroit: C. F. Clarke, 1903), 1064.

681. Ibid.

682. Ibid.

683. Aebra Coe, "A History of the Ironton Ferry," *Petoskey News*, January 17, 2013, articles.petoskeynews.com/2013-01-17/ironton-ferry_36400333.

684. Ibid.

685. Sign near the Ironton Ferry.

686. Coe, "A History of the Ironton Ferry."

687. Ibid.

688. "Ironton Ferry," *Charlevoix*, accessed October 23, 2017, www.visitcharlevoix.com/Ironton-Ferry.

689. "Home," *Summertime Rentals LLC of Lake Charlevoix*, accessed October 23, 2017, www.summertime-rentals.com.

690. U.S. Census Bureau, 2015 Demographic and Housing Estimates.

LAKE ANGELUS

691. U.S. Census Bureau, 2010 census.

692. "Short History," *Lake Angelus*, accessed October 25, 2017, www.lakeangelus.org.

693. Ibid.

694. Ibid.

695. "Short History," *Lake Angelus*; "Photos: Lake Angelus Summer Home is Now a Year-Round Retreat," *Detroit Free Press*, May 25, 2017, www.freep.com/picture-gallery/money/real-estate/michigan-house-envy/2017/05/25/photos-lake-angelus-summer-home-is-now-a-year-round-retreat/102101970/.

696. "Short History," *Lake Angelus*.

697. Ibid.

698. Ibid.

699. Ibid.

700. Ibid.

701. Michigan Municipal League, Sue A. Jeffers, ed., *Impact of Changing from a Village to a City*, n.d., www.mml.org/pdf/village_to_city.pdf.

702. "The 18 Tiniest Cities in Michigan," mlive, November 30, 2016, www.mlive.com/entertainment/index.ssf/2016/11/meet_michigans_smallest_cities.html.

703. "History," *McMath Hulbert Observatory*, accessed October 25, 2017, www.mcmathhulbert.org/history.php.

704. Ibid.

705. Ibid.

706. Ibid.

707. Ibid.

708. *The President's Report for 1937–1938* (Ann Arbor: University of Michigan, 1939), 267, accessed through Google Books.

709. Ibid.

710. Ibid.

711. Walter Romig, *Michigan Place Names* (Detroit: Wayne State University Press, 1986), 312.

LAKE ANN

1. U.S. Census Bureau, 2010 census.

2. Walter Romig, *Michigan Place Names* (Detroit: Wayne State University Press, 1986), 312.

3. Ibid.

4. "History," *Almira Township*, accessed October 26, 2017, www.almiratownship.org/history.asp.

5. Romig, *Michigan Place Names*, 312.

6. "History," *Almira Township*.

7. Romig, *Michigan Place Names*, 312

8. Ibid.

9. *Michigan State Gazetteer and Business Directory for 1897* (Detroit: C. F. Clarke, 1897), 1063.

10. Romig, *Michigan Place Names*, 312; "History," *Almira Township*.

11. "History," *Almira Township*.

12. Romig, *Michigan Place Names*, 312; "History," *Almira Township*; *Michigan State Gazetteer and Business Directory for 1907–1908* (Detroit: C. F. Clarke, 1908), 1302; *Michigan State Gazetteer and Business Directory for 1921–1922* (Detroit: C. F. Clarke, 1922), 1135; Richard Leary, "A History of Lake Ann's Disastrous Fires," *Grand Traverse Journal*, May 1, 2015, gtjournal.tadl.org/2015/a-history-of-lake-anns-disastrous-fires/.

13. *Michigan State Gazetteer and Business Directory for 1921–1922*, 1135.

14. "About Us," *Lake Ann Grocery*, accessed October 26, 2017, www.lakeanngrocery.net/about-us.html.

15. "Harmony Park, the Harm Farm," *Facebook*, accessed October 26, 2017, www.facebook.com/pg/TheHarmFarm/about/.

16. John Sinkevics, "Dunesville to Once Again Bring Music to Lake Ann Farm," *Traverse City Record Eagle*, July 14, 2017, www.record-eagle.com/news/local_news/dunesville-to-once-again-bring-music-to-lake-ann-farm/article_599ab383-3d62-51b1-b41e-2d837d38312c.html.

17. "History," *Almira Township*.

18. Michigan Pioneer and Historical Society, *Historical Collections*, vol. 31 (Lansing: Wynkoop Hallenbeck Crawford Co., 1902), 105–106.

LEONARD

19. U.S. Census Bureau, 2010 census.

20. Walter Romig, Michigan Place Names (Detroit: Wayne State University Press, 1986), 324–325.

21. Ibid.

22. Michigan State Gazetteer and Business Directory for 1887–1888 (Detroit: C. F. Clarke, 1888), 1140.

23. "Michigan, Oakland County," Jim Forte Postal History, accessed October 26, 2017, www.postalhistory.com/postoffices.asp?task=display&state=MI&county=Oakland&searchtext=&pagenum=3.

24. Michigan State Gazetteer and Business Directory for 1887–1888, 1140.

25. Ibid.

26. "History of the Leonard Grain Elevator," Leonard Mill, accessed October 26, 2017, www.leonardmill.com/page4.

27. Ibid.

28. Thaddeus D. Seeley, History of Oakland County, Michigan, a Narrative Account of its Historical Progress, its People, and its Principle Interests, vol. 1 (Chicago and New York: The Lewis Publishing Company, 1912), 463.

29. "History of the Leonard Grain Elevator," Leonard Mill.

30. Ibid.

31. "History of the Leonard Grain Elevator," Leonard Mill.

32. "History of the Leonard Grain Elevator," Leonard Mill

33. Walter Romig, Michigan Place Names (Detroit: Wayne State University Press, 1986), 324–325.

LEROY

34. U.S. Census Bureau, 2010 census.

35. *Local Acts of the Legislature of the State of Michigan Passed at the Regular Session of 1883, with an Appendix* (Lansing: W. S. George Co., 1883), 15–16.

36. *Portrait and Biographical Album of Osceola County, Containing Portraits and Biographical Sketches of Prominent and Representative Citizens of the County, Together with Portraits and Biographies of all the Governors of Michigan and of the Presidents of the United States. Also Containing a Complete History of the County, from Its Earliest Settlement to the Present Time* (Chicago: Chapman Brothers, 1884), 384.

37. Ibid.

38. Walter Romig, *Michigan Place Names* (Detroit: Wayne State University Press, 1986), 325; *Portrait and Biographical Album of Osceola County*, 386.

39. *Portrait and Biographical Album of Osceola County*, 384; *Local Acts of the Legislature of the State of Michigan*, 15–16.

40. *Michigan State Gazetteer and Business Directory for 1877* (Detroit: C. F. Clarke, 1877), 575.

41. *Michigan State Gazetteer and Business Directory for 1903* (Detroit: C. F. Clarke, 1903), 1200.

42. Ibid.

43. Charles E. Gasteyer, *Forest Ray Moulton, 1872–1952* (Washington DC: National Academy of Sciences, 1970), 341.

44. Gasteyer, 341–342.

45. Gasteyer, 342.

46. Gasteyer, 342–344; Thomas Hockey, Virginia Trimble, Thomas R. Williams, Katherine Bracher, Richard A. Jarrell, Jordan D. Marché, JoAnn Palmeri, Daniel W. E. Green, eds., *Biographical Encyclopedia of Astronomers* (New York: Springer, 2014), 810.

47. Gasteyer, 344.

48. Gasteyer, 343.

49. Gasteyer, 344.

50. Ibid.

51. Gasteyer, 345.

LINCOLN

52. U.S. Census Bureau, 2010 census.

53. Perry F. Powers, assisted by H. G. Cutler, *A History of Northern Michigan and Its People, vol. 1* (Chicago: Lewis Publishing Company, 1912), 504.

54. Alcona County Historical Society, *Driving Tours of Alcona County Historical Sites*, 2013, www.alconahistoricalsociety.com/2013%20Driving%20

Tour.pdf; "Josiah M. Donaldson," *Find a Grave*, accessed October 28, 2017, www.findagrave.com/cgi-bin/fg.cgi?page=gr&GSln=Donaldson&GSiman=1&G%20Scid=1766601&GRid=92371158.

55. Alcona County Historical Society, *Driving Tours*, 2013.

56. Ibid.

57. Ibid.

58. "Josiah M. Donaldson," *Find a Grave*.

59. Alcona County Historical Society, *Driving Tours*, 2013.

60. Ibid.

61. Ibid.

62. Ibid.

63. Ibid.

64. Powers, *A History of Northern Michigan and Its People*, 504.

65. Ibid.

66. "Home," *Lincoln, Michigan*.

67. Walter Romig, *Michigan Place Names* (Detroit: Wayne State University Press, 1986), 328; "Home," *Lincoln, Michigan*, accessed October 28, 2017, www.lincolnmi.com/1/170/index.asp.

68. Romig, *Michigan Place Names*, 328; "Home," *Lincoln, Michigan*.

69. "Home," *Lincoln, Michigan*.

70. Romig, *Michigan Place Names*, 328.

71. Ibid.

72. Powers, *A History of Northern Michigan and Its People*, 504.

73. "Home," *Lincoln, Michigan*.

74. *Michigan State Gazetteer and Business Directory for 1907–1908* (Detroit: C. F. Clarke, 1908), 1364.

75. Ibid.

76. Ibid.

77. *Michigan State Gazetteer and Business Directory for 1921–1922* (Detroit: C. F. Clarke, 1922), 1178–1179.

78. Ibid.

79. "Lincoln, MI, About" *Facebook*, accessed October 28, 2017, www.facebook.com/pg/Lincoln-MI-106939216083785/about/.

80. "About," *Lost Lake Woods Club*, accessed October 28, 2017, www.lostlakewoodsclub.com/about.

81. Ibid.

LUTHER

82. U.S. Census Bureau, 2010 census.

83. Perry F. Powers, assisted by H. G. Cutler, *A History of Northern Michigan and Its People, vol. 1* (Chicago: Lewis Publishing Company, 1912), 550.

84. "G. H. Gordon Biological Research Station," *Hillsdale College*, accessed October 28, 2017, www.hillsdale.edu/about/facilities/gordon-biological-station/.

85. Ibid.

86. "Lodging," *The Rockwell Lake Lodge*, accessed October 29, 2017, rockwelllakelodge.hillsdale.edu/lodging.

87. "Recreation," *The Rockwell Lake Lodge*, accessed October 29, 2017, rockwelllakelodge.hillsdale.edu/recreation.

88. "Luther, MI 49656," a postcard from Luther.

89. "Luther, MI 49656," a postcard from Luther; Walter Romig, *Michigan Place Names* (Detroit: Wayne State University Press, 1986), 337–338.

90. Romig, *Michigan Place Names*, 337–338.

91. Ibid.

92. *Michigan State Gazetteer and Business Directory for 1887–1888* (Detroit: C. F. Clarke, 1888), 1163–1164.

93. Ibid.

94. Ibid.

95. "History of Newkirk Township, Lake County, Michigan," *Newkirk Township*, accessed October 29, 2017, www.newkirktownship.com/history.html.

96. Powers, *A History of Northern Michigan and Its People*, 550.

97. Ibid.

98. Julie Morgan, in conversation with the author, August 13, 2017.

99. Ibid.

100. Ibid.

101. Morgan, 2017; Michigan Department of Natural Resources, *Michigan Natural Resources Trust Fund Recommendations*, December 7, 2012.

102. "Luther, MI 49656."

103. Ibid.

104. "Alonzo Woodruff," *Hall of Valor*, accessed December 17, 2017, valor.militarytimes.com/recipient.php?recipientid=129.

105. Ibid.

106. "SERG Alonzo Woodruff, Medal of Honor Company I, 1st US Sharp Shooters Union Army," *Faded Footsteps*, accessed December 17, 2017, www.fadedfootsteps.com/veteran/serg-alonzo-woodruff-medal-of-honor-company-i-1st-us-sharp-shooters-us-union-army.

107. Ibid.

108. "Luther Logging Days," *Cadillac, Michigan*, accessed October 28, 2017, www.cadillacmichigan.com/ events/4/855/; "Village of Luther," *Pure Michigan*, accessed October 28, 2017, www.michigan.org/ property/village-luther.

MACKINAC ISLAND CITY

109. U.S. Census Bureau, 2010 census.

110. Aaron Parseghian, "200 Years of History, City of Mackinac Island Celebrates Bicentennial," *9&10 News*, July 7, 2017, www.9and10news. com/2017/07/07/200-years-of-history-city-of-mackinac-island-celebrates-bicentennial/.

111. "An Island to Call Home," *City of Mackinac Island*, accessed October 29, 2017, www.cityofmi.org.

112. Mackinaw Area Visitors Bureau, "Living History. Making History.," accessed October 29, 2017, www.mackinawcity.com/area-info-2/living-history-making-history/.

113. Kathleen Lavey, "Mackinac Island Restores Its American Indian history," *Lansing State Journal*, March 7, 2017, www.lansingstatejournal.com/story/ travel/michigan/2017/03/07/restoring-mackinac-islands-native-american-history/98809484/.

114. Walter Romig, *Michigan Place Names* (Detroit: Wayne State University Press, 1986), 343–344; "Colonial Fort Michilimackinac," *Mighty Mac*, accessed October 29, 2017, www.mightymac.org/ michilimackinac.htm.

115. Romig, *Michigan Place Names*, 343–344.

116. Ibid.

117. "The City of Mackinac Island," *Mackinac State Historic Parks*, July 7, 2017, www.mackinacparks. com/the-city-of-mackinac-island/.

118. Lynn Armitage, "Mackinac Island Finally Telling Native Side of History," *Indian Country Today*, March 30, 2017, indiancountrymedianetwork.com/history/ traditional-societies/mackinac-island-finally-telling-native-side-history/.

119. Ibid.

120. Ibid.

121. *Michigan State Gazetteer and Business Directory for 1863* (Detroit: C. F. Clarke, 1863), 388; *Michigan State Gazetteer and Business Directory for 1877* (Detroit: C. F. Clarke, 1877), 588.

122. *Michigan State Gazetteer and Business Directory for 1877* (Detroit: C. F. Clarke, 1877), 588.

123. Mackinac Island," *Michigan.gov*, accessed October 29, 2017, www.michigan.gov/som/0,4669,7-192-29938_68915-54596--,00.html.

124. "An Island to Call Home," *City of Mackinac Island*, accessed October 29, 2017, www.cityofmi.org.

125. Frank Straus, "A Look at History," *Mackinac Island Town Crier*, August 29, 2009, www. mackinacislandnews.com/news/2009-08-29/ Columnists/A_Look_at_History_002.html.

126. "Highways 180 through 199," *Michigan Highways*, accessed October 29, 2017, www.michiganhighways. org/listings/MichHwys180-199.html#M-185.

127. Straus, "A Look at History."

128. Ibid.

129. Ibid.

130. "The History of a Timeless American Treasure," *Grand Hotel*, accessed December 17, 2017, www. grandhotel.com/about-grand-hotel/our-story/; "#GrandPhotoContest2017," *Grand Hotel*, accessed December 17, 2017, www.grandhotel.com/ category/130th-anniversary/.

131. "Mackinac Island Lodging and Accommodations," *The Official Website of Mackinac Island*, accessed October 30, 2017, www.mackinacisland.org/ lodging/.

132. Aaron Parseghian, "200 Years of History."

133. "Mackinac Island: Michigan's Top Summer Retreat," *The Official Website of Mackinac Island*, accessed October 29, 2017, www.mackinacisland.org/ mackinac-island-facts/.

MARENISCO

134. U.S. Census Bureau, 2010 census.

135. Dennis D. Rolando, *Marenisco* (Grass Lake Images, Inc., 2006), 10.

136. Ibid.

137. Ibid.

138. Rolando, *Marenisco*, 11; *Michigan State Gazetteer and Business Directory for 1903* (Detroit: C. F. Clarke, 1903), 1246.

139. Rolando, *Marenisco*, 15.

140. Rolando, *Marenisco*, 10–11.

141. Rolando, *Marenisco*, 11–12.

142. Rolando, *Marenisco*, 10–18.

143. Rolando, *Marenisco*, 18.

144. Rolando, *Marenisco*, 18–19.

145. Rolando, *Marenisco*, 22.

146. Ibid.

147. Rolando, *Marenisco*, 12–15.

148. Rolando, *Marenisco*, 12–15; "Marenisco," *Gogebic County, part of the MIGenWeb*, accessed October 30, 2017, hometownchronicles.com/mi/gogebic/cmtys/ marenisco.html.

149. Rolando, *Marenisco*, 12–15.

150. Ibid.

151. Ibid.

152. Rolando, *Marenisco*, 12–15; "Marenisco," *Gogebic County, part of the MIGenWeb*.

153. Rolando, *Marenisco*, 12–15.

154. "The Bad Guy of Gogebic," *Detroit Free Press*, June 24, 1984; "Black Bart Paroled," *The Diamond Drill*, January 7, 1911, accessed through the Library of Congress, chroniclingamerica.loc.gov.

155. Ibid.

156. "Black Bart Paroled," *The Diamond Drill*.

157. Ibid.

158. "Tourism," *Marenisco*, accessed November 2, 2017, marenisco.org/tourism/.

159. Rolando, *Marenisco*, 20.

160. Ibid.

161. Ibid.

162. "Economic Development," *Marenisco*, accessed November 2, 2017, marenisco.org/ economic-development/; Michigan Economic Development Corporation, "Renaissance Zones," *Michigan Economic Development Corporation*, accessed November 2, 2017, www.michiganbusiness.org/ renaissance-zones/.

MARTIN

163. U.S. Census Bureau, 2010 census.

164. Walter Romig, *Michigan Place Names* (Detroit: Wayne State University Press, 1986), 355.

165. "Early History of Martin," sign in village.

166. Ibid.

167. Ibid.

168. Ibid.

169. Ibid.

170. The Michigan Engineering Society, *The Michigan Engineers' Annual, Containing the Proceedings of the Michigan Engineering Society for 1897* (Lansing: Press of Robert Smith Printing, 1897), 42.

171. "Early History of Martin," sign in village.

172. "Plank Roads," *Kalamazoo Public Library*, accessed November 2, 2017, www.kpl.gov/local-history/ transportation/plankroads.aspx.

173. Romig, *Michigan Place Names*, 355; Henry F. Thomas, ed., *A Twentieth Century History of Allegan County, Michigan* (Chicago: Lewis Publishing Company, 1907), 51; "Early History of Martin," sign in village.

174. "Early History of Martin," sign in village.

175. Ibid.

176. Ibid.

177. "Early History of Martin," sign in village.

178. "Early History of Martin," sign in village; Romig, *Michigan Place Names*, 355.

179. Ibid.

180. *Michigan State Gazetteer and Business Directory for 1867–1868* (Detroit: C. F. Clarke, 1868), 294.

181. "Early History of Martin," sign in village.

182. Ibid.

183. *Michigan State Gazetteer and Business Directory for 1887–1888* (Detroit: C. F. Clarke, 1888), 1214–1215.

184. "Early History of Martin," sign in village.

185. Ibid.

186. Ibid.

187. "Early History of Martin," sign in village.

188. Ibid.

189. "Martin Public Schools Solar Project," *Martin Public Schools*, accessed November 2, 2017, www.martinpublicschools.org/content/martin-public-schools-solar-project.

MCBRIDE

190. U.S. Census Bureau, 2010 census.

191. Day Township," *Montcalm County MIGenWeb*, accessed November 3, 2017, www.migenweb.org/montcalm/townships/day.html.

192. John W. Dasef, *History of Montcalm County, Michigan, Its People, Industries and Institutions, vol. 2* (Indianapolis: B. F. Bowen & Company, Inc., 1916), 122.

193. Ibid.

194. Ibid.

195. Ibid.

196. Ibid.

197. Ibid.

198. Ibid.

199. Dasef, *History of Montcalm County*, 122–123.

200. Dasef, *History of Montcalm County*, 122.

201. Ibid.

202. Ibid.

203. Ibid

204. Ibid.

205. Ibid.

206. Dasef, *History of Montcalm County*, 123.

207. Ibid.

208. Ibid.

209. Ibid.

210. "Find Locations – McBrides," *USPS.com*, accessed November 4, 2017.

211. U.S. Census Bureau, 1920 census; U.S. Census Bureau, 2010 census.

212. "Welcome to McBride(s)," *UPI*, March 9, 1998, www.upi.com/Archives/1988/03/09/Welcome-to-McBrides/8684573886800/.

213. Ibid.

214. Gary L. Hauck, *The Story of Heritage Village: Celebrating 25 Years* (Bloomington: iUniverse, Inc., 2011), 59–60.

215. Ibid.

MELVIN

216. U.S. Census Bureau, 2010 census.

217. Walter Romig, *Michigan Place Names* (Detroit: Wayne State University Press, 1986), 361.

218. Ibid.

219. Ibid.

220. *Michigan State Gazetteer and Business Directory for 1887–1888* (Detroit: C. F. Clarke, 1888), 1226; *Michigan State Gazetteer and Business Directory for 1903* (Detroit: C. F. Clarke, 1903), 1279.

221. *Portrait and Biographical Album of Sanilac County, Containing Portraits and Biographical Sketches of Prominent and Representative Citizens of the County, Together with Portraits and Biographies of all the Governors of Michigan and of the Presidents of the United States* (Chicago: Chapman Brothers, 1884), 489; *Michigan State Gazetteer and Business Directory for 1887–1888*, 1226.

222. *Michigan State Gazetteer and Business Directory for 1887–1888*, 1226.

223. *Michigan State Gazetteer and Business Directory for 1903*, 1279.

224. Ibid.

225. Ibid.

226. Ibid.

227. *Michigan State Gazetteer and Business Directory for 1907–1908* (Detroit: C. F. Clarke, 1908), 1440.

228. "10th Annual Hog Town Run," *HCECM*, accessed November 4, 2017, www.hcecm.org/Events/10th-Annual-Hog-Town-Run.aspx.

229. Cathy Barringer, "Hog Town Run to Benefit Local Hospice," *The County Press*, August 2, 2017, thecountypress.mihomepaper.com/news/2017-08-02/News/Hog_Town_Run_to_benefit_local_hospice.html.

230. Ibid.

231. "10th Annual Hog Town Run," *HCECM*.

232. Ibid.

233. Ibid.

234. Beadel to Bealke," *Political Graveyard*, accessed December 17, 2017, politicalgraveyard.com/bio/beadle-beales.html#469.51.51.

235. Ibid.

MESICK

236. U.S. Census Bureau, 2010 census.

237. "Wexford County History," *Wexford County Historical Society Museum*, accessed November 4, 2017, www.wexfordcountyhistory.org/history/.

238. "Home," *Village of Mesick, Michigan*, accessed November 4, 2017, villageofmesick-public.sharepoint.com.

239. "Schedule," *Mesick Lions Mushroom Festival*, accessed November 5, 2017, www.mesick-mushroomfest.org/schedule.html.

240. "Home," *Mesick Lions' Mushroom Festival*, accessed November 5, 2017, www.mesick-mushroomfest.org/index.html.

241. "Wexford County History," *Wexford County Historical Society Museum*.

242. Walter Romig, *Michigan Place Names* (Detroit: Wayne State University Press, 1986), 364.

243. Ibid.

244. Ibid.

245. John H. Wheeler, comp., *History of Wexford County, Michigan, Embracing a Concise Review of Its Early Settlement, Industrial Development and Present Conditions* (Logansport: B. F. Bowen & Co., 1903), 298.

246. Ibid.

247. *Michigan State Gazetteer and Business Directory for 1903* (Detroit: C. F. Clarke, 1903), 1293.

248. "Wexford County History," *Wexford County Historical Society Museum*.

249. Wheeler, comp., *History of Wexford County*, 273.

250. Wheeler, comp., *History of Wexford County*, 273, 298.

251. Ibid.

252. *Michigan State Gazetteer and Business Directory for 1921–1922* (Detroit: C. F. Clarke, 1922), 1230–1231.

253. Ibid.

254. "About Mesick," *Mesick Consolidated Schools*, accessed November 5, 2017, mesick.org/district/about-mesick/.

255. Ibid.

256. Mark A. Tonello, *Hodenpyl Dam Pond, Wexford County* (Michigan Department of Natural Resources, 2012).

257. "Jeep Blessing," *Cadillac Jeepers*, accessed November 4, 2017, cadillacjeepers.com/jeep-blessing/.

258. Ibid.

259. "About Mesick," *Mesick Consolidated Schools*, accessed November 5, 2017, mesick.org/district/about-mesick/.

MICHIANA

260. U.S. Census Bureau, 2010 census.

261. Village of Michiana, accessed September 17, 2017, michianavillage.org/images/Michiana.pdf.

262. Village of Michiana.

263. "History of Village Organizations and the Community Center," Village of Michiana, accessed November 5, 2017, michianavillage.org/villagehome/michianahistory.html; Walter Romig, Michigan Place Names (Detroit: Wayne State University Press, 1986), 365.

264. "History of Village Organizations and the Community Center," Village of Michiana; Romig, Michigan Place Names, 365.

265. "History of Village Organizations and the Community Center," Village of Michiana.

266. Romig, Michigan Place Names, 365.

267. Ibid.

268. "History of Village Organizations and the Community Center," Village of Michiana.

269. Ibid.

270. Ibid.

271. "Michiana," Harbor Country Chamber of Commerce, accessed November 5, 2017, www.harborcountry.org/about-harbor-country/michiana/.

272. "Michiana," Harbor Country Chamber of Commerce; Village of Michiana, a Village Profile Document, 2009, michianavillage.org/images/Michiana_Village_Profile_2009.pdf.

273. "Michiana," Harbor Country Chamber of Commerce.

274. Village of Michiana, a Village Profile Document.

275. Ibid.

276. "Michiana," Harbor Country Chamber of Commerce.

277. Ibid.

278. Ibid.

MICHIGAMME

279. U.S. Census Bureau, 2010 census.

280. Don Moore, in conversation with the author, August 16, 2017; *Michigamme Museum 1900 Steamer*, museum pamphlet.

281. Michigamme Museum 1900 Steamer, museum pamphlet.

282. Moore.

283. Ibid.

284. Moore; *Michigamme Museum 1900 Steamer*, museum pamphlet.

285. Moore.

286. Michigamme Museum 1900 Steamer, museum pamphlet.

287. Ibid.

288. Ibid.

289. Ibid.

290. Ibid.

291. Walter Romig, *Michigan Place Names* (Detroit: Wayne State University Press, 1986), 365; Alvah L. Sawyer, *A History of the Northern Peninsula of Michigan and Its People, Its Mining, Lumber and Agriculture Industries, volume 1* (Chicago: Lewis Publishing Company, 1911), 437.

292. Ibid.

293. Mike Hosey, in conversation with the author, August 16, 2017.

294. Romig, *Michigan Place Names*, 365.

295. "Learn More about our U.P.," LMPO, accessed November 4, 2017, www.lmpowners.org/area-history.html.

296. Ibid.

297. *Michigan State Gazetteer and Business Directory for 1903* (Detroit: C. F. Clarke, 1903), 1294–1295.

298. Ibid.

299. Moore; *Michigamme Historical Museum*, museum pamphlet, n.d.

300. "Reviving Michigamme," *Mining Journal*, May 23, 2016, www.miningjournal.net/news/front-page-news/2016/05/reliving-michigamme/.

301. *Michigamme Historical Museum*, museum pamphlet, n.d.

302. Ibid.

303. Moore; *Michigamme Historical Museum*, museum pamphlet, n.d.

304. Moore.

305. *Michigamme Historical Museum*, museum pamphlet, n.d.

306. Ibid.

307. Ibid.

308. Ibid.

309. Ibid.

310. Hosey.

311. Ibid.

312. "Learn More about Our U.P.," *LMPO*.

313. "Michigamme Mine (Mt Shasta mine), Michigamme, Marquette Iron Range, Marquette Co., Michigan, USA." *Mindat*, accessed November 4, 2017, www.mindat.org/loc-12364.html.

MILLERSBURG

314. U.S. Census Bureau, 2010 census.

315. Walter Romig, *Michigan Place Names* (Detroit: Wayne State University Press, 1986), 369–370.

316. Romig, *Michigan Place Names*, 369–370; "Village of Millersburg," village sign, n.d.

317. "Detroit & Mackinac Railway Depot," village plaque; Romig, *Michigan Place Names*, 369–370.

318. "Village of Millersburg," village sign, n.d.

319. *Michigan State Gazetteer and Business Directory for 1907 1908* (Detroit: C. F. Clarke, 1908), 1472–1473.

320. Perry F. Powers, assisted by H. G. Cutler, *A History of Northern Michigan and Its People, vol. 1* (Chicago: The Lewis Publishing Company, 1912), 485–486.

321. Ibid.

322. "Village of Millersburg," village sign, n.d.

323. Powers, *A History of Northern Michigan*, 161, 485–486.

324. *Michigan State Gazetteer and Business Directory for 1907–1908* (Detroit: C. F. Clarke, 1908), 51472–1473.

325. Ibid.

326. Ibid.

327. *Michigan State Gazetteer and Business Directory for 1921–1922* (Detroit: C. F. Clarke, 1922), 1238.

328. "Detroit & Mackinaw Railway Depot," village plaque.

329. Ibid.

330. "History of the Fair," *Presque Isle County Fair Association*, accessed November 6, 2017, www.picountyfair.net/fair-history.html.

331. Ibid.

332. Ibid.

333. Ibid.

334. Ibid.

335. Ibid.

336. Ibid.

337. "River Drives," village sign, n.d.

338. Ibid.

339. "Providence: Destined to Become a Ghost Town," village sign, n.d.

340. Ibid.

341. Ibid.

MINDEN CITY

342. U.S. Census Bureau, 2010 census.

343. Walter Romig, *Michigan Place Names* (Detroit: Wayne State University Press, 1986), 372.

344. Michigan Department of Natural Resources, "The Wolverine," *Michigan Department of Natural Resources*, accessed December 17, 2017, www.michigan.gov/dnr/0,4570,7-153-10369_46675_57974-253814--,00.html.

345. Ibid.

346. Ibid.

347. Romig, *Michigan Place Names*, 372.

348. Esther L. Teeple, *Historical Souvenir of the Minden City Centennial, 1855–1955*, 3.

349. Ibid.

350. Teeple, *Historical Souvenir*, 4.

351. Ibid.

352. Romig, *Michigan Place Names*, 372.

353. Ibid.

354. Teeple, *Historical Souvenir*, 4

355. Ibid.

356. Romig, *Michigan Place Names*, 372; Teeple, *Historical souvenir*, 6.

357. Teeple, *Historical Souvenir*, 7.

358. *Michigan State Gazetteer and Business Directory for 1887–1888* (Detroit: C. F. Clarke, 1888), 1250–1251.

359. Teeple, *Historical Souvenir*, 6.

360. Romig, *Michigan Place Names*, 372.

361. Teeple, *Historical Souvenir*, 4.

362. Teeple, *Historical Souvenir*, 7–10; *Michigan State Gazetteer and Business Directory for 1887–1888* (Detroit: C. F. Clarke, 1888), 1250–1251.

363. Janis Stein, "Minden City Tractor Pull & Homecoming," *Lakeshore Guardian*, July 2015, www.lakeshoreguardian.com/site/news/557/Minden-City-Tractor-Pull--Homecoming#.WgeGcGVll-U; *Minden City Tractor Pull*, 2017 event flyer.

364. *Minden City Tractor Pull*, 2017 event flyer.

365. Teeple, *Historical Souvenir*, 5.

366. Ibid.

367. Teeple, *Historical Souvenir*, 7.

368. "Yellow Day, 1881," *Celebrate Boston*, accessed December 17, 2017, www.celebrateboston.com/disasters/yellow-day.htm.

MONTGOMERY

369. U.S. Census Bureau, 2010 census.

370. *Local Acts of the Legislature of the State of Michigan Passed at the Regular Session of 1907* (Lansing: Wynkoop Hallenbeck Crawford Co. State Printers, 1907), 1133–1134.

371. "History of Montgomery," *Hillsdale County Community Center*, accessed November 11, 2017, www.hillsdalecounty.info/history0065.asp.

372. Ibid.

373. Ibid.

374. Ibid.

375. Ibid.

376. *Montgomery Frogeye Days: July 14, 15 & 16, 2017*, event flyer, accessed on the Village of Montgomery Facebook page, www.facebook.com/153906237983057/photos/a.512388518801492.110956.153906237983057/1757132167660448/?type=3&theater.

377. Michigan State University Extension, *Michigan Natural Features Inventory*, "Oak Openings," a community abstract, published 2004, updated 2010; Crisfield Johnson, *History of Hillsdale County, Michigan, with Illustrations and Biographical Sketches of some of Its Prominent Men and Pioneers* (Philadelphia: Everts & Abbott, 1879), 307–308.

378. Johnson, *History of Hillsdale County*, 307–308.

379. Ibid.

380. Ibid.

381. Ibid.

382. Ibid.

383. Ibid.

384. Romig, *Michigan Place Names*, 377.

385. Johnson, *History of Hillsdale County*, 307–308.

386. Ibid.

387. Ibid.

388. Ibid.

389. *Michigan State Gazetteer and Business Directory for 1907–1908* (Detroit: C. F. Clarke, 1908), 1487.

390. *Michigan State Gazetteer and Business Directory for 1921–1922* (Detroit: C. F. Clarke, 1922), 1247.

391. "History of Montgomery," *Hillsdale County Community Center*.

392. "Halloween Celebrated Early in Montgomery," *Hillsdale Daily News*, October 23, 2017, www.hillsdale.net/news/20171023/halloween-celebrated-early-in-montgomery.

393. Andy Barrand, "Keegan Wins with Father, Son Team," *Hillsdale Daily News*, September 28, 2017, www.hillsdale.net/news/20170928/keegan-wins-with-father-son-team.

MULLIKEN

394. U.S. Census Bureau, 2010 census.

395. Walter Romig, *Michigan Place Names* (Detroit: Wayne State University Press, 1986), 384.

396. Thomas Merton, Robert E. Daggy, ed., *The Road to Joy: The Letters of Thomas Merton to New and Old Friends* (New York: Farrar, Straus and Giroux, n.d.).

397. Ibid.

398. Ibid.

399. Romig, *Michigan Place Names*, 354.

400. Dennis Baron, "America's War on Language," *The Web of Language*, September 3, 2014, blogs.illinois.edu/view/25/116243; Mary J. Manning, "Being German, Being American: In World War I, They Faced Suspicion, Discrimination Here at Home," *Prologue*, vol. 46, 2014, www.archives.gov/files/publications/prologue/2014/summer/germans.pdf.

401. "Stars and Stripes Protected with Honor," *Belding Banner*, April 11, 1917, accessed through the Library of Congress, chroniclingamerica.loc.gov.

402. Ibid.

403. Ibid.

404. Romig, *Michigan Place Names*, 384.

405. Ibid.

406. Ibid.

407. Vera Hogan, "Past and Present Collide in Murder Mystery Novel," *tctimes.com*, September 27, 2017, www.tctimes.com/news/past-and-present-collide-in-murder-mystery-novel/article_b6a78110-a383-11e7-93a7-07ebce5778ef.html.

408. "Hot Rods and Harleys," *Midwest Biker Events*, accessed November 11, 2017, www.midwestbiker-events.com/events/hot-rods-and-harleys.

NESSEN CITY

409. U.S. Census Bureau, 2010 census.

410. Walter Romig, *Michigan Place Names* (Detroit: Wayne State University Press, 1986), 391; Louis Yock for the Benzie County Historical Society, *Images of America: Lost Benzie County* (Charleston: Arcadia Publishing, 2011), 17–20.

411. Romig, *Michigan Place Names*, 391; Yock, *Images of America*, 17–20.

412. Yock, *Images of America*, 17–20.

413. Ibid.

414. Ibid.

415. *Michigan State Gazetteer and Business Directory for 1903* (Detroit: C. F. Clarke, 1903), 1362.

416. Ibid.

417. *Michigan State Gazetteer and Business Directory for 1907–1908* (Detroit: C. F. Clarke, 1908), 1530.

418. Ibid.

419. Ibid.

420. Ibid.

421. Ibid.

422. Ibid.

423. Yock, *Images of America*, 17–20.

424. *Michigan State Gazetteer and Business Directory for 1921–1922* (Detroit: C. F. Clarke, 1922), 1284.

425. Yock, *Images of America*, 17–20.

426. Karie Herringa, "Sightseeing in Northern Michigan: Nessen City Schoolhouse Renovation Project," *9&10 News*, May 18, 2016, www.9and10news.com/2016/05/18/sightseeing-in-northern-michigan-nessen-city-schoolhouse-renovation-project/.

427. Ibid.

428. Ibid.

429. Ibid.

430. Ibid.

431. Ibid.

432. Ibid.

433. Herringa, "Sightseeing in Northern Michigan."

434. Yock, *Images of America*, 17–20.

OAKLEY

435. U.S. Census Bureau, 2010 census.

436. Walter Romig, *Michigan Place Names* (Detroit: Wayne State University Press, 1986), 410.

437. Ibid.

438. Michael A. Leeson, *History of Saginaw County Michigan; Together with Sketches of Its Cities, Villages and Townships; Educational History, Religious, Civil, Military, and Political History; Portraits of Prominent Persons, and Biographies of Representative Citizens* (Chicago: Chas. C. Chapman & Co., 1881), 739.

439. Ibid.

440. Romig, *Michigan Place Names*, 410.

441. Ibid.

442. Ibid.

443. Ibid.

444. Romig, *Michigan Place Names*, 410; Leeson, *History of Saginaw County*, 741–742.

445. "Saginaw County Michigan: Brady," *MIGenWeb*, accessed November 12, 2017, www.mifamilyhistory.org/saginaw/brady/default.asp.

446. *Michigan State Gazetteer and Business Directory for 1887–1888* (Detroit: C. F. Clarke, 1888), 1349; *Michigan State Gazetteer and Business Directory for 1903* (Detroit: C. F. Clarke, 1903), 1385; *Michigan State Gazetteer and Business Directory for 1907–1908* (Detroit: C. F. Clarke, 1908), 1556; *Michigan State Gazetteer and Business Directory for 1921–1922* (Detroit: C. F. Clarke, 1922), 1299.

447. Ibid.

448. Leeson, *History of Saginaw County*, 743

449. Ibid.

450. Ibid.

451. Ibid.

452. Ibid.

453. Ibid.

454. Ibid.

455. Ibid.

456. Leeson, *History of Saginaw County*, 741.

457. "Home," *Oakley Community Church*, accessed November 12, 2017, oakleycommunitychurch.org.

458. Romig, *Michigan Place Names*, 410.

OMER

459. U.S. Census Bureau, 2010 census.

460. Walter Romig, *Michigan Place Names* (Detroit: Wayne State University Press, 1986), 415.

461. Ibid.

462. *History of Bay County Michigan, with Illustrations and Biographical Sketches of some of Its Prominent Men and Pioneers* (Chicago: H. R. Page & Co., 1883), 245.

463. Ibid.

464. Ibid.

465. Ibid.

466. Ibid.

467. Romig, *Michigan Place Names*, 415.

468. *History of Bay County Michigan*, 245.

469. Ibid.

470. Ibid.

471. *History of Bay County Michigan*, 245; *Michigan State Gazetteer and Business Directory for 1903* (Detroit: C. F. Clarke, 1903), 1389.

472. *Michigan State Gazetteer and Business Directory for 1907–1908* (Detroit: C. F. Clarke, 1908), 1560–1561.

473. Ibid.

474. *Michigan State Gazetteer and Business Directory for 1921–1922* (Detroit: C. F. Clarke, 1922), 1302.

475. "Ye Olde Courthouse Masonic Hall" Discover Heritage Route 23. www.us23heritageroute.org/arenac.asp?ait=av&aid=684., accessed January 14, 2018

476. Lindsey Russell, "The Witchy Wolves of Omer Plains," *Michigan's Other Side*, accessed November 12, 2017, michigansotherside.com/the-witchy-wolves-of-omer-plains/.

477. Ibid.

478. Ibid.

479. Tim Barnum, "Eerie Temperance Entertainment Calls Omer Plains Investigation a Great Success," *The Arenac County Independent*, March 23, 2009, www.arenacindependent.com/stories/Eerie-Temperance-Entertainment-calls-Omer-plains-investigation-a-great-success,79004.

480. Ibid.

481. Simon A. Thalmann, "What are The Most Haunted Places in Michigan? Here Are Some Suggestions," *mlive*, October 4, 2011, www.mlive.com/living/index.ssf/2011/10/what_are_the_most_haunted_plac.html.

482. "Omer Masonic Hall," *MichMarkers.com*, accessed November 13, 2017, www.michmarkers.com/startup.asp?startpage=L0444.htm.

483. "'Cussing Canoeist' Conviction Reversed in Michigan," *ACLU*, April 1, 2002, www.aclu.org/news/cussing-canoeist-conviction-reversed-michigan.

484. Jeff Seidel, "City Limits: Tiny Omer, Mich., Votes on Secession and What Community Really Means," *Detroit Free Press*, December 22, 2002, accessed through archive.org at web.archive.org/web/20021228193430/www.freep.com/features/living/omer22_20021222.htm.

485. Ibid.

ONEKAMA

486. U.S. Census Bureau, 2010 census.

487. Walter Romig, *Michigan Place Names* (Detroit: Wayne State University Press, 1986), 416.

488. "Onekama, Michigan," *Welcome to Onekama*, accessed November 13, 2017, www.onekama.info/about-onekama.

489. Anonymous surveyor, quoted in "Onekama, Michigan," *Welcome to Onekama*, accessed November 13, 2017, www.onekama.info/about-onekama.

490. Romig, *Michigan Place Names*, 416.

491. Ibid.

492. Virgil J. Vogel, *Indian Names in Michigan* (Ann Arbor: University of Michigan Press, 1986), 137.

493. Ibid.

494. Romig, *Michigan Place Names*, 416.

495. "Onekama, Michigan," *Welcome to Onekama; History of Manistee County, Michigan, with Illustrations and Biographical Sketches of Some of Its Prominent Men and Pioneers* (Chicago: H. R. Page & Co., 1882), 87.

496. *History of Manistee County*, 87.

497. Ibid.

498. "Onekama Springs," Michigan historical marker in Onekama, Michigan, 2012.

499. Ibid.

500. "Glen Park," Michigan historical marker in Onekama, Michigan, 2012.

501. *History of Manistee County*, 87.

502. Mark A. Tonello for the Michigan Department of Natural Resources, *Portage Lake*, survey document, June 1999, www.michigandnr.com/PUBLICATIONS/PDFS/ifr/ifrlibra/status/waterbody/00-9.htm.

503. Ibid.

504. Ibid.

505. Ibid.

506. Ibid.

507. Tonello; "Historical Marker, The Portage Lake Region," village historical sign.

508. Ibid.

509. Ibid.

510. Ibid.

511. Jane Mueller, in conversation with the author, August 13, 2017.

512. Ibid.

513. Ibid.

514. "1, - Onekama, Michigan" *Facebook*, accessed October 2, 2017, www.facebook.com/pg/onekamami/about/?ref=page_internal.

OTTER LAKE

515. U.S. Census Bureau, 2010 census.

516. Walter Romig, *Michigan Place Names* (Detroit: Wayne State University Press, 1986), 423.

517. "History of Otter Lake," *Welcome to the Village of Otter Lake Michigan*, accessed November 13, 2017, www.villageofotterlake.com/history.php.

518. Ibid.

519. *History of Lapeer County Michigan, with Illustrations and Biographical Sketches of Some of Its Prominent Men and Pioneers* (Chicago: H. R. Page & Co., 1884), 141.

520. Ibid.

521. Ibid.

522. Ibid.

523. Romig, *Michigan Place Names*, 423; *History of Lapeer County Michigan*, 141.

524. *History of Lapeer County Michigan*, 141.

525. Ibid.

526. Ibid.

527. Ibid.

528. *History of Lapeer County Michigan*, 141–142.

529. Ibid.

530. *History of Lapeer County Michigan*, 142.

531. Ibid.

532. Ibid.

533. *Village of Otter Lake Land Use Master Plan*, 2009, www.villageofotterlake.com/documents/communityinfo/Master%20Plan%20Text.pdf.

534. Krystal Johns, "Marathon Twp. Once Site of Medical, Surgical Sanitarium," *The County Press*, June 15, 2014, mcp.mihomepaper.com/news/2014-06-15/Community_View/Marathon_Twp_once_site_of_medical_surgical_sanitar.html.

535. Ibid.

536. Ibid.

537. Ibid.

538. Ibid.

539. *History of Lapeer County Michigan*, 142.

540. "Our History," *St. John the Baptist Episcopal Church*, accessed November 13, 2017, www.stjohnsotterlake.org/history.

541. Ibid.

542. Ibid.

543. Ibid.

544. "Civic Organizations," *Welcome to the Village of Otter Lake Michigan*, November 13, 2017, www.villageofotterlake.com/civic.php.

545. *History of Lapeer County Michigan*, 26.

OWENDALE

546. U.S. Census Bureau, 2010 census.

547. Walter Romig, *Michigan Place Names* (Detroit: Wayne State University Press, 1986), 424.

548. Ibid.

549. "Owendale," Michigan historical marker in Owendale, Michigan, 1976.

550. Ibid.

551. Ibid.

552. Romig, *Michigan Place Names*, 424.

553. "Owendale," 1976.

554. Ibid.

555. Romig, *Michigan Place Names*, 424.

556. Ibid.

557. "Owendale," 1976.

558. "Home," *Silver Bullet Speedway*, accessed November 13, 2017, www.silverbulletspeedway.com; Monica Drake, "Clarkston brothers revamp oldest operating race track in Michigan," *Oakland Press*, August 4, 2015, www.theoaklandpress.com/article/OP/20150804/NEWS/150809794.

559. "Schedule and Results," *Silver Bullet Speedway*, accessed November 14, 2017, www.silverbulletspeedway.com/schedule.

560. "A. J. Foyt," *AJ Foyt Racing*, accessed November 14, 2017, www.foytracing.com/ajfoyt.

561. "Parnelli Jones," *IMS*, accessed November 14, 2017, www.indianapolismotorspeedway.com/history/people-of-ims/indianapolis-500-drivers/parnelli-jones.

562. Drake.

563. "Bernhardt Barn / Old Maid's Puzzle Block," *Thumb Quilt Trail*, accessed November 13, 2017, www.thumbquilttrail.com/Bernhardt.

564. "Murphy Barn / Propeller Pinwheel," *Thumb Quilt Trail*, accessed November 13, 2017, www.thumbquilttrail.com/Murphy.

PERRINTON

565. U.S. Census Bureau, 2010 census.

566. Walter Romig, *Michigan Place Names* (Detroit: Wayne State University Press, 1986), 437.

567. Ibid.

568. Willard D. Tucker, *Gratiot County, Michigan. Historical, Biographical, Statistical. Chronicling the Events of the First Sixty Years of the County's Existence as the Abode of White Men; with County, Township, City and Village Matters Fully Detailed, and with Miscellaneous Events of Importance Duly and Suitably Treated; by One Who Has Been a Resident of the County Nearly Half a Century* (Saginaw: Seemann & Peters, 1913), 1157.

569. Ibid.

570. Ibid.

571. Ibid.

572. *Michigan State Gazetteer and Business Directory for 1903* (Detroit: C. F. Clarke, 1903), 1420.

573. Ibid.

574. Tucker, *Gratiot County*, 1163–1164.

575. *Michigan State Gazetteer and Business Directory for 1903* (Detroit: C. F. Clarke, 1903), 1420; Tucker, *Gratiot County*, 1167.

576. "William H. Sewell," *University of Wisconsin-Madison Sociology*, accessed November 14, 2017, www.ssc.wisc.edu/soc/alumni/sewell_bio.php.

577. Ibid.

578. Ibid.

579. Ibid.

580. Ibid.

581. Ibid.

582. Ibid.

583. Romig, *Michigan Place Names*, 437; Tucker, 1157.

584. "The Grand Army of the Republic and Kindred Societies," *Library of Congress Main Reading Room*, accessed December 17, 2017, www.loc.gov/rr/main/gar/appendix/mich4.html.

585. George B. Davis, Leslie J. Perry, and Joseph W. Kirkley, *The War of the Rebellion: A Compilation of the Official Records of the Union and Confederate Armies* (Washington: Government Printing Office, 1897), 1280.

586. "Charles A. Price," *Men of the Third Michigan Infantry*, April 18, 2010, thirdmichigan.blogspot.com/2010/04/charles-price.html.

PEWAMO

587. U.S. Census Bureau, 2010 census.

588. *Michigan Legislative Manual and Official Directory for the Years 1897–1898* (1897).

589. Cook, Mattie, "Former Pewamo Resident Joe Winkler Remembered as Early Evel Knievel," *Ionia Sentinel-Standard*, May 16, 2013, www.sentinel-standard.com/article/20130516/NEWS/130519596.

590. E. E. Branch, *History of Ionia County, Michigan: Her People, Industries, and Institutions*, vol. 1 (Indianapolis: B. F. Bowen & Company, 1916).

591. Ibid.

592. Ibid.

593. John S. Schenck, *History of Ionia and Montcalm Counties, Michigan, with Illustrations and Biographical Sketches of Their Prominent Men and Pioneers* (Philadelphia: D. W. Ensign & Co., 1881).

594. Branch, *History of Ionia County*.

595. Schenck, *History of Ionia and Montcalm Counties*.

596. Jackson D. Dillenback, comp., *History and Directory of Ionia County, Michigan: Containing a History of Each Township: the Name, Occupation, Location and Post-Office Address of Every Man in the County; a List of Post-Offices in the County; a Schedule of Population; and Other Valuable Statistics* (Grand Rapids: County History, Directory, and Map Publisher, 1872).

597. Branch, *History of Ionia County*.

598. Dillenback, *History and Directory of Ionia County*.

599. Branch, *History of Ionia County*.

600. Dillenback, *History and Directory of Ionia County*.

601. Dillenback, *History and Directory of Ionia County*; Schenck, *History of Ionia and Montcalm Counties*.

602. "Ionia County School Districts," accessed September 5, 2016, ionia.migenweb.org/schools/ioniaschools.htm.

603. Sandy Nestor, *Indian Placenames in America*, vol. 1 (Jefferson: McFarland & Company 2003).

604. Branch, *History of Ionia County*.

605. Ibid.

606. Ibid.

607. Sandy Wolniakowski, in discussion with the author, October 31, 2016.

608. "Parish History," *St. Joseph—Pewamo*, accessed September 5, 2016, www.stjosephpewamo.org/parish-history.

609. Sandy Wolniakowski, in discussion with the author, October 31, 2016.

610. Kristen Jordan Shamus, "The Miracles at Pewamo: 4 First-Graders Beat the Medical Odds," *Detroit Free Press*, May 1, 2016, www.freep.com/story/life/family/kristen-jordan-shamus/2016/04/30/miracle-class-pewamo-michigan/83605702/.

611. Ibid.

PIERSON

612. U.S. Census Bureau, 2010 census.

613. John S. Schenck, *History of Ionia and Montcalm Counties Michigan, with Illustrations and Biographical Sketches of Their Prominent Men and Pioneers* (Philadelphia: D. W. Ensign & Co., 1881), 480–481.

614. Ibid.

615. Ibid.

616. Ibid.

617. Ibid.

618. Walter Romig, *Michigan Place Names* (Detroit: Wayne State University Press, 1986), 441; Schenck, 480–481.

619. Romig, *Michigan Place Names*, 441; Schenck, 481–482.

620. Romig, *Michigan Place Names*, 441.

621. Schenck, *History of Ionia and Montcalm Counties*, 481–482.

622. Ibid.

623. Schenck, *History of Ionia and Montcalm Counties, 481–482; Michigan State Gazetteer and Business Directory for 1903* (Detroit: C. F. Clarke, 1903), 1437.

624. "Michigan Threatens Beavers Over Dams?," *Snopes*, accessed December 17, 2017, www.snopes.com/humor/letters/dammed.asp.

625. Ibid.

626. Ibid.

627. Ibid.

628. Ibid.

629. "Fred Meijer White Pine Trail State Park," *Michigan Trails*, accessed November 15, 2017, www.westmichigantrails.com/Fred-Meijer-White-Pine-Trail-State-Park_Entire-Trail-23.php.

630. "Railroads: G.R. & Indiana RR," *County of Montcalm Michigan*, accessed November 15, 2017, www.montcalm.us/community/community_a_-_1/railroads.php.

631. Ibid.

632. "Splashes and Splurges," *Motor Boat*, January 10, 1909, 62.

633. Ibid.

PORT HOPE

634. U.S. Census Bureau, 2010 census.

635. "History," *Port Hope*, accessed November 15, 2017, porthopemich.com/index.php/history/.

636. Florence McKinnon Gwinn, *Pioneer History of Huron County Michigan* (Huron County Pioneer and Historical Society, 1922), 28.

637. Ibid.

638. Ibid.

639. "Thumb Area Bottomland Preserve," *Rec & Tec Dive Charters, Inc.*, accessed December 17, 2017, www.rectecdivecharters.com/thumb.html.

640. Ibid.

641. Ibid.

642. Gwinn, *Pioneer History of Huron County Michigan*, 28.

643. Ibid.

644. Ibid.

645. Gwinn, *Pioneer History of Huron County Michigan*, 28; "Port Hope Chimney," historical marker in Port Hope, Michigan, n.d.

646. H. E. Baker, quoted in Florence McKinnon Gwinn, *Pioneer History of Huron County Michigan* (Huron County Pioneer and Historical Society, 1922), 29.

647. Ibid.

648. Gwinn, *Pioneer History of Huron County Michigan*, 30–31.

649. Ibid.

650. Gwinn, *Pioneer History of Huron County Michigan*, 30–31; "History," *Port Hope*.

651. "History," *Port Hope*.

652. Ibid.

653. Ibid.

654. T. J. Gaffney, "Thumb Depots: History of the Port Hope Depot - Part 1," *Lakeshore Guardian*, December 2015, www.lakeshoreguardian.com/site/news/667/Thumb-Depots--History-of-the-Port-Hope-Depot--Part-1#.WgyHj2Vll-U.

655. Ibid.

656. Ibid.

657. Ibid.

658. Ibid.

659. Ibid.

660. Ibid.

661. Ibid.

662. T. J. Gaffney, "Thumb Depots: History of the Port Hope Depot - Part 2," *Lakeshore Guardian*, March 2016, www.lakeshoreguardian.com/site/news/669/Thumb-Depots--History-of-the-Port-Hope-Depot---Part-2#.Wg0I6mVll-U.

663. Ibid.

664. T. J. Gaffney, "Thumb Depots: History of the Port Hope Depot - Part 3," *Lakeshore Guardian*, April 2016, www.lakeshoreguardian.com/site/news/688/Thumb-Depots--History-of-the-Port-Hope-Depot--Part-3#.Wjcbk7Q-d-U.

665. Ibid.

666. "Port Hope Chimney," historical marker.

667. "History," *Port Hope*.

POSEN

1. U.S. Census Bureau, 2010 census.

2. Perry F. Powers, assisted by H. G. Cutler, *A History of Northern Michigan and Its People, vol. 1* (Chicago: The Lewis Publishing Company, 1912), 486.

3. Powers, *A History of Northern Michigan*, 486.

4. "Our Polish Ancestory," *Welcome to Posen, Mi.*," accessed November 15, 2017, www.posenmi.org/?q=node/12.

5. Ibid.

6. Ibid.

7. Ibid.

8. Powers, *A History of Northern Michigan*, 486.

9. "Presque Isle Electric Cooperative Monument," historical marker in Posen, Michigan, 1988.

10. "Presque Isle Electric Cooperative Monument;" village plaque (near historical marker).

11. "Presque Isle Electric Cooperative Monument."

12. "66th Annual Posen Potato Festival," event flyer, 2017.

13. "Elowsky Mill," historical marker in Posen, Michigan, 2002.

14. Ibid.

POWERS

15. U.S. Census Bureau, 2010 census.

16. "From the History," *Spalding Township Michigan*, accessed November 16, 2017, www.powers-spalding.org/from-the-history.

17. Ibid.

18. "From the History"; Walter Romig, *Michigan Place Names* (Detroit: Wayne State University Press, 1986), 457.

19. "From the History."

20. George N. Fuller, ed., *Historic Michigan, Land of the Great Lakes, Its Life, Resources, Industries, People, Politics, Government, Wars, Institutions, Achievements, the Press, Schools and Churches, Legendary and Prehistoric Lore, Also a History of the Upper Peninsula of Michigan* (National Historical Association, Inc., n.d.), 100.

21. "From the History."

22. William John Cummings, comp., *All Aboard: Along the Tracks in Dickinson County, Michigan* (Iron Mountain: Ralph W. Secord Press, 1993), 5, accessed at www.uproc.lib.mi.us/SecordPress/Cummings/Complete2.htm.

23. Racketty, letter to the editor, June 9, 1877, in William John Cummings, comp., *All Aboard: Along the Tracks in Dickinson County, Michigan* (Iron Mountain: Ralph W. Secord Press, 1993), accessed at www.uproc.lib.mi.us/SecordPress/Cummings/Complete2.htm.

24. Racketty, letter to the editor, July 14, 1877, in William John Cummings, comp., *Along the Tracks in Dickinson County, Michigan* (Iron Mountain: Ralph W. Secord Press, 1993), accessed at www.uproc.lib.mi.us/SecordPress/Cummings/Complete2.htm

25. *Michigan State Gazetteer and Business Directory for 1903* (Detroit: C. F. Clarke, 1903), 1486.

26. "From the History"; *Michigan State Gazetteer and Business Directory for 1903*, 1486.

27. Racketty, letter to the editor, July 14, 1877; Racketty, letter to the editor, August 18, 1877, in William John Cummings, comp., *All Aboard: Along the Tracks in Dickinson County, Michigan* (Iron Mountain: Ralph W. Secord Press, 1993), accessed at www.uproc.lib.mi.us/SecordPress/Cummings/Complete2.htm

28. Ibid.

29. "From the History."

30. "Powers Badly Scorched," *The Diamond Drill*, November 21, 1914, accessed through the Library of Congress, chroniclingamerica.loc.gov.

31. Racketty, letter to the editor, July 14, 1877.

32. Tony Garcia, "Powers North Central Wins 3rd-Straight Class D Title with 78–69 Win over Buckley," *mlive*, March 25, 2017, highschoolsports.mlive.com/news/article/1403710133013558678/live-updates-powers-north-central-takes-on-buckley-in-class-d-boys-basketball-state-championship/.

33. Ibid.

34. Peter J. Wallner, "Longest Win Streak in Michigan High School Basketball History Comes to an End," *mlive*, December 14, 2017, www.mlive.com/sports/2017/12/lonngest_win_streak_in_state_p.html.

35. *Michigan State Gazetteer and Business Directory for 1903*, 1486; *Michigan State Gazetteer and Business Directory for 1921–1922* (Detroit: C. F. Clarke, 1922), 1367.

36. "Postmasters by City: Powers Post Office, Menominee County, Michigan," *United States Postal Service*, accessed November 18, 2017, webpmt.usps.gov/pmt003.cfm.

PRESCOTT

37. U.S. Census Bureau, 2010 census.

38. Walter Romig, *Michigan Place Names* (Detroit: Wayne State University Press, 1986), 459.

39. Ibid.

40. Cal Ennes, "Railroad Guided Moffatt History," unknown newspaper, unknown date, accessed November 18, 2017, www.algermichigan.com/docs/history/Railroad.htm; Rose City Area Historical Society, *Images of America: Ogemaw County* (Arcadia Publishing, 2009), 43–44, 50.

41. Rose City Area Historical Society, 50.

42. Rose City Area Historical Society, 44.

43. Ibid.

44. Ibid.

45. "Prescott," *The Political Graveyard*, accessed November 18, 2017, politicalgraveyard.com/bio/prescott.html.

46. Ibid.

47. Rose City Area Historical Society, 51.

48. Ennes, "Railroad Guided Moffatt History."

49. Ibid.

50. Ibid.

51. Ennes, "Railroad Guided Moffatt History"; Rose City Area Historical Society, 44.

52. Ennes, "Railroad Guided Moffatt History."

53. Romig, *Michigan Place Names*, 459.

54. Ennes, "Railroad Guided Moffatt History."

55. *Ogemaw County Master Plan*, November 10, 2016, 13, www.ocmi.us/wp-content/uploads/Zoning-County-Master-Plan.pdf.

56. *Michigan State Gazetteer and Business Directory for 1877* (Detroit: C. F. Clarke, 1877), 1443.

57. *Michigan State Gazetteer and Business Directory for 1893–1894* (Detroit: C. F. Clarke, 1894), 1323.

58. Ibid.

59. Rose City Area Historical Society, 50.

60. Lee Thompson, "Small-Town Pride Makes State Champ Whittemore-Prescott the Talk of the Town," *mlive*, June 6, 2017, highschoolsports.mlive.com/news/article/8460844348759552634/small-town-pride-makes-state-champ-whittemore-prescott-the-talk-of-the-town/.

61. Ibid.

62. Rose City Area Historical Society, 44.

ROSEBUSH

63. U.S. Census Bureau, 2010 census.

64. "Rosebush Elects Commission Charter," *Clare Sentinel*, January 25, 1968, digmichnews.cmich.edu/cgi-bin/michigan?a=d&d=ClareSENT19680125-01.1.1.

65. Walter Romig, *Michigan Place Names* (Detroit: Wayne State University Press, 1986), 484.

66. "Mid-Michigan History: Why Do They Call It Rosebush?," *Morning Sun*, December 20, 2011, www.themorningsun.com/article/MS/20111220/LIFE01/312209973; "History: 1908-Rosebush Banking Building Becomes Present Day Diner," *Morning Sun*, March 27, 2016, www.themorningsun.com/article/MS/20160327/NEWS/160329988.

67. Ibid.

68. "History: 1908-Rosebush Banking Building Becomes Present Day Diner."

69. "Mid-Michigan History: Why Do They Call it Rosebush?."

70. Ibid.

71. Ibid.

72. Ibid.

73. Ibid.

74. *Michigan State Gazetteer and Business Directory for 1903* (Detroit: C. F. Clarke, 1903), 373.

75. Ibid.

76. "History: 1908-Rosebush Banking Building Becomes Present Day Diner."

77. Ibid.

78. Malachi Barnett, "Roz's Diner Carries on Spirit of Owner's Mother," *Morning Sun*, May 30, 2014, www.themorningsun.com/article/MS/20140530/NEWS/140539983.

79. Ibid.

80. Emily Fox, "An Amish Community Modernizes in Michigan: Goodbye Horse and Buggy, Hello Minivans and Power Tools," *Michigan Radio*, January 12, 2016, michiganradio.org/post/amish-community-modernizes-michigan-goodbye-horse-and-buggy-hello-minivans-and-power-tools.

81. Adrian Hedden, "Rosebush Celebration is Fun and a Lesson on Freedom," *Morning Sun*, July 4, 2015, www.themorningsun.com/general-news/20150704/rosebush-celebration-is-fun-and-a-lesson-on-freedom.

ROTHBURY

82. U.S. Census Bureau, 2010 census.

83. "History," *Electric Forest Festival*, accessed November 19, 2017, www.electricforestfestival.com/history/.

84. Justine McGuire, "Good Vibes at Electric Forest is More than a Rumor," *mlive*, July 5, 2017, www.mlive.com/news/muskegon/index.ssf/2017/07/analysis_good_vibes_at_electri.html.

85. Anonymous Rothbury resident, in conversation with the author, August 12, 2017.

86. Erica Francis, "Rothbury Resident Upset after Electric Forest Acquires Neighbor's Land," *Fox 17 West Michigan*, June 17, 2017, fox17online.com/2015/06/17/rothbury-resident-upset-after-electric-forest-acquires-neighbors-land/.

87. Anonymous Rothbury resident, in conversation with the author, August 12, 2017.

88. David K. Petersen and the Oceana County Historical Genealogical Society, *Images of America: Oceana County 1850–1950* (Charleston, SC: Arcadia Publishing, 2012), 95.

89. Walter Romig, Michigan Place Names (Detroit: Wayne State University Press, 1986), 486; Petersen and the Oceana County Historical Genealogical Society, 95.

90. Petersen and the Oceana County Historical Genealogical Society, 95.

91. Ibid.

92. Ibid.

93. Ibid.

94. Romig, *Michigan Place Names*, 486.

95. *Michigan State Gazetteer and Business Directory for 1887–1888* (Detroit: C. F. Clarke, 1888), 1484.

96. *Michigan State Gazetteer and Business Directory for 1903* (Detroit: C. F. Clarke, 1903), 1517; *Michigan State Gazetteer and Business Directory for 1907–1908* (Detroit: C. F. Clarke, 1908), 1685.

97. Petersen and the Oceana County Historical Genealogical Society, 30.

98. *Michigan State Gazetteer and Business Directory for 1907–1908*, 1685.

99. Dan Todd, *The Community Church: A Brief History of Rothbury Community Church*, 2004, s3.amazonaws.com/churchplantmedia-cms/rothbury_community_churchrothbury_mi/the-community-church-port.pdf.

100. Ibid.

101. Ibid.

102. Anonymous Rothbury resident, in conversation with the author, August 12, 2017.

103. Susan Harrison Wolffis, "A Mammoth Tale: Unearthing Michigan's Ancient Beasts," *mlive*, April 20, 2011, www.mlive.com/news/muskegon/index.ssf/2011/04/a_mammoth_tale.html.

104. Ibid.

SAND LAKE

105. U.S. Census Bureau, 2010 census.

106. *History of Kent County, Michigan; Together with Sketches of Its Cities, Villages and Townships, Educational, Religious, Civil, Military, and Political History; Portraits of Prominent Persons, and Biographies of Representative Citizens* (Chicago: Chas. C. Chapman & Co., 1881), 1236.

107. "Sand Lake, Michigan and the Civil War," photo display in the Sand Lake bank.

108. Ibid.

109. Ibid.

110. Ibid.

111. Ibid.

112. Ibid.

113. "Sand Lake, Michigan and the Civil War," photo display in the Sand Lake bank.

114. Walter Romig, *Michigan Place Names* (Detroit: Wayne State University Press, 1986), 498.

115. Romig, *Michigan Place Names*, 498; History of Kent County, Michigan, 1235.

116. Romig, *Michigan Place Names*, 498.

117. Ibid.

118. *History of Kent County, Michigan*, 1235–1236.

119. Romig, *Michigan Place Names*, 498; *History of Kent County, Michigan*, 1235–1236

120. *History of Kent County, Michigan*, 1235–1236.

121. Ibid.

122. *History of Kent County, Michigan*, 440.

123. *Michigan State Gazetteer and Business Directory for 1907–1908* (Detroit: C. F. Clarke, 1908), 1767; *Michigan State Gazetteer and Business Directory for 1921–1922* (Detroit: C. F. Clarke, 1922), 1437–1438.

124. Ibid.

125. "Sand Lake 4th of July Celebration – June 29 thru July 4," *Cedar Springs Post*, June 23, 2017, cedarspringspost.com/2017/06/23/sand-lake-4th-of-july-celebration-june-29-thru-july-4th/.

126. Ibid.

127. Linda Gutzki, in conversation with the author, August 12, 2017.

128. *Memorial Record of the Northern Peninsula of Michigan* (Chicago: Lewis Publishing Company, 1895), 489–490.

129. Ibid.

130. Ibid.

131. Ibid.

132. "Michigan August 2010 Primary Election – Village of Sand Lake Proposal," *Election Magic*, accessed November 19, 2017, www.electionmagic.com/archives/mi/2010/augprim/K41results/K4100302sum.htm.

SHERWOOD

133. U.S. Census Bureau, 2010 census.

134. "Learn about the Branch County Historical Society," *Branch County Historical Society*, accessed November 19, 2017, www.branchcountyhistoricalsociety.org/learn.htm

135. Kristy Smith, "Kristy Smith Column: Stone Barn Brings Vision to Life," *Battle Creek Enquirer*, October 1, 2014, www.battlecreekenquirer.com/story/news/local/2014/10/01/kristy-smith-column-stone-barn-brings-vision-life/16542371/.

136. Bill Wood, "Jeff Stanton: The Road to the Top," *American Motorcyclist*, September 1989, 9–12.

137. Ibid.

138. "Learn about the Branch County Historical Society."

139. Walter Romig, *Michigan Place Names* (Detroit: Wayne State University Press, 1986), 512.

140. Ibid.

141. Henry P. Collin, *A Twentieth Century History and Biographical Record of Branch County, Michigan* (Lewis Publishing Company, 1906), 107.

142. Ibid.

143. Crisfield Johnson, *History of Branch County, Michigan, with Illustrations and Biographical Sketches of Some of Its Prominent Men and Pioneers* (Philadelphia: Everts & Abbott, 1879), 336.

144. Ibid.

145. Ibid.

146. Romig, *Michigan Place Names*, 512; Johnson, *History of Branch County, Michigan*, 336.

147. Johnson, *History of Branch County, Michigan*, 336.

148. Collin, *A Twentieth Century History*, 107, 146; *Michigan State Gazetteer and Business Directory for 1887–1888* (Detroit: C. F. Clarke, 1888), 1555; "Learn About the Branch County Historical Society."

149. *Michigan State Gazetteer and Business Directory for 1903* (Detroit: C. F. Clarke, 1903), 1621.

150. Michael Priestly, "Drawing on Childhood Memories: Why Farming Needs to Laugh," *The Sheep Site*, August 13, 2015, www.thesheepsite.com/news/1352/drawing-on-childhood-memories-why-farming-needs-to-laugh/.

151. Ibid.

152. "Learn about the Branch County Historical Society."

153. Ibid.

154. Johnson, *History of Branch County, Michigan*, 336.

155. *Michigan State Gazetteer and Business Directory for 1903*, 1621.

STANWOOD

156. U.S. Census Bureau, 2010 census.

157. Walter Romig, *Michigan Place Names* (Detroit: Wayne State University Press, 1986), 535.

158. Ibid.

159. Ibid.

160. Ibid.

161. *Michigan State Gazetteer and Business Directory for 1877* (Detroit: C. F. Clarke, 1877), 800.

162. *Michigan State Gazetteer and Business Directory for 1887–1888* (Detroit: C. F. Clarke, 1888), 1581.

163. Ibid.

164. *Michigan State Gazetteer and Business Directory for 1903* (Detroit: C. F. Clarke, 1903), 1645.

165. *Michigan State Gazetteer and Business Directory for 1921–1922* (Detroit: C. F. Clarke, 1922), 1448b.

166. Ibid.

167. *Portrait and Biographical album, Mecosta county, Mich., Containing Portraits and Biographical Sketches of Prominent and Representative Citizens of the County, Together with Portraits and Biographies of all the Governors of Michigan and the Presidents of the United States. Also Containing a Complete History of the County, from its Earliest Settlement to the Present Time* (Chicago: Chapman Brothers, 1883), 525–526.

168. Ibid.

169. Ibid.

170. Ibid.

171. Ibid.

172. Ibid.

173. Ibid.

174. Ibid.

175. Ibid.

176. "Morley Stanwood Elementary," *Morley Stanwood Community Schools*, accessed November 20, 2017, www.morleystanwood.org/schools/morleyelementary/.

177. Ibid.

178. Michigan Economic Development Corporation, "Stanwood," *Pure Michigan*, accessed November 20, 2017, www.michigan.org/city/stanwood#?c=44.4299:-85.1166:6&tid=665&page=0&pagesize=20&pagetitle=Stanwood.

179. "About Mecosta County," *A Secret Treasure Trove of Adventures Await you in Mecosta County!*, accessed November 20, 2017, www.bigrapids.org/about-mecosta-county.

180. *Portrait and Biographical album, Mecosta county, Mich.*, 616.

181. Ibid.

TURNER

182. U.S. Census Bureau, 2010 census,

183. *Local Acts of the Legislature of the State of Michigan Passed at the Regular Session of 1917 with an Appendix* (Lansing: Wynkoop Hallenbeck Crawford Co., State Printers, 1917), 21.

184. "Lumber Jacks and Lumbering Days," *Arenac County Independent*, March 16, 1966, accessed through "The Naming of Turner, Turner Township, Arenac County, Michigan," *Paul Turner*, accessed November 20, 2017, www.paulturner.ca/Turner/Turner/turnerville.htm.

185. Ibid.

186. Ibid.

187. Ibid.

188. Ibid.

189. Ibid.

190. Ibid.

191. Ibid.

192. Walter Romig, *Michigan Place Names* (Detroit: Wayne State University Press, 1986), 563.

193. James M. Reasoner, *Michigan Reports: Cases Decided in the Supreme Court of Michigan from May 29 to September 30, 1913, vol. 176* (Chicago: Callaghan and Company, 1914), 414–433.

194. Ibid.

195. Ibid.

196. Ibid.

197. *Michigan State Gazetteer and Business Directory for 1903* (Detroit: C. F. Clarke, 1903), 1679.

198. *Michigan State Gazetteer and Business Directory for 1903*, 1679; *Michigan State Gazetteer and Business Directory for 1921–1922* (Detroit: C. F. Clarke, 1922), 1458.

199. "Arenac County Dateline," *Arenac County Historical Society*, accessed November 20, 2017, www.rootsweb.ancestry.com/~miachs/museum/dateline001.htm

200. Ibid.

201. Ibid.

202. Ibid.

203. Ibid.

204. Ibid.

205. Ibid.

206. Ibid.

207. U.S. Census Bureau, 2010 Census.

208. "Arenac County Dateline," *Arenac County Historical Society*.

209. Ibid.

210. Ibid.

TUSTIN

211. U.S. Census Bureau, 2010 census.

212. Walter Romig, *Michigan Place Names* (Detroit: Wayne State University Press, 1986), 563.

213. Nils William Olsson, "The Swedish Settlement of Tustin, Michigan," *Swedish-American Historical Quarterly* 13, no. 3, (July 1962), 109–117, collections.carli.illinois.edu/cdm/ref/collection/npu_sahq/id/2941.

214. Ibid.

215. Ibid.

216. Ibid.

217. Ibid.

218. Jeffrey W. Hancks, *Scandinavians in Michigan* (East Lansing: Michigan State University Press, 2006), 1887.

219. Ibid.

220. Olsson, "The Swedish Settlement of Tustin, Michigan; 'Unto a New Land,'" historical marker in Tustin, Michigan, 1979.

221. Olsson, "The Swedish Settlement of Tustin, Michigan."

222. Ibid.

223. Ibid.

224. *Portrait and Biographical Album of Osceola County*, 363–364; Romig, Michigan Place Names, 563.

225. *Portrait and Biographical Album of Osceola County*, 363–364; *Michigan State Gazetteer and Business Directory for 1877* (Detroit: C. F. Clarke, 1877), 823.

226. *Michigan State Gazetteer and Business Directory for 1877*, 823.

227. *Michigan State Gazetteer and Business Directory for 1887–1888* (Detroit: C. F. Clarke, 1888), 1617–1618.

228. "His Experiences Overseas," *Charlevoix County Herald*, February 28, 1919, accessed through the Library of Congress, chroniclingamerica.loc.gov.

229. Ibid.

230. Ibid.

231. Ibid.

232. Ibid.

233. Kari DeVerney and Shaun Lausby, in conversation with the author, August 13, 2017.

234. Jessica Sequin, "Quaint, Little Tustin Rich in History," *The Marion Press*, October 2014, www.marion-press.com/2014/10/quaint-little-tustin-rich-in-history/.

235. "About," *Kettunen Center*, accessed November 21, 2017, www.kettunencenter.org/about/.

236. Sequin.

TWINING

237. U.S. Census Bureau, 2010 census.

238. Perry F. Powers, *A History of Northern Michigan and Its People, vol. 1* (Chicago: Lewis Publishing Company, 1912), 541.

239. "Lumber Jacks and Lumbering Days," *Arenac County Independent*, March 16, 1966, accessed through "The Naming of Turner, Turner Township, Arenac County, Michigan," *Paul Turner*, accessed November 20, 2017, www.paulturner.ca/Turner/Turner/turnerville.htm.

240. Ibid.

241. Walter Romig, *Michigan Place Names* (Detroit: Wayne State University Press, 1986), 564.

242. Ibid.

243. Ibid.

244. *Biographical History of Northern Michigan, Containing Biographies of Prominent Citizens* (B. F. Bowen & Company, 1905), 787–789.

245. Ibid.

246. Ibid.

247. Ibid.

248. *Michigan State Gazetteer and Business Directory for 1903* (Detroit: C. F. Clarke, 1903), 1680.

249. *Michigan State Gazetteer and Business Directory for 1921–1922* (Detroit: C. F. Clarke, 1922), 1459.

250. Ibid.

251. "Arenac County Dateline," *Arenac County Historical Society*, accessed November 20, 2017, www.rootsweb.ancestry.com/~miachs/museum/dateline001.htm.

252. *Biographical History of Northern Michigan*, 782–783.

253. Ibid.

254. Ibid.

255. Ibid.

256. Ibid.

257. Ibid.

258. "Arenac County Dateline," *Arenac County Historical Society*.

259. Alan Teelander, "Michigan Soldiers Killed in Action in World War 1," *Images of Michigan*, October 28, 2012, accessed November 20, 2017, www.imagesofmichigan.com/michigan-soldiers-killed-in-action-in-world-war-1.

260. Andrew Clyde Thompson. World War 1 Draft Card. 1917. Accessed via: www.familysearch.org

261. W. M. Haulsee, F. G. Howe, and A. C. Doyle, comp., *Soldiers of the Great War, vol. II* (Washington DC: Soldiers Record Publishing Association), 79; "1918 Flu Pandemic," *History*, accessed December 17, 2017, www.history.com/topics/1918-flu-pandemic.

262. "State News Notes," *Owosso Times*, August 24, 1906, accessed through the Library of Congress, chroniclingamerica.loc.gov.

263. "Arenac County Dateline," *Arenac County Historical Society*.

264. Ibid.

265. "Home," *Arenac Eastern School District*, accessed November 20, 2017, www.arenaceastern.org.

266. "Arenac County Dateline," *Arenac County Historical Society*.

267. Ibid.

268. Ibid.

VANDALIA

269. U.S. Census Bureau, 2010 census.

270. Walter Romig, *Michigan Place Names* (Detroit: Wayne State University Press, 1986), 569.

271. Ibid.

272. *History of Cass County, Michigan. With Illustrations and Biographical Sketches of some of its Prominent Men and Pioneers* (Chicago: Waterman, Watkins & Co., 1882), 255–256.

273. Ibid.

274. Romig, *Michigan Place Names*, 569.

275. *Michigan State Gazetteer and Business Directory for 1877* (Detroit: C. F. Clarke, 1877), 828.

276. Ibid.

277. Ibid.

278. Debra Haight, "History Buffs Explore Cass County Connections to Underground Railroad," *The Herald-Palladium*, July 16, 2000, www.heraldpalladium.com/history-buffs-explore-cass-county-connections-to-underground-railroad/article_91415047-51ce-5465-a1a5-a017385a26c0.html; "Home," *Village of Vandalia, Michigan*, accessed November 21, 2017, www.villageofvandaliami.com/home.

279. Ibid.

280. Haight, "History Buffs Explore Cass County Connections to Underground Railroad."

281. Ibid.

282. "Kentucky Raid of 1847," *Village of Vandalia, Michigan*, accessed November 21, 2017, www.villageofvandaliami.com/places_to_visit/kentucky_raid_of_1847.

283. Ibid.

284. Ibid.

285. Ibid.

286. "The Kentucky Raid: A Brief Description of the Infamous Kentucky Raid in August of 1847,"

Underground Railroad Society of Cass County, Michigan, accessed November 21, 2017, www.urscc.org/1847-kentucky-raid.html.

287. Ibid.

288. Ibid.

289. Christine Schwerin, "Tilling Up Fragments of History," *Seeking Michigan*, accessed November 21, 2017, seekingmichigan.org/look/2009/05/19/tilling-up-fragments-of-history.

290. Ibid.

291. Ibid.

VANDERBILT

292. U.S. Census Bureau, 2010 census.

293. "Timeline of Otsego County History," *Otsego County Historical Society*, accessed November 21, 2017, www.otsego.org/ochs/Articles%20Written%20History/Chronology%20of%20Events%202012comp.pdf.

294. "Vanderbilt," *Otsego County Historical Society*, accessed November 24, 2017, www.otsego.org/ochs/Towns%20Red%20Buttons/Vanderbilt/VanderbiltJumpPage.htm.

295. Ibid.

296. Ibid.

297. "A Chronology of Events Reaching Back Centuries," *Clear Water Land: A History of Otsego County for Michigan's Sesquicentennial*, August 20, 1987; "Timeline of Otsego County History"; "Vanderbilt," *Otsego County Historical Society*.

298. "Vanderbilt," *Otsego County Historical Society; Michigan State Gazetteer and Business Directory for 1887–1888* (Detroit: C. F. Clarke, 1888), 1626; "Timeline of Otsego County History."

299. *Michigan State Gazetteer and Business Directory for 1887–1888* (Detroit: C. F. Clarke, 1888), 1626.

300. *Michigan State Gazetteer and Business Directory for 1887–1888*, 1626; *Michigan State Gazetteer and Business Directory for 1903* (Detroit: C. F. Clarke, 1903), 1688.

301. "Vanderbilt, A Progressive Otsego County Village," *Gaylord Herald Times*, 1905 Special Edition, accessed www.otsego.org/ochs/Articles%20Written%20History/1905%20OC%20Herald/Vanderbilt.pdf.

302. Centennial Book Committee, *Otsego County: The Heritage Years 1875–1975* (Centennial Book Committee, 1975), 23–24.

303. Perry F. Powers, *A History of Northern Michigan and Its People, vol. 1* (Chicago: Lewis Publishing Company, 1912), 494.

304. Centennial Book Committee, *Otsego County*, 23–24.

305. Ibid.

306. "A Guide to Places Made Famous by Cornelius Vanderbilt and His Heirs," *Vanderbilt University*, September 26, 2014, news.vanderbilt.edu/vanderbiltmagazine/a-guide-to-places-made-famous-by-cornelius-vanderbilt-and-his-heirs/; "Cornelius Vanderbilt," *History*, accessed November 24, 2017, www.history.com/topics/cornelius-vanderbilt.

307. "Timeline of Otsego County History."

308. "Cornelius Vanderbilt," *Encyclopædia Brittanica*, accessed November 24, 2017, www.britannica.com/biography/Cornelius-Vanderbilt-1794-1877.

309. "Timeline of Otsego County History."

310. Centennial Book Committee, *Otsego County*, 23–24.

311. Ibid.

312. Ibid.

313. Ibid.

314. Kathleen Lavey, "Brr! Michigan's Coldest Temp Ever? 51 Below Zero," *Lansing State Journal*, February 19, 2015, www.lansingstatejournal.com/story/news/local/2015/02/19/brrr-michigans-coldest-temp-ever-zero/23683803/.

315. Ibid.

316. Ibid.

317. Village sign.

318. Jim Hanus, "Home," *The Pigeon River Country*, accessed November 24, 2017, www.pigeonrivercountry.com.

319. Austin Short, "Michigan MMA Fighter Brink Moving up in UFC World," *WKAR*, April 26, 2017, wkar.org/post/michigan-mma-fighter-brink-moving-ufc-world#stream/0.

320. John Robinson, "Haunted Michigan: Paranormal Activity in Tower Cemetery," *99.1 WFMK*, September 25, 2017, 99wfmk.com/towercemetery/.

321. Ibid.

WALKERVILLE

322. U.S. Census Bureau, 2010 census.

323. *Local Acts of the Legislature of the State of Michigan Passed at the Regular Session of 1909 with an Appendix* (Lansing: Wynkoop Hallenbeck Crawford Co., State Printers, 1909), 37–39.

324. Walter Romig, *Michigan Place Names* (Detroit: Wayne State University Press, 1986), 579–580.

325. Romig, *Michigan Place Names*, 579–580; L. M. Hartwick and W. H. Tuller, *Oceana County Pioneers and Business Men of To-Day. History, Biography, Statistics*

and Humorous Incidents (Pentwater: Pentwater News Steam Print, 1890), 153–154.

326. David K. Petersen and the Oceana County Historical and Genealogical Society, *Oceana County, 1850–1950* (Charleston: Arcadia Publishing, 2012), 579–580.

327. Romig, *Michigan Place Names*, 579–580.

328. Hartwick and Tuller, *Oceana County Pioneers*, 153–154.

329. Romig, *Michigan Place Names*, 579–580.

330. Leonore P. Williams, "Interesting Railway Saga," *Ludington Daily News*, December 17, 1953, accessed through www.newspapers.com.

331. Ibid.

332. Ibid.

333. Ibid.

334. Petersen and the Oceana County Historical and Genealogical Society, 579–580.

335. Ibid.

336. Williams, "Interesting Railway Saga."

337. Robert W. Garasha, "The Mason & Oceana Railroad," *The Railroad and Locomotive Historical Society Bulletin*, no. 89 (November 1953), 82–96.

338. Ibid.

339. Ibid.

340. "Walkerville Thrives – About," *Facebook*, accessed November 26, 2017, www.facebook.com/pg/WalkervilleThrives/about/?ref=page_internal.

341. Ibid.

342. "Tractor Fun," *Facebook*, accessed November 26, 2017, www.facebook.com/events/506692476338230/.

343. Ibid.

344. "Walkerville Kwik Mart Sells $4.7 Million Lottery Winner," *Oceana's Herald-Journal*, November 21, 2017, www.shorelinemedia.net/oceanas_herald_journal/news/top_stories/walkerville-kwik-mart-sells-million-lottery-winner/article_23d7f8f6-cee4-11e7-87b8-7b14a59e32ab.html.

345. "Santa Parade Saturday in Walkerville," *Oceana's Herald-Journal*, December 14, 2016, www.shorelinemedia.net/oceanas_herald_journal/lifestyle/stuff_to_do/santa-parade-saturday-in-walkerville/article_34f17288-c21b-11e6-830b-e305de55eeee.html.

WALLOON LAKE

346. U.S. Census Bureau, 2010 census.

347. Margaret Loftus, "Summer at the Lake: Walloon Lake," *National Geographic Traveler*, June/July 2012, www.nationalgeographic.com/travel/city-guides/michigan-walloon-lake/.

348. Ibid.

349. Ibid.

350. Ibid.

351. "Ernest Hemingway Cottage ('Windemere')," *Michigan State Housing Development Authority*, accessed November 26, 2017, www.michigan.gov/mshda/0,4641,7-141-54317_19320_61909_61927-54590--,00.html.

352. Rodeghier, 2017; Mark Alpert, "A Glimpse of Hemingway: Visiting the Windemere Cottage," *Criminal Element*, March 12, 2015, www.criminalelement.com/blogs/2015/03/a-glimpse-of-hemingway-visiting-the-windemere-cabin-walloon-lake-nick-adams-michigan-mark-alpert.

353. Walter Romig, *Michigan Place Names* (Detroit: Wayne State University Press, 1986), 580–581.

354. Ibid.

355. "History of the Walloon Lake Village," *Hotel Walloon*, accessed November 26, 2017, www.zhotelwalloon.com/history/.

356. Ibid.

357. Ibid.

358. Ibid.

359. *Michigan State Gazetteer and Business Directory for 1903* (Detroit: C. F. Clarke, 1903), 1699.

360. *Michigan State Gazetteer and Business Directory for 1907–1908* (Detroit: C. F. Clarke, 1908), 1876–1877; Catie L'Heureux, "Rejuvenating Northern Michigan's Walloon Lake," *MyNorth*, August 8, 2016, mynorth.com/2016/08/rejuvenating-northern-michigans-walloon-lake/.

361. *Michigan State Gazetteer and Business Directory for 1921–1922* (Detroit: C. F. Clarke, 1922), 1471.

362. L'Heureux.

363. Ibid.

364. Ibid.

365. Ibid.

366. Ibid.

367. L' Heureux; Garret Ellison, "How One Developer Singlehandedly Saved the Village of Walloon Lake," *mlive*, July 6, 2015, www.mlive.com/news/grand-rapids/index.ssf/2015/07/walloon_lake_village_borisch.html.

368. "Welcome to Walloon Lake," *Walloon Lake Michigan Wanderings*, accessed November 26, 2017, walloonlakewanderings.weebly.com/; Romig, *Michigan Place Names*, 580–581.

369. Romig, *Michigan Place Names*, 580–581.

370. Ibid.

371. Ibid.

372. Ibid.

373. Ibid.

374. Ibid.

375. Loftus, "Summer at the Lake: Walloon Lake."

376. "17 square meter," village sign, n.d.

377. Ibid.

WHITE PINE

378. U.S. Census Bureau, 2010 census.

379. Chris Chabot, "History of White Pine & Copper Mining," *Carp Lake Township*, accessed November 26, 2017, carplaketwp.com/page7.php?SessionID=5a49e17e5a1b3c7c498d3.

380. Ibid.

381. Ibid.

382. Ibid.

383. Ibid.

384. Ibid.

385. Ibid.

386. Ibid.

387. Ibid.

388. Chabot, "History of White Pine & Copper Mining"; *Michigan State Gazetteer and Business Directory for 1921–1922* (Detroit: C. F. Clarke, 1922), 1483.

389. Christian Holmes, *Company Towns of Michigan's Upper Peninsula* (Charleston, SC: History Press, 2015), 107–112.

390. Ibid.

391. Ibid.

392. Ibid.

393. Holmes, *Company Towns of Michigan's Upper Peninsula*, 107–112.

394. Ibid.

395. Rolland Craten Allen, *Mineral Resources of Michigan, with Statistical Tables of Production and Value of Mineral Products for 1918 and Prior Years*. Fort Wayne, Indiana, Fort Wayne Printing Co., 1920.

396. Ibid.

397. Ibid.

398. Ibid.

399. Ibid.

400. Ibid.

401. Ibid.

402. Ibid.

403. Holmes, *Company Towns of Michigan's Upper Peninsula*, 107–112; Larry Chabot, "'I'll Eat Every Pound of Copper from that Mine,'" *Michigan History Magazine* 84.1 (January–February 2000), 10, accessed through Gale.

404. Holmes, *Company Towns*, 107–112; Larry Chabot, "'I'll Eat…" *Michigan History Magazine.*

405. National Park Service, "Timeline of Michigan Copper Mining 1951 to Present," from the Keweenaw NHP Archives, Jack Foster Collection, *National Park Service*, accessed November 26, 2017, www.nps.gov/kewe/learn/historyculture/copper-mining-timeline-page-4.htm; Larry Chabot, "'I'll eat…" *Michigan History Magazine*

406. Garret Ellison, "Exploratory Drilling Begins for Copper Mine under Porcupine Mountains State Park," *mlive*, February 7, 2017, www.mlive.com/news/index.ssf/2017/02/porcupine_mountains_copper_min.html.

407. "Konteka Motel, Restaurant, & Bar, Black Bear Bowling Lanes," *Exploring the North*, accessed November 26, 2017, www.exploringthenorth.com/konteka/motel.html.

408. "About Us," *SubTerra*, accessed November 26, 2017, www.subterrallc.com/html/about.html.

409. Untitled plaque in White Pine, dedicated by the Porcupine Mountains Conservation and Sportsmen's Club, October 3, 1967.

410. Larry Chabot, "'I'll Eat…" *Michigan History Magazine.*

411. Ibid.

412. Larry Chabot, "'I'll Eat…" *Michigan History Magazine.*

413. Ibid.

414. Larry Chabot, "'I'll Eat…" *Michigan History Magazine.*

415. Larry Chabot, "'I'll Eat…" *Michigan History Magazine.*

WHITTEMORE CITY

416. U.S. Census Bureau, 2010 census.

417. Lugene Daniels, "Whittemore Incorporated as a City in 1907," *Iosco County Historical Museum*, accessed November 26, 2017, www.ioscomuseum.net/whittemore-incorporated-as-a-city-in-1907.html.

418. "History," *Whittemore Speedway*, accessed November 26, 2017, whittemorespeedway.org/?page_id=22.

419. Ibid.

420. Ibid.

421. Ibid.

422. Ibid.

423. Ibid.

424. Walter Romig, *Michigan Place Names* (Detroit: Wayne State University Press, 1986), 603; Huron Shores Genealogical Society, *Images of America: Iosco County: The Photography of Ard G. Emery 1892–1904* (Charleston, SC: Arcadia Publishing, 2015), 52.

425. Romig, *Michigan Place Names*, 603.

426. Ibid.

427. Huron Shores Genealogical Society, 52; *Michigan State Gazetteer and Business Directory for 1887–1888* (Detroit: C. F. Clarke, 1888), 1671–1672.

428. Huron Shores Genealogical Society, 52.

429. Perry F. Powers, *A History of Northern Michigan and Its People, vol. 1* (Chicago: The Lewis Publishing Company, 1912), 521.

430. *Michigan State Gazetteer and Business Directory for 1903* (Detroit: C. F. Clarke, 1903), 1725.

431. *Michigan State Gazetteer and Business Directory for 1907–1908* (Detroit: C. F. Clarke, 1908), 1889; Daniels, "Whittemore Incorporated as a City in 1907."

432. Powers, *A History of Northern Michigan and Its People*, 521.

433. Daniels, "Whittemore Incorporated as a City in 1907."

434. Ibid.

435. Ibid.

436. Ibid.

437. Ibid.

438. Ibid.

439. U.S. Census Bureau, 2010 census; *Michigan State Gazetteer and Business Directory for 1907–1908*, 1889.

440. "Home," *Whittemore-Prescott Area Schools – Home of the Cardinals*, accessed November 26, 2017, www.wpas.net/.

441. Eric Hammel, *Aces in Combat: The American Aces Speak* (Pacifica: Pacifica Military History, 2008), 228–231.

442. Ibid.

WOLVERINE

443. U.S. Census Bureau, 2010 census.

444. Perry F. Powers, *A History of Northern Michigan and Its People, vol. 1* (Chicago: Lewis Publishing Company, 1912), 457.

445. "History of Wolverine," *Wolverine*, accessed November 27, 2017, villageofwolverine.com/History.cfm.

446. Ibid.

447. Ibid.

448. Walter Romig, *Michigan Place Names* (Detroit: Wayne State University Press, 1986), 610; "Michigan Central Depot," historical marker in Wolverine, Michigan, 1991.

449. Ibid.

450. "Michigan Central Depot," historical marker in Wolverine, Michigan, 1991.

451. Ibid.

452. "History of Wolverine," *Wolverine.*"

453. Ibid.

454. Ibid.

455. Ibid.

456. Ibid.

457. Ibid.

458. Ibid.

459. John Cohassey, "Hemingway's 'Last Good Country,'" *Detroit Metro Times*, July 7, 2010, www.metrotimes.com/detroit/hemingways-last-good-country/Content?oid=2197733.

460. Ibid.

461. "Wolverine Lumberjack Festival," *Wolverine Lumberjack Festival*, accessed November 27, 2017, www.wolverinelumberjackfestival.org/.

462. Ibid.

463. Ibid.

464. "Home," *Wolverine*, accessed November 27, 2017, villageofwolverine.com/index.cfm.

465. Ibid.

466. "History of Wolverine," *Wolverine.*"

467. "Michigan," *World Atlas*, accessed November 27, 2017, www.worldatlas.com/webimage/countrys/namerica/usstates/misymbols.htm.

WOODLAND

468. U.S. Census Bureau, 2010 census.

469. W. W. Potter, *History of Barry County* (Grand Rapids: Reed-Tandler Company, date unknown), 52.

470. Ibid.

471. Ibid.

472. Ibid.

473. Ibid.

474. Ibid.

475. Ibid.

476. Walter Romig, *Michigan Place Names* (Detroit: Wayne State University Press, 1986), 612.

477. Potter, *History of Barry County*, 52.

478. Ibid.

479. *Michigan State Gazetteer and Business Directory for 1877* (Detroit: C. F. Clarke, 1877), 853.

480. Ibid.

481. *Michigan State Gazetteer and Business Directory for 1887–1888* (Detroit: C. F. Clarke, 1888), 1679.

482. Ibid.

483. Romig, *Michigan Place Names*, 612.

484. *Michigan State Gazetteer and Business Directory for 1891–1892* (Detroit: C. F. Clarke, 1892), 1549.

485. *Michigan State Gazetteer and Business Directory for 1891–1892*, 1549; *Michigan State Gazetteer and Business Directory for 1907–1908* (Detroit: C. F. Clarke, 1908), 1889K–1889L.

486. "Woodland Town Hall," historical marker in Woodland, Michigan, 1984.

487. Bonnie Mattson, "Seventy-Ninth Woodland Homecoming Still Offers Old-Time Fun," *Hastings Reminder*, August 27, 2016, hastingsreminder.com/ seventyninth-woodland-homecoming-still-offers-oldtime-fun-p12285-1.htm.

488. "Students Evacuated as Wind Blows off Roof of Barry Co. School," *Wood TV 8*, March 8, 2017, woodtv.com/2017/03/08/students-evacuated-as-wind-blows-off-roof-of-barry-co-school/.

489. Ibid.

490. *Michigan State Gazetteer and Business Directory for 1887–1888*, 1679.

491. Ibid.

ZEBA

492. U.S. Census Bureau, 2010 census.

493. Grenafore Westphal, Lola Menge, Madeline Holliday, Gertrude Cosgrove, Hans Tollefson, Elsie Lehto, Martin Almli, Oliver Thure, Eileen Lough, Henning Johnson, John McDonnell, Gordon Seavey, and Edward Westphal, *The History of L'Anse Township* (L'Anse Sentinel, 1922), n.p.

494. Ibid.

495. Walter Romig, *Michigan Place Names* (Detroit: Wayne State University Press, 1986), 618.

496. The Historical Society of the Detroit Annual Conference, *History of Methodism in the Upper Peninsula of Michigan* (The Historical Society of the Detroit Annual Conference, 1955); "Zeba Indian United Methodist Church History," *L'Anse United Methodist Church*, accessed November 27, 2017, lumc. umcchurches.org/?page_id=159.

497. "Zeba Indian United Methodist Church History," *L'Anse United Methodist Church*.

498. "Zeba Indian United Methodist Church," historical marker in Zeba, Michigan, 1979.

499. Ibid.

500. Grenafore Westphal, Lola Menge, Madeline Holliday, Gertrude Cosgrove, Hans Tollefson, Elsie Lehto, Martin Almli, Oliver Thure, Eileen Lough, Henning Johnson, John McDonnell, Gordon Seavey, and Edward Westphal, *The History of L'Anse Township* (L'Anse Sentinel, 1922), n.p.

501. "Zeba Indian United Methodist Church History," *L'Anse United Methodist Church*.

502. "Zeba Indian United Methodist Church," historical marker in Zeba, Michigan, 1979.

503. Ibid.

504. Ibid.

505. Romig, *Michigan Place Names*, 618.

506. Ibid.

507. "Ven. Bishop Baraga History," *Roman Catholic Diocese of Marquette*, accessed November 27, 2017, www. dioceseofmarquette.org/venbishopbaragahistory.

508. Ibid.

509. "Frederick Baraga among the Ottawas," *American Catholic Quarterly Review* vol. 21 (January–October, 1896), 106–129.

510. Ibid.

511. Marquette University, "Guide to Catholic-Related Records in the Midwest about Native Americans," published 1984 and revised in 2003 and 2013, www. marquette.edu/library/archives/NativeGuide/ MI/M-32.pdf; "Sainthood Cause of 'Snowshoe Priest' Heads to Vatican," *Catholic News Agency*, July 28, 2010, www.catholicnewsagency.com/news/ sainthood-cause-of-snowshoe-priest-heads-to-vatican.

512. John Fee, "Venerable Bishop Baraga's Cause for Canonization," *U.P. Catholic*, May 18, 2012, accessed through *Diocese of Marquette*, dioceseofmarquette.org/baragacause.

513. Alissa Pietila, "Michigan House to Unveil Portrait to Honor Former UP Representative," *TV6*, December 6, 2016, www.uppermichiganssource.com/ content/news/Michigan-House-to-unveil-portrait-to-honor-former-UP-Representative-405045026. html.

514. Ibid.

515. Ibid.

516. Ibid.

517. Westphal, *The History of L'Anse Township*, 1922; Romig, *Michigan Place Names*, 618.

518. The Historical Society of the Detroit Annual Conference, *History of Methodism*, 1955.

519. "Keweenaw Bay Indian Community," *Inter-Tribal Council of Michigan, Inc.*, accessed November 27, 2017, www.itcmi.org/blog/2012/10/11/ keweenaw-bay-indian-community/.

520. Ibid.

Towns/Villages and Their Respective Counties

Ahmeek: Keweenaw County

Akron: Tuscola County

Allen: Hillsdale County

Alpha: Iron County

Applegate: Sanilac County

Bancroft: Shiawassee County

Barryton: Mecosta County

Barton Hills: Washtenaw County

Bear Lake: Manistee County

Beulah: Benzie County

Big Bay: Marquette County

Bloomingdale: Van Buren County

Boyne Falls: Charlevoix County

Breedsville: Van Buren County

Burlington: Calhoun County

Carney: Menominee County

Carp Lake: Emmet County

Casnovia: Muskegon and Kent Counties

Cement City: Jackson and Lenawee Counties

Chatham: Alger County

Clarksville: Ionia County

Clayton: Lenawee County

Clifford: Lapeer County

Copemish: Manistee County

Copper City: Houghton County

Custer: Mason County

Daggett: Menominee County

Dansville: Ingham County

DeTour: Chippewa County

Eagle: Clinton County

Elberta: Benzie County

Ellsworth: Antrim County

Emmett: St. Clair County

Empire: Leelanau County

Estral Beach: Monroe County

Fife Lake: Grand Traverse County

Forestville: Sanilac County

Fountain: Mason County

Free Soil: Mason County

Gaastra: Iron County

Gagetown: Tuscola County

Gaines: Genesee County

Garden: Delta County

Grand Beach: Berrien County

Hanover: Jackson County

Harrietta: Wexford County

Harrisville: Alcona County

Hersey: Osceola County

Honor: Benzie County

Horton Bay: Charlevoix County

Hubbardston: Ionia and Clinton Counties

Ironton: Charlevoix County

Lake Angelus: Oakland County

Lake Ann: Benzie County

Leonard: Oakland County

LeRoy: Osceola County

Lincoln: Alcona County

Luther: Lake County

Mackinac Island: Mackinac County

Marenisco: Gogebic County

Martin: Allegan County

McBride: Montcalm County

Melvin: Sanilac County

Mesick: Wexford County

Michiana: Berrien County

Michigamme: Marquette County

Millersburg: Presque Isle County

Minden City: Sanilac County

Montgomery: Hillsdale County

Mulliken: Eaton County

Nessen City: Benzie County

Oakley: Saginaw County

Omer: Arenac County

Onekama: Manistee County

Otter Lake: Lapeer and Genesee Counties

Owendale: Huron County

Perrinton: Gratiot County

Pewamo: Ionia County

Pierson: Montcalm County

Port Hope: Huron County

Posen: Presque Isle County

Powers: Menominee County

Prescott: Ogemaw County

Rosebush: Isabella County

Rothbury: Oceana County

Sand Lake: Kent County

Sherwood: Branch County

Stanwood: Mecosta County

Turner: Arenac County

Tustin: Osceola County

Twining: Arenac County

Vandalia: Cass County

Vanderbilt: Otsego County

Walkerville: Oceana County

Walloon Lake: Charlevoix County

White Pine: Ontonagon County

Whittemore: Iosco County

Wolverine: Cheboygan County

Woodland: Barry County

Zeba: Baraga County

About the Author

Born and raised in mid-Michigan, Kathryn Houghton has spent most of her life in the Mitten State. She can't imagine living anywhere else, and not just because no one in Michigan looks at her funny when she calls it pop instead of soda. It's the people that make Michigan feel like home. She teaches writing and editing at Michigan State University. She lives in Holt with her sister and three dogs.